Great BIG BOOK of Children's Games

Great BIG BOOK *of* Children's Games

OVER 450 INDOOR AND OUTDOOR GAMES FOR KIDS

written by DEBRA WISE
illustrated by SANDY FORREST

Reader's Digest

The Reader's Digest Association, Inc.
Pleasantville, New York / Montreal

A Reader's Digest Book
Conceived and produced by Round Stone Press, Inc.

Round Stone Press
Directors: Marsha Melnick, Susan E. Meyer, Paul Fargis
Editorial Director: Nick Viorst
Editor: Judy Pray
Design: Sandy Forrest
Design Concept: Charles Kreloff
Production Design: Steven Rosen, Laura Smyth
Project Editor: Sue Heinemann
Text Editors: Virginia Croft, James Waller

Reader's Digest General Books
Vice President, Editor-in-Chief: Christopher Cavanaugh
Art Director: Joan Mazzeo
Editorial Director: Tad Harvey
Design Director: Irene Ledwith
Editor: Susan Bronson

Library of Congress Cataloging in Publication Data

Wise, Debra.
The Reader's Digest great big book of children's games : over 450 indoor and outdoor games for kids / Debra Wise : illustrations by Sandy Forrest.
p.cm.
Includes index.
Summary: A collection of more than 450 games including complete instructions for playing the game and a thumbnail overview with details on number of players, appropriate age level, best playing location, and necessary equipment.

ISBN 0-7621-0094-X
1. Games—Juvenile literature.   2. Indoor games—Juvenile literature.   3. Outdoor games—Juvenile literature.   [1. Games.]   I. Forrest, Sandra, ill. II. Reader's Digest Association.
III. Title.
GV1203.W7526   1999
790.1–dc21   98-44582

Printed in USA

CONTENTS

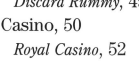

Mind Games 53

Word Games 69

Pencil-and-Paper Games 93

Tabletop Games 107

Sidewalk and Blacktop Games 137

Ball Games 199

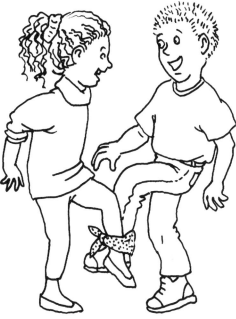

Strength and Wrestling Games 237

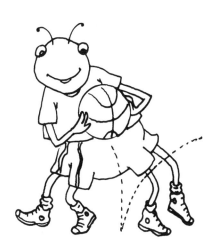

Introduction

Play is the work of childhood. It is a child's job to explore the world and figure out how he or she fits into it. This journey of discovery begins when an infant first bats at a string of toys and sees their bright colors, feels (and often tastes) the smooth plastic, and hears the sound of the rattle. As children move into toddlerhood, they become social beings, and as they discover each other, they also discover games. Although games can be enjoyed throughout a person's life, it is during the toddler to teenage years that they play a crucial role in an individual's development. Kids play games to have fun, rarely realizing that all the while they are learning about organization, role playing, strategy, spontaneity, etiquette, patience, problem-solving, concentration, coordination, confidence, creativity, and how to follow rules.

Parents, grandparents, aunts and uncles, teachers, coaches, babysitters, and counselors have a job too. It is every adult's task to make sure that a child's childhood is as rich, stimulating, and joyful as possible. That's not so easy in this technological age, when television and computer programs mesmerize young minds and discourage physical activity. While there's certainly a time and a place for both television and computers in a child's life, it is only through play—both organized and spontaneous—that kids' bodies, minds, and spirits can fully develop and thrive. This book is meant to be a resource for filling the hours, days, and years of childhood with fun.

The Reader's Digest Great Big Book of Children's Games is a collection of more than 300 games and 150 variations especially selected for children between the ages of 3 and 14. The clear and complete instructions should refresh adults' memories of the rules of such childhood favorites as Kick the Can, Marco Polo, Spud, Hangman, Checkers, Capture the Flag, Simon Says, Crazy Eights, Musical Chairs, Hopscotch, and Telephone. The book also introduces dozens of lesser-known but equally enjoyable pastimes, such as Snip Snap Snorem, Spoof, Shove Winter Out, Seega, Dizzy Izzy, O'Leary, and Tangram.

The games are grouped into chapters according to certain basic similarities, whether in equipment, location, or type of action. The chapters "Card Games," "Pencil-and-Paper Games," and "Ball Games" are clearly characterized by the equipment needed to play the games. "Tabletop Games," "Sidewalk and Blacktop Games," "Water Games," and "Road Games" all reflect the locations where the games are usually played. Similarly, the chapter "Party Games" reflects an event at which the games are played. "Hunt and Hide-and-Seek Games," "Tag and Chase Games," "Strength and Wrestling Games,"

and "Races and Relays" are organized according to the action involved. Two other chapters—"Word Games" and "Mind Games"—deal with the manipulation of words and ideas. There are, of course, infinite possibilities for crossover between the chapters. Many of the races and relays, for example, make excellent party games, and all of the card and pencil-and-paper games might be considered special tabletop games.

Each chapter opens with a quick survey of the category covered in the chapter. Then each entry not only gives clear and complete instructions for playing the game but also provides a thumbnail overview with details on number of players, appropriate age level, best playing location, and necessary equipment. (The games are also cross-listed in the index according to age and number of players.) The age range for a game, however, is always flexible, and the suggestions in this book are meant only as guidelines for choosing games. A precocious 6-year-old may excel at Checkers or Knockout Whist, and a group of rambunctious 13-year-olds may delight in a fast and furious game of Dodge Ball. And children aren't the only ones who will enjoy the games in this book. Many of the card and tabletop games, in particular, offer challenges to the entire family, from toddlers on up through great-grandparents. Playing games can be a great way to bring the family closer together.

The playing environment, like the age range, is subject to change. Many of the sidewalk and blacktop games, for example, can be played indoors on a large sheet of paper, just as many of the other active outdoor games—Obstacle Course or Follow the Leader, for instance—can be modified for indoor play. Needless to say, almost any indoor game can be enjoyed outdoors on a beautiful day. Moreover, many of the games—not just those listed under "Road Games"—are great for trips. All the mind games, many of the word games, and some card games travel well. Families may even want to take this book along on trips for lots of fun both along the way and at the final destination.

Because this book aims to provide opportunities for spontaneous play, almost all of the games require only basic equipment that can be found in most households: a deck of cards, pencil and paper, chalk, a checkers set, coins, rope, a source of music, and all sorts of balls. Any necessary purchases—a set of jacks, pickup sticks or dominoes, a Chinese Checkers or Tiddlywinks game, marbles, or a baseball

bat—are inexpensive investments sure to serve the family well for years to come.

Just as the information on the who, what, and where of the games is flexible, so are the rules of play. As is inevitable with anything that is handed down mainly through verbal folklore, the rules of children's games vary slightly (or in some cases hugely) from location to location and from generation to generation. This book includes many of these variations, so kids can select a version that they really enjoy playing. Even if the rules are flexible, it's a good idea for an adult to explain the instructions given here to the players before the game begins. That gives kids a chance to ask questions about "What happens if...?" and it ensures that an adult is involved from the start and on hand to supervise. (Needless to say, an adult should always be nearby whenever kids play any of the games in this book.) While explaining the rules, the adult should feel free to tailor the games to the needs and desires of a particular group. It's also fine if children use creativity and imagination to invent different versions and rules of their own—as long as these are within the bounds of safety and common sense.

Many experts characterize games as being microcosms of real life: To be successful, one must play within the structure and the rules, but at the same time there is room for enormous physical, mental, and social experimentation and development. Many of the games in this book are competitive, drawing kids into the excitement of winning, but also helping them to accept inevitable defeats. In all, good sportsmanship is to be encouraged. Most important, the games in this book teach children how to have fun *together*—something no computer or television can do. It's this capacity for pleasant interaction that will serve kids well as they move into adult life and begin to differentiate work from play. Ready or not, here they come!

The Pre-Game Show

Before beginning a game, the players must decide which team they will be on, who will go first, or who will be "it." Settling these questions can be fun. One player may quickly shout, "Not 'it!' " and the last player to echo this cry becomes "it." For a card game, players may follow tradition and let the person on the dealer's left go first. When teams are needed, a supervising adult may handpick them to assure a good balance of abilities. In other situations kids can try the following ideas to put on their own pre-game show.

Heads or Tails

Flipping a coin is the most random way to make a decision and a very fair way to decide which player or team goes first in a game. One player places a coin on his palm or the top of his thumb, flips it up into the air, and catches it in his hand. The other player (or a player from the other team) calls out "heads" or "tails." The flipper then slaps the coin onto the back of his other hand and shows it. If the caller guessed right, she—or her team—goes first. If not, the flipper or his team is number one. A playing card may be substituted for the coin. In this case, the card is tossed, the call of "up" or "down" is made while it is in the air, and the decision is made when it lands face up or down on the table or floor.

Which Hand?

Much like a coin toss, Which Hand? relies on chance to determine who will go first. One player grasps a small object (marble, pebble, shell, blade of grass, etc.) in one fist and then passes it from hand to hand behind her back. She then holds both fists out in front and challenges the other player to guess which hand the object is in. If the guesser is right, he goes first. If not, the hider goes first.

Rock, Paper, Scissors

Rock, Paper, Scissors (also called Scissors, Paper, Stone) can be played as a game in itself or used by two players to determine who (or whose team) will go first or be "it." Two players stand facing each other, each with one hand hidden behind his back. At the count of "one, two, three, go!" each thrusts the hidden hand into the center and makes one of three gestures (see diagram): a closed fist (which stands for

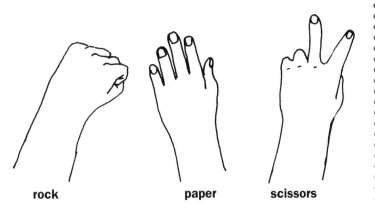

rock   paper   scissors

a rock), an open hand with fingers together (which stands for paper), or a fist with two fingers held out in a V shape (which stands for scissors). Since a rock can crush a pair of scissors, rock beats scissors. Since scissors can cut paper, scissors beat paper. Since paper can wrap around a rock, paper beats rock. The winner goes first, or the loser is "it." If both players use the same gesture, they try again.

High Card/High Roller

This method is a good way to determine who will deal or go first in card or dice games, although it works for any type of game as long as cards or dice are available. For High Card, each player chooses one card from the deck, and the one with the highest card (Ace is highest) goes first. In High Roller, each player rolls one die. The one with the highest number goes first. Tie-breaker picks or rolls are sometimes necessary.

Odds and Evens

Odds and Evens is a way to choose who will go first (or who will be "it") when only two players (or two teams) are involved. One player is designated "odd" and the other, "even." The two stand facing each other with their hands behind their backs. On the count of "one, two, three, go!" each player displays a hand with zero (closed fist) to five fingers showing. (In some versions, players may "shoot" only one or two fingers.) If the total of the fingers shown is odd, the odd player goes first, and vice versa. Players may agree to hold more than one shoot, with the winner taking two out of three shoots or three out of five.

Counting Off

Counting Off is the best way to divide into teams when there is no need to consider a balance of skills or strength on a team. Players line up side by side, preferably against a wall. Starting at one end, they count off in sequence according to the number of teams. If two teams are needed, for example, the children count off "one, two, one, two," to the end of the line. All the players who call out "one" make up one team; the "twos" make up the other. For three teams, players count off from one to three; for four teams, from one to four; and so on.

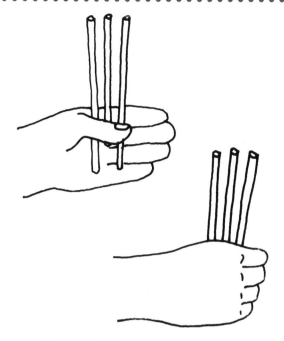

Drawing Straws

Drawing Straws is a fast way to determine who will be the first "it" in a tag or chase game. Originally straws from a haystack were used, but drinking straws or twigs of roughly equal length are fine. One straw is needed for each participant, and one straw should be cut shorter than the rest. One player then holds the straws, with the short end hidden in the fist, so the straws appear to be of equal length (see diagram). Each player draws one straw. Whoever gets the short straw is "it."

Eeny, Meeny, Miney, Mo

Reciting a rhyme is a fun way to choose who will be "it." The players stand in a circle or loose group, and one (usually the child who initiated the game) is selected to be the counter. The counter chants the rhyme, tapping or pointing to a different player (including herself) as each word is said. Sometimes the players hold out one or both fists, and the counter taps each with her own fist. (This is known as "dipping.") Players are eliminated when they are tapped on the last beat of the rhyme. They then leave the circle, secure in the knowledge that they will not be "it." The counting continues until only one player is left. That player is "it." Here are four of the most popular rhymes:

Eeny, meeny, miney, mo,
Catch a tiger by the toe,
If he hollers, let him go,
Eeny, meeny, miney, mo.
My mother says to pick the very best one,
And you are not "it."

One potato, two potato,
Three potato, four,
Five potato, six potato,
Seven potato, more.

One, two, three
Out goes he (or she)*!*

Engine, engine number nine,
Going down Chicago line,
If the train goes off the track,
Do you want your money back?
N-O spells "no," and you are not "it."

For the final line of this last rhyme, the chanter can substitute "Y-E-S spells 'yes,' and you are 'it.'"

Pick a Number

Pick a Number is a good way to determine the order of play in a large group. Slips of paper should be numbered to correspond to the number of players (1 through 20 for 20 children, for example). The pieces of paper are then folded in half to conceal the numbers and placed in a hat, bowl, or bag. Each player picks out a piece of paper and checks the number to find out if she goes first, second, third, and so on. Pick a Number can also be used to choose teams. In this case, a slip of paper is set aside for each participant. These slips are then divided equally into "teams" and numbered according to the number of the team (team 1, team 2, and so on). When players pick a number, they discover which team they are on.

Rotten Egg

"Last one in is a rotten egg!" is a call that can be heard all summer at the beach and pool. While this ploy is a very effective way to make sure everyone gets wet, Rotten Egg can also be used to decide who will be "it." The initiator of the game simply calls out, "Last one to the slide [or the tree, the stoop, etc.] is a rotten egg!" The group races for the goal and the last one to reach it—the "rotten egg"—is "it."

Hand Over Hand

Hand Over Hand is a good way to choose which team will be up first in a game (such as Stickball) that requires a bat. One player starts by holding the bat upside down in one hand, about halfway up the bat. A second player, from the other team, grasps the bat right above (and just touching) the first player's hand; the first player now does the same with the second player's hand, and so on, hand over hand, until there is no more room on the bat (see diagram). The team of the player whose hand is the last on the bat goes first. For Kickball and other games that do not use a bat, Hand Over Hand may be done on a stick or a broom handle.

Volley for the Serve

In many of the ball games that use a net (or a line representing an imaginary net), the two teams (or two players) volley to determine which side will go first. The ball is served by either side and hit back and forth over the net. The ball must travel over the net three times before the volley is considered valid. After that, the first team to miss the ball forfeits the serve to the other side.

Card Games

A deck of cards can provide endless hours of enjoyment for players of almost any age. Card games are more than just a fun way to spend a rainy afternoon or winter evening—they refine mental skills such as memory, observation, and logic. All of the games in this chapter require a flat playing surface and at least one standard deck of 52 cards (which should be shuffled before kids draw for the deal). A pencil and paper may be handy for keeping score.

Here are a few basic card terms kids should know: *Throwing a card* means laying it down on the table—not literally throwing it! Each card belongs to one of four *suits* (clubs, diamonds, hearts, or spades) and has a specific *rank* (its number value or the kind of face on it). *Standard scoring* follows the rank order, from Two up to Ten, followed by the *face cards* (Jack, Queen, King). In some games the Ace ranks above the King; in others, it counts as a lowly One.

Go Fish

This classic card-matching game can be fun for everyone!

Players: 2 to 6

Ages: 4 to 8

Place: Table or other flat surface, with seating for all players

Equipment: Standard deck of cards

It is possible to purchase a Go Fish game with specially printed picture cards for children too young to deal with numbers. But kids will be proud to move up to using a real deck of cards. The game can be modified for little children by requiring them to collect only pairs instead of four-card books. A *book* is all four cards of any rank—all four Sevens, say, or all four Jacks.

Everyone picks a card, and the one who draws the highest card deals. If there are two or three players in the game, each player gets seven cards, face down. If there are four or more players, each gets five cards. The remaining cards are spread out face down in haphazard fashion in the middle of the table—this is the fishing pond. Each player then arranges her hand so that cards of the same rank are next to one another. The goal of the game is to capture as many groups of four matching cards of the same rank as possible.

The player to the dealer's left starts by asking any other player for the cards she needs to fill out a group of four. For example, if she happens to have two Kings, she may ask another player if he has any Kings. And if he does, he has to turn them over. She can then go again, asking that same player, or any other, for other cards. If he doesn't have the cards, however, he cries out, "Go Fish!" With that, the first player selects a card from the fishing pond and adds it to her hand. Her turn is now over, and the next player to her left goes.

Picking from the pond can be good or bad. It's good if a player is lucky enough to get something he needs to help fill out a group of four. It's bad if it just adds another useless card to his hand.

Throughout the game, players should pay attention to what the other players are asking for. A player who is looking for Aces, for example, should ask the player who asked someone else for an Ace earlier in the game. Of course, it's important to keep in mind that someone could have added a valuable card to his hand when he fished in the pond. A player's hand changes every time he picks up a card from the center.

When a player collects four matching cards, she lays them, face up, on the table in front of her. The winner is the first player to get rid of all her cards.

Authors

This matching game delights even young children.

Players: 2 or more

Ages: 8 to 14

Place: Table or other flat surface, with seating for all players

Equipment: Standard deck of cards

In Authors, the rank of each card stands for a different "author," and the suit stands for a "chapter" in one of that author's "books." Each Three card, for example, represents one of the four chapters in Mr. Three's book; each Queen stands for one chapter in the Queen's book. The object of Authors is to collect all four chapters in as many books as possible —to collect, in other words, all four Sevens or all four Kings, and so on.

To start, each player draws a card from the deck. The player with the highest card shuffles and deals. The dealer deals out the whole deck, face down. It's fine if some players have more cards than others. Privately, each player now sorts his cards to place cards of the same rank next to each other in his hand; this way, it's easy to see which cards he needs to complete a book.

has the card, he must hand it over. The player who asked for the card then gets to go again, asking the same player or another player for another card and, if that player has it, adding that card to her hand. Whenever she acquires a complete book, she immediately lays all four cards face up on the table. The asking player's turn continues as long as each player she asks has the card she requests. When she asks for a card that the other player does not have, her turn is over.

Play goes around to the left, with each player, in turn, laying down any complete books he already holds in his hand and then asking other players for the cards he needs. As he acquires more complete books, he lays them face up on the table.

Each player should listen carefully to what the others are asking for on every turn and pay attention to which cards get handed over. That's the way to figure out who has what—valuable information when it's a player's turn to ask again!

Once a player has completed all the books in her hand and no longer holds any cards, she is free to sit back and watch the others go on. The game ends when all of the books have been completed and everyone is out of cards. The player with the most books wins.

The player on the dealer's left goes first. If she already holds any complete books in her hand, she lays them face up on the table. She then can ask any other player for any one card that she needs to complete or help complete a book. If, for example, she already has the Sixes of clubs, spades, and hearts, she'd want to ask for the Six of diamonds. If the other player

Slapjack

Sharp eyes and speedy reactions earn victory in this lightning-quick game.

Players: 2 to 5

Ages: 4 to 8

Place: Sturdy table or the floor, with seating for all players

Equipment: Standard deck of cards

Probably the easiest card game of all, Slapjack does not require any matching or sequencing skills. Players don't even have to know their numbers! All they have to do is be able to recognize the Jacks. The real thrill of this game—especially for preschoolers—is that (gentle) hand

slapping is not only allowed by the rules, it's required.

Everyone picks a card, and the one who draws the highest card shuffles and deals out all the cards, one at a time, face down, to the players. It's fine if some players receive more cards than others. Each player then places her cards—without looking at them—in a face-down stack in front of her. The object of the game is simply to win all the cards.

The player on the dealer's left goes first by laying the top card on his pile

face up in the center of the playing area. The next player does the same, placing her card face up on the previous player's card. This pile continues to build until a player lays down a Jack. As soon as a Jack appears, all the players try to slap their hands on top of it.

The first one to slap the Jack takes the whole pile and mixes it with his own pile. The player to the successful slapper's left then starts a new pile in the center. If someone gets overeager and slaps any card other than a Jack, she must give a card to each of the other players.

A player who runs out of cards is not automatically out. Instead, he must watch carefully while the others play on. And if he's the first person to slap the next Jack that appears, he can take the pile and continue to play. But if he misses this chance, he's out for good. The first player to collect all the cards is the winner.

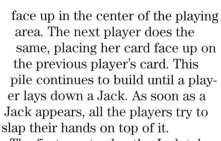

Snap

This noisy card-matching game is a snap to learn and a blast to play.

Players: 2 to 4

Ages: 4 to 8

Place: Table or other flat surface, with seating for all players

Equipment: Standard deck of cards

Snap is a game in the Slapjack family, and, like Slapjack, it's suitable for preschoolers. The most important difference is that, to play Snap, children do need to be able to match numbers. Also, this game promotes shouting rather than slapping—not a bad tradeoff.

Everyone picks a card, and the one who draws the highest card shuffles and deals out all the cards, one at a time, face down. Each player then neatens his cards into a stack but does not look at them. The object is simply to win all the cards and to make a lot of noise in the process.

The player on the dealer's left goes first by turning over the top card on her stack and laying the card face up beside her pile. One by one, the other players do the same. The cards keep piling up until a card appears that is the same in rank as another face-up card. When that happens, all the players (including the player who turned up the matching card) race to yell "Snap!" The first player to cry out "Snap!" gets to snatch both face-up piles and add them to the bottom of his own face-down stack. The play then continues around the circle (to the left of the player who turned up the matching card).

Any player who gets overeager and shouts "Snap!" at the wrong time must give each of the other players a card from her face-down stack. If two players yell "Snap!" at exactly the same time, the piles with the matching cards are stacked on top of one another in the middle. This is the "Snap pool." Play goes on as before, except that now the first player to call out "Snap pool!" when someone turns over a card matching the one on top of the Snap pool gets to add all those cards to his face-down stack. If two players yell out at the same time, a second Snap pool is created and both are up for grabs.

When a player runs out of face-down cards, she turns over her face-up pile and continues playing. Anyone who runs out of all his cards is out of the game. The player who collects all the cards is the winner.

Animal Noises

This version of Snap is a noisy barnyard of fun. The game is played just like Snap, except that animal noises replace the yelling of "Snap!" Each player takes on the role—and the voice— of an animal of her choice, ideally one that makes a funny noise. A game with six players might include a quack, a meow, an oink, a baa, a cheep, and a moo, for example.

Everyone should know which animal every other player is supposed to be before beginning the game. Play proceeds as in Snap, with the players turning over cards and looking for matches.

When a match occurs, the players quickly make the animal sound of the player whose card the new one matches. The first player to do so three times takes both face-up stacks. If a player makes the wrong noise, he must give his whole face-up stack to the player who turned up the card that made the match. As in Snap, the player who gathers up all the cards is declared the winner.

War

It's not hard to win a battle in this game, but it takes a lot of luck and stamina to win the whole "war."

Players: 2

Ages: 4 to 12

Place: Table or other flat surface, with seating for all players

Equipment: Standard deck of cards

War is a very simple card game with absolutely no skill involved. Children seem to delight in its elements of chance and surprise in much the same way that many adults savor bingo. War is also ideal for introducing young card novices to the concept of rank.

The classic game of War is between two players, each aiming to capture all the opponent's cards. Each player picks a card, and the one who draws the higher card shuffles and deals the entire deck, one card at a time, face down. Next, each player places his cards in one face-down stack in front of him (no peeking!). To begin, both players turn over their top cards simultaneously and place them side by side, face up, in the center. The one who plays the higher-ranking card gets to keep both cards. (Aces are high in this game.) The cards are added to the bottom of the winner's stack, and play continues in this manner.

When both players turn over cards of the same rank (two Kings, for example, or two Eights), "war" is declared and the fun begins! Each player places the top three cards from his stack face down on the original card. Then each places a fourth card face up on top of the three face-down cards. The higher face-up card wins all ten cards. If the cards match again, it's "double war," and the battle continues in the same manner until there is a victor.

The player who captures all 52 cards is the winner. A player also wins if her opponent runs out of cards in the middle of a war. Since every game of War has the potential of dragging out into something akin to the Hundred Years' War, it's not a bad idea to set a time limit before beginning. Then, if there's no outright victor, the winner is the player with the most cards at the end of that time.

World War

In this variation, three or four nations (players) clash. In a three-person game, each player is dealt 17 cards—the leftover card goes to the winner of the first pot. In a four-player game, each gets 13 cards. Play proceeds as in War. When any two equal-rank cards are turned up, all three or four players wage war.

Pisha Pasha

Pisha Pasha is a game for players who like to send lots of soldiers into battle. As in War, the two combatants use a single deck, and each aims to vanquish her opponent's army. Play proceeds exactly as in War, except that the battle continues until both of the turned-up cards are of the same suit. Only then does the higher-ranking card win the battle. The winner adds all the cards to her deck.

It's not unusual for a dozen or more cards to be up for grabs at any moment. This makes for a very fast-paced and dramatic game.

Persian War

In this somewhat more peaceful version of War, players place their turned-up cards next to their face-down piles rather than in the middle of the table. Instead of going to war over rank, in this game the players win battles involving the same suit. When two turned-up cards are of the same suit, the higher-ranking card immediately wins, and that player takes the other's face-up pile to add to the bottom of his own face-down stack. The person with the most cards at the end of a predetermined time period wins.

Snip Snap Snorem

Snip Snap Snorem is a loud and rowdy, fast and furious card-matching game.

Players: 3 or more

Ages: 4 to 8

Place: Table or other flat surface, with seating for all players

Equipment: Standard deck of cards

Snip Snap Snorem is, like Snap, a noisy, action-packed game.

Players must try to get rid of all their cards while calling out a sequence of nonsense words.

Everyone picks a card, and the one who draws the highest card shuffles and deals out all the cards, one at a time, face down. It's fine if some players have more cards than others.

Players then arrange their hands by rank. Their aim is to get rid of all their cards during the game.

The player to the dealer's left starts by laying any one card from his hand face up in the center of the table. The next player to the left looks in her hand for a card of the same rank, regardless of suit. If she has one, she lays it down next to the first card and shouts "Snip!" (Any other matching cards in her hand are saved for later.) If she doesn't have one, she passes and it's the next player's turn.

Play goes around the circle with each player matching or passing. The player who makes the second match yells "Snap!" and the player who makes the third match calls out "Snorem!" That cry ends the first round of play. Often, one player will get a match more than once in a single round.

The "Snorem" player then starts the next round by playing a new card onto the center pile. It's a good idea, when leading, for a player to start with a card in which he has at least one match. The first one to get rid of all his cards wins.

Jig

This game is a little tougher than Snip Snap Snorem because, instead of matching cards by rank, players build sequences. For instance, if there is a Three in the center, players build on it with a Four, then a Five, then a Six, and so on. Sequences must always go up; players may not add to the bottom. Aces are low. Suit doesn't matter. For this variation, the words "Jiggety," "Joggety," and "Jig" replace "Snip," "Snap," and "Snorem." A new four-card sequence begins after each "Jig." For a more challenging game, players can follow both the sequence and the suit.

Beggar Your Neighbor

Lucky players with face cards and Aces demand "payment" from their neighbors in hopes of winning all the cards in the deck.

Players: 2 to 6

Ages: 5 to 10

Place: Table or other flat surface, with seating for all players

Equipment: 1 or 2 standard decks of cards

Like its cousin War, Beggar Your Neighbor is a game of pure luck. The role of luck, combined with the way the game is always changing, makes Beggar Your Neighbor a certain winner for the 10 and under set. A player can be down and out one minute and king of the cards the next!

To begin, each player draws a card from the deck. The player with the highest card is the dealer. The dealer shuffles the deck and deals out all the cards, one at a time, face down. It's fine if some players have more cards than others. If there are more than three players, the game is better with two decks of cards mixed together.

Each player arranges his cards in a neat stack, face down, on the table and does not look at the cards. The player to the dealer's left goes first by turning over the top card on her pile and laying it face up in the middle of the table. Play continues with each player turning up his top card and putting it on top of the center pile. The real action starts as soon as a face card (Jack, Queen, King) or an Ace is turned over.

The player who turns over the face card or Ace stops turning over cards and demands "payment" from the player on her left. That player pays up by adding some of his cards, face up, one at a time to the center pile: four cards for an Ace, three cards for a King, two for a Queen, and one for a Jack. If the paying player turns up a face card or an Ace as he's paying up, he stops and demands payment from the player on his left. This goes on until a player fails to turn up a face card or an Ace. Then the center pile goes to whoever turned over the last Ace or face card. That player adds the center pile to the bottom of her face-down pile and starts a new round by turning over the top card in her stack.

Any player who loses all his cards is out of the game. Play goes on until one player has collected all the cards in the deck. The winner shuffles the cards and deals the next game.

Because this game tends to go on so long, a time limit should be set so that the person with the most cards at the end of that time is the winner. Removing all the Twos, Threes, Fours, and Fives from the deck is another way of shortening the game. (If that makes the game too short, put the Fives back in.)

Chase the Ace

No one wants to be left with the lowest card in this betting and trading game.

> **Players:** 5 or more
>
> **Ages:** 5 to 10
>
> **Place:** Table or other flat surface, with seating for all players
>
> **Equipment:** Standard deck of cards; 3 counters (such as peanuts, small candies, pennies, or buttons) for each player

In Chase the Ace, players don't need to know "when to hold 'em and when to fold 'em," but they nonetheless get the thrill of collecting a pot after winning a round (or the agony of losing all their booty if the numbers are not so lucky). Blocks, chips, or paper clips can be used as counters, but why not sweeten the pot with something that is really fun to win, like nuts, candies, or pennies?

Each player picks a card, and the one who draws the highest card deals the first hand. The dealer starts the game by giving each player three counters, each of which represents a "life." The deck is shuffled and each player is dealt one card, face down. On each round, the object is to avoid being left with the lowest card dealt. (In this game, Kings are high and Aces are low.) Each player looks at her card and decides whether she wants to keep it. The player on the dealer's left starts, saying "stand" if she wants to keep her card and "change" if she wants to get rid of it.

If a player decides to change her card, she slides it, face down, to the player on her left. That player must now exchange cards with the player sliding her card over—unless the card he is holding is a King. In that case, he declares, "King!" (and shows it to everybody) and the first player must change instead with the next player over. Changing a card is, of course, the big gamble, because unless the player is holding an Ace, there's always a risk of getting a lower card.

After the change has occurred, the player looks at her new card. If it is an Ace, Two, or Three, she must tell the other players. The game is called Chase the Ace because, as the lowest card, the Ace will keep moving around the table. The player who has just been forced to trade then decides whether to stand or change with the person on his left.

This continues until it is the dealer's turn. Since the dealer is last in the round, she can't ask to trade with anyone. If the dealer wants to get rid of her card, she buries it in the middle of the deck and chooses another card from the top, which she then shows to the other players. If the dealer picks a King, she automatically loses the hand and a "life," and must put one counter into the pot (the pile of counters in the middle of the table).

After the dealer's card is shown, the rest of the players must turn over their cards. The person with the lowest card also loses a "life." If there is a tie for lowest card, both players put a counter into the pot.

Now the player on the original dealer's left becomes the dealer. The cards from the last round are simply added to the bottom of the deck, and another hand is dealt. Any player who loses all his lives (counters) is out of the game. The last player to have a remaining counter wins and gets to collect the rewards.

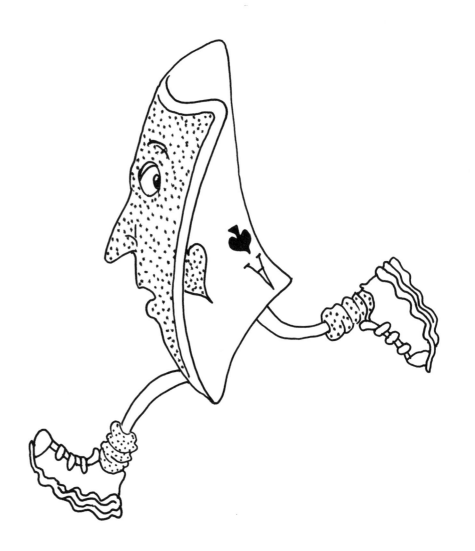

Old Maid

Nobody wants to be stuck with the Old Maid
in this well-loved matching game.

Players: 3 to 6

Ages: 5 to 10

Place: Table or other flat surface,
with seating for all players

Equipment: Standard deck of cards

Old Maid is the quintessential childhood card game and probably the easiest to learn and play. It's also 100 percent luck—no skill at all is required to win—which means a lot to a 5-year-old pitted against his elders. That must be why the game has survived unchanged through so many generations.

Before starting, three of the Queens are removed from the deck. The remaining Queen, usually the Queen of spades, is called the Old Maid; she stays in the deck.

Everyone picks a card, and the one who draws the highest card shuffles and deals out all the cards, one at a time and face down. It's fine if some players have more cards than others.

The players look at their hands and pull out any two cards that match in rank. Each player lays his matches face down in a pile beside him. If a player has three cards of the same number, one stays in his hand. If he has four, he can put down both pairs.

After everyone has sorted out their matches, the player to the dealer's left makes a fan out of the cards in her hand, making sure that no one can see which cards she holds. The player to her left must then choose a card from the first player's hand, hoping that the new card will match a card in his own hand. If a match is made, the pair goes into the player's face-down pile. Now the player who just chose offers up his cards to the next player to the left. Play goes around in a

circle, with players picking cards from one another and making matches to lay down. Since there is only one Queen, the Old Maid, no match can be made for her. At the end of the hand, the player left holding the Old Maid loses the game.

Over the course of the game, the Old Maid is likely to change hands several times. If a player picks the Old Maid from another player's hand, he can only hope that another player will pick it from him before the hand is over.

Le Vieux Garçon

This French version of Old Maid switches the traditional stereotype and makes it the "Old Boy" (*le vieux garçon*) that everyone is trying to avoid. Play is the same as in Old Maid except that three Jacks are removed and the Jack of spades is the odd card.

Le Pouilleux

This slightly more complicated version of Old Maid has a "lousy" name—quite literally, since *le pouilleux* means "the lice-infested man" in French. To begin play, the Jack of clubs is removed from the deck. Play is the same as in Old Maid except that the pairs must match in color as well as number. Hearts must match diamonds, in other words, and clubs must match spades. The player left holding the odd Jack—the "lice man"—is the loser.

Go Boom

A matching game for card novices, Go Boom has quite an explosive ending!

Players: 2 to 7

Ages: 5 to 9

Place: Table or other flat surface, with seating for all players

Equipment: Standard deck of cards

Go Boom, also known as Dig, requires a simple skill: the ability to match cards. Young players who have learned to match numbers may need a careful explanation of how to match suits.

First, everyone picks a card, and the player who draws the highest card shuffles and becomes the dealer. Each player is dealt seven cards, one at a time and face down. The remaining cards are piled face down in the center. Next, each player arranges his hand of cards from high to low, regardless of suit. Cards are ranked in the standard way, with Aces high. The players now try to get rid of all their cards during the game.

The player to the dealer's left starts by placing any card from her hand face up next to the face-down pile in the center. The next player to the left then puts down a card that is either of the same rank or of the same suit as the first card. If a player can't match the first card in either rank or suit, he must pick cards from the face-down pile until he gets one he can use. If all the cards in the face-down center pile are gone, the player must say "pass," and the next player takes a turn. The round ends when each player has taken a turn.

The dealer then clears away the face-up cards from the center and puts them aside. The player who threw the highest card in the first round starts the next round by placing a card face up in the center. If there was a tie,

whoever threw the first high card starts the next round. Play continues round after round until one player gets rid of all her cards. That player then shouts, "Boom!" and is declared the winner.

Scoring Go Boom

There's no need to score Go Boom, but scoring makes the game more interesting (and requires a pencil and paper). The game is played the same way, except that each card is worth a certain number of points. In this variation, the game does not end when a player gets rid of all her cards. Instead, the other players hand over their cards and the value of the cards they were holding is tallied up and credited to the "Boomer." Every card, from Two to Ten counts for its number value; Aces and face cards each count as 10.

The deck is then shuffled and dealt by the Boomer, and play continues. The game is over when one player wins by reaching a predetermined number of points (say, 200).

Donkey

This card-matching game is like a cross between Musical Chairs and Ghost—and a player who isn't on the alert will end up as the "donkey."

Players: 3 to 13

Ages: 5 to 9

Place: Table or other flat surface, with seating for all players

Equipment: Standard deck of cards; small unbreakable objects (such as spoons, buttons, or coins), 1 fewer than the number of players; pencil and paper for scoring

Donkey is a speedy game complete with animal noises and sneaky moves. Kids will be full of giggles as they try to avoid being dubbed the donkey at the end of the game. The whole deck of cards is not needed to play Donkey—just pull out four cards of the same rank for each player. If there are three players, for example, use the Aces, Kings, and Queens and put the rest of the deck aside. Several small unbreakable objects without sharp edges are needed; they should number one fewer than the number of players (five objects for six players, for instance). Spoons are most commonly used, but buttons or quarters will also do the trick. The objects are placed in the middle of the table.

One of the players should volunteer to keep score. The scorekeeper should list each player's name on a piece of paper and leave plenty of room to write beside it.

To begin, each player picks a card from the deck, and the one who draws the highest card deals the first round. The cards are shuffled and dealt one at a time, face down, until each player has four cards. The goal during each round is to collect four matching cards before anyone else does. Each player looks at his cards and chooses one to get rid of, then slides the unwanted card, face down, to the player on his left. As quickly as possible now, each player glances at his incoming card and immediately decides whether to keep it or pass it along. Either way, he again passes a card to the player on his left. This goes on until someone has a set of four matching cards. At once, that player quietly lays his cards face down on the table and picks up one of the objects from the center. (Sometimes, more than one person gets a match at the same time.)

This is when the mad scramble begins! As soon as the other players see someone pick up an object, they immedi-ately put down their cards and scramble to pick up an object too. They had better pay close attention and move fast, because the player left without an object loses the round. The loser of the round then shuffles the cards and deals the next round.

When a player loses a round, she is assigned a letter in the word "donkey" —a D for the first round she loses, an O for the second, and so on. As the game unfolds, scorekeeper writes each letter down. The first player to complete D-O-N-K-E-Y is the game loser and must bray, "Hee-haw!" three times.

Pig

Pig is played just like Donkey, except that there are no objects involved. Instead of picking something up from the table, the first player to get a matching set of four cards puts her finger beside her nose. Everyone else does the same as quickly as possible, because the last person to react is the pig and must say, "Oink, oink!" The first person to lose ten rounds becomes the prize pig and must squeal three times.

Concentration

The player with the best concentration skills wins in this memory and matching game.

Players: 2 or more

Ages: 5 and up

Place: Large table or other large flat surface, with seating for all players

Equipment: Standard deck of cards

Concentration is a playing-card version of an old TV game show, except there are no fabulous prizes offered at the end. It is a great game for honing the powers of memory and observation. It also teaches kids to pay attention during the whole game, not just when it's their turn.

To set up the game, all the cards are laid face down and side by side in even rows to form a neat, more or less rectangular arrangement. If players want to have exactly the same number of cards in each row, they should remove three Twos from the deck and arrange the cards in a seven-by-seven square—in that case, though, there will always be one extra card left at the end of the game.

The players now take turns flipping over two cards from the rectangle. Their aim is to find two that match in rank, regardless of suit. If a player finds a matching pair, she not only gets to keep it but also gets to take another turn. If the cards don't match,

however, the player simply flips the cards down again, and the next player gets a try.

During one player's turn, it is crucial that all the other players pay attention to which cards are revealed and where they are in the rectangle. They can use this information when it's their turn to make a match. As the game progresses and more and more cards are removed from the board, it becomes easier to remember what is where. When all the cards are gone, the player with the most pairs wins.

For young players, it's a good idea to use only a small portion of the deck—say, 16 cards—but every card should have a match. Expert Concentration players can make things more challenging by picking up only pairs that are of the same rank and color (a Seven of clubs and a Seven of spades, for example).

Stealing Bundles

In this card-matching game, opponents may rob each other of victory up to the very end.

Players: 2

Ages: 6 to 12

Place: Table or other flat surface, with seating for both players

Equipment: Standard deck of cards

Stealing Bundles is a game for anyone who's good at matching cards. A one-on-one game, Stealing Bundles has the added fun of allowing a player to foil her opponent by capturing his cards unexpectedly.

Each player picks a card, and the one who draws the higher card shuffles and deals out four cards, one at a time and face down, to both his oppo-

nent and himself. Next, four cards from the deck are laid out, face up and side by side, in the center of the table; the rest of the deck is put aside. The players arrange their hands by rank, regardless of suit.

The dealer's opponent goes first by scanning her hand for a card that matches (in rank) any of the four cards in the center. If she has one, she throws it on top of the matching card, gathers up the two-card bundle, and stacks it face up to one side. Throughout the game, she adds all other captured bundles, face up, to this pile. If two or more center cards are the same rank and match a card in her hand, she may use the one card to collect all the center matches. If she

has no matching cards, a card from her hand must be added to the ones in the middle.

Once the opponent has taken her turn, the dealer tries to capture a card. He, however, has another option. He may either match and take one from the middle or "steal" his opponent's bundle (if she has one) by matching the card on top of her bundle pile.

Play continues back and forth, with players matching cards from their hands with cards from the center or using a card to steal the top bundle on the other player's pile. When both players have played all four cards from their hands, four more cards are dealt to each from the stack that was set aside at the beginning. No more cards are dealt into the center.

When all the cards have been dealt and played, the game is over. If one player runs out of cards first, the other player may continue to try to play cards from his hand. The player who has the most cards in her bundle pile at the end wins the game.

Card Dominoes

Sevens are lucky in this sequencing game, which blends chance and skill.

Players: 2 or more

Ages: 6 to 12

Place: Table or other flat surface, with seating for all players

Equipment: Standard deck of cards

Also called Sevens, Parliament, or Fan Tan, Card Dominoes is simple to learn. The goal is to be the first player to get rid of all his cards. In a good game, some pretty fierce strategizing goes on.

Each player picks a card from the deck, and whoever has the highest card deals. The dealer shuffles the deck and deals out all the cards, one at a time, face down. Depending on the number of players, some may end up with more cards than others; that's fine. Players take up their cards and,

to make play easier, arrange the cards by suit and rank, with Aces high.

Then, the player holding the Seven of diamonds starts the action by laying that card face up in the middle of the table. Everyone now must build upon that card to create a stack of all the diamonds in order of rank. (Players will later do this with the other suits as well.)

The next player to the left gets the ball rolling. She does this by laying the

Eight of diamonds, if she has it, on top of the Seven of diamonds, or by sliding the Six of diamonds, if she has it, beneath the Seven. If the player does not have either card, she has one more option at this point: to start a new stack with a Seven from another suit. And if she doesn't have that, she must pass, and the player to her left gives it a shot.

Once the game is truly under way, players can add to the top or bottom of any stack, with the goal of getting rid of all their cards. This is where strategy comes into play. As a general rule, it's a good idea for a player to hold onto his Sixes, Sevens, and Eights for as long as he can. If he has any other cards that can be played, he should play them first. Sevens, especially, should be saved for as long as possible—they're insurance guaranteeing future plays. But holding onto Sixes and Eights is also a good strategy, since this will prevent anyone else from adding to new columns in either direction. Of course, if a player is holding an Eight as well as a Nine and Ten of the same suit (or a Six, Five, and Four), he shouldn't hold back, since he can still block others from playing their cards.

The first person to use up all her cards is the winner, but the other players can continue the game until all four suits have been built.

Giveaway

Players try to give their cards away as quickly as possible in this fast and easy sequencing game.

Players: 2 or more

Ages: 6 to 12

Place: Table or other flat surface, with seating for all players

Equipment: Standard deck of cards

This game requires a sharp mind that can pay attention to several things at once. Everyone must keep track of his own cards while also keeping an eye on the other players' cards and the piles in the center. It's almost as much fun to try to keep others from winning as it is to win!

Each player picks a card from the deck, and the one who draws the highest card deals. The dealer shuffles and deals the whole deck, one card at a time and face down. It's fine if some players end up with more cards than others. Without looking at their cards, the players pile them face down in a stack in front of them. The goal is to get rid of the entire pile over the course of the game.

The player to the dealer's left starts by turning over the top card on her pile. Unless this card is an Ace, she simply lays it face up next to her face-down stack. If it is an Ace, of any suit, she sets it face up in the center of the table and turns over another card in her pile. In most cases, she will simply place this card face up

next to her face-down stack. But if this card is an Ace, she puts it beside the other Ace in the center of the table, or if it's a Two in the same suit as the first Ace, she lays it face up on that Ace. As long as she can start a new pile (with an Ace) or add to the sequence in an existing pile, she continues to draw cards. When she comes to a card she can't play in the center, she places it face up next to her face-down stack and her turn ends.

The next player then turns over a

card from his pile, and he has a few more choices than the first player. He can put an Ace into the center of the table, and he can add sequentially (in suit) to any existing pile(s) in the center. In addition, he can play on the face-up pile of the first player. If the card he turns over is either one above or one below the top card in the first player's face-up stack—it doesn't matter what suit—he can add his card to that pile. If, for example, the first player's face-up card is a Six, the next player can drop a Five or a Seven of any suit on top of it. Anytime a player can play a card, he gets to draw from the pile again. If he can't make any play, he has to start a face-up pile of his own.

Play proceeds clockwise with each player turning over a card from his face-down pile and trying to give it away to either the center pile(s) or to any other player's face-up pile. Once all the Aces have surfaced, there are four active center piles along with each player's face-up pile to work off of, so the players have quite a few options. Players must play a card onto a center pile if at all possible. But when they can't do this, they can strategize to keep other players from getting rid of all their cards (including the face-up pile). If a player has a card that could go on more than one of his opponent's face-up piles, he'd be smart to put it on the pile of the player with the fewest cards in both her face-up and face-down stacks. When a player's face-down pile runs out, her turn ends. But the next time around, she must turn over her face-up pile and play with that. The game continues until one player has given away all her cards.

Comet

In this sequencing game, which can be won or lost in a flash, everyone tries to catch and play the "comet."

Players: 2 to 8

Ages: 6 and up

Place: Table or other flat surface, with seating for all players

Equipment: Standard deck of cards; pencil and paper for scoring

Legend holds that Comet was invented in France when Halley's comet visited in 1758–59. But Comet is also known as Commit, and which name came first is lost in the mists of time. A sequencing game with a twist, Comet requires players to pay attention to who has which cards. Anyone who holds the "comet" (Nine of diamonds) for too long gets burned.

The game is not played with a full deck. The Eight of diamonds should be removed from the deck first. Then, additional Sevens and/or Eights—it makes no difference which—of any suit come out until the number of cards is divisible by the number of players. So if two or five are playing, one other Seven or Eight is removed; with seven players, two other Seven or Eights are removed; with three, four, six, or eight players, three extra Sevens or Eights are removed.

Next, everyone picks a card, and the player who draws the highest card shuffles and deals all the cards out, one at a time and face down. Each player should then arrange his hand by suit and rank with alternating black and red suits. Aces are low and Kings are high in this game.

The player on the dealer's left starts. He places the lowest card he has of any suit into the center face up and announces the card as he plays it. He then lays on top of that card, face up and in sequence, any other cards he

has in the same suit, announcing as he goes. A player, for example, might start with the Three of clubs and then add the Four and Five of clubs before running out of cards in sequence. When no more cards in that suit and

in sequence can be played, the turn is over.

Play proceeds clockwise, with each player trying to build on the sequence and eventually get rid of all her cards. If a player doesn't have the necessary card, she must announce this, saying, "Without the Five" (or Six, or whatever is missing), and pass. If everyone has had a turn and no one can add to the sequence, the game reaches a "stop." That happens whenever the sequence reaches a Seven or Eight that has been removed from the deck. Then, the player who put down the last card starts a new sequence by

playing the lowest card in another suit from his hand. The same rule applies whenever a sequence makes it all the way up to a King, but this time the player who threw the King also scores a point.

The "comet" for which the game is named is the Nine of diamonds. The lucky comet-holder may play the card at any time he cannot continue a sequence, including any time the game reaches a "stop." Throwing the comet wins the player 2 points. After playing the comet, the comet-holder may continue by putting down either a Ten of diamonds or the next card in the sequence after the "stop" (in this case, the comet substitutes for the missing card).

Obviously, it's smart to hold on to the comet until it can be used to play several cards in sequence. But a player must take care not to keep the comet too long, or he may not get a chance to play it at all and will end up paying a penalty.

The first player to get rid of all her cards wins the round, and points are now tallied. The winner gets 1 point for each card in the other players' hands, plus an extra 2 points for every unplayed King. Points earned by those who earlier played Kings or the comet should not be forgotten. If the comet was not played, everyone but the comet-holder gets 1 point. The rounds continue until one player or more passes a predetermined total—100 is the most common; high scorer wins.

Rolling Stone

Like a rock tumbling downhill, Rolling Stone gains momentum as it goes along. Players may be hit with an avalanche of cards at any point in the game.

Players: 4 to 6

Ages: 6 to 12

Place: Table or other flat surface, with seating for all players

Equipment: Standard deck of cards

Rolling Stone is always an unpredictable game—anyone can be down to his last card and suddenly find himself with a new handful! That's why the game is called *Enflé* ("inflated") in French and *Schwellen* ("swollen") in German.

The game is not played with a full deck. If there are four players, all Twos, Threes, Fours, Fives, and Sixes are removed before dealing; if there are five players, just the Twos, Threes, and Fours are removed; and if there are six players, it's just the Twos that go. Everyone picks a card, and the one who draws the highest card shuffles and deals out all the cards, one at a time and face down. Each player ends up with eight cards.

Players arrange their hands by suit. The player on the dealer's left gets the stone rolling by laying any card from his hand face up in the center. On top

of that card the next player must lay another card of the same suit, if she has one. Then the next player to her left does the same. If a player cannot "follow suit," he must take all the cards in the face-up pile and add them to his hand. The person who takes the pile continues the play by laying down a card from any suit except the one that has just been played—even though that is the suit he will probably most want to get rid of. Of course, whenever possible, it's a good idea for a player to lead with a suit in which he holds a lot of cards; that way, he's less likely to run out of cards with which to follow suit.

Play continues until one player gets rid of all her cards and is declared the winner.

Crazy Eights

Eights are wild in this easy-to-learn but hard-to-master suit-sorting game.

Players: 2 to 4

Ages: 6 and up

Place: Table or other flat surface, with seating for all players

Equipment: Standard deck of cards; pencil and paper for scoring

Crazy Eights—also called Switch, Eights, or Swedish Rummy—is a classic "wild card" game, which keeps everyone guessing until the very end. The beauty of this game is that although it is simple enough for a first grader to grasp, it involves enough skill and strategy to fascinate more mature minds.

Each player picks a card from the deck, and the one who draws the highest card deals the first round. The dealer shuffles the deck and deals seven cards to each player, one at a time and face down. The rest of the deck is placed face down in the middle of the table. This pile is called the "stock" pile. The top card of the stock is turned over and placed face up beside the stock. This card is called the "starter." If the starter is an Eight, it is buried in the stock and a new card is chosen. Each player's aim over the course of the game is to get rid of all the cards in his hand and, at the same time, to force others to hold on to as many of their cards as possible.

Players arrange their cards by suit and rank. The cards are ranked in the standard way, with Aces high. Eights, however, are in a class all their own, because they are wild. This means that they can stand for any card their holder wants them to.

The player on the dealer's left goes first and must play a card that is of the same suit as the starter, which she does by simply laying it face up on top of the starter. If the starter is the Jack of diamonds, for example, she may play any diamond. The next player to the left follows by adding another card of the active suit. If a player does not have a card of that suit, or if he wants to change the active suit, he can instead play a card of the same rank as the face-up card, if he has one—throwing, for example, a Jack of clubs on the Jack of diamonds. Clubs then becomes the active suit. If a player doesn't have a card of either the same suit or rank of the face-up card (or if he chooses not to play it), he still has another option: to play any Eight he holds.

No matter what suit the Eight is, the player who throws an Eight has the right to select what the new active suit will be. Usually a player will choose a suit in which he holds a lot of cards in the hope that that suit will still be active when his turn comes again.

A player who can't follow suit or rank and doesn't have any Eights must pick cards from the stock and add them to her hand one at a time until she draws a card she can play. If the stock runs out before a playable card is drawn, the player must pass.

It's good strategy for a player to save his Eights as long as possible. A player is never required to play an Eight just because he has one—and, at the beginning of the game, it may be better to pick from the stock than to play an Eight. One possible trick is to save an Eight until all the cards in a suit have been thrown and then name that suit when throwing the Eight. Because the other players will have no cards they can play, they'll be forced to pick cards from the stock. Of course, this trick works best when there's a sizable stock left.

Savvy players keep track of what's been played and figure out what must still be in their opponents' hands. Using this knowledge, they try to get rid of a lot of cards while preventing other players from getting rid of any. One other word of advice: It's best to play high cards before low cards because of the way this game is scored.

The round ends either when a player has no more cards or when no one can make any more plays, in which case the player holding cards with the lowest total value wins the hand. The round winner is awarded points based on the cards left in the other players' hands: 50 points each for any Eights, 10 points each for any face cards (Jacks, Queens, Kings) or Aces, and face value for all other cards. (If the winner still holds some cards, their value is subtracted from the total.)

The winner of the round shuffles and deals the next round. The game continues until the first player reaches a predetermined total—say, 500 points—and wins the game.

For a quicker, easier game, players can forget about keeping score. The winner of each round is the winner of the game. In another version of the game, which requires more skill, a player may choose to draw a card from the stock even when he has cards that he could play.

Quango

This game should be called Crazy Aces because this time Aces are wild. And there are a few other twists, too: anyone who plays a Jack or an Eight gets to go again. If someone plays a Seven, the next player must also play a Seven. If he can't, he has to pick two cards from the stock. When that happens, the next player must then play a Seven if she can or pick cards from the stock. Only after a second Seven has been played does the game go back to "normal," and the second Seven's suit becomes the active one. Sound difficult and a bit confusing? It is—and that's what makes it so much fun!

Catch the Ten

It may be called Catch the Ten, but it's the Jack everyone's after in this game of tricks and trumps.

Players: 4 to 6

Ages: 6 to 14

Place: Table or other flat surface, with seating for all players

Equipment: Standard deck of cards; pencil and paper for scoring

Another name for Catch the Ten is Scotch Whist, although it is not whist and did not come from Scotland. The object is to win as many "tricks" as possible—that is, to beat all the other cards that are thrown in one round of play—while also trying to capture valuable Tens and face cards (Jacks, Queens, Kings).

The game is not played with a full deck. Before dealing, all the Twos, Threes, Fours, and Fives are removed from the deck. If there are five players, one of the Sixes is removed, too. This ensures that every player gets the same number of cards. The players each pick a card, and the one who draws the high card shuffles and deals all the cards, one at a time and face

down. If there are four players, each will have nine cards; if there are five, each will have seven cards; and if there are six, each will have six cards.

When all the players have their cards, the dealer turns over the last card that was dealt and shows it to everyone. This card's suit will be the "trump" suit, which means that a card from this suit will beat any card from any other suit during that hand. The turned-over card is then returned to the player's hand.

The player on the dealer's left leads by putting a card into the center. This card cannot be from the trump suit. The next player must follow suit (play a card from the same suit). If and only if that player cannot follow suit, she may play a trump card or, if she has no trump card (or does not wish to use it), a card from another suit.

Play proceeds to the left until everyone has played a card. If no trump card has been played, the highest-ranking card of the suit that led wins the trick. (The cards are ranked in the standard way, with Aces high.) If only one player has thrown a trump card, he wins the trick. If more than one

player has thrown a trump card, the highest trump card wins. The winner puts his trick aside and starts the next round with one of the cards he is still holding. The hand is over when all the cards have been played.

At the end of each hand, the players count up their points. Anyone who ends up with more cards than he had at the beginning of the hand gets a bonus point for each extra card, no matter what it is. The Ten and the face cards in the trump suit also carry points: the Jack is worth 11; the Ten, 10; the Ace, 4; the King, 3; and the Queen, 2. After scoring, the cards are shuffled and redealt by the player to the original dealer's left. Play continues until one player wins by reaching more than 40 points; if more than one player passes 40, the player with the highest score wins.

Because it is not permissible for a player to play a trump card until she has no more cards of the suit that was led, she should try to get rid of the suits with the fewest cards first. Also, the Ace, King, and Queen from the trump suit should be saved and used to capture the more valuable Jack and Ten from the trump suit. The player who holds the Jack and Ten of the trump suit should try to save them until they can definitely win a trick. One of the ways to do this is to play lower trump cards, if possible, when everyone else is playing high trumps.

I Doubt It

Great bluffers take the lead in I Doubt It.

Players: 3 or more

Ages: 6 to 12

Place: Table or other flat surface, with seating for all players

Equipment: Standard deck of cards; pencil and paper for scoring

In I Doubt It, players compete to pull the wool over one another's eyes by claiming to hold cards that may or may not be in their hands. And lest anyone be too suspicious, there are penalties for false accusations.

Each player picks a card, and the one who draws the highest card shuffles and deals out the entire deck, one card at a time, face down. It's fine if some players have more cards than others. Players sort their cards by rank, regardless of suit. Each player's goal is to be the first to get rid of all her cards.

The player on the dealer's left goes first by throwing any Aces he holds face down in the center, then calling out what he has thrown ("Two Aces," for example). If he doesn't have any Aces, he can (and must) fake it. To do this, he throws any other card face down and claims it's an Ace; in fact, he can throw two, three, or even four "Aces" if he wants. Unless another player calls his bluff—by loudly declaring, "I doubt it"—the fake Ace-thrower gets away with his deception. Even if a player does have Aces, he can do some bluffing, by adding extra cards to the real Aces and pretending they're Aces too.

Play goes around to the left, with the next player laying down and calling Twos, then Threes, and so on by rank, all the way up to Kings—at which point Aces start again. If at any time a thrower is challenged, she must flip over the cards in question. And if she has been bluffing, she pays the price for it: she has to take all the cards that have accumulated in the center pile. If, however, she has told the truth, the challenger is stuck with all the cards. The first player to get rid of all her cards wins.

Obviously, bluffing is risky. But if a player doesn't have the necessary cards, he has no choice. Bluffing even when a player does have the necessary cards may be reckless, but it's a great way to empty out a hand quickly—that is, if the player gets away with it. In either case, successful bluffing depends on being believable. The more cards a player claims to have, but doesn't, the more likely he is to have his bid challenged.

Players should be encouraged to keep a straight face, no matter what. Giggly or shifty-eyed bluffers won't be very good at this game. Very crafty players may pretend to be bluffing when they're not and stick the other players with the penalties of false accusations. As the game goes on, players should try to make honest plays, if they can, because more players will find it necessary to bluff and more will get caught.

Early in the game it may be a good idea to accuse another player of bluffing, even when it's almost certain she's telling the truth. The reason for this is that it's desirable to acquire at least one card of every rank, so a player does not need to bluff. The only way to fill in gaps in a player's hand is to pick up the pile. This strategy should not be used, however, when the pile gets too large or else you'll be stuck holding all the cards.

Commerce

This precursor of poker is a workout for the knuckles, as players announce their great hands with good, hard knocks!

Players: 3 or more

Ages: 6 and up

Place: Table or other flat surface, with seating for all the players

Equipment: Standard deck of cards; equal number of counters (such as candies, sticks of gum, buttons, or toothpicks) for each player

Three-card Commerce is a simple poker-type game that will delight young card buffs and introduce them to concepts like rank and suit. The object is to collect the most counters by getting one of the three special Commerce hands, which is similar to how hands in poker are won.

Before the game begins, every player receives the same number of counters. To start the first round, each player "antes up" by contributing one counter to the "pot" (the center pile where winnings collect). Everyone picks a card, and the one who draws the highest card shuffles and deals three cards, face down, to each player. Three more cards are placed face up on the table to form what is called the "widow" hand.

The goal in each round is to collect the strongest of three possible Commerce hands: a tricon (three of a kind); a sequence (three-card straight flush, which means three cards of the same suit in rank order); or a point (more than one card of the same suit, whose point values are added together). Three Aces is the highest tricon hand, and three Twos is the lowest. Ace-King-Queen is the highest sequence, and Three-Two-Ace is the lowest. In a point, Aces count as 11, face cards (Kings, Queens, Jacks) count as 10, and the other number cards equal their face values. The highest point would be

an Ace and two face cards (or a Ten) of the same suit, and the lowest point would be a Two and a Three of the same suit and a third card of a different suit. In Commerce, the worst hand is one that has three cards of different, nonsequential rank and all of different suits.

The dealer may exchange her entire hand for the widow before play begins, in which case the dealer's hand becomes the widow. The player on the dealer's right starts play off and may exchange any one of his cards for any one from the widow. Play continues to the right with each player having the chance to trade a card with the widow. A player may also opt to pass, but then may not exchange again for the rest of the round. When a player has a Commerce hand with which he is satisfied, he knocks on the table and stops playing ("stands"). The others go on, and after a second player stands, the round ends.

During any round, a player need not stand the instant he gets a Commerce hand; he may fear that this hand is so weak that the next player to get a Commerce hand will easily beat him. So he can stay in the round and try to strengthen his hand. Of course, this gives the other players further chances to strengthen their hands, too. So it's a gamble.

The second player's knock brings the moment of truth: each player shows her hand to the others. Tricon beats sequence and sequence beats point. A high tricon beats a low tricon; a high sequence beats a low sequence; and a three-card point beats a two-card point. Of course, a high three-card point beats a low three-card point, and a high two-card point beats a low two-card point. The best hand wins the round, and the winner takes the pot.

The player on the dealer's right deals the next round. The game may go on for as many rounds as desired. The person with the most counters at the end of the game is the winner.

Trade and Barter

In Trade and Barter, there is no widow hand. Instead, the players trade with the dealer's stack of undealt cards or barter with each other, and may do one or the other on each turn.

To make a trade, a player gives the dealer a counter and a card, face up, and receives a face-down card from the stack of undealt cards. (His old card is now no longer in play for the rest of the round.)

To barter, a player offers a face-down card from his hand to the player on his right for any face-down card in her hand. That player may refuse the barter, but if she does, she must knock on the table and "stand" with her hand. In that case, the round ends immediately, and everyone must show his hand. The winning hand is determined just as in Commerce. Needless to say, a player should be very satisfied with her hand before refusing a barter.

The dealer keeps the counters she received in trades, but must pay one counter to the winner at the end of the round. If, however, the dealer holds a tricon, sequence, or point but does not win the pot, she must pay a counter to those with better hands—or, according to some versions, to every other player. The dealer's aim, then, is to try to secure the best hand (to win the pot) or a non-Commerce hand (to avoid having to give away any counters).

Play or Pay

In this sequencing game, if there's no card to play, it's time to pay.

Players: 3 to 7

Ages: 7 to 12

Place: Table or other flat surface, with seating for all players

Equipment: Standard deck of cards; 20 counters (such as candies, sticks of gum, cookies, or pennies) for each player

Play or Pay, also known as Round the Corner, is a fun, quick card game with the bonus of a pot of goodies for the winner. Even the losers usually end up with a few rewarding treats.

Each player starts with 20 counters. Everyone picks a card, and the one who draws the highest card shuffles and deals out all the cards, one at a time and face down. All the players then sort their cards by suit and rank. The player on the dealer's left starts by laying a card from his hand face up in the middle. The player to his left must now follow by playing the next highest card in that same suit. If, for example, the first player has played the Nine of hearts, the second player must follow with the Ten of hearts, if she has it. If, however, she doesn't have the necessary card (which is pretty likely), she has to put one counter in the center of the table, next to the face-up pile. Then the next player to the left goes, either playing the necessary card, if he has it, or paying into the ever-growing pot of counters, if he doesn't. The Ace is both the high card and the low card in any suit. So whenever a King is played, the Ace follows—and then the Two follows the Ace. This is called "rounding the corner."

The person who plays the last card of a suit starts the next suit with any card from his hand. The first player to get rid of all her cards wins the round and takes the pot of goodies. The losers must give the winner one counter for each card left in their hands. After round one, the cards are shuffled and redealt. The player with the most counters after ten rounds wins the game.

Play or Pay is mostly a game of luck. The only strategy suggestion is that the player who leads should start with a suit in which he holds a lot of cards. By using this strategy, he'll have to pay as little as possible during that round.

Muggins

Muggins players must be wary—each is
just waiting for the other to slip up.

Players: 4 to 8

Ages: 7 to 14

Place: Table or other flat surface,
with seating for all players

Equipment: Standard deck of cards

The card version of Muggins—not
to be confused with the classic
dominoes version—originated in
Victorian times. The special feature of
this game is that each player polices
the other players' every move, trying
to catch someone in an innocent mistake. Kids will love the idea of "catching" their opponents in a wrong move.

Everyone picks a card, and the one
who draws the highest card shuffles
and deals. Four cards are laid out,
face up in a row, in the middle of the
table. These cards start piles that will
grow larger as play progresses. The
dealer then deals each player an equal
number of cards, face down. Players
neaten up their cards in a stack but
may not look at them. Leftover cards
are placed face up on any of the center piles. Each player's aim is to get
rid of all her cards during the game.

The player on the dealer's left starts
by turning over the top card in his
stack. If the card happens to be one
number higher or lower than any of
the face-up cards in the center, he lays
his card face up on that stack. The
suit doesn't matter. If, for example, he
turns over a Jack, and a Ten or a
Queen is showing on a center pile, he
places the Jack there. For any card
that could go on more than one stack,
the player may take his pick. The Ace
is low, so it can be played only on a
two, and the King is high, so only a
Queen can be played on a King.

If the first player can't play his card
onto one of the piles in the middle, he
places the card face up next to his
face-down pile. Then the next player
to the left tries to play a card from her
stack. If she can't play a card onto one
of the other piles, however, she has
another option: she can play onto the
first player's new face-up pile. If she
can't do that either, play passes on to
the next player.

The game continues in this way,
with players flipping over cards and
playing them (or not playing them)
onto center piles or onto other
players' face-up piles. But this is
not a free-for-all. A player must put
his card on a center pile whenever
possible. Also, if a card cannot be
placed on a center pile but can
be placed on more than one opponent's pile, the player must always
choose the opponent who is closest to his left.

If this sounds complicated, that's
just the point. Players watch each
other carefully to make sure
nobody breaks any of the rules
of sequence or tries to play an
inappropriate card. If someone
does trip up, the player who
notices shouts, "Muggins!" As
a penalty, the offending player
must take one card from the
face-down pile of each of the
other players and add it to
her own.

Play continues in this fashion.
If someone uses up all his
face-down cards, he turns his
face-up pile over and begins
playing those cards. The first
one to get rid of all her cards is
declared the winner.

Spit

In this race to get rid of all the cards, the hands must be as quick as the eyes.

Players: 2

Ages: 8 to 14

Place: Table or other flat surface, with seating for both players

Equipment: Standard deck of cards

Spit is also known as Speed for good reason—it's the fastest-paced card game of all. Exciting and challenging for school-age children, Spit demands completely focused attention and a fair amount of hand-eye coordination.

The opponents each pick a card, and whoever draws the higher card shuffles and deals out the deck, one card at a time, face down. Without looking at their cards, the players now each choose ten at random and lay them out in a grid in the following manner: First, each makes a row of four cards, left to right, with the first card face up and the other three face down. Then each makes a second row of three cards, overlapping the three face-down cards in the first row; in this new row, the first card is again face up and the others face down. A third overlapping row consists of just two cards, on the two face-down cards of the second row; the first card is face up and the second is face down. Finally, in a fourth row, one face-up card overlaps the face-down card of the third row. The rest of each player's cards are stacked face down to the left of the grid. This pile is the "spit" pile.

When both players are ready, they yell out together, "One, two, three. Spit!" At the shout "Spit!" both players take the top card from their spit piles and put it face up in the middle. As quickly as possible, both players try to play face-up cards from their grids onto their center piles. This can be done only if the face-up card in their grid is one above or one below the center card. The suit does not matter. If, for example, one of the center cards is a Six, a player may lay a Five or a Seven on top of it—if she has one face up in her grid. If a face-up card can be played, the face-down card just below it on the grid is immediately turned face up, and it becomes eligible for a trip to the center pile. If one of the four rows in a player's grid is played completely into the center, she may place a card from her spit pile face up in the newly empty spot. Players keep playing cards into the center pile, going up and down in sequence. They move at lightning speed, trying to beat their opponent to any spot for which they both have a card. This goes on until neither can play any more cards from the grid.

When both are stopped, the players again shout "Spit!" and each puts the top card from his spit pile into the center. Play continues, with players trying to play the cards from their grids onto the piles in the middle. If both stop because they've run out of possible plays, they once again shout "Spit!" and put out new cards from their spit piles. This sequence may be repeated as many times as necessary over the course of the game. If a player uses up his entire spit pile but still has cards in his grid, he must "spit" with the face-up card farthest to the left. The first player to get rid of all her cards is the winner.

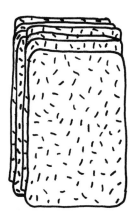    

Knockout Whist

This relatively simple game teaches several basic card-playing concepts.

Players: 2 to 7

Ages: 8 to 12

Place: Table or other flat surface, with seating for all players

Equipment: Standard deck of cards; pencil and paper for scoring

Playing Knockout Whist helps teach children such card-playing moves as winning tricks, following suit, and playing trumps. One way to explain these concepts is to say that winning a trick means beating all the other cards played in one round of play. To follow suit means playing a card in the same suit as the first card played in a round. And playing a trump is using a card from a suit whose cards, it has been agreed, will beat any cards from any other suit during that round. Players also need to know that they cannot play a trump card unless they do not have any cards from the suit that was led.

The object of Knockout Whist is to win the most tricks and to be the last player still "standing" at the end of the game. Each player picks a card, and the one who draws the highest card shuffles and deals seven cards, one at a time and face down, to each player. The players arrange their hands in order by suit and rank. The rest of the deck is placed face down in the center, and the dealer turns over the top card of the center stack. This card determines the trump suit for that hand: for instance, a Jack of diamonds means that diamonds are trump cards; a Seven of spades means that spades are trump.

The player to the dealer's left throws the first card. Proceeding clockwise, the other players must then each play a card that follows suit until every player has thrown a card.

If a player has no cards of the suit that was led, he may play a card from the trump suit or, if he has no trump cards (or does not wish to play them), any other card from his hand. If no trump card has been played, the card of the highest rank of the suit that was led wins the trick. (The cards are ranked in the standard way, with Aces high.) If only one player has thrown a trump card, she wins the trick; even the smallest trump card beats any card from any other suit. If more than one player has thrown a trump card, the highest trump card wins. Each player makes a pile of the tricks that she has won

and sets it to the side. The winner of each trick leads the next play.

The hand is over when all seven tricks have been played. Players who don't win any tricks are "knocked out" of the game, and any player who wins all seven tricks automatically wins the game. If no one wins all seven tricks, the winner of the last round gathers up all the cards, reshuffles them, and deals six cards to each player.

Play continues as before, with players who win no tricks during the hand dropping out. Again, if one player wins all the tricks, that player wins the game. As long as there is no single winner, however, play continues, hand after hand, with the number of cards dealt being reduced by one with each hand. In the third hand, five cards are dealt; in the fourth, four; and so on until each player receives only one card. Whoever wins the last trick then wins the game.

It's best for a player to lead with a card from a suit in which he holds either very many or very few cards. A high card should not be led unless it's an Ace, which is high and will guarantee winning the trick.

Knaves

"Knave" is another word for "Jack," and that's the card to avoid in this game.

Players: 3

Ages: 8 to 14

Place: Table or other flat surface, with seating for all players

Equipment: Standard deck of cards; pencil and paper for scoring

Knaves is a straightforward game in the spirit of Knockout Whist and Hearts, but there's a special twist. In this game two players can join forces against the third if it looks as if she's getting close to winning. In the end, though, it's every player for himself, so alliances can shift in the blink of an eye.

Each player picks a card, and the one who draws the highest card shuffles and deals 17 cards to each player, one at a time and face down. The players arrange their hands in order by suit and rank. Fifty-one of the 52 cards have now been dealt, and the dealer turns over the last card to determine the trump suit for that hand. The trump suit is the suit whose cards will beat any cards from any other suit during that hand. If the card turned over is a Jack, the hand is played without a trump suit ("no trump"). This card is then put aside. The aim of each player over the course of the game is to win as many "tricks" as possible—except any trick with a Jack. To win a trick means to beat all the other cards that are thrown in one round of play.

The player on the dealer's left leads by throwing any card. The next player to the left follows by adding another card of the same suit, if she has one. If she doesn't have a card of that suit, she may throw a card from the trump suit or a card from another suit. The third player faces the same alternatives. If no trump cards are played,

the highest card in the suit that led wins the trick; if trump cards are played, the highest trump card wins the trick, with the Ace beating the King. The winner stacks the cards in a pile beside him and then starts the next round by leading with any card. The hand is finished when all the cards have been played.

Now the points are tallied. Players get 1 point for every trick they take, but points are subtracted for the Jacks. The Jack of hearts carries a penalty of –4 points, the Jack of diamonds –3, the Jack of spades –2, and

the Jack of clubs –1. There is one big exception, though: if a player manages to capture all four jacks, he is rewarded with 10 points. After the score for that hand is totaled, the player to the left of the first dealer gathers all the cards, shuffles, and deals a new hand. The game continues in this way until a player wins by reaching at least 20 points; if two or more players do this, the high scorer wins.

Top Knaves players keep a few

simple strategies in mind. A player who has only one card from a suit should lead with it (if she's the one leading). That way, she can use a trump card (if she has one) to win the trick the next time a player leads with that suit. She should also consider leading from a suit in which she has a lot of cards—that keeps what's in her hand a secret for a little while longer. Finally, a player should try not to play an Ace, King, or Queen unless the Jack of that suit has been played in a previous trick; otherwise, another player will probably stick her with the Jack. Of course, this doesn't apply if she's the last to throw on a trick that has no Jacks.

It's common in Knaves that when one player takes a strong lead, the other two temporarily forget their differences and join forces to thwart the leader. They will, for example, try

not to beat out each other for tricks the leader is bound to lose; this way, they can save their high cards for later tricks. And they'll go out of their way not to dump any Jacks on each other, throwing only a harmless card when the other is poised to win a trick. Instead, they'll save their Jacks for when the leader is set to win a trick. Of course, these partnerships inevitably break down once the score starts to even out and the game is on the line.

Linger Longer

In Linger Longer, as the name implies, the victor is the player with the most staying power.

Players: 4 to 6

Ages: 8 and up

Place: Table or other flat surface, with seating for all players

Equipment: Standard deck of cards

Linger Longer, like Knockout Whist and Knaves, is a great game for teaching young players about tricks and trumps. But there's no hurry to finish the game. In Linger Longer, all the players try to hold on to their cards rather than racing to get rid of them.

Everyone picks a card, and the one who draws the highest card shuffles and deals. Each player receives the same number of cards as there are players in the game, one at a time and face down. If there are four players, for example, each player gets four cards. The rest of the cards go in a stack—called the "stock" pile—in the center of the table. The dealer then reveals, but still holds on to, the last card he dealt to himself: this card's suit is the trump suit for the game—the suit whose cards will beat any cards from any other suit. Every player should arrange his cards by suit and rank. Throughout the game each player tries to win as many tricks as possible. To win a trick means to beat all the other cards that are thrown in one round of play.

The player on the dealer's left starts by laying any card face up in the center of the table. The next player plays a card in the same suit, if she has one. If she can't follow suit, she may play any other card in her hand, including a card from the trump suit. Once each player has thrown a card, the highest card from the suit that led wins the trick, unless a card from the trump suit has been played. In that case, the highest trump card—Aces beat kings—wins the trick. The winner of each trick makes a pile of the cards she has won and sets it off to one side. She then draws a card from the stock pile (no one else does) and leads the next round.

One by one, players who go for long stretches without winning a trick will find they have no cards left in their hands. That puts them out of the game. The last player left with cards wins the game.

Blackout

A game for the seasoned cardplayer, Blackout teaches concepts like bidding and trumping.

Players: 3 to 7

Ages: 9 and up

Place: Table or other flat surface, with seating for all players

Equipment: Standard deck of cards; pencil and paper for scoring

Blackout, sometimes called Oh Pshaw, is from the whist family of card games, which originated in the eighteenth century. Blackout, which should be taught only to children who have mastered simpler card games, features a complicated bidding system in which each player tries to predict, before play gets under way, the number of "tricks" he expects to win. To win a trick means to beat all the other cards that are thrown in one round of play. Points are won by predicting correctly.

To select the dealer, each player picks a card from the deck; the player who draws the highest card shuffles and deals to the left. For the first hand, each player is dealt one card, face down. For each subsequent hand, the job of dealing shifts to the next player on the left, all the cards are reshuffled, and the number of cards dealt to each player is increased by one. When the size of the deal cannot be increased by one card per player, the last hand has been dealt. So for four players, the cards will be dealt a total of 13 times; for five players, 10 times; and so on.

At the end of each deal, the top card of the "stock" pile (the pile being dealt from) is turned over to indicate the "trump suit"—the suit whose cards will beat any cards from any other suit during that hand. If there are no leftover cards in the last hand, there is no trump suit.

Before the game begins, one player should be assigned the job of recording all the bids and toting up the score at the end of each round. After the deal, the players pick up their cards and engage in bidding before the play of the cards begins. Starting with the dealer, each player bids the number of tricks she expects to win. If she does not expect to win any, she bids "nullo" (a special word for "nothing").

Bidding accurately is difficult, so it's important to understand beforehand how the cards will be played. Each trick will be won by the player who either plays the highest card in the suit that was led for that round or throws the highest trump card. In the first hand, 1 and nullo are the only possible bids because each player has only one card, so there will only one round of play before the next deal. As the size of the hand increases, the number of possible bids increases accordingly: for instance, in a hand where seven cards are dealt, the bid may range from nullo up to 7.

Since it's more difficult to win tricks than to lose them, it's usually a good strategy to "underbid" a hand by 1 point: for example, if a player thinks he can win seven tricks, he bids 6; if he thinks he can take only one trick, he bids nullo. This gives the bidder a little room for error. After all, if a player finds herself winning more tricks than expected, she can intentionally try to lose one.

The first card is played by the player to the dealer's left. Each of the other players must then put down a card of the same suit until every player has thrown a card. If he has no cards of the suit that was led, a player may play a card from the trump suit or, if he has no trump cards (or does not wish to play them), any other card from his hand. If no trump card has been played, the card of the highest rank of the suit that was led wins the trick. (The cards are ranked in the standard way, with Aces high.) If only one player has thrown a trump card, she wins the trick; even the smallest trump card beats any card from any other suit. If more than one player has thrown a trump card, the highest trump card wins. Each player makes a pile of the tricks that she has won and sets it to the side. The winner of each trick leads the next round of play.

Because trump cards (especially high ones) are so valuable, players are advised to use them sparingly—generally throwing them only when they can be sure to win a trick. This requires remembering what other trump cards have been played. It's not usually a good idea to lead with the trump suit.

The game continues until all the hands have been dealt and played. A running tally of the score is kept after each hand. Players win points only when their bids exactly match the number of tricks taken. (No score is given if a player takes more or fewer tricks than she bid.) When a player

has bid correctly, she gets 1 point for each trick taken plus a bonus of 10 points. (For example, if she has made a bid of 3, her score for that hand is 13 points.) The "nullo" bid is an exception to this rule. Because it becomes more difficult to make nullo as the number of cards dealt increases, a player who accurately bids nullo (that is, who bids nullo and takes no tricks) gets 5 points plus the entire

number of tricks in that hand. (For example, if a player bids nullo in a round of ten tricks and, in fact, wins no tricks, she scores 15.) The winner is the player with the highest score after all the hands have been played.

Hearts

Players battle to score the fewest points in this classic game.

Players: 3 to 6

Ages: 9 and up

Place: Table or other flat surface, with seating for all players

Equipment: Standard deck of cards; pencil and paper for scoring

A sophisticated Hearts match involves a lot of strategy, but the game can also be played on a much more basic level. Convincing children that the player who ends up with the most points is the loser is sometimes difficult—it may help to present the points earned as marks against you.

Hearts is played with a full deck only if there are exactly four players. Otherwise, one or more cards must be removed before play begins. If there are three players, the Two of clubs is removed; if there are five players, both the Two of clubs and the Two of diamonds are out; if there are six players, the Twos of clubs, diamonds, and spades are out, and so is the Three of clubs. This way, when the deck is dealt, each player will have an equal number of cards.

To start, each player picks a card, and the one who draws the highest card deals. The dealer deals out all

the cards, one at a time and face down. Everyone should arrange her hand by suit and rank.

The aim of each player is to avoid winning any "tricks" that contain any hearts or the Queen of spades. A trick consists of all the cards played in one round. Hearts and the Queen of spades are to be avoided because they are all worth points, and in this game the object is to accumulate as few points as possible.

Before play gets under way, each player selects three cards from his hand and passes them, face down, to the player on his right, who now must add these new cards to his hand. (A variation of the game skips the pass.)

The real action begins differently depending on the number of players.

If there are four players, the player with the Two of clubs starts by throwing that card face up into the center. In games with three, five, or six players, the person to the dealer's left leads with any card—except a heart or the Queen of spades.

In either case, the next player to the left follows by throwing another card of the same suit as the starter, if he has one. If he doesn't have a card of that suit, he may throw any other card at all, including a heart. But there's one exception: no one is allowed to throw the Queen of spades in the first round. After all the players have thrown one card, the first round is over. The player who threw the highest card in the suit that started the round takes the trick, which is not good news if the trick contains any hearts. (Later in the game, the news may be even worse—if the trick contains the Queen of spades.)

The taker of the trick picks up the cards, puts them face down in a pile beside him, and leads the next round. He can open with any club, diamond, or spade in his hand. He can even open with a heart—but only if a heart has been played in the earlier round. No one can lead with a heart until hearts have been "broken."

When all the cards have been played, it's time to tally up the scores. Each heart is worth 1 point and the Queen of spades is worth a whopping 13. The one quirk in this scoring system is that if a player happens to have captured all the hearts *and* the Queen of spades, too, she actually gets a big reward: 26 points are deducted from her score. This is called "shooting the moon." Sometimes it will happen by accident, but it usually takes a lot of planning. But going for it is very risky, because if a player fails to capture just one heart, all the other hearts she has captured (and the Queen of spades) will count against her.

After tallying the score, the player to the left of the original dealer shuffles and deals the next hand. Play continues until one or more players reaches a total of 50 points. The person with the lowest score wins.

The tricky rules of Hearts require smart strategizing from the moment players first pass cards. The Queen of spades should not necessarily be passed at the beginning of the game, since the player who possesses the unlucky lady has control over when she will be played. To avoid being stuck with her, however, a player should be sure to have some low spades, so he can save the Queen until someone else plays the Ace or King. The Ace and King of spades should be passed to another player during the passing round unless a player thinks his hand is so good that he might be able to shoot the moon.

Since no one wants to win hearts, a player should try to lead with low hearts (once hearts have been broken) and discard them whenever possible. A few high cards should be kept on hand for winning tricks without any hearts in them. But a player should not hold on to too many high cards toward the end of the hand—that's when the others are sure to start dumping their unwanted cards.

Rummy

Rummy players need clear heads if they hope to win. And if they tire of one version of the game, there are many variations to try.

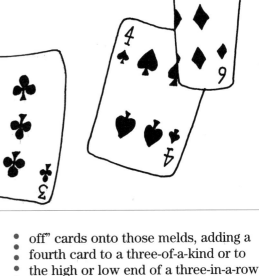

Players: 2 to 6

Ages: 10 and up

Place: Table or other flat surface, with seating for all players

Equipment: Standard deck of cards; pencil and paper for scoring

R ummy is one of the most popular card games around—and for good reason! Although relatively uncomplicated, a good game of Rummy requires a lot of strategic thinking. Paying attention to what the other players are doing and having the flexibility to rethink positions constantly are the two most important paths to success in this game.

Everyone picks a card, and the one who draws the highest card shuffles and deals one card at a time, face down, to all the players. If there are two players, each gets ten cards; if there are three or four players, each

gets seven; if there are five or six, each gets six cards. The rest of the cards are then placed face down in a stack in the middle. This is the "stock" pile. The top card of the stock pile is turned over and set alongside the stock to start a discard pile.

Each player's object is to get rid of all her cards during the game. The only way to do this is to collect certain combinations of cards, called "melds." Melds include any group of three or four cards of the same rank, or any sequence of three or four cards of the same suit. Four Sixes or three Queens, for example, make a meld, as do the Two, Three, and Four of clubs or the Nine, Ten, and Jack of diamonds. (Aces are low when putting together sequences, so a player can use sequence Ace, Two, Three but not Queen, King, Ace.)

The player to the dealer's left begins by picking the top card from either the face-down stock pile or the face-up discard pile. He then discards any card from his hand onto the discard pile. (If he has picked a card from the discard pile, however, he can't discard the same card.) Play proceeds clockwise, with each player picking and discarding a card. Whenever a player gets a meld, she lays it face up on the table. A player may even have a meld to lay out right after the initial deal, and that's fine.

As players begin putting out their melds, the other players on their turns may "lay

off" cards onto those melds, adding a fourth card to a three-of-a-kind or to the high or low end of a three-in-a-row sequence. (A four-card sequence may not be added to.) For example, if someone has played three Aces and another player has the fourth, that player may lay down her Ace when her turn comes. If someone has melded the Five, Six, and Seven of hearts, someone else may lay off the Four or the Eight of hearts. Players may lay off as many cards as possible during a turn.

If the stock runs out and the player does not want the top card in the discard pile, the discard pile is turned over and used as a new stock. The first player to "go out" (play all his cards) wins the hand. A player does not have to discard when he goes out, unless he wants to.

Now the score is tallied. The value of all the cards left in other players' hands (the "deadwood") is awarded to the winner. Aces are worth 1, face cards (Jack, Queen, King) are worth 10, and the number cards are worth their number value. The winner doubles his score on the hand if he manages to win by "going rummy." Going rummy means putting out every one of his cards on a single turn. To do this, he must not yet, up to that point in the hand, have laid out any melds or laid off any cards on opponents' melds. Usually, going rummy happens early in the hand if it happens at all—

unless some bold player holds back any melds in hopes of being able to go rummy later in the hand.

After the first hand is scored, the player on the dealer's left shuffles the cards and deals the next hand. It's especially important in this game to shuffle the cards well. The game continues until one player reaches a predetermined score, usually 500 points. If two or more players top 500 simultaneously, the high scorer wins.

During any hand, players should pay attention to what everyone else is doing. A player should try not to discard a card that she thinks the player to her left can use. By keeping track of which cards each opponent picks up and puts down a player can know what others need and avoid helping them out.

It's important for a player to change tactics if other players seem to be snatching up all the cards that he needs. The more flexible a player is about changing the groups and sequences he's trying to collect, the more successful he'll be. If his opponents seem to be going for group melds, a player should try to do sequence melds, and vice versa. Finally, to keep the hand winner's score low, players should avoid getting caught holding a lot of high-point cards at the end of a hand. Unwanted face cards should be discarded early in the game.

Knock Rummy

Knock Rummy, also called Poker Rummy, requires players to take a gamble. Instead of laying down melds as they occur, all are held until the end of the hand. There is thus no laying off on other players' melds. Each player is dealt six cards no matter how many players are in the game, and play proceeds as in ordinary Rummy, with each player trying to make melds and reduce the amount of deadwood (unused cards) in his hand. Any player who has a good hand and thinks she will have less deadwood than her opponents can end the hand by knocking on the table when it's her turn. She then discards one card and shows her other cards. The other

players then show their cards.

If a player who has knocked does turn out to have the least deadwood, she wins the hand, and her score is calculated by deducting her deadwood from that of each of the other players' hands and then totaling these differences. If the player who knocks has rummy (only melds—no deadwood—in her hand), she gets 25 bonus points from each of the other players, even if another player also has a rummy hand.

Except in the case of rummy, if someone knocks but then ties with another player, the other player wins

and gets the big points. If, however, a player knocks but it turns out that someone else has the least deadwood, the player who knocked actually loses 10 points, and the winner gets the 10 points as a bonus.

Round-the-Corner Rummy

Also called High-Low Rummy, this game differs from classic Rummy in that, in a sequence, an Ace may serve as a high card, a low card, or both. King-Ace-Two, for example, is a valid meld, going "round the corner." Aces always count for 11 points in this version. Otherwise, scoring is the same as usual.

Boathouse Rummy

This game is played in the same way as classic Rummy, except that each time a player draws from the discard pile, she must also draw from the stock. The player then discards only one card. Also, melds are not shown until one player goes rummy, so cards cannot be laid off on other players'

melds. As in Round-the-Corner Rummy, an Ace may serve as a high or a low card and melds may be made "round the corner" (King-Ace-Two, for example). When a player cries out "Rummy!" the other players reveal their melds. Aces count for 11 points, but otherwise Boathouse Rummy is scored in the same way as classic Rummy, with only the unmelded cards in the players' hands counting toward the winner's score. There is no bonus for going rummy.

Queen City

Queen City is also called One-Meld Rummy. As in Boathouse Rummy, players may go out only by going rummy. In this version the score is based not on the opponents' deadwood, but on the value of the winner's hand. Aces count as 11 points. In this variation, as players scramble to go rummy, they will want to work as many high cards as possible into their melds.

Call Rummy

In this louder-than-usual version of Rummy, players need to keep an eagle eye on what their opponents discard. The object is to catch another player discarding a card that could have been laid off. The player who notices the mistake calls out "Rummy!" and grabs the card. That player then lays off the card and replaces it with a discard from his own hand. If two players yell "Rummy!" at the same time, the card goes to the player whose turn is coming up sooner. Otherwise, the rules are the same as they are in classic Rummy.

Discard Rummy

True to its name, in this version of Rummy a player can go out only if her turn ends with a discard. The last card cannot be played by melding or laying off. Otherwise, play and scoring are the same as in classic Rummy.

Casino

In this ancient game requiring good math skills, the winner is the one who captures the most cards.

Players: 2 to 4

Ages: 10 and up

Place: Table or other flat surface, with seating for all players

Equipment: Standard deck of cards; pencil and paper for scoring

Casino, which dates back to fifteenth-century France, was one of the most popular card games in the United States roughly 100 years ago. Although it seems straightforward, players need considerable mathematical prowess to compete successfully. Kids who are old enough to grasp the math and remember the somewhat intricate rules will enjoy learning a card game that involves some real thinking.

Each player picks a card from the deck, and whoever has the highest card shuffles and deals. The dealer deals four cards, two at a time and face down, to each player. Four more are laid face up on the table. The players now try to use cards in their hands to capture the face-up cards. There are four ways to do this: pairing, combining, building, and calling.

Pairing is exactly what it sounds like. Any card on the table may be captured by pairing it with a card of the same rank from the player's hand. An Ace, for example, takes any and all Aces on the table.

Combining is where the math comes in. A player can take two or more cards on the table whose numerical values add up to any single card in his hand. For example, a Ten in a player's hand can take a Five, Three, and Two from the table. In these calculations, Aces count as Ones. Face cards (Jacks, Queens, Kings) cannot be taken in combinations. Two combinations can be captured at the same time, as long as each combination adds up to the value of the card from the player's hand. An Eight can take a Seven and an Ace as well as a Five and a Three, if they're all face up on the table. A player can also pair and combine in a single play —using a Six, for example, to take a Six and two Threes.

Building involves planning future combinations. To build, a player lays a card from her hand on top of one on the table. The pair is collected on the next turn with another card that equals their total value. If there is a Six on the table, for example, and the player has a Three and a Nine in her hand, she can place the Three on the Six, call out "Nine," and then hope to capture the pair with the Nine on her next turn. It's risky, though. Another player can either add onto the build or collect the cards with his own Nine before the original builder's turn comes around again. Although an opponent can raise another's build, no one can raise her own.

Calling (or duplicating) is a sort of multiple building. In calling, a player creates a build (adding a Two to a Seven, for example, to make a Nine) that is equal to another build (say, a Three and a Six) already on the table. Or he creates two builds (or a build

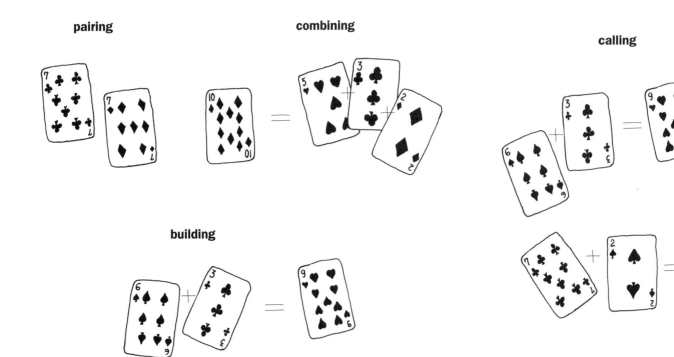

pairing

combining

calling

building

Casino Scoring

7 or more spades in pile = 1 point

"little casino" = 1 point

"big casino" = 2 points

27 or more cards in pile = 3 points

"sweep" = 1 point

and a pair) of the same value. He then stacks both builds into a single pile and calls out their shared value ("Nines!"). Like a standard build, the stack cannot be collected until the next turn and may be captured by another player with the right card in the meantime. Unlike a standard build, however, once a call is made, the cards cannot be built upon further; they can only be captured by a card of the specified value.

Play starts to the dealer's left. Captured cards are placed in a pile in front of each player. If a player's turn comes and she cannot build or capture, she must add one card from her hand to the face-up cards on the table. With all the picking up and laying down of cards on the table, the number of cards there can vary a great deal during the game; sometimes all the face-up cards will have been captured, leaving the center of the table empty. In that case, the player whose turn it is has no choice but to give up a card from her hand.

After the original hands have been played, four more cards are dealt to each player in the same manner, but no more are laid in the center. If there are fewer than four cards left in the deck, these are dealt out anyway—some players simply won't get another

card. Play continues until the whole deck has been dealt out and the players have made all the plays they can. If any face-up cards are still left on the table, the last player to have captured a card gets them. This ends the round.

Each player's score is tallied up at the end of the round, and points are awarded based on what's in a player's capture pile. Here's how to score: 1 point for the Two of spades ("little casino"); 2 points for the Ten of diamonds ("big casino"); 1 point for a pile with seven or more total spades; 3 points for a pile with 27 or more total cards. One point is also awarded to any player who, during the course of the round, captures all the cards on the table in a single move (a "sweep"); so the players should be sure to keep track of this as the round goes on.

Obviously, players will be angling to capture as many cards as possible on any round in hopes of reaching the valuable total of 27. But because the "little casino" and "big casino" cards are also worth points, a special effort should be made to grab them by including them in any pairs, combinations, builds, or calls. The same is true of spades, if a player has any hope of getting seven of them.

Generally, Casino continues until, at the end of a round, at least one player has reached a score of 21 (or some other predetermined total); high scorer wins. But each round can also count as a game in itself.

Royal Casino

In this variation, the face cards are given numerical values and can therefore be built upon and captured like the other cards. Jacks are worth 11 points; Queens are worth 12 points; and Kings are worth 13 points. Aces can be treated as either 14 points or 1 point on any given play. The rest of the game is played the same way as regular Casino.

Mind Games

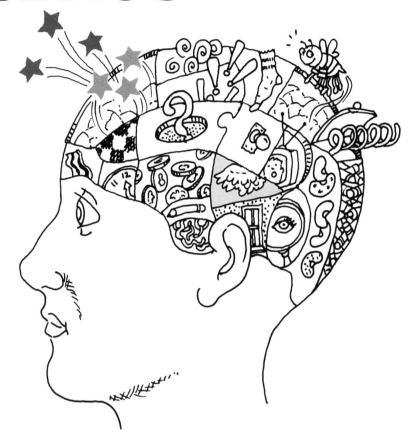

Whether they rely on the power of imagination, observation, memory, or logic, mind games develop thinking skills *and* provide lots of fun. Some mind games could also be categorized as word games, but even the games in this chapter that involve words are based more on the manipulation of ideas than on the manipulation of the words themselves. And just because these are games of the mind doesn't mean the body doesn't get involved, too! Acting games like Charades and Dumb Crambo get everyone up and moving. Most of these games can be played almost anywhere, and the only equipment needed is a dash of creativity and a nimble brain. A few, as noted, require paper and pencil and small objects. In some cases, a clock or other timer with a second hand may be helpful to monitor time limits.

I Spy

This classic guessing game is good training for future sleuths.

Players: 3 or more

Ages: 3 to 10

Place: Anywhere

Equipment: None

Generations of children have played and enjoyed I Spy. The game is so much fun because it has few rules and can be played anywhere—in fact, it's a wonderful travel game. It's also educational for younger children who are in the process of learning to identify objects by color and initial letters.

To play, one person chooses an object that is in view of all the players and says, "I spy, with my little eye, something that is _____." The blank is filled in with the name of a color. For example, if the object is a houseplant, the player would say, "I spy, with my little eye, something that is green."

The other players now try to guess the object. Each takes a turn naming something green until the mystery is solved. The player who guesses right is the winner and gets to choose the next object. To keep the other players guessing, it's best to choose an object with a common color—if there is only one thing in sight that is lavender, for example, the game will be too easy.

Alphabet I Spy

In this version of I Spy, suited for slightly older children (5 to 10), the clue is the first letter of the object's name rather than its color. For example, if the object is a sheep, the player would say, "I spy, with my little eye, something that begins with S." For a more challenging game, players are assigned a letter of the alphabet and must pick an object that begins with that letter. The object is then identified by its color: "I spy, with my little eye, something that is blue." If the player has the letter B, the guesses could be berry, bird, book, ball, and so on. Going through each letter in the alphabet makes for a great time-filler while traveling.

Wrong!

In Wrong! players test their skills at detecting errors in a story.

Players: 2 or more, plus an adult or older child to serve as storyteller

Ages: 4 to 10

Place: Anywhere with seating for all players

Equipment: Pencil and paper for writing story and scoring (optional)

Wrong! is similar to the old children's challenge What's Wrong with This Picture? But instead of trying to find the inconsistencies in a picture, players must listen carefully to discover flaws in a story that is told to them. This game can be tailored to the age and ability level of the players, with obvious errors being put in for young listeners and subtle ones for older, savvier players. Wrong! delights children by offering a silly story and some chuckles, but it's also a great exercise in listening and logic.

Before the game begins, an adult or older child makes up a short story that is filled with errors of common sense. Most storytellers will want to write down the tale, and that's fine. The storyteller may stick in blatant errors and say, for example, "Last summer, in the middle of a terrible blizzard . . ."; "I picked the bluest apple on the tree"; "The cat next door had puppies yesterday." Or the storyteller may make the errors harder to detect—for example, "The curtains on my windowsill are yellow and white," or "I went to the library and bought three books."

After the story is composed, the storyteller reads or tells it to the other players. The players listen carefully and shout "Wrong!" whenever they hear an error. The first player to detect each mistake scores a point. If more than one player catches an error at the same time, all the error-catchers get a point. Any player who calls out "Wrong!" when there is no error loses a point. (The storyteller may wish to point out any errors that go unnoticed.)

The player with the most points at the end of the story wins the game.

Up, Jenkins!

Is the hand quicker than the eye? Players test their powers of observation in this fast-paced game.

Players: 8 or more

Ages: 5 to 9

Place: Long table, with seating for all players

Equipment: Quarter; pencil and paper for scoring (optional)

Up, Jenkins! is like the old gambling game where a pea is hidden under one of three shells. In this case, though, the goal is to guess which hand is holding a quarter. This is a great party game for school-age kids because it's based on teamwork and cooperation.

Players split up into two teams, which sit facing each other on opposite sides of a long table—the longer, the better. Each team chooses a captain or the players can take turns being captain. One team takes possession of the quarter first and begins passing it back and forth from hand to hand under the table, out of sight of the opposing team.

The captain of the team without the quarter slowly counts from 1 to 10 and then yells, "Up, Jenkins!" At this call, all the players on the team with the quarter raise their fists in the air. Then the captain of the other team calls, "Down, Jenkins!" and all the members of the team with the quarter must open their fists as they slap their hands down on the table, all the time trying to keep the coin hidden.

Now the team without the quarter confers and tries to figure out who has the quarter. This is where being an astute listener and observer pays off. Players need to have listened for the sound of the coin clinking against the table and to have watched the faces and hands of the opponents as they tried to conceal the quarter.

After the team without the quarter has reached their decision, the captain calls out the names of all the players on the other team except the one thought to be hiding the quarter. As each player's name is called, that player must turn over his hands. If the quarter shows up before the last player is called, the team hiding the quarter earns a point and gets to hide it again. If the other team guesses correctly, they get a point and the chance to pass the quarter.

The team with the most points after a specified period of time (usually between 5 and 15 minutes) is the winner of the game.

For a more challenging game, players may be required to guess not only the player who is holding the quarter, but also the hand in which the quarter is hidden.

Odd Bean

In this game of chance, players must guess the number of beans in their opponents' hands.

Players: 2 or more

Ages: 6 to 10

Place: Anywhere

Equipment: 12 dried beans per player; 1 small bag per player (to hold the beans)

Odd Bean is a guessing game to some, a test of psychic powers to others. Either way, kids who understand the concept of odd and even numbers will enjoy trying to win every last one of their opponents' beans.

Each player is given a small bag—a plastic sandwich bag or paper lunch bag works well—containing 12 dried beans.

The first player reaches into her bag, fills her fist with any number of beans (except zero), and asks the second player, "Odds or evens?" The second player takes a guess. If the guess is correct, the second player wins the beans in the hand of the first player. If the guess is wrong, the second player must give the first player the same number of beans that the first player is holding.

The second player then repeats the process, asking the third player (or the first if there are only two players), "Odds or evens?" The game continues in this manner. Any player who loses all his beans is out of the game. (Obviously, it's not a good idea to risk too many beans on a turn.) The winner is the first one to collect all the beans or the player who has the most beans after a specified period of time.

Numbers

This number game resembles a mathematical version of Musical Chairs.

Players: 10 or more, plus an adult or older child to serve as leader

Ages: 6 to 10

Place: Indoors in large room (cleared of furniture and breakable objects) or outdoors

Equipment: None

The more people involved in a game of Numbers, the more fun it is, and that makes for a wonderful party game. If the game is played indoors, it's a good idea to clear a large space in the middle of the room, because the game involves a lot of rushing around.

An adult or older child acts as the leader and counts the number of players. The leader then begins the game by calling out, "Mix into twos!" Everyone in the group must find and join hands with a partner as quickly as possible. Anyone left out is out of the game. If there is an even number of players, everybody will survive the first round.

Next, the leader calls out, "Mix into threes!" Anyone who cannot find two partners is out of the game. The leader continues calling out numbers—not necessarily in sequence—as long as there are enough players left in the game to make at least one group of that number. The leader needs to make some quick calculations as the group gets smaller so that it can eventually be whittled down to only two players. The last pair to remain in the game is the winning team.

For example, a group of ten may be mixed into twos, which produces five groups with no one eliminated. Then they might be mixed into threes, which produces three groups, with one player eliminated; in other words, they're down to nine players. Then come fours, producing two groups, with one player eliminated; they're down to eight. Then come threes again, producing two groups, with two players eliminated; now they're down to six. Then fours again, producing one group, with two players eliminated; down to four. Then threes, producing one group, with one player eliminated; down to three. Then twos, producing one group, with one player eliminated. Clearly, the more players there are, the more creative the caller can be.

To make Numbers more challenging for older players, the leader can use fractions. If the leader calls out, "Mix into groups of one-third of nine!" players must quickly figure out that they need to form groups of three.

Orchestra

Players learn to follow the conductor's lead in this silent symphony.

Players: 5 or more

Ages: 6 to 12

Place: Anywhere with seating for all players

Equipment: None

Orchestra is a wonderful observation game that also teaches children about different musical instruments. Parents will appreciate the fact that even if the room is full of kids playing Orchestra, there won't be a sound.

One player is chosen to be the conductor, and the rest of the group sits facing him in a row or a semicircle. Each child, including the conductor, chooses a different imaginary instrument to play. Violin, flute, trombone, drums, trumpet, tuba, saxophone, harp, piano, banjo, harmonica, and xylophone are all good choices.

The conductor begins the game by pretending to play his instrument, and the orchestra follows by pretending to toot, strum, and beat their own instruments. No one is allowed to make a sound. After all the other players have begun their motions, the conductor suddenly switches from playing his own instrument to playing one of the other musicians' instruments. The members of the orchestra observe this change and everyone, except for the player whose instrument it is, switches to the same motions as the conductor.

The player whose instrument is being imitated must stop playing and put her hands over her ears. For example, if the conductor switches from the harp to the tuba, the tuba player covers her ears while the rest of the orchestra toots the tuba.

After a bit, the conductor resumes playing his original instrument, and

the other players—including the one with her hands over her ears—do the same. This goes on for a few seconds and then the conductor switches to another instrument again.

A player who fails to make the right motion—who either continues to play her own instrument when the conductor is playing it or who doesn't change instruments at the correct time—is out of the game.

The last remaining orchestra member is the winner and becomes the conductor for the next round.

Total Recall

This game demands a keen eye and a sharp memory.

Players: 2 or more, plus an adult or older child to set up the game

Ages: 6 to 10

Place: Table or other flat writing surface, with seating for all players

Equipment: Large tray, with cloth to cover it; assortment of 20 to 25 small objects; pencil and paper for each player

Total Recall, also called the Memory Game, is a simple exercise in short-term memory and observation. It's a good idea to start out with just a few objects for young children and gradually build up to a large assortment for the real memory demons.

Before the game gets under way, an adult or older child prepares, out of sight of the other players, a tray with an assortment of 20 to 25 small objects on it. The objects can be anything: coins of different denominations, pieces of jewelry, small toys, teacups, pens, flowers—the more diverse the assortment of objects, the better! After spreading the objects on the tray, the preparer covers the

whole display with a dish towel or similar cloth.

Players now gather around the tray and the preparer removes the cloth for 1 to 3 minutes. During that time the players must memorize as many of the objects as they can. When the

time is up, the tray is covered again and players are given another 3 minutes to write down all the things they remember seeing.

The player who lists the most correct objects wins the game. If two or more players list the same number, the more precise description determines the winner: for instance, "a gold earring" beats "an earring," and "a pink rose" beats "a flower."

If the players become very good at the game, the number of objects can be increased to make it more challenging for everyone.

Going on a Picnic

Don't forget anything when packing for this picnic, or it's back to the beginning of this alphabetical memory game.

Players: 2 or more

Ages: 6 to 12

Place: Anywhere

Equipment: None

It's fortunate that Going on a Picnic is just a mind game because the imaginary picnic basket involved can get extremely heavy. This game reinforces alphabetizing skills and is also an excellent workout for young memories. Although it can be played almost anywhere, Going on a Picnic is a wonderful way to pass the time on a long car ride.

The game begins with the first player reciting the sentence "I'm going on a picnic and I'm bringing _____." The player must fill in the blank completing the sentence, with an appropriate word or short phrase beginning with the letter A, such as "apples" or "American cheese."

The second player must repeat the sentence just as the first player said it and add an item that begins with B. For example, "I'm going on a picnic and I'm bringing apples and bread." The game continues, around and around, with each player repeating the complete list of items and then adding something that begins with the next letter of the alphabet.

As the list lengthens, it becomes more and more difficult to remember: "I'm going on a picnic and I'm bringing apples, bread, cake, doughnuts, eggs, figs, grapes, a hat, ice cream, juice, kidney beans, lamb chops, and macaroni." And that's only half the alphabet! (If the players agree beforehand, the letter X and other difficult letters, like Q and Z, can be left off the list.)

If a player makes a mistake, he's immediately out of the game. The winner is the last person left, provided she can repeat the whole basketful of items collected without making any mistakes.

"Categories" Going on a Picnic

In this variation, instead of adding items that begin with the next letter of the alphabet, players decide on a category that all the items must fit. Toys, names, animals, or vehicles are all examples of categories that can be used. The items don't have to follow in alphabetical order, but the whole chain must be remembered in the correct sequence, so this variation can be much more difficult than the standard version of the game. It can truly test memory skills.

Grandmother's Trunk

This memory game, which is also called I Went on a Trip or I Packed My Bag, is suitable for slightly younger players (ages 5 to 10) because it doesn't require alphabetizing or fitting answers into specific cat-

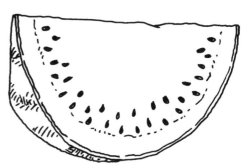

egories. Instead, kids can pack their trunks with anything under the sun.

The first player begins by saying, "I put a _____ in Grandmother's trunk." (Or "I went on a trip and took _____" or "I packed my bag with _____.") The blank can be filled with just about any noun (or adjective and noun). For example, "I put a snowman in Grandmother's trunk." The next player repeats the first player's sentence, adding another item. For instance, "I put a snowman and a rotten egg in Grandmother's trunk." Players continue repeating the contents of the trunk and adding new items to the list.

If a player misses any object in the sequence, the next player starts a new list from the beginning. Players are out of the game after making three mistakes. The last player to remain is the winner.

Rigmarole

Awesome alliteration is the key to this tongue-twisting memory game.

Players: 2 or more

Ages: 8 to 12

Place: Anywhere

Equipment: None

Rigmarole is a memory game using a counting sequence in which the central concept is alliteration—that is, beginning consecutive words in a phrase with the same letter sound ("five flying fish," for example, or "ten tall trees"). The repetition of a list makes this game similar to Going on a Picnic or Grandmother's Trunk. In this game, however, players must remember a string of phrases rather than a string of just words, so the task is more challenging. Even though players' memories are helped by the counting order and the repetition of the initial letter sound, this is definitely a game for older children interested in mighty mental maneuvers.

The first player says a three-word alliterative phrase beginning with the word (and number) "one," such as "one outraged ostrich" or "one old orange." The second player must repeat that phrase and add a three-word phrase beginning with "two," such as "two tired tigers." The next player repeats both phrases and adds a third one beginning with "three," such as "three thirsty throats" (in this case, the alliterative sound is "th" not just "t").

Play goes around and around up to "ten," then starts at "one" again. Any player along the way who does not repeat the chain correctly or fails to add an appropriate phrase is out of the game. The last remaining player is the winner and gets to start the next round of play.

For a more challenging game, players may decide to make their phrases contain the same number of words as the number beginning the phrase. The second player might offer the phrase "two tulips," and a later player might come up with "six scary, slimy, soggy, silly seahorses."

Name Six

In this circle game, players race the clock to complete a six-item list.

Players: 10 to 20

Ages: 7 to 14

Place: Indoors in large room or outdoors

Equipment: Small ball, beanbag, or similar unbreakable object

Name Six is a good party game because it requires so many players. To play, participants form a circle and begin passing around a small ball (a beanbag or other unbreakable object works just as well). One player, designated the leader, stands outside the circle and calls out a letter of the alphabet. The person holding the ball when the letter is called must name six things that begin with that letter before the ball travels around the circle and is passed back to him. For example, if the leader calls out the letter M, the player may answer, "Money, milk, man, monkey, maple syrup, monorail." The letter S may elicit "Soap, straw, sand, sack, sink, stop sign."

Whether or not the player can come up with the answers in time, he remains in the circle and the ball keeps moving. When the ball is in a new player's hands, the leader calls another letter. (The leader has to keep an eye on the ball, making sure to call out the letter when it reaches someone who hasn't yet had a chance to answer.)

After all the players have had a chance to answer, the ones who failed to call out their six words in time drop out and the game begins again with a smaller circle. Clearly, the game is now more difficult because it doesn't take as long for the ball to travel around the circle. The game continues with the circle getting smaller and smaller. The last player to be able to name six before the ball comes around again is the winner.

Name Six may be expanded to Name Ten or shrunk to Name Four, depending on the size as well as the skill level of the group.

Associations

In this fast-moving word-association game, victory belongs to the player with the quickest answers.

Players: 2 or more

Ages: 7 to 14

Place: Anywhere

Equipment: None

Associations requires quick and imaginative thinking. As kids fire words back and forth at each other, they give their mental reflexes a good workout. The associations they make between words are often amusing—and at times revealing.

The first player starts by calling out a word. The next player must immediately say the first word that comes to mind. For example, if the first word is "dog," the second might be "house," "bone," or "cat." If the second word is "house," the third might be "plant," "home," or "igloo," and so on.

Completely unrelated words don't count. For instance, to follow the word "dog" with the word "bread" would be considered unacceptable by the other players unless the person who said it could prove it was associated in some way. If differences of opinion arise, a majority vote decides a word's acceptability.

Play goes clockwise, with each player trying to come up with an association for the previous word without hesitation. If a player pauses before giving an association or gives an unacceptable association, he is out of the game. The last player to remain in the game is the winner.

Association Chain

This variation is usually played as an add-on to Associations and requires excellent memory skills. After a game of Associations has been completed, the last player to have contributed a word starts to say the chain backward—that is, listing all the words from the previous game in reverse order. If a mistake is made, that player is out and the next player starts back at the end of the chain of words. The first player to complete the chain is the winner. If no one is able to do it, everybody loses.

Who Am I?

There are lots of cases of mistaken identity in this personality guessing game.

Players: 3 or more

Ages: 7 to 14

Place: Anywhere

Equipment: None

Who Am I? is a straightforward guessing game that's lots of fun for a big group. Kids love this game because it's a group effort—all the players except one know the secret identity. It's also fun to hear all the different impressions a group of players can have about the same person. One player leaves the area (or covers his ears) while the rest of the group agrees on a well-known person who may be real (Shaquille O'Neal) or fictional (Aladdin), living (Tom Cruise) or dead (Cleopatra). The personality must, however, be someone who will be recognized by everyone participating.

The player then returns to the group and asks everyone, "Who am I?" Each of the other players in turn makes a statement giving a clue to the mystery person's identity. For example, if the person is Abraham Lincoln, one clue might be "You have a beard." Another might be "You are from Illinois." A third could be "You work as a lawyer at one point."

The clues should be accurate and informative enough to give the guesser a chance at figuring out who the person is. But they should not be too obvious (unless the players are very young), or the game will be over too quickly. For example, "You give the Gettysburg Address" or "You are the president of the United States during the Civil War" makes the mystery person a bit too easy to guess.

After each player has given one clue, the guesser has three chances to name the correct person. If the guesser is stumped, the other players claim victory. Play should go on long enough to give each person a chance to play the guesser.

What's My Thought Like?

Although technically a word association game, What's My Thought Like? requires players to stretch their minds for some creative thinking.

Players: 3 or more

Ages: 8 to 14

Place: Anywhere

Equipment: Pencil and paper for scoring (optional)

Despite its name, What's My Thought Like? is not a mind-reading contest. Instead, it's a game of associations that trains players to use their imagination and think in abstract rather than literal ways. Kids are sure to come out of these mental calisthenics with nimbler brains.

To start, one player thinks of any object or any person at all—a kangaroo, a rubber band, Amelia Earhart, anything—then asks, "What's my thought like?" Each of the other players, who have absolutely no clues about the first player's thought, then takes a totally random guess as to what it might be.

This guessing can be amusing in itself, but then the thinker tells the others his thought and the real fun starts. Now the other players must "justify" their earlier questions by finding some way to associate their guesses with the thinker's thought. One at a time, each player uses her imagination to reveal a connection between her guess and the thinker's thought. For example, if the thought was "clock" and one player's guess was "leaf," the association might be "A leaf is like a clock because they both mark the passing of time." If

another player's guess was "gorilla," the answer might be "A gorilla is like a clock because they both have hands and a face."

It takes a lot of ingenuity to come up with legitimate associations, and sometimes a player's answer may be a bit too farfetched. If, for example, a player tries to connect "banana" to the word "clock" by explaining that "they can both be eaten," the response is a little hard to accept. If the other players agree that an answer isn't appropriate, that player gets a penalty point. If all the players can give acceptable answers, the player with the original thought gets a penalty point. The player who has the fewest points at the end of a specified time period is the winner.

Assassin

In this elimination game, players disappear in a wink! It's up to the survivors to expose the killer.

Players: 6 or more

Ages: 8 and up

Place: Anywhere with seating for all players

Equipment: Pencil and paper

Assassin, also known as Murder or Killer, is a surprisingly nonviolent game. Intrigue and subtlety are what make it so much fun.

Assassin can be played on its own or, for older and more experienced players, during a card or board game. The more players, the better. This game is a wonderful exercise in observation and restraint. As players "disappear," the others try to figure out who's assassinating everyone before being "rubbed out" themselves.

First, a piece of paper is torn into as many pieces as there are players; one piece is marked with an X, and all the pieces are folded in half. The scraps of paper are then mixed up and distributed, one to each player. Everyone now peeks at her scrap, without showing anyone else. The player who holds the paper with the X is the secret "assassin." If the game is being played alone, the players sit in a circle. If it's being played during another game, the other game is now begun.

For the assassin, the object of the game is to "kill" off the other players, which he does by slyly winking at them, one at a time. For the other players, the object is to catch the assassin in the act of winking at another player, before being winked at themselves. As the players scan each other's faces in search of the assassin, the assassin tries to catch the eye of one person—his victim. If a player is winked at, she must wait 10 seconds, then say, "I'm dead," and drop out of the game. This waiting period between being killed and announcing it is important—otherwise it's much too easy to identify the assassin.

The assassin tries to kill off as many players as possible before getting caught. If someone thinks she knows who the killer is, she may make an accusation. If she is right, she wins the game; if not, she's out. If no one discovers his identity, the assassin wins.

Buzz

When this counting game really gets rolling, it sounds as if a swarm of bees had invaded the room!

Players: 2 or more

Ages: 8 to 12

Place: Anywhere with seating for all players

Equipment: Pencil and paper for scoring

Buzz is a counting game that requires both quick calculating and constant concentration. Kids must have their multiplication tables down pat—or this game will only frustrate them. Those adept with numbers, however, can show off their mathematical prowess. And everyone will get a kick out of the funny noises.

Players sit in a circle and begin counting in sequence. Play goes clockwise, and each player calls out one number per turn. When any multiple of 7 comes up or any number with the digit 7 in it, the number is replaced by the word "Buzz!" Play sounds like this: "One," "Two," "Three," "Four," "Five," "Six," "Buzz!" "Eight," "Nine," and so on. The numbers 14, 17, 21, 27, and 28 would be the next ones to be buzzed. When the seventies are reached, they are all buzzes. Any number that both is a multiple of 7 and has a 7 in it (such as 70 and 77) gets a double buzz.

Play continues at as quick a pace as possible. If a player hesitates too long, misses a "Buzz!" or supplies one at an inappropriate time, he gets a penalty point and the game restarts at "One."

The game continues until the counting has reached 100. The player with the fewest penalty points wins. For a quicker game, or if it seems that 100 will never be reached, players can be permitted two mistakes before elimi-nation from the game. The last player to remain is the winner.

Fizz

Fizz is a slightly simpler version of Buzz, based on multiples of 5 rather than 7. Play starts in the same way as in Buzz, but when a player reaches a multiple of 5 or a number with 5 in it, "Fizz!" is substituted. Play sounds like this: "One," "Two," "Three," "Four," "Fizz!" "Six," "Seven," "Eight," "Nine," "Fizz!" "Eleven," and so on. The fifties are handled in the same way as the seventies in Buzz. And, as in Buzz, any number that is a multiple of 5 and has a 5 in it (15, 25, 35, etc.) gets a "Fizz-Fizz!" Scoring is the same as in Buzz.

Buzz-Fizz

Buzz and Fizz champions can move on to Buzz-Fizz, a challenge which combines both of these counting games. Players say "Buzz!" at multiples of 7 and numbers with 7 in them, "Fizz!" at multiples of 5 and numbers with 5 in them, "Buzz-Buzz!" at multiples of 7 with a 7 in them, "Fizz-Fizz! at multiples of 5 with a 5 in them, and "Buzz-Fizz!" at multiples of both numbers (35 and 70) and numbers with both a 7 and a 5 in them (57 and 75). Whew! Scoring is the same as for Buzz.

Twenty Questions

Players have 20 chances to deduce a mystery word.

Players: 2 or more

Ages: 8 to 14

Place: Anywhere

Equipment: None

This classic guessing game—also called Animal, Vegetable, or Mineral—can easily be adjusted to different skill levels. Kids can have so much fun playing Twenty Questions that they barely notice that they're learning to ask pertinent questions and to deduce answers from the responses. The game is a great traveling companion—it can make the road to anywhere seem shorter and more interesting.

The game begins with one player thinking of an object—any object—that can be classified as an animal, a vegetable, or a mineral. The object can be very general (a dog, for example) or very specific (a cocker spaniel, or even a particular cocker spaniel belonging to someone whom all the players know). An animal is defined as anything that moves and breathes or happens to be made out of an animal. A butterfly counts as an animal, of course, but so does a sausage or a leather briefcase. A vegetable is defined as a plant or anything made with plants, from a dandelion to a wicker chair to a cotton t-shirt. A mineral is anything "inorganic" (not an animal or a plant)—like rocks, metal, or plastic—or anything made from such materials, like helicopters or even salt. If an object is made up of a combination of elements, it is classified by its most dominant element. A book, for example, would be considered vegetable because its dominant element, paper, is made from wood,

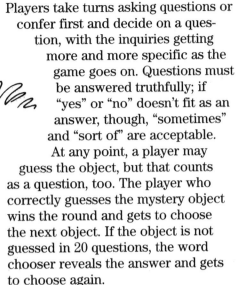

even though it might be bound in a leather case.

The word chooser declares whether the object is animal, vegetable, or mineral, and then the other players ask yes-or-no questions to try to identify the mystery object. Altogether the players are allowed to ask only 20 questions. "Is it bigger than a lunchbox?" might be a good first question.

Players take turns asking questions or confer first and decide on a question, with the inquiries getting more and more specific as the game goes on. Questions must be answered truthfully; if "yes" or "no" doesn't fit as an answer, though, "sometimes" and "sort of" are acceptable.

At any point, a player may guess the object, but that counts as a question, too. The player who correctly guesses the mystery object wins the round and gets to choose the next object. If the object is not guessed in 20 questions, the word chooser reveals the answer and gets to choose again.

Virginia Woolf

This version of Twenty Questions is played like the original game, except that players try to guess the name of a famous person rather than an object. The person may be real or fictional, living or dead, but must be well enough known for all the players in the group to recognize the name. To narrow down the possibilities, good starter questions are "Is this person female?" and "Is this person living?"

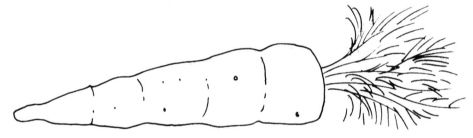

Charades

Body language speaks louder than words in this classic pantomime and guessing game.

Players: 6 or more

Ages: 8 and up

Place: Large room or outdoors

Equipment: Pencil and paper for each player; bowl, hat, or similar container

It's hard to decide what's the most fun about playing Charades—the acting or the guessing. Both parts take imagination, creativity, and a lot of energy—three traits that children

possess in abundance. Charades is a great game for mixed-age groups, as long as kids are old enough to understand and follow the rules.

Before beginning the game, each player is given several scraps of paper on which to write words or phrases that fall into any of several categories: foods (soufflé, artichoke), places (Timbuktu, Mount Rushmore), famous people (Albert Einstein, Oprah Winfrey), song titles ("Yellow Submarine"), books (*The Cat in the Hat*), movies (*101 Dalmatians*), TV

shows (*The Simpsons*), and proverbs or slogans ("A bird in the hand is worth two in the bush," "Bet you can't eat just one"). Players should list the category of the word or phrase and sign their names to the bottom of each scrap. If the players have decided beforehand to play with only one category, the category does not need to be written on the paper. The scraps of paper are then folded in half and mixed up in a bowl (or hat). These are the charades.

To begin, one player picks a charade out of the bowl. She announces the name at the bottom of the scrap

of paper and that player sits out the round. Then, the player who picked the charade proceeds to act out the word or phrase so that the others can guess it.

The actor must follow certain rules and use standard gestures as she tries to convey the word or phrase. Talking or mouthing words is strictly forbidden. This is a purely pantomime game. Using props, pointing, and doing just about anything else that will convey the message is fine.

First, the actor must indicate the category. Here's a guide to some standard gestures she can use:

• *Food:* Pretends to shovel food into her mouth.
• *Famous person:* Puts a hand inside her shirt (like Napoleon).
• *Place name:* Puts hands in circles in front of her eyes (as if looking through binoculars).
• *Song:* Pretends to sing (silently), with her mouth open and one hand raised in the air.
• *Book:* Puts her hands together, palms up, forming an open book.
• *Movie:* Turns the crank on an old-fashioned movie camera.
• *TV show:* Draws a square in the air in front of her face.
• *Proverb or slogan:* Makes quotation marks with her fingers.

When someone in the audience guesses the correct category, the actor puts a finger on the tip of her nose to indicate that the guesser is right—he's hit it on the nose. She'll do this throughout the game whenever another player makes a correct guess. Now the actor proceeds to communicate the word or phrase in question. When there's more than one word involved, she can act them all at once or one at a time. Sometimes a word may have to be broken down into syllables to get it across to the audience. Here are standard gestures the actor can use for this part of the game:

• *Acting out entire phrase at once:* Crosses her arms over her chest. Then does her acting.
• *Number of words in the phrase:* Holds up the appropriate number of fingers. If she now wants to act out the words one at a time, she again holds up a specific number of fingers to indicate which word she's focusing on. (She doesn't have to do the words in order.) If she wants to break a word into syllables, again she puts up the appropriate number of fingers to show which syllable she's focusing on.
• *Little word:* Holds her index finger and thumb close together. This is usually for words like "a," "an," "the," "is," and "it," which are impossible to act

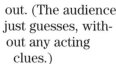

out. (The audience just guesses, without any acting clues.)
• *Word "sounds like":* Cups her hand around her ear or pulls her earlobe, then points to or in some other way indicates an object or action that her word sounds like.

Maybe the sound-alike word rhymes with her word ("jump" for "stump"), or maybe it just has some letters in common ("stamp" for "stump").
• *Longer or shorter form of a word:* Makes a stretching-out motion with her hands when audience guesses one word and she wants a longer version of that word—for example, "walking" instead of "walk." Brings her palms toward one another when she wants a shorter version—"walk" instead of "walking."
• *Past or future tense of a word:* Looks forward (with her hand over her eyes, like a visor) or backward (over her shoulder).
• *Getting close to the answer:* Makes a beckoning motion.

As the actor acts, the audience calls out its guesses. The actor must simultaneously react to their calls—shaking her head at incorrect guesses—and continue to act out the charade. If an audience member guesses a word or syllable correctly, the actor touches her finger to her nose and then begins to pantomime another part of the word or phrase. The game can get pretty loud and raucous, but that's all part of what makes it so much fun!

When the word or phrase is finally guessed, another actor takes his turn. There are no losers in charades.

Team Charades

This variation is meant for an even number of players (at least six) and requires some additional equipment: a bowl for each team, a timer with a second hand, and pencil and paper for scoring. The players split into two equal teams and compete to see which team is faster at guessing the charades. Each team has its own bowl of charades, and the player whose charade is selected is "out" so as to not give the answer away. That player serves as timekeeper.

The actors perform only for their fellow team members, with the timekeeper keeping track of how long it takes the team to get the answer. After each charade, the timekeeper notes the time it took on a score sheet. The teams take turns going until each player has acted at least once and both teams have acted out the same number of charades. At that point, the team that has accumulated the least time—that is, has gotten across its messages in the shortest amount of time—wins.

Dumb Crambo

To guess the word that fits the rhyme, act it out in pantomime.

Players: 4 or more

Ages: 8 and up

Place: Large room or outdoors

Equipment: Pencil and paper for scoring (optional)

Dumb Crambo is a game in the Charades family; as in Charades, the players act out words. Unlike Charades, however, it's the actors who are trying to guess a word that the audience knows and to convey their guesses through mime. A popular Victorian parlor game, Dumb Crambo is a good introduction to pantomime games because actors don't have to act out whole phrases, just single words.

First, players divide into two teams—the audience and the actors. The actors leave the area while the audience decides on a word for the actors to guess. Once the word is decided on, the audience chooses a word that rhymes with the mystery word to give to the actors as a clue. For example, if the mystery word is "book," the audience may choose the rhyming word "took." When choosing a word, it is to the audience's advantage to pick one that has a lot of possible rhymes.

The actors then return to the area and are given the clue. Their job is to use pantomime to check their guesses about the mystery word with the audience. Before they begin, they confer about the first word they plan to act out. If, for example, they've been given the clue "took," the actors may guess that the word is "cook" and decide to act this out by pretending to open an oven and put something in or to stand at a stove and fry something in a pan. If the actors are any good, the audience can tell what they're doing and calls out, "No, it's not 'cook'!" Next, the actors might try the word "hook" and pretend to be fishing. The audience would respond, "No, it's not 'hook'!"

The actors are allowed up to three guesses. If the third guess is wrong, the audience scores a point for stumping the other team. If the actors do get the word in three guesses, they get the point. After the first round, actors and audience switch roles, and the new audience chooses a word. The teams continue alternating between being the actors and being the audience. The first team to score 10 points is the winner.

Botticelli

This two-tiered guessing game tests players' knowledge of famous and infamous people.

Players: 3 or more

Ages: 12 and up

Place: Anywhere, preferably with seating for all players

Equipment: None

Botticelli is an ingenious game that some players find difficult to understand at first. Once mastered, however, it never seems too easy or boring. A mind game for older children and adults, Botticelli requires logical reasoning, quick thinking, and—most important—an extensive knowledge of famous personalities. The more a player knows about history, art, literature, politics, and popular culture, the better a Botticelli player he'll be.

To begin the game, one person becomes the chooser. The chooser thinks of a famous person and tells the others in the group the initial of that person's last name. The famous person can be real (Woody Allen) or fictional (Peter Pan), living (Stephen King) or dead (Jane Austen), remembered by all (Mother Teresa) or forgotten by many (Chester A. Arthur). People who are commonly known by only one name (Moses, Dante, Michelangelo, Cher, Madonna) are fair game. The only condition is that the person must have achieved fame or a certain level of renown. For a more interesting game, choosers should steer clear of people with very unusual initials such as I, Q, O, U, X, Y, and Z. The game is a lot harder when the initial is a very common one, like B, C, M, or S.

The other players' goal is to work together to discover the identity of the mystery person. This is done by asking two levels of questions. The first questioner thinks of a person with the same initial as that of the mystery person, and then asks the chooser a question that describes that person without using his name. For example, if the mystery person is Thomas Jefferson and the announced letter is J, the questioner might think of Jesse James and ask, "Are you an outlaw?" The questioner's aim is to stump the chooser, and he should think of a name with that intention; fair play requires that the questioner have a real name in mind. If the chooser can come up with the figure the questioner is thinking of—or with any figure at all who fits the descrip-

tion in the question—she replies, "No, I'm not Jesse James" (or, "No, I'm not Frank James [Jesse's equally bad brother]"). Then another questioner takes a turn.

But if the chooser can't come up with an acceptable answer, the ques-

tioner reveals who he was thinking of and then gets to ask a more specific yes-or-no question about the mystery person. Examples of these are "Are you male?" "Are you living?" "Are you fictional?" The chooser must answer "yes" or "no" truthfully.

After the yes-or-no question is answered, players go back to asking descriptive "Are you . . ." questions. Every time the chooser is stumped and has to answer a yes-or-no question, the players learn more about the mystery person. Little by little, their own questions get more and more specific, such as "Are you a politician?" "Are you alive in the late eighteenth and early nineteenth century?" or "Are you a president of the United States?"

This goes on—sometimes for hours—until someone figures out the secret identity. The player who does so keeps it to himself until his turn comes around, then asks an "Are you . . ." question intended to make the chooser reveal the mystery person's name: "Are you the third president of the United States and the author of the Declaration of Independence?" Once the chooser has replied, "Yes, I'm Thomas Jefferson," the questioner wins the game and gets to be chooser for the next round.

If the questioners seem to be getting closer and closer to figuring out the mystery person, an expert chooser may throw her opponents off course by using the following tactic. Say the person's initial is M, and the chooser has thought of the French artist Claude Monet. A questioner might ask, "Are you a famous French artist?" It's 100 percent acceptable, in this case, for the chooser to say, "No, I am not Henri Matisse"—that is, to attempt to deceive the questioner by giving the name of another famous French artist whose last name begins with M. A good questioner, however, won't be thrown off the track so easily; as long as he knows another artist whose name begins with M, he can keep asking the same question, hoping the chooser will eventually run out of alternatives and be forced to reveal the mystery person's name.

Proverbs

Questions and answers provide clues to hidden proverbs in this guessing game.

Players: 3 or more

Ages: 12 and up

Place: Anywhere with seating for all players

Equipment: None

In this challenging detective game for older children, the words of a proverb are hidden within the answers to one player's questions to the others. It's the guesser's task to figure out the right words and piece together the adage. To enjoy playing this game, kids need well-developed reasoning skills and a good knowledge of common proverbs.

One player is sent out of the room (or covers her ears) while the others decide on a proverb—an old saying or maxim such as "The early bird catches the worm" or "You can lead a horse to water but you can't make him drink." The guesser then returns and seeks clues to the proverb by asking the other players questions. The questions don't need to have anything to do with the proverb at all; they can be on any subject—for example, "What did you do on Saturday?" or "How do you make tasty pancakes?" The questions themselves are not the point; the answers are.

Yet actually the answers don't have to directly reflect the proverb either. Instead, it's the words used in the answers that provide clues for the guesser. Specifically, each answer must contain a word from the proverb. The first answer must contain the first word; the second, the second word, and so on.

As long as the answers make some sense and contain the key word, they don't have to be true or accurate. If the proverb chosen is "The early bird catches the worm," for example, the first player might answer the question "What did you do Saturday?" by saying "I went to the zoo." (The player, however, should not stress the key word; he doesn't want to give the guesser extra help.) If asked, "How do you make tasty pancakes?" the next player may answer, "I make a rich batter and start flipping them early in the morning." The third question might be: "What is your favorite hobby?" And the answer: "I like baseball, stamp collecting, and bird watching."

The questions and answers continue until all the words of the particular proverb have been spoken. The player who uses the last word of the proverb tells the guesser that all the words have now been used. If the guesser can't figure out the proverb, she can ask more questions, and the other players can again use the words of the proverb, one by one, starting with the first word in the proverb, in their answers.

The guesser is allowed three run-throughs of all the words in the proverb. If she is unable to guess the proverb after that, she is told the answer. Another player takes over as guesser for the next round with a new proverb.

Proverbs can be played noncompetitively, or the player who has guessed the most proverbs after a certain number of rounds can be declared the winner.

Word Games

In addition to being lots of fun, word games help sharpen young minds and build vocabulary and spelling skills. The games in this chapter will appeal to children of many ages and abilities, although most require at least a basic knowledge of reading, spelling, and writing. Word games are wonderful for passing the time on a long car trip, jazzing up a party, or engaging kids when they're bored. For many of these games no equipment is needed at all. Others, as noted, require pencils and paper or a dictionary, atlas, or thesaurus. Some of the games are more exciting if time limits are set, so a timer, such as a kitchen timer or a watch or clock with a second hand, may be useful. Many of these games are portable and can be played anywhere, although a table or other flat writing surface is necessary for some.

Tongue Twisters

Tongue Twisters tangles talkers with terrific talent—try saying that fast, five times.

Players: 2 or more, plus an adult or older child to provide tongue twisters

Ages: 4 and up

Place: Anywhere

Equipment: Watch or other timer with second hand

ongue Twisters is a contest to see who can repeat the most tongue-numbing phrases at lightning speed. Kids go into hysterics over the silly-sounding slip-ups. This game can be enjoyed equally by a wide variety of ages.

The rules are simple: An adult or older child gives each player a tongue twister to repeat as many times as possible before making a mistake. Using a watch with a second hand, another player times the talker. For maximum fairness, players should all be given the same phrase. For more variety, they can be given different

ones. Here are some tried-and-true tongue twisters:

She sells seashells by the seashore.

Peter Piper picked a peck of pickled peppers.

Rubber baby buggy bumpers.

How much wood would a woodchuck chuck if a woodchuck could chuck wood?

Toy boat.

Unique New York.

One smart man, he felt smart; two smart men, they felt smart; three smart men, they all felt smart.

Red leather, yellow leather.

Six thick thistle sticks.

The winner is the player who correctly repeats the tongue twister the most times or who goes the longest without making a mistake or faltering.

Word Lightning

Players are on the spot to think up as many words as possible beginning with the same letter—in just a minute.

Players: 2 or more

Ages: 4 to 14

Place: Anywhere

Equipment: Watch or other timer with second hand

ord Lightning sounds easy to play: contestants reel off as many words as possible beginning with a given letter in 1 minute. Just try it. It's harder than it seems because all too often the brain freezes up just when you want it to perform well. This little exercise is one of the few games that can chal-

lenge kids as young as 4 and as old as 14 (or even older). In fact, Word Lightning is an excellent tool for helping preschoolers with word skills. Two or three appropriate words in a minute is quite respectable—even impressive—for a 4-year-old.

Players take turns picking a letter for everyone to use. Each player gets a minute to call out as many words as possible that begin with the letter chosen for the first round. One player acts as the timekeeper, counting the words being called out.

After everyone has had a turn, the player who called out the most words is named the winner. The winner gets to choose the letter for play in the next round.

Crambo

It takes some skill to make a rhyme to guess the secret word in time.

Players: 2 or more

Ages: 6 to 12

Place: Anywhere, preferably with seating for all players

Equipment: None

This 400-year-old game of guesses and rhymes teaches kids how to compose rhymes and deduce answers in a fun, straightforward fashion. The more players, the better.

The first player thinks of a word and another word that rhymes with it. Then she tells the group, "I am thinking of a word that rhymes with _____." The other players try to discover the mystery word by asking questions that define words that also rhyme with the first word. The first player must answer the questions with the new rhyming words.

For example, if the first player announces, "I'm thinking of a word that rhymes with 'cat,'" the next player may ask, "Does it fly at night?" The first then responds, "No, it's not a bat." Another player may ask, "Do you wear it on your head?" The first player answers, "No, it's not a hat." A third player questions, "Does it look like a mouse?" The first player replies, "No, it's not a rat."

Players keep asking questions until someone uncovers the secret word. In our example, a guesser might ask, "Is it another word for barrel?"—to which the first player would have to respond, "Yes, it's a vat!"

If the players are stumped, the one who thought of the word wins the round. If not, the player who uncovers the mystery word wins the round and thinks of the next word. There's one other possibility—which is that the person who thought of the word may not be able to come up with the correct rhyming word to answer another player's question. For example, a questioner might ask, "Is it a small bug?" but the player who knows the secret word may not be able to think of "gnat." In this case, the questioner wins the round and thinks of the next mystery word.

Coffeepot

"Can you coffeepot in the rain?" Fun is brewing in this silly-sounding guessing game.

Players: 2 or more

Ages: 6 and up

Place: Anywhere, preferably with seating for all players

Equipment: Watch or other timer with second hand

offeepot is a great word game for beginners because it's not complicated, but it's not too easy. Substitution is the principle here. The object is to guess the activity that the other players are thinking of by substituting the word "coffeepot" for the verb.

To begin, one player leaves the area (or covers his ears) while the others think of a verb describing an activity —"run," "climb," "laugh," "eat," and "swim" are all good choices. When the first player returns, it's his task to figure out what the secret verb is. To do this, he asks questions with the word "coffeepot" substituting for the mystery verb. For instance, he might ask, "Can a dog coffeepot?" or "Do people coffeepot on TV?" The other players must answer "yes" or "no" truthfully.

The first player's innocent but silly-sounding questions can make this game truly hilarious. Sometimes just the reactions of the other players can be a good hint about what the secret activity is (or isn't!).

If the first player guesses the word, the last player to answer a question becomes the next guesser. If the original guesser can't figure out the word within a predetermined period of time (say, 3 minutes), that player must take another turn at guessing another verb. Someone should be chosen to keep an eye on the watch or other timer to make sure this time deadline is met.

Teakettle

Teakettle—a trickier version of Coffeepot—is for more experienced players. Instead of choosing an activity, players must select homophones—words that sound alike but have different meanings. "Bear" and "bare" are examples, as are "to," "too," and "two," and "rain," "reign," and "rein."

As in Coffeepot, the guesser leaves the area while the homophones are chosen. When the guesser returns, each of the other players must use one of the sound-alike words in a sentence, but with the word "teakettle" substituted for the secret word. If the words are "plane" and "plain," one player might say, "I saw a teakettle flying over my house today." The next might add, "I saw it too, but it wasn't very pretty; it was really quite teakettle." A third player might contribute, "It flew over rivers, mountains, and teakettles."

The conversation goes on until the guesser figures out what "teakettle" stands for. If the guesser is right, another player takes a turn as the guesser. If not, the first guesser must try again, with a new "teakettle."

Preacher's Cat

Every letter of the alphabet is used
to describe this friendly feline.

Players: 2 or more

Ages: 6 to 10

Place: Anywhere

Equipment: None

Themes of repetition and use of
the alphabet make Preacher's
Cat—known in more formal circles as Minister's Cat—a natural for
young children just getting the hang
of word games. Although it can be
played anywhere, this pretty kitty is
an especially great diversion for back-
seat squabblers.

To play, each player takes a
turn creating a sentence centered
around a letter of the alphabet.
The basic framework of the sentence is: "The preacher's cat is a(n)
_____ cat, and his/her name is _____."
This framework remains the same
throughout the game. Players must fill
in the first blank with an adjective and
the second with a name, each beginning with the same letter.

Everybody starts with the letter A.
The first player might say, "The
preacher's cat is an awesome cat, and
his name is Arthur." The second
player might follow with: "The preacher's cat is an active cat, and her name
is Annie."

After each player has a
turn with A, the round moves
to B ("The preacher's cat is a bad
cat, and his name is Bert") and
continues through the alphabet.
Some letters are a lot more challenging than others—try thinking of an
adjective that begins with the letter
X! (Players may agree to skip very
difficult letters.)

This game works well as a noncompetitive activity, but it can also be
played as a contest. In that case,
players must drop out if they repeat a
word that someone else has already
used or if they cannot come up with
an appropriate new word. The last
player left is the winner.

Hangman

Figuring out a mystery word is the goal of
this old favorite, and players who get
hung up for too long are doomed.

Players: 2 or more

Ages: 6 and up

Place: Table or other flat writing surface, with seating for all players

Equipment: Pencil and paper or black-
board and chalk

This beloved fill-in-the-blank game
was the inspiration for the TV
program *Wheel of Fortune*, in
which players also seek to uncover a
mystery word, letter by letter. In the
original Hangman, however, only
writing tools, a sharp mind, and a

strong grasp of the process of elimination are required. Hangman hones
memory, concentration, vocabulary,
and spelling skills.

To begin, one player thinks of a
word and on a piece of paper draws a
line of dashes to represent the letters
of the word. If, for example, the player thinks of the word "kangaroo," she
draws a series of eight dashes. Now
the other players must figure out what
this word is.

To do this they take turns guessing
at the letters that belong in the word.
Whenever someone guesses correctly,
the letter is written in the appropriate
blank—or blanks if the letter appears

more than once in the word (like A or
O in "K-A-N-G-A-R-O-O"). At any time
as the letters get filled in, a player
may use his turn to guess the whole
word. Savvy players always begin the
game by calling out vowels.

Danger arises when a player guesses
a letter that is not in the word. In that
case, the invalid letter is written down
in a "scrap heap" below or to the side
of the dashes. Then, the round head of
a stick figure is drawn hanging from a
gallows (see diagram on next page).
(The gallows can be just an upside-
down L, with a little line of "rope"
dangling off the end of the short part
of the L.) Each incorrect guess adds
another body part to the hanging
stick-figure: after the head comes a
body, a right arm, a left arm, a right
leg, and a left leg. (Players can agree,
before the game, to a more elaborate
victim, with facial features, hands and
feet, and articles of clothing.)

Players keep calling out letters in
turn until the word, or the hanging
figure, is complete. The player who

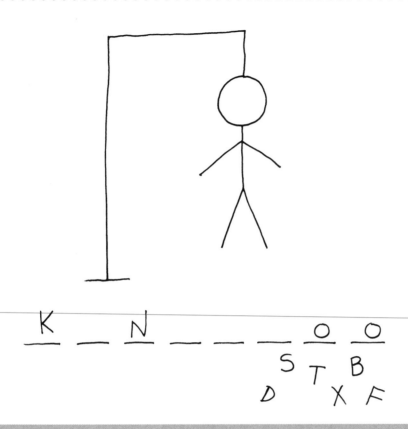

completes the word before the stick figure is drawn is the winner. The drawer wins if the stick figure is completed before the word is guessed.

For a more challenging game of Hangman, players may use a phrase or title rather than a single word. The player who is drawing the hanging figure should give the others a hint by announcing the category of the group of words. Examples of categories are movie titles, quotations, or clichés.

Grab on Behind

In this alphabet category game, one word's final letter is transformed into another's first letter at breakneck speed.

Players: 2 or more

Ages: 6 to 12

Place: Anywhere

Equipment: None

Grab on Behind, also known as Alpha and Omega or Last and First, is similar to the classic word game Geography. A word chain is formed using the last letter of one word as the first letter of the next word. The difference is, instead of being well versed in locations, players must have a wide knowledge of whatever category they choose. This is a great game for a large group because the variety of answers makes it a fun and interesting learning experience for all.

First, the players decide on the category. Some possibilities include food, entertainers, athletes, plants, and animals (or a smaller subcategory such as insects, mammals, birds, or fish).

The first player chooses any word that fits the category. The next player must think of another appropriate word that begins with the last letter of the first word. If the category is food and the first word is "soup," the second may be "peas," the third, "sugar," the fourth, "rice," and so on. Play continues, around and around, with players having only about 5 seconds to come up with the next word.

Any player who fails to add a word in time, repeats a word already used, or uses a word that is not appropriate for the category is out of the game. The last remaining player wins.

Spelling Bee

This classroom classic is fun as a spelling sport at home.

Players: 2 or more, plus an adult or older child to play "teacher"

Ages: 6 to 12

Place: Anywhere

Equipment: Dictionary (optional)

Although a spelling test is often a dreaded activity in elementary school, a Spelling Bee is usually enthusiastically anticipated. That's because children love the thrill of competition and the delicious tension that a Spelling Bee can provide.

To stage a home Spelling Bee, an adult or older child should serve as the "teacher." To make the game go more smoothly, the teacher may want to prepare a list of words appropriate to the players' abilities in advance. Players first line up in a row and face the teacher (the game can also be played with two teams that line up opposite each other or with children sitting rather than standing next to each other). Next, the child farthest to the teacher's left is given

a word to spell. In answering, the player should say the word, spell it, then say the word again: "Special, S-P-E-C-I-A-L, special."

If the word is spelled correctly, the next player is given a new word. If, however, the first player spells the word incorrectly, he is out of the game and must sit down (or put his head down if already sitting). The next contestant is then given a chance to try the same word. It's a good strategy to begin with relatively easy words and gradually increase their difficulty.

The last player (or team member) to remain standing wins the game. An alternative way to play is to award a point for each correctly spelled word. The first person to reach a predetermined score is named the winner.

Greedy Spelling Bee

This version of Spelling Bee can keep a demon speller on her feet for a long time. If a player spells a word correctly, she scores a point and is given another word to spell. This goes on until a mistake is made. Then the next player starts with the last player's incorrectly spelled word. Play continues this way, with players scoring a point for each word they spell right. The player with the most points at the end of the game is declared the winner.

Backward Spelling Bee

This game is played the same way as regular Spelling Bee, except that the

words must be spelled backward. It's important to start the game with relatively short, simple words to help the players get the hang of spelling backward. The teacher should begin with simple words and gradually move up to longer, more difficult words.

Right or Wrong Spelling Bee

This variation requires at least six players and is always played in teams. The two teams line up opposite each other, and the teacher calls out the first word to one of the players. After that contestant has attempted to spell the word, the person standing opposite him must decide if the player has spelled the word correctly and call out "right" or "wrong." If the second

player misjudges (calls a correctly spelled word "wrong" or an incorrectly spelled word "right"), that player is out of the game and must sit down. If the correct call is made, the caller gets the next word to spell. The speller stays in the game even if she spelled the word incorrectly. A savvy speller might even spell a word incorrectly on purpose and fool her opponent into judging it as "right."

As players drop out, their places are filled by their teammates so that a speller is always standing opposite a caller. The last team with a player still standing is the winner of this Spelling Bee game.

Initials

In this game, players use their own initials to answer questions. A guy named Xavier Quincy is at a definite disadvantage.

Players: 2 or more

Ages: 7 and up

Place: Anywhere with seating for all players

Equipment: None

Initials challenges each player to answer questions with words beginning with the initials of his own name. Kids will get a kick out of the silliness that ensues as the answers get more and more outlandish.

Players sit in a circle (or similar formation), and one person is chosen to be the questioner for the first round. It is the questioner's job to ask each player a question, which must be

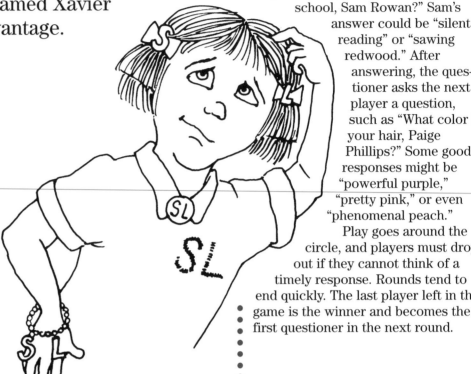

responded to using the initials of the answerer's first and last names. (The answers don't actually have to be true.)

For example, the questioner might ask, "What is your favorite subject in school, Sam Rowan?" Sam's answer could be "silent reading" or "sawing redwood." After answering, the questioner asks the next player a question, such as "What color is your hair, Paige Phillips?" Some good responses might be "powerful purple," "pretty pink," or even "phenomenal peach."

Play goes around the circle, and players must drop out if they cannot think of a timely response. Rounds tend to end quickly. The last player left in the game is the winner and becomes the first questioner in the next round.

Initial Answers

An initial letter and a definition are the clues to a secret word.

Players: 2 or more

Ages: 8 and up

Place: Anywhere with seating for all players

Equipment: None

Initial Answers can be played anywhere by virtually any number of people, although the more players involved, the more interesting the game. It is perfect for the car, as well as for a big group at a party. Nimble-

minded children delight in thinking up ever more complex words and clues.

Players sit in a circle (or similar formation), and one person chooses a letter of the alphabet. That player then thinks of a three-letter word beginning with the letter and a one-sentence clue that is a definition of the word. If, for example, the player chooses the letter C and the word "cat," he might say, "C plus two letters is an animal that catches mice." The second person then tries to guess the mystery word. If the

guesser is correct, she must now think of a four-letter word beginning with the same letter. If the word is "corn," she might say, "C plus three letters is a yellow vegetable." Play continues clockwise around the circle, with an extra letter being added after each correct guess. The next clue might be:

"C plus four letters is where the ocean meets the land" ("coast").

Whenever a player is stumped or guesses the wrong word, he is out of the game. A player is also out if he can't make a new word that begins with the chosen letter and has the right number of letters for that turn;

the task of doing so then passes to the next player. Needless to say, coming up with appropriate words gets harder and harder as the game goes on and the words get longer.

The last person left after all the others have dropped out is declared the winner.

Traveler's Alphabet

In this verbal excursion through the letters of the alphabet, players get a lesson in alliteration.

Players: 2 or more

Ages: 8 and up

Place: Anywhere

Equipment: None

Playing Traveler's Alphabet is like taking a trip through the 26 letters. A sentence-building exercise, this game requires players to know a little bit about geography and a lot about vocabulary.

Each player must create a sentence that begins with the phrase "I'm going to . . ." followed by the name of a place, then a verb, and then an adjective and a noun—all starting with the same letter of the alphabet. (The word "to" is used before the verb, but it doesn't count as an alphabet-letter word.) The first player starts with A and says, for example, "I'm going to Alaska to acquire amazing art." The next contestant might continue, "I'm going to Bavaria to buy burnt buns." The third player might respond, "I'm going to Connecticut to catch curried catfish." And so on until "I'm going to

Zanzibar to zap zany zebras." The letter X is usually eliminated.

Players who want a more challenging journey may decide that each sentence must relate in some way to the location it names—for example, "I'm going to Egypt to excavate embalmed elephants" or "I'm going to Switzer-land to ski spectacular slopes." This requirement, though, is usually a tall order even for well-traveled grownups.

The players travel through the alphabet until one hits a mental roadblock. Contestants may challenge

one another if they feel that someone's sentence is inappropriate—that it doesn't make sense, for example, or uses made-up words. If the majority of the players agree that someone's sentence is faulty and the challenger can supply a sentence that everyone thinks is better, the voted-down player must drop out of the game. If not, the player stays in. Players are also eliminated if they cannot come up with a suitable sentence within about a minute's time. The last person to remain in the game is the winner.

Geography

Players who know their geography
and spelling will go places in this game.

Players: 2 or more

Ages: 8 to 12

Place: Anywhere, preferably with
seating for all players

Equipment: Atlas or dictionary with
place names

The concept of Geography is easy, but it's not so simple to play. This game requires quick thinking, a good knowledge of geography, and the ability to spell the places that are named.

The game begins with one player naming a city, a state or province, a country, or a continent. The next player must immediately name another place that begins with the same letter with which the first named place ended. If, for example, the first player opens with "Antarctica," the second might follow with "Arkansas," the third with "San Francisco," and the fourth with "Oklahoma City." In this four-player game, the first player would now have to start with Y, perhaps offering "Yukon Territory."

It's a good idea to have an atlas or similar reference book—some dictionaries give place names—available to settle any arguments over spelling or whether a place really exists. Alternate spellings, so long as they can be found in a reference book, should be considered acceptable (Peking and Beijing, the old and new spellings of China's capital, for example).

Players are not allowed to repeat place names that have already been used. If a player can't come up with an answer within 30 seconds or so, he is out of the game. The last player to remain in the game is the winner.

Ghost

In this challenging spelling game, the idea
is to *avoid* completing words. Anyone who
spells the word "ghost" disappears.

Players: 2 to 4

Ages: 8 to 14

Place: Anywhere, preferably with
seating for all players

Equipment: Dictionary (optional)

Despite its scary name, Ghost remains one of the most popular word games ever. Besides being fun and challenging, the game enhances a player's memory, visualization ability, powers of concentration, mental dexterity, spelling skills, and word knowledge. As pencil and paper are not required, Ghost can make its appearance anywhere, at any time.

It is not a good idea to have more than four players in the game because each player needs enough turns per round to make the game an interesting one. The players should decide beforehand on the order of play and, if possible, arrange

themselves in a row or circle to correspond with that order.

In Ghost, the players try to build a lengthening chain of letters that could form part of a real word without actually completing the spelling of a word. Here's an example of how it works: The first player calls out a letter of the alphabet, such as C. The second player adds a letter, such as R, and calls out, "C-R," perhaps thinking of the word "crook." The next player must add a letter to this sequence, but must avoid any letter that would spell out a complete word (for instance, Y, which would spell "cry"). A good choice for the third player would be C-R-A, for the word "crab." The next player would be well advised to continue the chain with C-R-A-C, giving the person who follows no choice but to add the letter K, thereby spelling the word "crack" and losing the round.

Whenever a person adds a letter to the sequence, he must have at least one word in mind that this letter fits. For example, if someone says, "C-R-A-C-O," the next player in line may well doubt that there is any word beginning with these five letters, and she has the right to challenge. If the play-

er who added the O cannot come up with a permissible word containing the letters C-R-A-C-O in that order, then he loses the round. If the player can come up with a permissible word, however, the challenger loses the round. A dictionary should be used to settle any disputes over legitimate words. Proper nouns—names of people, place names, brand names, and so on—are not permitted. Therefore, in the example just given, the name "Cracow" (a city in Poland) would not be acceptable after C-R-A-C-O was challenged.

A player who thinks he has no choice but to complete a word may give up—or, if he denies that he has completed a word but another player thinks that he has done so, he may be challenged. The challenge can come from any other player, and a dictionary (if one is available) should be used to settle the matter. In any case, the loser—either the person who has completed the word or the unsuccessful challenger—starts the next round by offering the first letter.

A player whose turn it is may not stall for too long (say, for more than a minute or any other agreed-on time limit) or she loses the round. Bluffing

is perfectly acceptable in Ghost. There is no law against adding a letter that either forms a real word or that could not possibly lead to a real word, so long as it goes unnoticed and unchallenged by any opponent.

Any player who loses a round is penalized by receiving a letter from the word "ghost." After losing one round, he is assigned the letter G; the second time, the letter H; and so on until he has earned all five letters spelling "G-H-O-S-T" and thus vanishes from the game. The last player remaining in the game after the others have turned into ghosts is the winner.

Double Ghost

This challenging and thrilling version of Ghost is highly recommended for expert spellers. In Double Ghost, players can add a letter to either end of the chain, in other words, before or after the existing letter(s).

Using the example C-R-A-C, the next player would not be stuck having to add a K at the end, but would have the option of continuing with, say, O-C-R-A-C, with an eye toward spelling "democracy," or he might propose C-R-A-C-I, with words like "democracies" or "bureaucracies" in mind.

Letter Ladder

Players climb a word-building ladder one letter at a time.

Players: 2 or more

Ages: 8 and up

Place: Anywhere, preferably with seating for all players

Equipment: Pencil and paper for scoring (optional)

In a sort of reverse Ghost, players compete to build complete words by adding one letter at a time—but instead of trying to leave words unfinished, the goal is to complete them. A bit easier than its spooky cousin,

Letter Ladder is good training for more complex word-building games.

To start, the first player thinks of a word ("game," for example) and calls out its first letter (G). The second player then thinks of a word that begins with the same letter ("groundhog," for instance) and calls out the second letter (R, in this case). Play continues with each player building another letter onto the word with the aim of completing a word that cannot be made any longer. It is not permissible to add an S to the end of the word simply to make a plural. But it is acceptable to add an S if the player has a word that is not plural in mind.

A player thinking of "damsel," for example, might add an S to D-A-M. Other ways to continue a word include turning it into a compound word (like "leftover") or adding a suffix (such as "-ed" or "-ing"). Hyphenated words (like "left-handed") and proper nouns (names like "Calgary" or "Connecticut") are not acceptable.

The first player to be unable to add a letter collects 1 penalty point and begins the next word. At any time a player adding a letter may be challenged and asked to prove that her new letter builds a word. If she cannot supply the word, she receives a penalty point—but if she does have a word, the challenger is stuck with the penalty. Whoever gets the penalty starts a new word.

After everyone has had a turn to start a word, the player with the lowest score makes it to the top of the Letter Ladder.

Name Game

The race is on to guess hidden
identities without naming names.

Players: 4 or more (even number)

Ages: 8 and up

Place: Anywhere with flat writing
surface and seating for all players

Equipment: Pencil and about 20 slips
of paper for each player; large bowl,
hat, or other container; watch or other
timer with second hand

Name Game is a rip-roaring race
to identify mysterious celebri-
ties or friends without uttering
any part of their names. Kids have a
ball describing their favorite athletes,
movie stars, friends, or teachers for
teammates to identify. Gestures and
innuendo can be used to give hints,
but the best clue-givers are masters of
quick, right-on description.

This game takes a bit of preparation
to create the pool of names. Each
player takes about 20 slips of paper,
writes one name on each, folds the
slips in half, and drops them into a big
bowl or hat. The names can be those
of famous people or characters, real
or fictional—Michael Jordan, for
example, or Hercules. They can also
be ordinary people whom everyone
in the group knows. It is not permissible, however, to include names that
will be recognized by only some of
the players.

After writing down the names, the
players split into teams of two. A time
limit is set—3 minutes works well—
and one player from the team that
will go second acts as the timekeeper.
At the timekeeper's signal, the first
team starts its turn, with one player
acting as clue-giver and the others as
guessers. The clue-giver picks a name
from the bowl or hat and must
describe the chosen person to the
guessers without saying any part of
the name. If the name "Michael

Jordan" is picked,
the clue-giver
might say, "He's a
great basketball
player who also
played baseball." If
that's not enough, the
clue-giver could add, "He
has a brand of sneakers
named after him."

If the guessers are still in
the dark after these kinds of
descriptions, the clue-giver can
resort to other methods. One such
method is to associate the first and
last names with other people whom
the guessers might have an easier
time identifying. For example, "His
first name is the same as the King of
Pop" (Michael Jackson) or "His last
name is the same as a country in the
Middle East" (Jordan).

As a last resort, the clue-giver can
turn to another method: breaking the
name down into syllables. For example, "The first syllable is the shortened
name for something that a singer
sings into to make his voice louder"
(mike), or "The second syllable is like
a word meaning 'everyone' or 'everything.'" (all). Rhymes cannot be used:
"The first name rhymes with 'cycle'"
is not a valid clue. As soon as the
guessers get the right name, the
clue-giver picks another scrap from
the bowl.

The team tries to guess as many
names as possible in the allotted time.
A clue-giver may not pass on a name;
if the guessers are stumped, they have
to keep trying until time runs out.
Then the unguessed name goes back
in the bowl. When the first team's turn
is up, its score is the number of correct guesses. A member of the second
team now acts as clue-giver, and a
member of the first team takes over
as timekeeper. Each team should have
the same number of turns. The team
with the highest total wins.

Synonyms

Searching for similar meanings is fun, besides being good practice for standardized tests.

Players: 2 or more, plus an adult or older child to serve as leader

Ages: 8 to 12

Place: Table or other flat writing surface, with seating for all players

Equipment: Pencil and paper for each player; watch or other timer with second hand; thesaurus or dictionary (optional)

Synonyms are words with the same or very similar meanings. "Jump" and "hop," for example, are synonyms, as are "goofy" and "silly." Learning to identify and use synonyms is a foundation of a good vocabulary. Although Synonyms could easily be mistaken for a quiz in English class, many children enjoy this game and find that the challenge of competition makes *thinking* about words fun.

Before the game begins, an adult or older child serving as the leader prepares a list of 10 to 20 words, which is handed out to each player. The leader may also read the words for the players to copy down. Then, at a signal, all the players write down as many synonyms for each word as they can think of. Next to the word "sleep," for example, a highly skilled player might write "slumber," "doze," "drowse," "snooze," "nap," "hibernate," and "rest."

The leader also acts as the time-keeper—a limit of 5 minutes is about right. After calling "Time!" the leader checks the players' lists for accuracy, using a thesaurus or dictionary if necessary, and crosses out any words that aren't correct synonyms. (Spelling doesn't count as long as it's clear what a word is, although the leader may choose to point out and correct any such mistakes.)

Once the lists are checked, the players count up the total number of *letters* in their correct synonyms. The player who has the highest total of letters is declared the Synonyms champion.

Hidden Words

This is a challenging contest to make one word into many.

Players: 2 or more

Ages: 8 and up

Place: Table or other flat writing surface, with seating for all players

Equipment: Pencil and paper for each player; watch or other timer with second hand; dictionary (optional)

Hidden Words is a great mental exercise that can be played on many levels, although a good working knowledge of spelling is required. Using the letters of a single key word, players compete to see how many other words they can create.

Before starting, everyone agrees on the key word, which must be at least seven letters long. A time limit of 3 to 5 minutes is set, and players compete to see how many new words of two to seven letters they can create out of the letters of the original word. Here's an example: If the key word is "kitchen," some hidden words are "it," "net," "kite," "nice," "etch," "tin," "hit," and "itch." (Keep looking—there are many more!)

The new words must contain at least two letters, and each letter may only appear in the new word as often as it appears in the key word. For example, if the key word is "kitchen," the word "entice" is not allowed because it contains an extra letter E. Proper nouns—names of people and places, brand names, and so on—and abbreviations are not allowed. For a more challenging game, players may agree not to accept any word shorter than four letters. It's not a bad idea to keep a dictionary on hand to settle disputes.

Players should write down all of the words they can find. The player with the longest list of words when the time is up is the winner and picks the next key word.

Anagrams

Anyone who plays newspaper jumble games will love the letter-unscrambling challenge of the game Anagrams.

Players: 2 or more
Ages: 8 and up
Place: Table or other flat writing surface, with seating for all players
Equipment: Pencil and paper for each player

A genuine anagram is a word whose letters can be rearranged to form another word. "Scat," for example, is an anagram of the word "cats"; "miles" and "limes" are anagrams of "smile." The game Anagrams, however, does not actually involve anagrams—or at least

not as a rule. Instead, it involves jumbled words. A jumbled word mixes up the letters of a real word, but not (necessarily) in such a way as to spell another word. For example, "gfeirn" is a jumble of "finger," and "opson" is a jumble of "spoon." But neither is a true anagram.

In Anagrams, players take turns choosing a word (which they keep secret) and then creating a jumble from this word, which the other players must unscramble as quickly

as they can. The game begins with one player selecting a category of words to jumble—say, animals, fruits, or countries—and then preparing a list of up to ten (or even more) jumbles. A list of animal jumbles, for example, might rearrange "zebra" into "bazer," "elephant" into "pelaneth," "octopus" into "scootup," "monkey" into "koymen," and "sheep" into "hepes." These jumbles should be written out on a sheet of paper, clearly and in big letters, with the category name written at the top of the page.

The jumbler shows his list to the group and keeps it in full view while they race to unscramble the words on sheets of their own. The first to unscramble all the words wins the round. Then another player gets to be the jumbler. (If every player wants to create jumbles, and

there's time for that many rounds, a few minutes can be devoted to list making before the game begins.)

If there are only two players in the game, each should make a list with the same number of jumbles. Then the two exchange their lists, and the race is on to unscramble the words.

Jumbled Words

Another way to play Anagrams with three or more players is to have each player write one jumbled word on a slip of paper and then pass it to the player on the left. The first player to unscramble a word wins. To make this a fair game, all the players should choose words that have the same number of letters.

Categories

Only the fastest thinkers win
this brain-stretching word race.

Players: 2 or more

Ages: 8 and up

Place: Table or other flat writing surface, with seating for all players

Equipment: Pencil and paper for each player; watch or other timer with second hand

In Categories, players fill in a grid with words that fit into certain designated categories. It's a great game for those who work well under the pressure of a time deadline, with victory often going to the coolest—rather than the most brilliant—head.

Each player begins by drawing a grid on a piece of paper, with five boxes across and down, for a total of 25 boxes (see diagram). (Actually, the grid can consist of as many boxes in either direction as the players want.) Then the players together select five categories of people, places, or things. These categories can range from the obvious to the obscure, but should be broad enough for players to know plenty of examples for each. Colors, animals, boys' names, cities, and flowers are possible categories. Once the categories are selected, each is assigned to a row in the grid and the appropriate name is written to the left side of that row. Next, the players

choose letters to put at the head each of the grid's five columns. These represent the initial letters for the fill-in words. Common letters such as S, T, A, R, and D are easiest. Each letter should be different.

Players now have a set time period in which to complete the grid, usually 5 to 15 minutes. Each box must be filled in with a word that fits into the category of its row and starts with the letter at the top of its column. In the category "boys' names," for instance, S, T, A, R, and D might be filled in with Sam, Tony, Adam, Roberto, and Daniel. The players should try to be as original as possible; the more ingenious their answers, the more points they're likely to earn in the end.

When time is up, the players put down their pencils and take turns reading off their answers. Any word that fits the category and the initial letter earns 1 point—but if no one else came up with the same word, it merits a full 2 points. Blank boxes and words that don't fit the category or the initial letter get 0 points. The high scorer wins.

Exchange Categories

In this variation, each player makes up her own grid, complete with letters and categories, then passes it to the player on her right. The players then race to complete the grids and the first player to do so wins. For this game to work, however, all players do have to play in a fair-and-square spirit. It's not much fun if someone makes a grid that is too hard for another player to fill out. No grids asking for tightrope walkers whose names begin with the letters Q and X, please!

Guggenheim

Guggenheim is played like Categories but with one difference: instead of choosing letters for the grid columns randomly, one player chooses a key word with four, five, or six letters, and the letters of this word are used to head the columns.

The players prepare by making a grid with as many squares across and down as there are letters in the "key word." If the word chosen is "king," a

	S	T	A	R	D
Colors	SEA GREEN	TEAL BLUE	AZURE	RED	DUSTY ROSE
Animals	SKUNK	TIGER	ARMADILLO	RHINO-CEROS	DOG
Boys' Names	SAM	TONY	ADAM	ROBERTO	DANIEL
Cities	ST. LOUIS	TORONTO	ATLANTA	RIO DE JANIERO	DUBLIN
Flowers	SUNFLOWER	TULIP	ASTER	RHODO-DENDRON	DAFFODIL

chart with four boxes horizontally and four vertically is drawn (see diagram). The players then label their columns with the letters K, I, N, and G. Then they choose four categories, such as the names of states, sports, actors' last names, and girls' names, and write these to the left of each horizontal row.

The players try to fill in their charts within a predetermined time limit. Working with the letters K-I-N-G and the category "states," a player might fill in "Kansas," "Iowa," "New York," and "Georgia." When time is called, players put down their pencils and read off their answers in turn. Scoring is the same as in Categories.

	K	I	N	G
States	KANSAS	IOWA	NEW YORK	GEORGIA
Sports	KICKBALL	ICE HOCKEY	NETBALL	GOLF
Actors	(NICOLE) KIDMAN	(JEREMY) IRONS	(PAUL) NEWMAN	(CARY) GRANT
Girls' Names	KATE	ISABEL	NANCY	GRACE

Acrostics

Everybody wins in this quick test of word-building skills.

Players: 2 or more

Ages: 9 and up

Place: Table or other flat writing surface, with seating for all players

Equipment: Pencil and paper for each player; dictionary; watch or other timer with second hand (optional)

A little game that makes full use of the brain, Acrostics is a perfect challenge for times when there are only a few minutes to play.

To begin, the players agree on a key word of at least three letters. (They can also take turns choosing the key word for each game.) They then write the word vertically down the left side of their own sheets of paper, and down the right side, they write the same word, but with the letters in reverse order. For example, if the key word is "spell," each player writes S-P-E-L-L down the left side of the paper and L-L-E-P-S down the right

(see diagram). There should be plenty of space left between the two columns of letters.

The players now race to fill in the space between the two columns with words that begin with a letter on the left and end with the letter opposite it on the right. If the key word is "spell," the first word to be filled in must begin with an S and end with an L. The key word itself may not be used again, but similar words like "still" or "spill" are perfectly fine. Moving down the columns, the following words could be "pill," "erase," "leap," and "loss." (Actually, players can fill in the slots in any order they wish, not only top to bottom.) The longer the key word and the more vowels it has, the

more challenging the game. The game becomes especially stimulating if all filled-in words must have more than three or four letters. There are several ways to determine the winner in Acrostics—including simply naming everyone who completes the whole sheet (or does so within a set time limit) a winner. If the challenge alone isn't enough, players can decide that the winner will be the first person to complete all the words. Or each filled-in letter can count as 1 point, with victory going to the player who tallies the most points. This system rewards players who come up with long words. Keep a dictionary close at hand to settle disputes.

Crosswords

Crosswords is the classic easy-to-learn but hard-to-master puzzler.

Players: 2 or more	
Ages: 9 and up	
Place: Table or other flat writing surface, with seating for all players	
Equipment: Pencil and paper for each player; dictionary (optional)	

The name "Crosswords" may make you think of a puzzle in which words are filled into a maze of squares in answer to a set of clues. This game of Crosswords game, however, is a totally different animal. Although its object is to fill in words both horizontally and vertically in little squares, the similarity ends there.

First, each player makes a grid of five squares across by five squares down (see diagram). Then each player takes a turn calling out a letter at random. Everyone must write the letter in any box on his grid. The object is to use the letters to form as many words as possible both horizontally and vertically. Abbreviations and proper nouns do not count. Players call out letters until all 25 squares have been filled. Letters may be called more than once, but once a letter is written

down, it cannot be moved. It's a good idea to limit the number of times that any particular letter can be called out to, say, three times.

After the charts are complete, players add up their scores. Horizontal and vertical words each score 1 point for each letter. (One-letter words don't count.) Any five-letter word earns a bonus point. There can be two words on one line, but no letter may be scored more than once across and once up and down. For

example, I-T-A-L-L is scored as 5 points for "it" and "all," but no extra points are collected for the word "tall." The points scored in each horizontal and vertical line are written at the end of each line, down and across, and then added up. The player with the highest total wins. A dictionary can help settle disputes over whether a particular combination of letters is really a word.

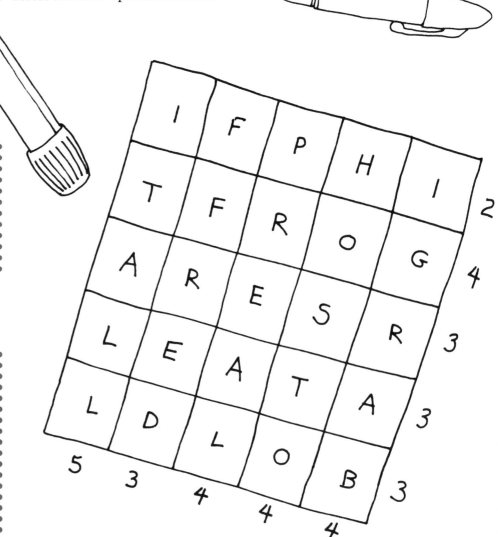

Sentences

In this tricky game, players must make a sentence using all the letters in one word.

Players: 2 or more

Ages: 9 and up

Place: Anywhere

Equipment: Watch or other timer with a second hand; pencil and paper for each player (optional)

While the concept of Sentences is simple and straightforward, this is one of the more difficult word games to master. It demands quick thinking and a lot of creativity, as well as an excellent vocabulary.

To begin, players agree on a four- to six-letter word. Now each player must create a sentence using each of the letters of the chosen word, in order, as the first letter of each of the words in the sentence. If the word is "paper," for example, the sentence might be "Peter and Paul eat rice" or "People actually painted every room." The original word may not be used, nor may any word in the sentence be repeated.

The sentences may be written down or simply said aloud.

After each player has had a turn using the first word, a new word is chosen and another round is played. To simplify the game for young players, nonsensical (though grammatically correct) sentences may be accepted. In contrast, to make the game more difficult, players can be required to relate the sentence's meaning to the original word. For instance, if the word is "food," the sentence might be "Fried okra offends dogs."

Players earn 1 point if they can create a valid sentence within a specified amount of time (usually 2 or 3 minutes). The first player to reach an agreed-on number of points wins.

Telegrams

This is a telegram with a twist: the message must be made from the letters of one word.

Players: 2 or more, plus an adult or older child to serve as judge (optional)

Ages: 9 and up

Place: Table or other flat writing surface, with seating for all players

Equipment: Pencil and paper for each player; watch or other timer with second hand (optional)

Telegrams is an entertaining word challenge for older kids. But before playing the game, children may need an explanation of what a telegram is. An electronic message transmitted in code over telegraph wires, the telegram was a major means of communication across the country and overseas before long-distance phone service became both cheap and widely available. Because, in a telegram, the message is transmitted in code and the sender is charged by the word, the sender tries to condense the information into as few words as possible. Most telegrams are written in a terse language and usually leave out articles ("the," "a," and "an") and any other nonessential words. The word "stop" is used instead of a period.

To start the game Telegrams, play-

TELEGRAM

TAKE OTHER ORANGUTAN TO HOUSE STOP BROTHER REMAINING UPPER SAHARA HABITAT STOP

ers decide on a 10- to 15-letter word (or they can come up with a random list of 15 letters). Another possibility is for an adult or older child to provide the word.

Now the players must each try to compose a telegram using all the letters of the key word, in order, as the initial letters for each word in the telegram. The telegram can include personal and place names. The sender can also use the last letter to "sign"

his name. "Stops" do not require a letter, and a player is permitted to use as many "stops" as are needed to make the message clear. The only requirement, beyond the use of the designated letters, is that the telegram communicate some piece of information, as ridiculous as it may be.

If, for example, the key word is "T-O-O-T-H-B-R-U-S-H," one telegram might read: "Take Other Orangutan To House stop Brother Remaining

Upper Sahara Habitat stop." Another, using the same key word, might say: "Tell Oliver Our Truck Has Broken stop Really Unbelievable stop Staying Home stop."

The first person to complete a coherent telegram is the winner. Experienced players may want to set a time frame for completing the telegrams; an adult or older child can then judge which telegram contains the best message.

Taboo

In this question-and-answer game, one letter is off-limits.

Players: 2 or more

Ages: 9 and up

Place: Anywhere

Equipment: None

In this word game, also known as Poison Letter, the object is to answer another player's question without using any words that contain a certain "taboo" letter. This is not an easy task, but with practice, players can become whizzes at this game.

One player is designated the questioner and decides which letter will be taboo. After announcing this letter, the questioner asks each player, in turn, a question that must be answered without using the forbidden letter anywhere in any word in the reply. (The questioner, by the way, is free to use the taboo letter.) The questioner tries to devise questions that will force the others to slip up, but there is always a creative way to answer without violating the taboo. The answers must be full sentences, not just "yes" or "no."

Let's say the game is being played

with G as the poison letter. The questioner might ask, "What's that green stuff on the ground on a baseball field?" in hopes of forcing the other player to answer using the word "grass." A savvy player, however, might respond, "Often it's artificial turf." The questioner might then try, "What color is Kermit the Frog?" To avoid saying "green," a player might reply, "Kermit is a lovely emerald

hue." But the player better be careful not to use the word "frog" (with its taboo G) in her sentence.

If a player hesitates for too long, gives an answer containing the taboo letter, or gives a nonsensical response, he must drop out of the game. The last player to remain is the winner. The winner then assumes the role of questioner in the next round and play continues.

Password

A teammate's clues—and maybe even some mind reading—help players guess the secret "password" in this popular game.

Players: 5

Ages: 10 and up

Place: Anywhere, preferably with seating for all players

Equipment: Pencil and paper (optional); watch or other timer with second hand (optional)

Whether Password originated as a television game show or was modified to become one is a matter of some dispute. What is important is that Password is a simple yet challenging game that is still fun years after the TV program went off the air. Twenty years ago, Password sets were available in stores, complete with a pile of word cards and a red plastic card holder just like the ones they used on TV. Today pencil and paper work just as well—but they're not even necessary.

To play Password, the players divide into two two-person teams. The leftover player is the leader, or emcee. It's the leader's job to think of "secret" words (nouns work best), which are then whispered to one member of each team. An alternative way to play is for the leader to write the same word down on two scraps of paper and then pass the word to one member of each team.

The object of the game, of course, is for the other member of each team to guess the secret word. The teams take turns. On the team that goes first, the player who received the secret word gives his partner either a synonym or a word associated with the secret word as a clue (the player may pass if he finds the word too difficult to describe). The partner tries to guess the mystery word. If she's right, her team gains a point. If not, the other team gets a turn, and another clue is given. Play continues in this way, back and forth between the two teams, until the word is guessed. It's a good idea to set a time limit—say, 15 seconds—for each turn. The leader acts as timekeeper.

Here's an example of how the game might progress: The leader whispers the word "penguin" to the first player, who then gives his partner the clue "bird." The partner guesses "fly." The next team offers the clue "tuxedo," and the word is guessed correctly. If it remains a mystery, the next clue could be "cold" or "ice."

The team that discovers the word gets a point, and then the two players on each team switch roles, so that the guessers are now giving the clues. Sometimes—and this happens more often than you'd think—a clue-giver will make the mistake of saying the secret word. If this happens, the opposing team wins a point. Also, sometimes neither guesser is able to discover the secret word; if no one guesses the word after each team has had five turns, the round is declared a draw, the players switch roles, and the leader chooses a new word. The first team to reach an agreed-on number of points (like 10) wins. Playing five short (5-point) games gives each player the chance to be the emcee.

Word to Word

How do you turn a pig into a boy? By transforming one word into another, one letter at a time.

Players: 2 or more

Ages: 10 and up

Place: Table or other flat writing surface, with seating for all players

Equipment: Pencil and paper for each player

Word to Word—also known as Smith to Jones, Doublets, and Transformation—challenges players to turn one word into another. To begin, one player chooses two words with the same number of letters, and each participant writes both words down. All the players now try to transform the first word into the second. They do this in steps, each time changing a single letter in the word to create another word.

This process isn't as confusing as it sounds. If the starting word is "pig" and the ending one "boy," the progression might be: "pig," "big," "bog," "boy." A more difficult transformation might be to turn "flour" into "bread" in seven steps: "flour," "floor," "flood," "blood," "brood," "broad," "bread." Until players become skilled at the game, words should be kept to three or four letters.

Players may take as long as they like (within reason) to work with their words. The one who completes the transformation in the fewest steps is the winner. Although it is surprising how many words can be transformed (given enough steps), it is not always possible to do so. If no one can figure out a transformation, the round is considered a draw.

Dictionary

Creativity is essential in Dictionary, the classic definition-bluffing game.

Players: 4 or more

Ages: 12 and up

Place: Table or other flat writing surface, with seating for all players

Equipment: Pencil and scraps of paper for each player; dictionary (preferably unabridged)

Dictionary is an old parlor game that has inspired such board games as Balderdash and Slang Teasers. In Dictionary, players come up with fake definitions to real (but little-known) words with the aim of fooling others into believing that the bogus definition is genuine. Not for young children, this game appeals to those who are intrigued by words and like to pull the wool over other people's eyes. Dictionary can be hilarious and even educational. It's hard to tell whether the best players are those with a great vocabulary or those who are good bluffers.

To start, one player looks through the dictionary and picks out a word that nobody is likely to know. The weirder or more obscure the word, the better. "Popliteal" (the part of the leg behind the knee) is a good choice, as is "coypu" (a South American aquatic rodent), "lithophane" (a type of decorated porcelain), or "tuque" (a knitted stocking cap). The word is announced to the other players, and everyone writes it down on a scrap of paper. The player who found the word then copies down the correct definition on his own scrap, while all the others try to come up with phony but plausible-sounding meanings to write on theirs.

A player should not get too carried away, because the point of this game is to make the others believe that her definition is the true definition. The best fake definitions are concise and authoritative-sounding. A player who is asked to come up with a definition of "popliteal," for example, might write: "An organic chemical used in the production of oil paints" or "Of or pertaining to the respiratory system."

When they're finished writing, the players all write their names next to the definitions on their scraps, fold

them up, and hand them to the person with the dictionary. He mixes up the papers and then reads each definition aloud (with a straight face, please!). After all the definitions have been read—including the real one—everyone, except for the reader, declares which one she thinks is real. The reader writes each player's initials on the definition she picks and, once all the votes are in, reveals the true answer.

Any player who identifies the true definition earns 1 point. A player gets 3 points for every other player who votes for his bogus definition. If no one votes for the real definition, the player who chose the word from the dictionary scores 5 points. Now it's another player's turn to choose a word. The first player to score 25 points wins.

Adverbs

Adverbs is a Charades-like acting game that focuses on vocabulary.

Players: 4 or more

Ages: 10 and up

Place: Anywhere with open area to serve as small stage

Equipment: None

The dictionary defines an adverb as "a word serving as a modifier of a verb, an adjective, another adverb, a preposition, a phrase, a clause, or a sentence, and expressing some relation of manner or quality, place, time, degree, number, cause, opposition, affirmation, or denial." But players of Adverbs can think of adverbs simply as words that end in "ly" and describe an action: "loudly," "slowly," "crazily," and so on.

To bring out the theatrical element in Adverbs, it's best to gather everyone around an area that can serve as the "stage." One by one, the players take to the stage to act out a selected adverb, while the others try to figure out what the adverb in question is.

One player starts by thinking up an adverb. The choices are endless, and it can be really fun to choose a less familiar word, such as "poetically" or "independently"—but if it's too unusual it may be impossible to act out. The starting player steps onto the stage, and the others, one at a time, ask her to carry out an action "in the manner of the word." Someone, for example, might tell her to "eat in the manner of the word" or "talk in the manner of the word" or "hop in the manner of the word." If the adverb she has picked is "loudly," she then acts out "eating loudly" or "talking loudly" or "hopping loudly."

The guessing begins as soon as the action does, with the watching players calling out guesses as often as they like. The first player who guesses the adverb correctly gets a point. If, after 30 seconds or so of "eating loudly," no one has guessed the adverb, one of the watching players can

ask for another action to be performed "in the manner of" the mystery adverb. If everyone in the group has made a request and the adverb has still not been guessed, the player on stage has to pick another adverb and try again.

After every player has gone on stage once (or as many times as the group decides), whoever has guessed right most often is the Adverbs champion.

Team Adverbs

In the team variation—which calls for paper and pencil, a timer, and a big bowl (optional)—the participants split into two groups, and players take turns acting out adverbs for their group only. This time the player must write down his chosen adverb on a scrap of paper and give it to the opposing team to hold onto. The adverb actor's team yells out requests to him and guesses at his word, and if anyone on that team guesses correctly within a set time limit (say, 1 minute), the team scores a point. If not, the other team goes, with their own adverb actor. The winning team is the one with the most correct guesses after every player on both teams has performed an adverb.

This team version of Adverbs can also be played with adverbs selected not by the performers themselves, but by the group as a whole. Before the start of the game, everyone writes an adverb on a scrap of paper (or several adverbs on several scraps of paper), folds it up, and tosses it into a big bowl. Then, before taking the stage, a player plucks an adverb at random from the bowl— and that's the one she has to act out.

Pencil-and-Paper Games

Pencil-and-paper games are almost as portable as games that need no equipment at all, and the ability to create patterns and game boards opens up a whole new scope of play. The games in this chapter are contests of strategy and creativity. All are played on paper and require a writing utensil. An ordinary No. 2 pencil or a black or blue ballpoint pen is good enough for most, but felt-tip markers or crayons in different colors are sometimes required. A few of the games are much easier to play on graph or lined paper than on blank sheets, although a conscientious and steady-handed player *can* create a homemade grid. Because writing is involved, the most comfortable place to play pencil-and-paper games is at a table. If a table and chairs are not available, however, these games can be played on the floor or on large books set on the players' laps.

Tic-Tac-Toe

This game has one simple aim: to get three in a row and yell "tic-tac-toe!"

Players: 2

Ages: 4 to 12

Place: Table or other flat writing surface, with seating for both players

Equipment: Pencil for each player; paper

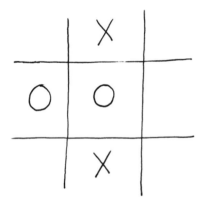

Tic-Tac-Toe's origins lie in ancient Egypt, where the nine-square grid, or "magic square," was filled with numbers that were believed to contain mystical power. Today's more down-to-earth game is still fascinating to players of all ages—even those who know the secret to winning! The fact that Tic-Tac-Toe—known as Noughts and Crosses in Great Britain—takes only seconds to play makes it hard to stop after just one game.

Creating a Tic-Tac-Toe board is as easy as drawing two vertical lines crossed with two horizontal lines (see diagram above). The nine squares that result should be roughly the same size. Now the two players decide who will be O's (noughts) and who will be X's (crosses) and who will go first. Each player aims to get three of his own marks in a row—horizontally, vertically, or diagonally.

To play, the first player makes an X or an O in one of the squares. Because the first player has the advantage, it's only fair for the other player to go first in the next game. The players continue to alternate starting positions, making their marks as they try to get three in a row and block their opponent from doing the same.

The first player to get three in a row draws a line through her marks and calls out "tic-tac-toe!" to win the game. If neither player is able to complete a line of three marks, the game is considered a draw.

Children should be encouraged to play offensively, if possible. Any player who makes marks in three corners or in the center square and two corners is guaranteed to win. This is because even if the opponent blocks the row in one direction, the other row will still be available on the next turn. If the first player knows this strategy, the second player should place his first mark in the middle square and hope to make the game a tie by playing defensively. If both players are adept at the strategy, however, all games will turn out to be draws.

Magic Square Tic-Tac-Toe

This version of Tic-Tac-Toe is played not with X's and O's, but with coins—five each of two different denominations of coins (such as pennies and dimes). The playing board in this game is not a grid, but a square crossed by four lines: one horizontal, one vertical, and two diagonals (see diagram to right).

The four lines intersect at the center, but they also intersect the square's perimeter at the corners and at the middle of each side of the square. Players take turns placing their coins at any of these intersections. The goal is the same as in Tic-Tac-Toe: to complete three in a row. The first to complete a horizontal, vertical, or diagonal line is named the winner.

Expanded Tic-Tac-Toe

This variation is played on a larger grid of 16 squares (three vertical lines and three horizontal ones) or 25 squares (four lines each way; see diagram below). Using X's or O's, each player competes to get three, four, or five of her marks in a row. Instead of winning with just one line, players try

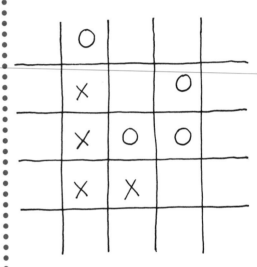

to form as many lines as possible. A mark may be counted several times: as part of a horizontal, a vertical, or a diagonal line. The scoring is as follows: three marks in a row scores 1 point; four in a row, 3 points; and five in a row, 5 points. The game ends when all the spaces are filled. The player with the highest score is the winner.

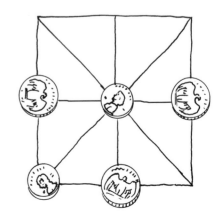

Go-Moku

With its X's and O's, Go-Moku is a close cousin of Tic-Tac-Toe, but there's a twist.

Players: 2

Ages: 8 to 14

Place: Table or other flat writing surface, with seating for both players

Equipment: Pencil for each player; paper

There are several versions of Go-Moku, which can most accurately be described as Tic-Tac-Toe "on the lines." The original game, called Go or I-Go, is a complicated strategy game played with black and white stones on a grid carved into a wooden board. The version described here is played with pencil and paper on a grid which can be completed in minutes and is easily mastered by children in the middle grades.

First, the players draw a playing grid with 19 vertical and 19 horizontal lines (see diagram). Next, they decide who will be X's and who will be O's. X's go first. Each player is trying to mark a series of five X's or O's on the intersections of the lines. The series may run horizontally, vertically, or diagonally.

Players take turns writing their symbols on the grid, trying to complete a series or block their opponent's markings. It's important to block an opponent's line the minute there's a chain of three with both ends open. Once a player gets four in a row with both ends still open, her opponent will be stymied. Even if he manages to close off one end, she'll still be able to get her fifth mark in.

The first player to get five in a row, vertically, horizontally, or diagonally, wins the game.

Magic Square

The magic number is 15 in this number puzzle.

Players: 2 or more

Ages: 8 to 12

Place: Table or other flat writing surface, with seating for all players

Equipment: Pencil and paper for each player

This nifty little puzzle is a great workout for young brains. Once the secret pattern is unlocked, players will be ready to move on to more challenging brain teasers.

Each player draws a square on a sheet of paper and then divides it into nine smaller boxes (three across and three down). The object is to fill in each square with a number from 1 to 9 (each number may be used only once) so that the sum of any three numbers in a line (horizontally, vertically, or diagonally) is 15.

Children compete to be the first one to solve the puzzle. If nobody is able to figure it out, players can be given the hint that the center number should be 5. The first player to complete their square correctly wins.

There are several ways to play Magic Square that will challenge players who have solved the original problem. In one version, an identical nine-box square is used. Players must try to fill in the boxes with the numbers 1, 2, 3, 10, 11, 12, 19, 20, and 21 so that any horizontal, vertical, or diagonal line totals 33.

In another version of Magic Square, players draw a large square and divide it into 16 equal boxes (four down and four across). The numbers 1 through 16 are used to fill in the boxes so that the sum of each horizontal, vertical, and diagonal line is 34.

Number Tic-Tac-Toe

Math makes this version of Tic-Tac-Toe much more challenging than the original.

Players: 2

Ages: 9 to 14

Place: Table or other flat writing surface, with seating for both players

Equipment: Pencil for each player; paper

Standard Tic-Tac-Toe is a great diversion for very young players, but once they find out the secret of winning, the fun may run a little thin. Number Tic-Tac-Toe brings the challenge back into the game by requiring each player to finish a line of numbers adding up to exactly 15 while her opponent tries to prevent her from doing so.

First, players make a standard nine-square Tic-Tac-Toe board by drawing two parallel vertical lines crossed by two parallel horizontal lines. One player is assigned the four even numbers between 1 and 9 (2, 4, 6, and 8), and the other gets the five odd numbers (1, 3, 5, 7, 9). The player with odds goes first because he has one extra number. This player writes one odd number in any square. Next, the player with evens does the same, with an even number.

The object is to complete a line of numbers with the sum of 15. The line may be vertical, horizontal, or diagonal. Each number may be used only once.

For example, if the first player starts by putting a 5 in the top left, the second player might put a 6 in the middle square, with the intention of putting a 4 in the bottom right square on his next turn—making a line that adds up to 15. The odd player, however, will want to prevent this, and she can do so by putting one of her numbers, like a 3, into that bottom right square.

The game continues until one player wins by totaling 15 or all the squares are filled, in which case there's a draw. Players switch odd and even numbers for the next game.

Tip-Tap-Toe

Tip-Tap-Toe is like playing darts with a pencil and paper—a bull's-eye wins the game.

Players: 2 to 6

Ages: 5 to 10

Place: Table or other flat writing surface, with seating for all players

Equipment: At least 2 pencils (1 for the game, 1 for keeping score); paper

Although the names sound similar, Tip-Tap-Toe is completely unrelated to Tic-Tac-Toe. In fact, in both play and spirit it bears much more resemblance to Pin the Tail on the Donkey. The difference is that there are numbers involved, so players need to be able to add.

Before playing, the children make a game board by drawing a large circle on a piece of paper and dividing it into 10 to 12 pie-shaped wedges (see diagram). The wedges are numbered in clockwise order. One player is designated as scorekeeper and, on a separate piece of paper, notes each player's score after every turn.

To play, each player takes a turn closing his eyes and touching a pencil to the target. He then scores the number of points in that segment. That section of the board is crossed off and not worth any points to any player who might later touch it.

Each player gets only one touch per turn. If she hits a crossed-out wedge or goes outside the circle, no points are scored. If a player hits the bull's-eye—the exact center of the circle—he instantly wins the game.

If no one makes a bull's-eye, the player with the most points after all the wedges are crossed out is the winner.

Boxes

Players try to make boxes by connecting the dots on a grid while preventing their opponent from doing the same.

Players: 2

Ages: 7 to 12

Place: Table or other flat writing surface, with seating for both players

Equipment: Pencil for each player; paper

This simple little game can be played almost anywhere at any time, and it's addictive! That's why so many teachers have banned Boxes from study halls over the years. Opponents compete to make the greatest number of boxes out of a dot grid. As players catch on to the strategy, they can vary the game to make it more challenging.

To begin, players draw a square grid of 16 dots, with four even rows of four dots. More experienced players may prefer a 100-dot grid.

Players now take turns drawing lines connecting any two dots that are next to each other. The lines must be either horizontal or vertical (no diagonals), and each player may draw only one line per turn—at the outset. As the lines accumulate, each player tries to be the one who can close up a four-dot box by drawing the fourth line. When a player completes a box, she claims that box with her initial and then draws another line (see diagram). And she can keep going again as long as she keeps completing boxes. Sometimes, drawing the fourth line on one box can start a chain reaction; that fourth line might be the third line on another box, to which the player can then add a fourth line, which might again be the third line on yet another box, and so on. When that player cannot complete any more boxes, it's finally the other player's turn again.

The game is over when all the dots are connected and all the boxes filled in. The player with the most boxes is the winner.

In a variation of the game, players try to complete the smallest, rather than the greatest, number of boxes. In this case, the player who has the fewest boxes at the end of the game is the winner.

Drawing in the Dark

The dimly lit setting of this illustrating game makes for some hilarious art.

Players: 2 or more, plus an adult or older child to serve as storyteller

Ages: 6 to 10

Place: Dark room with table or other flat writing surface and seating for all players

Equipment: Pencil, crayon, or marker and paper for each player

Many very young children's artwork looks as if it were done in a blackout. In Drawing in the Dark, this really will be true. Children will have a wonderfully silly time comparing their mixed-up masterpieces. Adults can rest assured that this game fosters creativity and enhances fine motor skills.

To prepare for the game, each child is given paper and a pencil, crayon, or marker. Then the lights are turned out. The storyteller proceeds to tell a short, simple tale that the players must illustrate. The story should include different people, animals, and objects that the storyteller instructs the players to draw.

For example, a story might start out like this: "Once upon a time, there was a small kitten named Whiskers. Please draw Whiskers." The players are given a minute or so to draw a cat, then the story continues—with the storyteller pausing for a few moments after each new element is added to the tale.

"Whiskers lived in a barn. Please draw the barn with Whiskers inside. Every day the farmer's son, Jack, would bring Whiskers a fish to eat. Please draw Jack feeding Whiskers a fish. One day a hungry little mouse asked Whiskers if she could share his fish. Whiskers said 'yes,' gave the mouse some of the fish, and didn't even chase the mouse. Please finish your picture by drawing Whiskers and the mouse both eating the fish."

When everyone has finished drawing, the lights are turned on. The children should get a big kick out of examining their garbled drawings. There is no need to name winners and losers in Drawing in the Dark. The storyteller, however, may act as a judge, or the whole group may vote on the illustration that comes closest to depicting the story.

The Snake

This serpent grows as dots are connected but, above all, it must avoid biting its own tail.

Players: 2 or more

Ages: 8 to 13

Place: Table or other flat writing surface, with seating for all players

Equipment: Pencil for each player; paper

The Snake makes its home on a dot grid just like the one used in Boxes. The object here is just the opposite, though: in The Snake, players try to avoid closing a box at all costs!

Before playing, make a grid of 100 dots, with ten even rows of ten dots. The first player then connects any two dots next to each other with a horizontal or vertical line (no diagonal lines allowed). The next player must connect one end of the first line to another dot. This goes on and creates a growing "snake" slithering along the grid (see diagram). The line must be continuous, with no branches or crossing over from one part of the snake to another. Players try to avoid connecting either end of the snake to itself.

The first person who can't connect the snake's tail to an adjacent dot—and instead has to make the snake "bite" its own tail—loses the game.

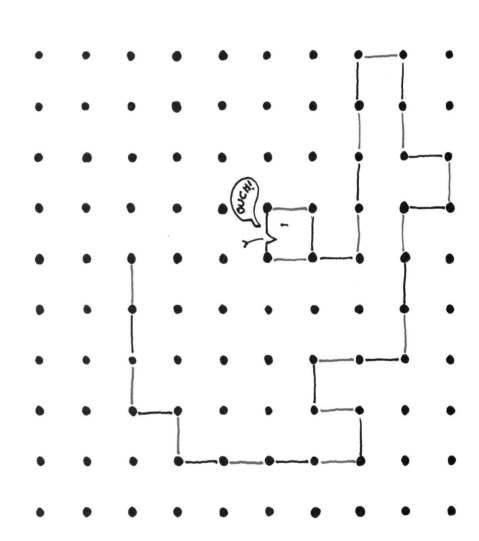

Two-Color Snakes

In this snake race, the victorious viper is
the one that slithers across the grid first.

Players: 2

Ages: 8 to 13

Place: Table or other flat writing
surface, with seating for both players

Equipment: 2 pens of different colors
(preferably black and red); paper

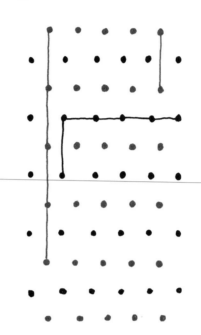

Two-Color Snakes takes its inspiration from The Snake, but it's very
much a unique game in its own
right. From start to finish, it has all the
excitement of a flat-out race.

Two pens of different colors (black
and red are best) are necessary to
play. Before beginning, the players
must create a grid they will both use.
To make the grid, the player with the
black pen starts by drawing a row of
five black dots. Below this row, and
evenly spaced between the black dots,
the other player draws a row of six
red dots. Then another row of five
black dots, and another row of six
red, and so on until there are six rows
of black dots and five rows of red
(see diagram).

Now the race begins, with the black-
penned player trying to draw a continuous line connecting the black dots
from the top to the bottom and the
red-penned player trying to create a
continuous line connecting the red
dots from one side to the other. The
players take turns drawing lines
between adjacent dots, but they must
connect only dots of their pen color.
A player is free to start a new line at
any time. A line may turn and branch,
but it may not cross the opponent's
line or head back the way it came or
cross over itself.

The first player to complete a continuous line from the top of the grid to
the bottom, or from one side of the
grid to the other, is the winner.

Sprouts

This unusual connect-the-dots game seems
simple but requires a lot of ingenuity.

Players: 2 or more

Ages: 7 to 14

Place: Table or other flat writing
surface, with seating for all players

Equipment: Pencil for each player;
paper

Sprouts is one of those wonderful
games that can be played at
many levels of skill, making it
accessible to relatively young children
and intriguing even to adults. The size
of the playing field dictates the difficulty of the game, so keep it small for
beginners. Veteran players often
spread the dots over a poster-size
sheet of paper.

To create a Sprouts board, players
put down any number of dots at random on a sheet of paper. Anywhere
from 5 to 30 dots make for a good
game. Players take turns drawing
lines to connect two dots or curving
lines that begin and end on the same
dot (see diagram). After drawing a
line, the player marks its halfway
point with another dot. This dot is
now part of the game.

Lines can be any shape or size and
can go in any direction. But a new line
may never cross another line or pass

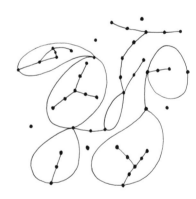

through a dot. Only three lines may
lead from any one dot (a line that doubles back counts as one line, though).
Players continue taking turns drawing
lines and connecting dots until all permissible moves are made. The last
player to draw a legitimate line wins.

Learning to plan ahead is crucial to
mastering this game. To prevent opponents from making easy connections,
players can isolate dots with long,
curvy lines or create lines that double
back to the same dot.

Find the Fort

In this imaginary attack game, settlers beat a path to their fort without crossing one another's lines.

Players: 2

Ages: 7 to 10

Place: Table or other flat writing surface, with seating for both players

Equipment: Pencil and paper for each player

Find the Fort is a simple but exciting game that appeals immensely to children. In it, settlements are being attacked and "settlers" must seek cover in a make-believe fort. Players must have steady hands and good visual tracking skills.

Before beginning, each player prepares a playing sheet for her opponent. The fort, a square with a small opening in one side, is drawn in the center (see diagram). Then the settlements—represented by 15 circles—are randomly scattered around the page. Each of the circles is then numbered from 1 to 15. The numbering, too, should be quite random. The two players then trade papers.

The players imagine that the settlements are under attack and that they must get all of the settlers into the fort before the assault begins. To do this, each player must draw a line connecting each number, in sequence (first 1,

then 2, and so on), to the opening in the fort. This must be done in such a way that none of the lines touch or cross any of the other trails. One penalty point is scored for every crossed path.

It's likely that some lines will cross, but the idea is to cross as few as possible. The game continues until each of the players has herded all the settlers into the fort. Penalty points are then totaled, and the player with the fewest points is the winner.

Pairing Numbers

There's no fort in Pairing Numbers, but there are two sets of numbers from 1 through 15 circled and scattered at random about the page. The object is to connect each number with its match without crossing or touching lines. Players take turns drawing lines to connect the numbers in sequence (1 to 1 first and 15 to 15 last). The first player to cross a line loses the game.

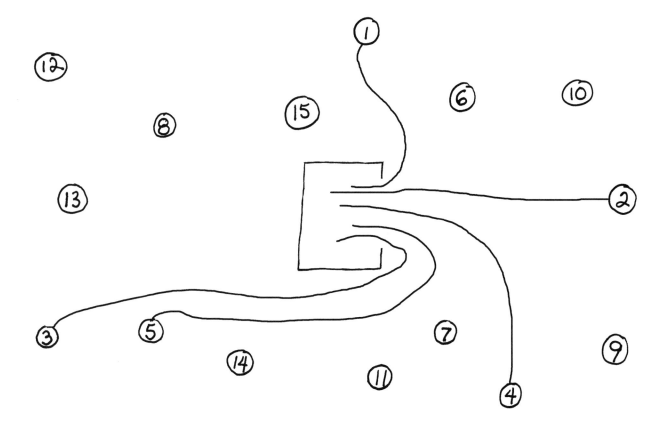

Buried Treasure

In this graph-paper game, opponents search for "buried treasure" through a process of elimination.

Players: 2

Ages: 7 to 12, plus an adult or older child to help out

Place: Table or other flat writing surface, with seating for both players

Equipment: Pencil and graph paper for each player

Buried Treasure is a simpler version of Swiss Navy (see next page). It's a good introduction to logic and strategy for younger children. The game is played on two graph-paper grids, each consisting of 81 squares. Eighty of these squares are assigned to one or the other player; the object is to uncover the only square on the board without an owner.

Before the game begins, each player marks off a nine-square by nine-square area on his paper and labels the grid with the numbers 1 through 9 from top to bottom down the left side and the letters A through I from left to right across the top (see diagram). The top left corner is therefore called A-1; the square directly below it is A-2; the square to the right of A-1 is B-1, and so on to the last square on the bottom right, I-9.

Next, the adult or older child who's helping out takes both papers and shades in four vertical columns and four horizontal rows on each. One player's grid may be shaded, for example, on vertical columns A, D, F, and H and horizontal rows, 1, 2, 7, and 9. The other paper must be shaded on completely different columns and rows. This leaves only one square that's unshaded on both sheets—that's the buried treasure. Players do not see each other's sheets and therefore don't know which squares are shaded on the other's paper.

The helper then returns the papers to the players, whose mission is to figure out where the buried treasure is located. The opponents take turns asking one another whether they have a particular square shaded, identifying the square by letter and number. Players must answer truthfully. Each time a player admits that a particular box is shaded, the opponent should mark it off on her own grid. The game goes back and forth in this manner until one of the players identifies the buried treasure by process of elimination and wins the game.

Swiss Navy

In this game of strategy, opponents use persistence (and a bit of luck) to try to locate each other's fleets on a hidden grid.

Players: 2

Ages: 9 to 14

Place: Table or other flat writing surface, with seating for both players

Equipment: Pencil and sheet of graph paper for each player; book or cereal box to serve as screen

This pencil-and-paper game has a tongue-in-cheek name because Switzerland—a landlocked country—has no navy! Using deductive reasoning and a healthy dose of imagination, players wage war on a sea of graph paper, with the aim of destroying the opponent's "fleet."

This game takes a little more preparation than most. First, on her graph paper, each player maps out two grids—one labeled "home fleet" and the other, "enemy fleet." Each grid should be ten squares by ten squares. The squares on both grids are identified by numbering the boxes down the left side 1 through 10 and labeling the boxes across the top A through J (see diagram). The top left box is thus A-1, the bottom right is J-10.

Next, without allowing her opponent to see, each admiral positions her fleet of ships anywhere on the grid marked "home fleet." The fleet consists of one battleship (four consecutive horizontal or vertical squares), two cruisers (three consecutive squares each), three destroyers (two adjacent squares each), and four submarines (one square each). The squares representing each ship in the fleet are outlined and shaded in. Ships may not be located on the diagonal. There must be at least one empty square between ships, and once they are positioned, they cannot be moved.

Now, the battle begins! Players sit so they cannot see each other's papers during play—a book or cereal box propped up in the middle of the table between the players works well. Each admiral's goal is to sink the enemy fleet through a series of "hits." With players taking turns, shots are fired by calling out three locations on the enemy grid—G-8, B-3, and I-10, for example. The defending player responds to each shot by saying "miss" if the shot lands on an empty space in his home grid or by saying "hit" if a ship is located. If a hit occurs, the defending admiral marks a dark X across that square on his "home fleet" grid—and must reveal the category of the craft (battleship, cruiser, destroyer, or sub) that was hit. The attacking player marks those shots on the grid labeled "enemy fleet" by crossing out the misses and coloring in the hits. For a ship to sink, it must be hit on all the squares it occupies. When that happens, the defending admiral declares, "Sunk!"

The battle continues, back and forth, until one player sinks the enemy's entire fleet and wins the game. Players generally start out taking shots all across the opponent's grid. Once a hit occurs, however, the smart strategy is to home in on surrounding squares in order to sink the ship.

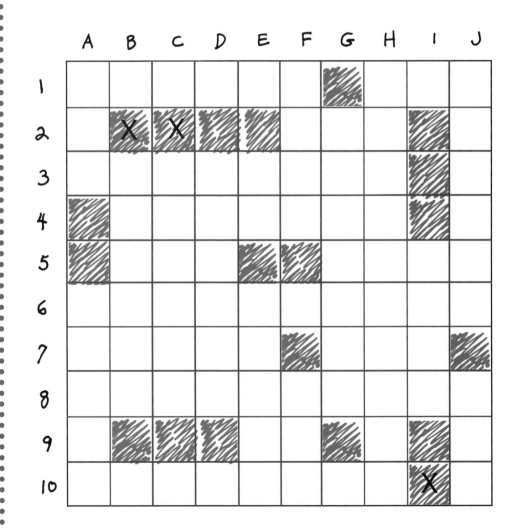

Aggression

It's army against army in this imaginary
battle to capture the most territory.

Players: 2 or more

Ages: 10 to 14

Place: Table or other flat writing
surface, with seating for all players

Equipment: Large sheet of paper;
pencil for each player; different color
of crayon or marker for each player or
team; 2 dice

Aggression is a battle for "world
domination" fought on a piece
of paper. The object is for a
player to conquer as many "countries"
as possible by making the best use
of the armies under her control. It
appeals to kids who are interested in
battles and military strategy. Children
need a good command of addition and
subtraction to participate, and each
child's understanding of strategy is
sure to get better after playing the
game more than a few times.

First, players gather around a large
sheet of paper to draw an imaginary
map of the world. They roll the dice to
decide on their order, with the highest
score going first and the lowest last.
Using an ordinary lead pencil, the first
player draws a country of any size or
shape. Players then take turns drawing
adjoining countries (see diagram). A
new country may touch as many or as
few of the existing countries as its cre-
ator wishes; it may not, however, completely surround all the existing countries. Each player should draw no
more than 10 countries. For two players, 20 total countries makes for a perfect game; for more than two, the total
number of countries per player should
be reduced considerably. Each country
is then labeled with a different letter
of the alphabet.

Now it's time for the "occupying
forces" to march in. Each player
chooses a different colored crayon or

marker, and each is given a total of
100 armies to command. These 100
armies may be divided up in any manner to occupy the countries. The dice
are rolled, and the "general" rolling
the highest score chooses one territory to occupy and deploys however
many of her armies she wishes (up to
100) inside its boundaries, writing in
the number of armies allocated to it in
her colored crayon or marker. Once a
country has been occupied, no other
player may add forces to it, and each
time a general uses any of the armies
assigned to her, that number is
deducted from the total of 100. (It
may be a good idea to keep track of
how many armies have been deployed
on a separate scrap of paper.)

After the first general has made her
decision, each of the other generals
has a chance to choose a country and

to deploy as many armies as he wishes (up to 100) inside its borders. This
"deployment" part of the game goes
on, around and around in clockwise
order, until all the countries have
been occupied or all the forces have
been deployed (whichever comes
first). Now the quest for world domination begins!

The goal of each general is to capture the largest number of territories
(the respective sizes of the different
countries don't matter). The player
who occupied the first country goes
first. Choosing any one of the countries in which she has deployed
forces, she begins her "attack" on her
"enemies"—the countries in which the
other players have deployed their
forces. She does this by conquering
any bordering countries that have
smaller numbers of armies than the
country she is attacking from. For
instance, if the attacking country (G)
has 17 armies and two bordering
defending countries (E and F) have 6
armies each, G can conquer both E
and F, which are crossed out of the
game, using the attacking general's
color to show that these territories

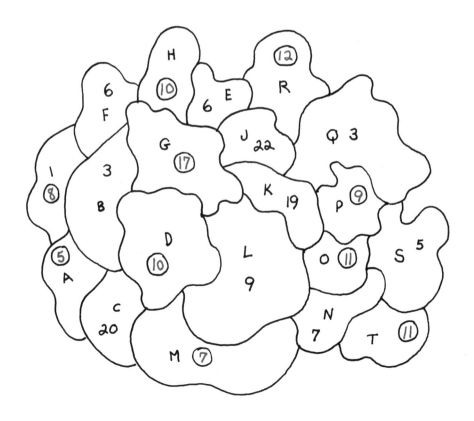

now belong to her. The attacking country can also conquer any bordering country that has no occupying forces in it.

The attacking general cannot conquer her own territories (and, of course, wouldn't want to), nor can she conquer territories that have the same number of forces as the country she's attacking from. Also, the attacking country remains vulnerable to attack from other adjacent countries: for instance, if country G (with its 17 armies) also has a border with country J, which has 22 armies, J may conquer G later in the game. (But J would win only the country G, not the countries E and F, which G had conquered earlier.)

After the first general has conquered all the countries she can from country G, play passes to the general on her left, who chooses any of his countries that has not yet been conquered to mount an attack on his enemies. The play continues, around and around, until all the countries that can

be attacked have been conquered. (It's quite possible that there will be a number of standoffs—adjacent countries that have equal numbers of forces and that therefore cannot be taken by any enemy.) The general who ends up with the greatest number of countries (including countries that have been conquered and countries that were invulnerable to attack) wins the game.

The initial deployment of forces can be a major factor in determining who wins Aggression, so players must take care right from the start. The best strategy for deploying forces differs from game to game and depends largely on what other players do. Thus, each player in each game must vary her strategy accordingly. If an opponent seems to be concentrating large numbers in a few countries while leaving many others empty or nearly so, a good approach would be to spread out forces in smaller numbers across as many countries as possible. In contrast, if an opponent's tactic is to spread out her armies, then placing

large numbers of armies in countries that have a lot of bordering countries may be the way to go.

Team Aggression

Aggression can be a lot of fun to play with teams—though team play may lead to some arguments about strategy! Teams should have equal numbers of players. Although the method of play is basically the same, players should decide ahead of time how the teams will make their decisions regarding which countries to occupy, how many armies to assign to particular territories, and where to begin the attempt to conquer the world. In one variation, all the members of each team decide together where and how to deploy and use their forces. In another variation, each team member acts individually (with no coaching or signaling from the others) as his turn comes up—while always trying to stay aware of how his actions may be helping or hurting his team as a whole.

Crystals

In this challenging pattern-visualizing game, players grow imaginary crystals corresponding to the "laws of nature."

Players: 2 or more

Ages: 11 and up

Place: Table or other flat writing surface, with seating for all players

Equipment: Sheet of graph paper; different color of crayon or marker for each player

rystals is an intriguing exercise that calls for imagination, the power to visualize, and strategic planning skills. It's best suited for older children who have well-developed powers of concentration and reasoning. Indeed, some adults may find this game difficult to grasp and master. A precocious 12-year-old may well become the Crystals champion in the family.

Only one sheet of graph paper is required to play. If there are two players (the best number for this game), one player marks off a grid of 20 squares by 20 squares. If there are more than two players, the size of the field should be increased by 10 squares in each direction per player. (In other words, three players need a grid of 30 by 30 squares; four players,

a grid of 40 by 40 squares; and so on.) Each player now tries to build perfect crystals by coloring in squares with a crayon or marker.

These imaginary crystals, like the real ones, are made up of "atoms" (individual squares, in this case). They must also follow the "laws of nature," which in this game dictate that a crystal be perfectly symmetrical. To make sure a crystal is symmetrical, players must visualize four axis lines through its center—one horizontal, one vertical, and two diagonal—and then mentally "fold" the crystal along each axis. An acceptable crystal will form a mirror image when "folded" along any axis (see diagram on next page).

Besides being symmetrical, crystals must be made up of four or more atoms filled in by only one player. In each crystal, each atom must touch at least one other atom along at least one of its sides (that is, atoms can't be joined only at the corners). Finally, crystals may not contain any empty atoms (holes). Squares, crosses, and an infinite variety of far more elaborate shapes are all legitimate crystals.

To play, participants take turns coloring in one atom at a time, with the aim of growing crystals. During the early part of the game, players usually scatter atoms across the board to establish places where potential crys-

tals might grow. Players continue coloring one atom per turn, gradually trying to grow crystals that cover as much of the playing surface as possible. To gain the upper hand, players should try to block the growth of their opponent's crystals and make their own crystals as large as possible.

The game is over when there are no

more empty squares left or when it is not possible to form any more crystals. To score, each player counts the number of atoms in her acceptable crystals. Crystal-like shapes that do not meet all the requirements do not count. The player with the highest total number of atoms in his crystals (not necessarily the most crystals) is the winner.

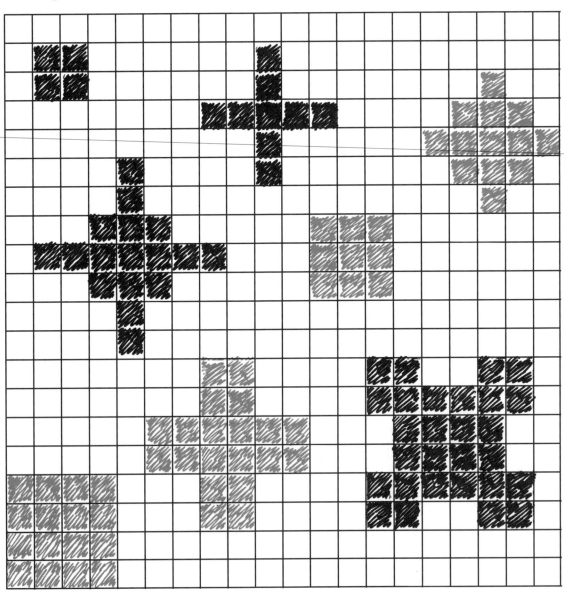

Tabletop Games

Tabletop games encompass highly diverse kinds of activities, help develop concentration, and offer entertainment for every age and skill level. Kids can compete at various board games or enjoy tabletop versions of baseball, football, and soccer. For even more tabletop ideas, check the listings under Card Games and Pencil-and-Paper Games.

The games in this chapter make use of a variety of equipment: dominoes and dice, sticks and buttons, checkers and checkerboards, paper and table tennis balls, rulers and coins. What's needed is noted in every entry. The most important requirement is usually a sturdy table, one that will stand up to the wear and tear of exuberant play, chalk marks, and masking tape (although many of these games can, in a pinch, be played on the floor).

Bingo

No money need change hands to make this classic number-matching game loads of fun.

Players: 3 or more

Ages: 5 and up

Place: Table or other flat surface, with seating for all players

Equipment: Sheet of paper for each player plus 75 small scraps of paper; pencil for each player; large bowl, hat, or similar container; 25 place-markers (such as pennies, buttons, small candies, or pebbles) for each player

What's one of the most popular and often-played games in North America? Bingo! Sure, most adult Bingo players are hoping to win a pot of money, but kids don't need a prize to enjoy this game. Its delicious tension and dramatic ending are enough to make it a hit with any kid who can read numbers and spell B-I-N-G-O.

Stores offer Bingo sets ranging from simple to ornate, but the homemade version is just as much fun. All that's needed are 75 scraps of paper numbered 1 through 75 and a large bowl, hat, or other container to hold them. The letter B is written on numbers 1 through 15, the letter I on numbers 16 through 30, N on numbers 31 through 45, G on numbers 46 through 60, and O on numbers 61 through 75.

Each player makes herself a Bingo card, which consists of 25 square boxes, 5 across and 5 down (see diagram). The word "B-I-N-G-O" is printed in capital letters across the top of the card, with one letter at the top of each column. The first column (under B) is filled in with any five numbers between 1 and 15, with the chosen numbers getting progressively higher going down the column. The second column (under I) gets any five numbers from 16 through 30; the third (under N), any four from 31 through 45 (the center square is designated a "free" space and does not get a number); the fourth (under G), any five from 46 through 60; and the fifth (under O), any five from 61 through 75. (Players should make sure no two cards are exactly the same—if they differ by as little as a single number in a single position, that's just fine.) Finally, each player receives 25 place-markers.

Before play gets under way, each player may use a place-marker to cover his free space in the center. One player, designated the "caller," picks a piece of paper from the bowl and calls out the letter and number on it. If the letter-number combination is G-58, for example, any player with a 58 (under G) on his card covers it with a place-marker.

The caller continues picking numbers until one player has covered five squares in a line, either horizontally, vertically, or diagonally. At that point, the player with the line shouts "Bingo!" and wins the game. (If more than one player calls "Bingo!" the faster mouth wins.) For a longer and more nerve-racking game, players can be required to fill up the whole card before shouting "Bingo!" Advanced players should try two cards at once.

Tiddlywinks

Players test their target skill by flipping small plastic disks into a cup.

Players: 2 to 6

Ages: 5 and up

Place: Cloth-covered table or floor covered by a flat rug, with seating for all players

Equipment: Tiddlywinks set or, for homemade set: 4 small disks (coins, cardboard disks, buttons) for each player; 1 larger disk (poker chips, bigger coins, or buttons) for each player; "cup" (jar lid or shallow bowl); and pencil and paper (optional)

Tiddlywinks is a hopping, skipping, jumping, and flipping party of a game. Despite its frivolous name, enthusiasts (including many adults) have been known to take their wink-flicking quite seriously. It takes a lot of fine motor skill to use a small plastic disk to flip an even smaller plastic disk into the air and make it land in a little cup a few feet (about 1m) away. The best Tiddlywinks playing surface is a cloth-covered table or a flat rug.

The easiest way to play Tiddlywinks is with a packaged set that comes with plastic winks (small disks) and shooters (larger disks) of various colors, a cup, and a cloth or plastic sheet printed with a target—the cup goes in the center. Homemade Tiddlywinks may not flip as well, but they do the job. Try using quarters as shooters and dimes as winks. Smooth poker chips, cardboard disks, or flat buttons can also be pressed into service. A jar lid or shallow bowl can be used as the cup. Playing with a target is optional; a homemade target—with

the number 25 in the bull's-eye and 20, 15, 10, and 5 in the rings extending out from the center—can be drawn on a large sheet of paper (see diagram). The bull's-eye should be about the same diameter as the cup, which is placed on top of it.

Once the equipment is assembled, each player is allotted a shooter and four winks. The cup is placed in the center of the table (or floor area), and players sit around this with their winks in a horizontal line in front of them. Each player takes a preliminary shot by holding her shooter between her thumb and index finger and pressing the shooter down on the edge of a wink (see diagram). The wink should pop up in the air and fly toward the cup. The player whose wink lands closest to the cup (or in it) goes first.

Each player "squidges" (shoots) one wink per turn. When someone "pots the wink" (gets a wink in the cup), he gets to take another shot. Opening shots should be made at least a foot

(30cm) from the cup—farther for more expert players. Play continues, with players squidging their winks from the starting line or from wherever they have landed, until one player pots all her winks. If a wink flies off the table or goes off the target, it must be put back at the starting line. Seasoned squidgers know that it's more effective to take many small hops toward the cup rather than one flying leap.

If one wink lands on top of another, the bottom wink is "squopped." A player must wait until the top wink is moved before playing the bottom one. Therefore, leaving a wink on top of someone else's is a good strategy for preventing him from potting all his winks. A player whose last wink is squopped must "pass" on his turn until the wink is free.

If a wink lands propped up against the cup, it may not be played until it is flat. Its owner must shoot other winks to knock it down. If a player's last wink is stuck this way, she must pass on her turn until an opponent knocks it down. If it is never knocked down, she's out of luck.

If the game is being played without a target, the first player to pot all his winks is the winner. If a target is used, players add up their scores according

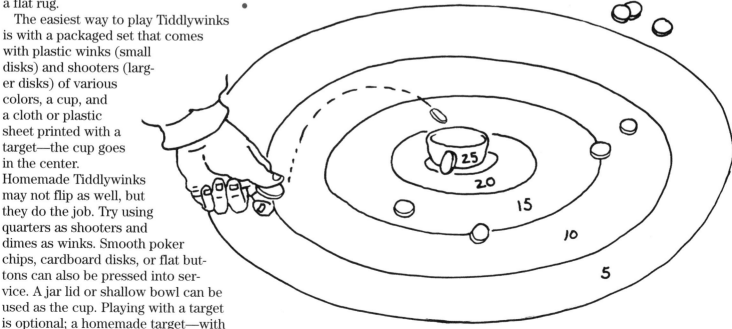

crumpled paper or opened books placed under the cloth make for rough terrain. Water traps can be created by filling jar lids with water and should be avoided.

Players take turns shooting each of their four winks, keeping track of how many "strokes" it takes to sink each hole. The player with the fewest total strokes after everyone has completed the course is the winner.

Tiddlywinks Race

This lively floor game—which calls for a wink and shooter for each player, as well as masking tape or string to mark the course—is well suited to a group of three or more small children. Contestants line up their winks at a starting line and attempt to shoot them over a finish line about 8 feet (2.4m) away. The two lines can be delineated with tape or string. Play progresses by turns, with each player continuing to shoot her wink from the spot where it landed on the previous turn. This game requires a lot of space because the route will be anything but direct. The player whose wink crosses the finish line first is the winner.

---

to where their winks are at the end of the game, and the highest score wins.

Castle

For this more challenging Tiddlywinks game, a target is drawn with concentric circles 2, 5, and 10 inches (5, 12.5, and 25cm) in diameter on a sheet of paper. The cup—the "castle" in this game—goes in the middle, and should fill up almost the whole central circle. Players shoot from the edge of the outer circle. The object is to reach

the castle. But beware of the moat! If a wink lands in the second circle, it is gobbled up by crocodiles and disappears from the game. The first player to get a wink in the cup conquers the castle.

Tiddlywinks Golf

The Tiddlywinks links are laid out on a large cloth, using a small cup or napkin ring for each of the nine holes. Obstacles can be added for a fancier, more realistic course; for example,

---

Blow Soccer

In this lively free-for-all, players propel a "soccer ball" by blowing through drinking straws.

Players: 2 to 10 (even number)

Ages: 4 to 8

Place: Table (preferably long and rectangular) or floor

Equipment: Table tennis ball; drinking straw for each player; pencils, pens, or toothpicks to mark the goal; strips of cardboard and masking tape (optional)

Blow Soccer is a raucous game that doesn't take much skill, just a good set of lungs. The action is fast-paced and the rules are simple and few, making this a good party game or a fun rainy-day activity for young kids.

Best played on a long, rectangular table, Blow Soccer can also be played on a square table or a marked-off area on the floor. A goal a few inches (cm) wide and deep is marked by pencils, pens, or toothpicks at each end of the table.

Especially motivated Blow Soccer players may want to tape strips of cardboard along the edges of the table, leaving only one narrow opening on each end for the ball to smash through the goal. This setup helps keep the ball in play continuously and really picks up the pace.

Blow Soccer can be played one on one or between two teams. To start play, the ball is placed in the center of the table. The players or teams stand at opposite ends of the table and must stay on their side throughout the match. (If playing on the floor, the players sit or kneel at opposite ends of the "field.") At a signal, all the players blow through their straws in an attempt to propel the ball through the opposing goal. When necessary, they must also use their breath to defend their own goal from attack. No one may touch the ball with the straw or with face, hands, or any other body part. And there's no blowing on the ball directly, without using the straw.

If the ball makes it through the goal-posts, the scoring team gets a point. The ball is then placed back in the middle of the table and play resumes. If the ball is blown off the table and thus out of bounds (which can happen even with the cardboard strips in place), it is replaced at the spot where it went out and the opposing team gets a "free blow"—after which the game resumes.

The player or the team scoring the most points within a given time period is the winner.

Paper Football

This exciting paper-flicking football game is a favorite of gridiron fans.

Players: 2

Ages: 7 to 12

Place: Table (preferably rectangular)

Equipment: Sheet of paper (to be folded into the "football"); chalk or masking tape; coin for tossing; pencil and paper for scoring; clock or watch for timing

In Paper Football, the ball is a triangle of folded paper, the field is a table, and the goalposts (when needed) are fingers. This simulated football game is a favorite of school-age fans because it retains the suspense and excitement of the real game. Parents like Paper Football, too, because the worst injury a player is likely to sustain is a paper cut.

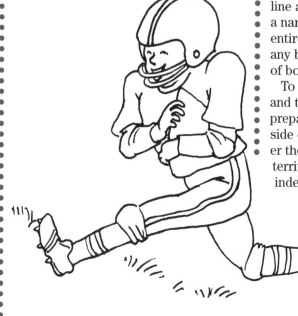

Before the kickoff, a ball must be created from a piece of paper (see diagram on next page). An $8\frac{1}{2}$ x 11 inch (21 x 28cm) sheet of plain white paper is best.

Paper Football is best played on a rectangular table, although a square table can be used. Mark the 50-yard line at the halfway point with chalk or a narrow strip of masking tape. The entire table is the playing field, and any ball that goes off the table is out of bounds.

To start, the two players toss a coin and the loser gets the kickoff. In preparation, the football is laid on its side on the 50-yard line. The first player then propels it into the opponent's territory by flicking the ball with her index finger as far as possible without knocking it off the table.

After the kickoff, the players take turns flicking the ball back and forth, with each player being allowed three flicks (or "downs") per turn. Each player aims to score a "touchdown," by making the football hang partway off the opponent's end of the table. When a touchdown is scored, the player is awarded 6 points and the chance to try for an "extra point." (If the player makes the ball hang off the edge on a kickoff, this counts as a "safety," which is worth 2 points.)

To prepare for the extra point attempt, the opponent sets up a goalpost: resting his fists on his edge of the table, with the palms toward him, he makes a "crossbar" by touching his index fingertips together in a straight line, and "uprights" by sticking his thumbs straight up. The player who just scored now stands the paper football on one corner at the 50-yard line and, holding it in place with one hand, flicks it through the air with the index finger of the other hand. If it sails over the crossbar and between the uprights, she gains the extra point (for a total of 7 on the touchdown). The scorer now gets to kick off.

During the game, if the player flicks the football off the table edge three times, his opponent may attempt a "field goal." The field goal is made in the same fashion as the extra point, but if successful, it's worth 3 points. A player who scores a field goal kicks off. If the field goal is missed, the opposing player starts again on the 50-yard line.

The game is divided into two halves of a specified time—5 minutes apiece works well. The players switch sides at halftime. The player who has scored the most points when the clock runs out is the winner.

1. Fold the paper in half lengthwise.

2. Fold it in half lengthwise again to create a long strip.

3. With the strip laid out vertically on the table, bring the bottom right corner up to the edge of the opposite side and fold again.

4. Now fold again, bringing the point on the bottom right up along the right edge.

5. Keep folding the paper over and over as if it were a flag —until the piece left at the top of the strip is too small to make a complete triangle (this is usually after seven total folds).

6. The leftover can now be tucked back into the folds of the triangle (or it can be taped in place).

Voilà, a football!

Shovelboard

This tabletop shuffleboard game uses rulers as cues and coins as pucks.

Players: 2 to 10 (even number)

Ages: 7 to 14

Place: Table (preferably long and rectangular)

Equipment: Ruler; 4 quarters for each player or team; chalk; masking tape (optional); pencil and paper for scoring (optional)

Kids are drawn to shuffleboard courts like Winnie the Pooh to honey, so why not bring the fun indoors with Shovelboard? This simple coin-shoving game is actually the ancestor of both shuffleboard and Shove Ha'penny, which was an old English tavern game.

A long, rectangular table makes the best Shovelboard court, although a wider rectangle or even a square table will do. The court is marked off by drawing two lines lengthwise down the table with chalk or using thin strips of masking tape, about 6 inches (15cm) from the table edges (see diagram). The two narrow strips of "land" between the lines and the edges of the table make up the out-of-play area. Next, a crosswise line is drawn about 6 inches (15cm) from one end of the table. Between this line and the near end of the table is the high-scoring area. Finally, one more crosswise line is drawn about 12 inches (30cm) down from the last line—that is, about 18 inches (45cm) from the same end of the table. Between these two lines is the low-scoring area. The area between the second line and the other end of the table is the no-score area, but it is fair territory.

Shovelboard may be played one on one or between two teams. Starting

from the end of the table with the no-score area, players (or teams) take turns trying to propel each of their four coins ("pucks") toward the low-scoring and high-scoring areas with a ruler. It takes some practice to get the hang of pushing a coin hard enough to get it into the scoring areas but gently enough to keep it on the table. If a coin flies off the table or goes more than halfway over an out-of-play line, that coin is removed from play. Once a player has a coin or two on the court, she may, in propelling a new coin, try to knock her previously played coins into

more favorable positions. But she should be careful not to hit her opponent's coins into more favorable positions while doing so.

The round is over when both players or teams have played all four of their pucks. Three points are awarded for any coin in the high-scoring area that is partly over the edge of the table. Two points are earned for any coin completely in the high-scoring area. One point is added for any coin completely in the low-scoring area or on the line between the high- and low-scoring areas. No other coin positions score points.

The player or team that reaches a predetermined number of points first is the winner. The game can also be played in rounds. In this case, the player or team with the highest score after a certain number of rounds wins.

Shove Soccer

The shoving involves rulers and coins in this simulated soccer game.

Players: 2 to 10 (even number)

Ages: 8 to 14

Place: Table or other flat surface

Equipment: Plastic ruler for each player or team; 4 quarters for each player or team; 1 penny; 4 pencils or toothpicks to mark the goals; masking tape (optional)

This tabletop game mimics a real soccer match, but some of the rules have been modified because the players are coins. Shove Soccer devotees have been known to spend weeks on multilayered tournaments, but the game can just as easily be played in less than 10 minutes, from the kickoff until the clock runs out.

shove the "players" (quarters) on her team into the "ball" (penny). One side may wish to mark the tops of its quarters with bits of masking tape to tell them apart from opposing players. The game is divided into two halves of 2 to 5 minutes each.

Participants toss a coin to decide which team gets the ball first. The penny is then placed in the center of the table. Next, a soccer player (quarter) from the starting team is placed anywhere on the table, although obviously the best position is behind and not too far from the ball. The rest of the soccer players are then also set anywhere on the table—as long as none is within 3 inches (7.5cm) of the coin making the kick.

One child now "kicks" the designated quarter by tapping it with the ruler (held flat on the table), so that the quarter bumps into the

"free kick." A free kick is like a kick-off. The ball is left where it is and the kicking team sets down a kicker; then both teams reposition all their other players anywhere on the field—at least 3 inches (7.5cm) from the kicker. The team taking the free kick always gets to set its players in place first. After the free kick, that same team gets another turn. If, during the free kick or the next kick, a team manages to pass successfully again, they get yet another free kick. With good passing skills, a team's turn can go on indefinitely.

The rules must be very carefully observed. Any one of the following violations is considered a foul: touching the ball (penny) with the ruler; touching an opposing soccer player with the ruler; shoving a player into an opposing player before making contact with the ball; moving a player by hand; pushing, rather than flicking, a player; playing out of turn; and interfering with the game in any way. (Bumping the ball into an opposing player is not a foul.) Whenever a foul is committed, the opposing team is awarded a free kick, with the ball being placed on the spot where the foul occurred. The same team still gets its regular turn before the opposing team plays again.

If the ball flies off either side of the table during play, the opposing team gets a "kick on," a free kick 2 inches (5cm) in from where the ball went out of play. The same rule holds if a team kicks the ball off the opposite end—unless the ball bounced off an opposition player before going out. In that case, the offensive team earns a "corner kick"—a free kick from the corner of the table nearest where the ball went off.

Shove Soccer can be played one on one or between two teams. As in real soccer, the object is to score as many goals as possible. In this case, though, the playing field is a table. Goals 3 inches (7.5cm) wide are set up at opposite ends of the table and marked with pencils, toothpicks, or masking tape. The ends of the tables themselves are the opposing teams' goal lines. Each participant uses a ruler to

penny, ideally sending the penny in the direction of the opposing goal. The two opponents or sides then take turns kicking the ball, using any quarter on the team to do so.

Generally a team's turn consists of a single kick. But a team may keep its turn going by "passing" from one teammate to another. To pass, the ball must bump into another player on the team. If successful, the team earns a

Goals are scored when the ball is shoved through the opposing team's goalposts and off the table. Teams switch sides at halftime. To begin the second half, there's a new kickoff, with the team that did not kick off first having the chance to do so now. After a goal, the team that scored gets to kick off from the center of the table. The team that scores the most goals in the time allotted wins.

Squails

In this tabletop bowling game, teams compete to propel their markers toward a target.

Players: 4 to 8 (preferably an even number)

Ages: 8 to 14

Place: Table (preferably round), with seating for all players

Equipment: Small, round metal object (such as a silver dollar); 4 small, round objects (coins, poker chips, coasters, etc.) for each team; masking tape (optional); ruler (optional); pencil and paper for scoring (optional)

Although Squails originated in English taverns, this form of tabletop bowling translates well into a children's game. Kids enjoy trying to push their markers close to the target in this active and noisy contest. The game can be played on any kind of table, but a round table that can withstand a bit of wear and tear is the best choice.

Originally, "squails" were special wooden markers 1¹/₂ inches (3.8cm) in diameter and raised in the center, but almost any type of flat disk can be used. Coins work well because they're suitably heavy, but it's important to differentiate between the teams' squails (try heads for one team, tails for the other, or marking one team's coins with bits of masking tape). Different-colored poker chips—especially the heavier clay chips—are also a good choice. The target may be a 50-cent piece, a silver dollar, a medal, or a large metal washer.

Players are divided into two teams, which occupy alternating seats around the table. The target is put in the center of the table. Each team chooses a player to place a squail so that it hangs partway over the edge of the table and then to try, in one sweep, to push it with the palm of his hand toward the target. The player whose squail ends up closest to the target goes first.

The object of Squails is for each team to hit the target with its squails, or at least to get close to the target.

Players try not only to push their own squails toward the target but also to knock the other team's squails out of the way. Each player gets to shoot a single squail per round.

Play goes clockwise, with the teams taking turns. If a squail hits the target and moves it more than 6 inches (15cm), the target is returned to the center of the table, and the squail that knocked it out of place is taken out of play. A squail that goes off the table or lands within 3 inches (7.5cm) of the edge is out of the game for that round. The game continues until all of the squails have been played.

At the end of the round, each team's points are tallied. The squail farthest away from the target earns 1 point, the next-farthest squail gets 2 points, and so on. If a squail has at any time during the round knocked the target off the table, or within 3 inches (7.5cm) of the edge of the table, the opposing team gets 2 points. (A ruler may be needed to measure this.) Under this scoring system, the team with the squail closest to the target does not necessarily win the round. The team with the most points after a predetermined number of rounds wins the game.

Pick-up Sticks

Pick up one stick without moving the rest of the pile—easier said than done!

Players: 2 to 4

Ages: 7 to 12

Place: Table or floor, with seating for all players

Equipment: Pick-up Sticks set (41 thin, pointed plastic or wooden sticks in various colors); pencil and paper for scoring (optional)

Pick-up Sticks is a direct descendant of the ancient Chinese game of Spellicans, which was played with carved ivory sticks. The sticks in modern Pick-up Sticks sets look like huge colored toothpicks. This game requires a steady hand, concentration, and a high tolerance for frustration. It's too hard for most preschoolers, but older kids will relish the challenge.

Before beginning, the players decide who will go first, second, and so on. The player who will go last grasps all the sticks in his hand (like a bunch of spaghetti going into the pot). He sets the bottom of his fist on the table or floor so that all the sticks rise straight up, then he opens his hand and lets them fall. If possible, this should be done in one smooth motion. (Beginners should hold the bundle a few inches [cm] off the table or floor so the sticks spread out more.)

Now the players take turns trying to pick up the sticks, one by one, without touching or moving any of the other sticks. The sticks may be pinched with two fingers or lifted by placing a finger on each pointy end. The players take their turns with the others watching closely and calling out if any other stick moves—even a fraction of a millimeter. Each turn lasts as long as the player can pick up a stick without disturbing any others. As soon as another stick is jiggled, it's the next player's turn. The game continues until all of the sticks are picked up. The player with the most sticks at the end of the game is the winner.

For a more challenging game, assign point values to each color stick. Five points for red, 10 points for yellow, and 20 points for green, for example. Players try to pick up the more valuable sticks and then tally their points at the end of the game. The highest score wins.

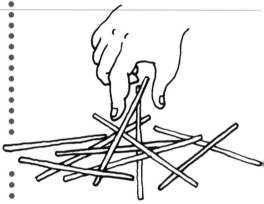

Nim

This unusual game, played with toothpicks, requires some serious strategizing.

Players: 2 or more

Ages: 8 to 14

Place: Table or other flat surface, with seating for all players

Equipment: Box of toothpicks

Nim is an ancient game that was traditionally played with piles of stones. Today, wooden toothpicks are used, which makes the game more portable—not to mention easier on the back.

Any number of toothpicks may be used to play Nim. The toothpicks are divided up into piles on the table—it doesn't matter how many piles there are or how many toothpicks are in each pile. The object of the game is to be the last player to pick up a toothpick from the table.

Each player takes a turn picking up one, several, or all the toothpicks in any one pile. Or, instead of picking up toothpicks, a player may use her turn to divide any *one* pile into two or more separate piles. A player may not pick up toothpicks from more than one pile or divide more than one pile during a single turn.

Playing this game requires a great deal of thinking ahead. If, for example, there are two piles on the table, a player would not want to pick up one entire pile. Otherwise, all his opponent would have to do to win would be to pick up the remaining pile. A better tactic would be to pick up just part of one pile (maybe just a single toothpick) or to divide one of the piles, creating a total of three piles. A smart player tries to think through the next several moves—figuring out not only what she plans to do, but also what her opponent is likely to do.

The player who picks up that last toothpick is the winner. The object of the game can also be reversed, so that the last person to pick up a toothpick is the loser.

Draw Dominoes

Matching numbers is the hallmark of this classic domino game, but the strategy is far from black and white.

Players: 2 to 5

Ages: 6 and up

Place: Table or other flat surface, with seating for all players

Equipment: Standard set of 28 dominoes

Dust off those old dominoes (or buy some new ones) and round up the kids—this is one of the best games for the whole family to play together. Kids can play as long as they're able to count to six and match the patterns on the dominoes, although older kids are more likely to appreciate the subtleties of strategy.

A dominoes set consists of 28 flat, rectangular tiles (usually black). One face of the tile is divided in half crosswise by a line; on either side of the line there are one to six dots (usually white) or a blank space. The numbers represented by the dots on each side of the line are called "suits." There are seven "doubles," which have an equal number of dots on each side of the line (double blank through double six); these are also called "one-number suits." Each of the 21 remaining dominoes shows a different number of dots on either side of the line (or dots on one side and a blank on the other); these are "mixed suits."

Before the game begins, the dominoes are turned face down and mixed

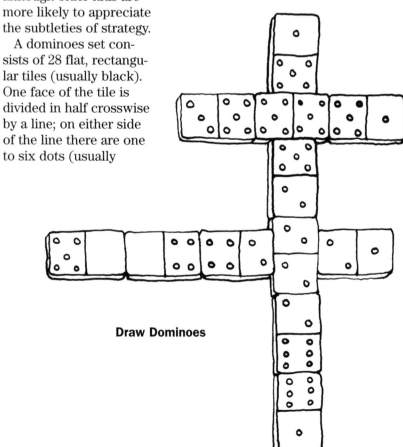

Draw Dominoes

up in a pile. This pile is called the "boneyard." Each player draws one domino (or "bone"), and the one whose domino has the highest total number of dots—usually referred to as the "heaviest" domino—goes first. Now, if there are two players in the game, each player draws a hand of seven dominoes; if there are three or more players, each draws five dominoes. Each player then sets up her hand of dominoes, standing the tiles up on their edges, in a row with the dots facing her so no opponent can see them.

To start, the first player lays any domino face up in the center of the table. The player to his left goes next; from her hand, she selects a domino that, on one side, has the same number of dots as there are on one side of the domino on the table. If, for example, the domino on the table has one dot on one side and six on the other (1:6), the second player can select a domino from her hand with six dots on one side and two on the other (6:2). She then lays the short end of her domino up against the short end of the other domino so that the ends with the same number of dots touch (see diagram).

If the second player happens to have a double that matches one end of the layout, she can play this, too. But instead of laying the domino end

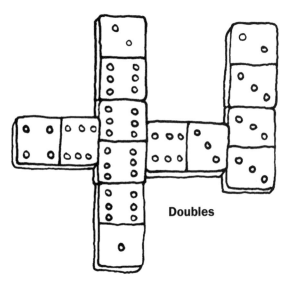

Doubles

to end, she lays the domino across the path, to create a sort of "T." If a player cannot put down a match for the domino on the table, she keeps drawing from the boneyard until she finds one she can use.

After a domino has been played, the next player takes a turn, using one of his dominoes to add to either end of the "layout." If a previous player has played a double (creating a "T" on the end of a domino), any following player may either jump across the "T" and continue the layout, or play off in one of the new directions created by the "T".

The first player to use up all her dominoes calls "Domino!" and wins the game. If the boneyard is emptied before any player uses all his dominoes, the player with the lowest score (the total number of dots left in his hand) is the winner.

Since players are trying simultaneously to get rid of all their dominoes

and to force their opponents to build up their hands, a good strategy is for a player to lay down tiles she does not think the others will be able to match. If, for example, one player holds four dominoes with 6 as one of the suits, the others are less likely to be holding 6s. It would, therefore, be wiser to add a 3:6 to a 2:3 than it would be to add a 3:4—unless, of course, several 4s have already been played.

Block Dominoes

This variation is played much like regular Draw Dominoes. The difference is that there is no boneyard. If there are two or three players in the game, hands of seven are drawn. Four or five players choose five dominoes each. A player who can't match either end of the layout must pass for that turn. The winner is determined in the same way as in Draw Dominoes.

Doubles

In this version of Draw Dominoes, the player with the "heaviest" double (double 6 is the heaviest) goes first. Play is then continued on all four sides of the starting double—on both short ends, and to each side of the middle. A mixed-number domino may be played only after the double of the number that is being matched has

been played. For example, after that initial double 6, the next player may lay down a mixed-number tile such as 6:3. The next player to build on *that* domino, however, must have a double 3 (see diagram), after which the next player may use a mixed number tile, and so on until all the doubles have been played, players may need to draw from the boneyard even if they have a one-sided match. Once all the doubles have been played, the game proceeds as in Draw Dominoes and the winner is determined in the same way.

Bergen

In Bergen, players score points when they make a move that puts matching dominoes at the ends of the layout. If there are two or three players in the game, each draws six dominoes. Four or five players draw five each. The player with the heaviest double goes first. Play then continues only to each side of the middle of the starting domino. The layout in this game has only two ends. A player scores 2 points whenever he puts down a domino that makes the two ends of the layout match (see diagram). For example, he might lay down a 4:5 on one end of a layout that has a 1:5 at the other end, with both 5s on the outside. Three points are scored when there is a double at one end and a matching domino at the other (a double 5 added to one of the 5s in the previous example). If a player is unable to add a domino to the layout, she must draw from the boneyard. The round ends when one player uses up all his dominoes.

Because players score points throughout the game, it is essential to keep track while playing. But more points can be gained once the round is over. A player scores 2 points for getting rid of all the dominoes in her hand, ending the round. If the game is "blocked" (no moves can be made) before someone empties his hand, the player with the fewest dots scores 2 points. The first player to reach 10 points (with two or three players) or 15 points (with four or more players) wins the game.

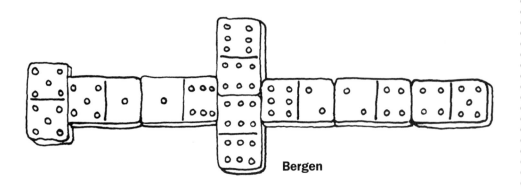

Bergen

Fifty

Dice doubles are nifty
in the game of Fifty.

Players: 2 or more

Ages: 5 to 10

Place: Table or other flat surface, with seating for all players

Equipment: 2 dice; pencil and paper for scoring

Fifty is an easy dice game that children of almost any age or ability level can play, although kids do need to know their numbers. The goal is to be the first player to reach 50 points. The way to do it is to keep rolling doubles.

Each player rolls one die before starting, and the player with the highest number goes first. That player then shoots both dice. The player scores only if doubles (two identical numbers) are thrown.

All doubles except 3s and 6s score 5 points. Double 6s are worth a whopping 25 points. Double 3s, however, are incredibly unlucky—they wipe out the player's entire score, and she must start again from 0. Players should use a pencil and paper to keep track of the score as the game goes on.

Play continues with each player taking one roll per turn. The first player to score 50 or more points is declared the winner.

Chicago

Success in this simple adding game
depends on the roll of the dice.

Players: 2 or more

Ages: 5 and up

Place: Table or other flat surface, with seating for all players

Equipment: 2 dice; pencil and paper for scoring

Two dice and the ability to add up to 12 are all that's needed to play Chicago. It's a game of pure luck, but young children find it exciting simply to "play the numbers."

The object of Chicago is to roll the 11 possible combinations of the two dice in sequence (2, 3, 4, 5, 6, 7, 8, 9, 10, 11, 12). The first player throws the dice with the aim of getting two 1s. If successful, that player is awarded 2 points. After each player has had one chance to roll for the 2, the round ends—and now everyone tries to roll for the 3, then the 4, and so on. Each time a player rolls the appropriate combination, he is awarded that number of points. Any combination that adds up to the desired total is fine; for the round of 7, a 6 and a 1 are just as good as a 4 and a 3 or a 5 and a 2.

At the end of the game, everyone adds up her points. The player with the highest total wins.

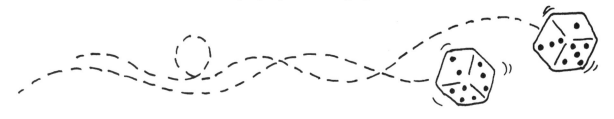

Round the Clock

Players travel around the face of the "clock" as they shoot the dice in sequence from 1 to 12.

Players: 3 or 4

Ages: 6 to 12

Place: Table or other flat surface, with seating for all players

Equipment: 2 dice

A simple but satisfying dice game, Round the Clock requires only basic addition skills. And unless it's a particularly unlucky day, it takes only a few minutes to beat the clock. The object of the game is to roll the numbers 1 through 12 in the correct sequence.

Each player rolls one die, and the player with the highest roll goes first; the second highest roller goes second, and so on. (If any players roll the same number, they roll again until the tie is broken.) Each player may roll the dice only once per turn. The first player begins by rolling both dice, hoping to get a 1 on either of the dice. If he doesn't get the 1, he has to try again on his following turns until he succeeds. But if he does get a 1, on his next turn he shoots for a 2. Now, however, he can get his 2 either on a single die or through a combination of both dice (with a 1 on each). If he gets the 2, on his next turn, he shoots for 3, and so on, all the way up to 12.

If a player manages to get two of the numbers he needs (in the sequence) on a single roll, he can count them both. If, for example, he's up to 3, and he rolls a 3 and a 4, they both count. On his next turn he skips up to 5. Obviously, once a player has gotten up to 6, he can't get any of the numbers he needs on one die alone; players can roll numbers 7 through 12 with combinations involving both of the dice.

Players continue taking turns rolling the dice. The first one to go "round the clock" is the winner.

Going to Boston

In this simple dice game, it's the high roller who prevails.

Players: 3 or more

Ages: 6 to 11

Place: Table or other flat surface, with seating for all players

Equipment: 3 dice; pencil and paper for scoring

If the kids are restless on a rainy day, Going to Boston may be just the thing to do! Also known as Newmarket and Yankee Grab, this relatively simple dice game is a good exercise in addition skills. It can be played in minutes or stretched out into a marathon.

All players roll one die before starting, and the player with the highest number goes first. (If any players roll the same number, they roll again until the tie is broken.) The first player rolls all three dice at once and sets aside the die with the highest number. If the highest number comes up on two dice, only one is set aside; if the same number comes up on all three dice, again only one is set aside. The same player then rolls the remaining two dice and again sets aside the higher one. The last die is thrown one more time, and the total of the three dice is the player's score. When each player has taken a three-roll turn, the round is over. If two or more players are tied, they go head to head in a playoff round.

The game may be played for as many rounds as the participants wish. It's important to keep track of the score as the game goes on. The player with the highest score at the end of the game is the winner. Play can continue to establish second place, third place, and so on.

Multiplication

Multiplication is played in the same way as Going to Boston, but the scoring is different. Instead of simply adding the values of the three dice, the sum of the first two dice is multiplied by the value of the third. For example, if the highest die on the first throw is 6, the second is 5, and the third is 2, the score is $(6 + 5) \times 2$, or 22 points. This takes a bit of mathematical prowess, but the power of that final roll makes for a very unpredictable game. Consider the score if the numbers from these throws are reversed, giving $(2 + 5) \times 6$, or 42 points.

Beetle

The rolls of the die determine who triumphs in this "buggy" contest.

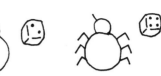

Players: 2 to 6

Ages: 6 to 12

Place: Table or other flat surface, with seating for all players

Equipment: 1 die; pencil and paper for each player

Even kids who hate creepy-crawly things will love playing Beetle. A simple but exciting game, it's a great introduction to throwing dice. In Beetle each number rolled allows a player to add another body part to his drawing of a beetle.

Each player begins with a blank sheet of paper on which a beetle will be drawn during the course of the game. Sitting around a table or even on the floor, everyone rolls the die once, and the player with the highest number goes first. (If any players roll the same number, they roll again until the tie is broken.) The first player opens the game by again rolling the die. If a 1 is thrown, the player may start her picture of the beetle by drawing a big round circle on the page—the beetle's body (see diagram). If any other number comes up, however, the die passes to the next player to the left. Each player gets one roll per turn.

To complete the beetle, the numbers must be rolled in order from 1 through 5. After rolling a 1 and drawing the body, each player must wait until he rolls a 2 to draw the head: a little circle attached to the body. Next, a roll of 3 is required for a player to draw three legs on one side of the body, and another 3 is needed to draw three legs on the other side. Then the player tries for a 4, in order to add one antenna to the head; another 4 is needed to add the second antenna. Finally, the player is allowed to add one eye for each roll of 5. The first player to complete an entire beetle wins the game.

Hearts Due

This Hearts game is played with dice rather than cards, and it's just as much fun.

Players: 3 or more

Ages: 6 to 11

Place: Table or other flat surface, with seating for all players

Equipment: 6 dice; pencil and paper for scoring

This is *the* dice game to play on Valentine's Day. In this game, the numbers on each die correspond in order to the letters of the word "HEARTS"—1 for H, 2 for E, and so on. The more completely the word can be spelled on each roll, the higher the score.

Players shoot one die to determine who goes first. (If any roll the same number, they roll again until the tie is broken.) The one who throws the highest number starts by rolling all six dice at once. To score anything at all, this player must roll at least one 1. If he does get a 1, he scores 5 points. If there's a 2 as well as a 1, he scores 5 more points. As long as the numbers follow in sequence, the roller gets 5 more points for each additional letter (represented by a number) in the word "HEARTS." Plus, he gets a 5-point bonus if he is lucky enough to spell the whole word in a single roll (35 total points).

If more than one die shows the same number (doubles, triples, and so on), only one of the repeat numbers counts toward scoring. For example, if a player rolls 1, 2, 2, 3, 5, 5, the score is 15 points for 1, 2, 3 (H-E-A). There is one exception to this rule: a roll of three 1s (Hs) wipes out a player's entire score up to that point.

Each player gets one roll per turn. The letters scored on the previous turn do not carry over; players must begin each time with 1 (H).

The winner may be the player with the highest score after a predetermined number of rounds or the first one to reach an agreed-on score, such as 100.

Drop Dead

Stay away from 2 and 5 if you want to stay alive in this fast-paced dice game.

Players: 2 or more

Ages: 7 to 12

Place: Table or other flat surface, with seating for all players

Equipment: 5 dice; pencil and paper for scoring

Disappearing dice are the hallmark of this quick and exciting game. Drop Dead is a fun way to develop or hone addition skills.

Before starting, each player rolls one die and the lowest scorer goes first. (If any players roll the same number, they roll again until the tie is broken.) To play, each player takes a turn rolling all five dice. If no 2 or 5 shows up, the player adds the numbers showing on the dice; this is the number of points he earns on the roll. But if a 2 or a 5 is thrown, the player scores nothing and the die that showed the forbidden number is eliminated. Whatever has happened on the previous roll, the same player then rolls the remaining dice, adding points to his score or eliminating dice. He keeps on rolling the dice until all five dice are "dead."

Here's a sample turn: The first roll is 1, 3, 4, 4, 5—there is no score and the die showing the 5 is removed. The next roll is 3, 4, 4, 6, giving the player a score of 17 points. The next roll is 1, 2, 3, 5—there is no score and two dice (2 and 5) are removed. The next roll is 2, 6—again no score and one die is eliminated. The next roll is 6, so 6 points are scored. The next roll is 1, so 1 point is scored. The next roll is 2, and the player "drops dead" and is out of the game with a final score of 24 points. It is now the next player's turn.

The player with the most points after everyone has "dropped dead" wins. Alternately, one game can consist of an agreed-on number of rounds.

Pig

In this simple dice game, players must choose to play it safe or take a gamble.

Players: 2 or more

Ages: 8 to 14

Place: Table or other flat surface, with seating for all players

Equipment: 1 die

The dice game called Pig—not to be confused with the card game of the same name—derives its excitement from the element of risk. Every time a player rolls the die, she comes one step closer to winning or losing everything. Although the game itself requires no more than the ability to add, players are expected to do the math in their heads and remember their scores.

Before the game begins, each player rolls the die once. The player with the *lowest* number goes first, the one with the second-lowest number goes second, and so on. (If any players roll the same number, they roll again until the tie is broken.) The order of play is important in a game with more than two players, because the first player and the last player have small advantages. In fact, the fairest way to play is to have enough rounds so that each player has a chance to go first. The players must also decide on a winning score—usually 100.

To play, the first player rolls the die as many times as he wants. The value of each throw is added onto the score until the player decides to end his turn and passes the die to the next player. The catch to this system is that if the player rolls a 1, his entire score is erased, his turn automatically ends, and he has to pass the die. Each player must decide for himself when to stop. At one extreme, any player who gets a 1 on his first roll is immediately out. At the other extreme, the first player could theoretically reach the winning score on his first turn, as long as he doesn't throw a 1. If he succeeds, the game ends there.

But if the first player stops before 100 (and before being knocked out), the next player knows there is no point in stopping her turn until she has at least reached the first player's score. If she manages to accomplish that, the next player knows what score he has to beat. Play continues until one player reaches 100 or until all have had a chance to roll, in which case the player with the highest score is the winner.

Shut the Box

This dice game challenges kids to use simple math skills as they compete to cover all the numbers on a game board.

Players: 2 to 4

Ages: 8 to 12

Place: Table or other flat surface, with seating for all players

Equipment: 2 dice; pencil and paper; 9 counters (such as coins, buttons, or slips of paper)

Shut the Box is a popular game in France, where commercially manufactured sets are available. The homemade version works just as well. Children should have a good command of addition, as well as the ability to do some basic strategizing, before attempting to play this game.

To make the game board, one player (or the players together) draw nine squares on a sheet of paper. Squares may be arranged in a strip or a grid—it doesn't really matter. The squares are numbered 1 through 9 in order. Although all the players may use the same nine counters, players may prefer to have their own sets, with one player using buttons, another using coins, and so on.

Each player rolls one die, and the player with the highest number goes first. (If any players roll the same number, they roll again until the tie is broken.) The object of Shut the Box is to roll as many as possible of the nine numbers in the squares during a single turn. To do this, the first player rolls the dice and adds up his score. This number may then be split up in any way to get one or more of the nine numbers, as long as the entire score is used. For example, if the player's roll totals 8, it could be used to cover boxes 1, 2, and

5; 1, 3, and 4; 1 and 7; 2 and 6; 3 and 5; or 8. He then uses his counters to cover the squares with the appropriate numbers.

The first player continues rolling the dice and covering numbers as long as he can use his whole score. Numbers that are already covered cannot be recovered. After 7, 8, and 9 are covered, the player throws just one die. When the first player can no longer use his whole score, the numbers in the remaining squares are totaled as penalty points. If, for instance, the first player's turn ends with boxes 1 and 5 still uncovered, he gets 6 penalty points. To keep the penalty points down, it's good strategy to try and cover the highest numbers on the board first.

When the first player is finished, the counters are cleared from the board and the next player takes her turn. The player with the fewest penalty points after one round is the winner. If there's a tie between two or more players, playoff rounds can be used to determine the winner.

Centennial

The roll of the dice determines who wins the race up and down the Centennial board.

Players: 2 to 8

Ages: 8 to 14

Place: Table or other flat surface, with seating for all players

Equipment: 3 dice; plastic cup; pencil and paper; distinctive marker (different coins, different-colored buttons, candies, or pieces of chalk) for each player

Also known as Ohio and Martinetti, Centennial is a dice game that involves moving markers along a board. It's the granddaddy of all the race-to-the-finish board games. Although the game does not require any skills beyond addition, players must be quick at totaling different combinations of numbers.

Before play begins, a game board must be drawn on a piece of paper (a small chalkboard, laid flat, works well, too). The board is simply a strip of 12 connected boxes, numbered 1 through 12 in order. The squares should be big enough to hold the markers. The object of the game is to be the first player to move his marker from 1 to 12 and back again.

To begin, each player throws a die and the player with the highest number goes first. (If any players roll the same number, they roll again until the tie is broken.) The first player puts all three dice into the cup, shakes the cup, and then rolls the dice. If one of the dice shows a 1, the player moves her marker to the number 1; if not, the cup is passed to the next player. Each player must throw the numbers from 1 to 12 in sequence to move his markers up the board. An individual number (if it's the needed one) on any of the die is enough to move a marker along. But, of course, after square 6, that's no longer an option. But numbers can be combined on two or all three dice to get the needed sum. If, for example, a player needs a 5, and happens to roll a 2, a 3, and a 4, she can add the 2 and the 3 together to get 5.

A player may use every possible combination of dice to advance, so certain throws enable a player to move more than one space on a single turn. The dice numbers can be used alone and combined to allow a player to advance as many as six squares in one turn. A very lucky player, for example, might roll 1, 2, and 3 on the first try. This player could then move not only up the first three squares, but also to number 4 (3 + 1), 5 (3 + 2), and 6 (1 + 2 + 3).

Players must police each other constantly, because if one player overlooks a usable total, the player who notices the mistake can use the roll. If, for example, one player throws the 1-2-3 combination just described, but moves only to 5 because she doesn't notice that the total of all three dice is 6, the next player may claim the 6 on his next move—but only if he's already on square 5. Then he can roll again.

Any time a player is able to advance, she gets to roll again. Only when a roll is completely unusable is the cup passed. The first player to travel from 1 to 12 and back again wins.

Dice Baseball

No bats, balls, or gloves are needed for this dice game that die-hard baseball fans can play all year.

Players: 2

Ages: 9 to 14

Place: Table or floor, with seating for both players

Equipment: 2 dice; 8 markers (coins, buttons, or the like, representing baseball players), 4 for each player; pencil and at least 2 sheets of paper

For Little Leaguers depressed because their game's been rained out, Dice Baseball is sure to score an instant homer. This is a game for children who are well grounded in the rules of baseball and whose memory, adding, and association skills are well developed. The list of dice combinations to remember is long, so even older children are likely to need some coaching for the first few innings.

Before the opening pitch, a simple diagram of a baseball diamond is drawn on a sheet of paper. One corner of the diamond represents home plate. The other corners, moving counterclockwise around the diamond, represent first, second, and third bases. Another piece of paper serves as the scoreboard. The object, as in real baseball, is to score as many "runs" as possible during a nine-inning game. Markers (such as coins or buttons) stand in for base runners.

To decide who starts, each player rolls a die; the player with the highest number "bats" first. The first batter rolls both dice and adds their numbers to get one of the following "hits":

2–Home run: Batter and all runners on base advance to home.

3–Triple: Batter advances to third base. All runners on base advance to home.

4–Single: Batter advances to first base. Any runners on first and second base advance to the next base. Similarly, any runner on third base makes it home.

5–Sacrifice out: Player gets an out. However, any runners on first and second base advance to the next base. Similarly, any runner on third base makes it home.

6–Out: No base runners advance.

7–Sacrifice out: Same as 5, but in this case, if there are two or more runners on base, the lead runner—the one nearest home plate—is out, in addition to the batter. In other words, there might be two outs on the play.

8 (double 4s only)–Walk: Batter advances to first base. Other runners advance only as necessary to make room for the batter. For example, a runner on first base must advance to the next base. If there are runners on both first and second base, both advance to the next base. And if the bases are loaded, with runners on first, second, and third, all advance to the next base, with the runner on third base making it home. However, if there are runners on second and third, but no runner on first, only the batter advances.

8 (any other combination)–Out.

9–Out.

10–Single.

11–Double: Batter advances to second base. Any runner on first base advances to third base. Any runner on second or third base makes it home.

12–Home run.

The innings are played as in baseball, with a side retiring after three outs. Players move their markers around the bases according to the rolls of the dice. The player with the highest score after nine innings wins the game.

Checkers

This block-and-capture board game is an excellent introduction to strategic thinking.

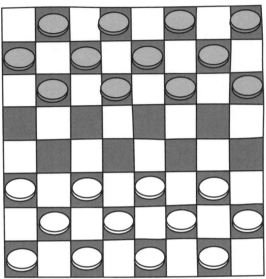

Checkers—starting position

Players: 2

Ages: 7 to 14

Place: Table or other flat surface, with seating for both players

Equipment: Checkerboard; 24 checkers (12 light, 12 dark)

Played in many different forms all over the world, Checkers is a strategy game that is fairly easy to learn but remains an intellectual challenge even after years of playing. The 64-square checkerboard serves as a "battleground" for the 12 black and 12 red (sometimes black and white) disks that players try to move from one side of the board to the other. The object of Checkers is to capture or block the opponent's 12 pieces so that the enemy is not able to make any more moves. Children usually have the patience and intellectual ability to start playing Checkers around age 7. It takes a while, however, to master strategy—thinking one or more moves ahead—so adults and older children should make allowances for beginners.

Checkers is played on a square board divided into eight rows of eight alternating dark- and light-colored squares. Pieces are placed only on the dark (usually black) squares. To set up the game, players sit across from each other with the board between them so that each has a black corner on the lower left. Each player gets a set of 12 pieces (one player gets the dark-colored pieces, the other the light-colored ones), which they then place on the black squares in the three rows closest to them (see diagram). When playing with checkers that feature a star on one side and a crown on the other, all the checkers should have their stars face up to start. The two center rows remain empty.

The player with the black (or dark) pieces always goes first. Since the pieces must stay on the black squares, all moves in Checkers are diagonal (from corner to corner). Each player is allowed one move per turn. Players take turns moving their pieces forward, one at a time, to adjacent empty squares, with the goal of making it all the way to the opponent's back row. Until a piece reaches that back row, it can only be moved forward (never backward). Also, a piece may not be moved onto a square already occupied by another piece. But if one of the adjacent squares is occupied by an enemy piece, and the square beyond that is vacant, the player may *jump* over the opponent's piece to the square beyond and remove the opponent's piece from the board. On a single turn, a player may jump over two or more pieces if there is an empty square before and after each one—these moves are called double and triple jumps (see diagram on next page).

If it is possible to jump, a player must do that rather than moving another checker or moving the checker in question in another direction. If there are two separate possible jumps, the player chooses one and loses the other. If a player fails to notice a jumping opportunity, the opponent may take the piece that should have made the jump. This is called "huffing." In this situation, the opponent also has the option of pointing out the missed jump and requiring the first player to go back and take it. Why on earth would an opponent do this? The only good reason would be if it set up an opportunity for the opponent to take multiple jumps.

When a piece makes it all the way to the opponent's back row, it becomes a "King" and is "crowned" by placing a captured piece of the same color on top of it. (Or, if the checkers bear stars and crowns, the checker is now flipped over to reveal its crown.) Kings have a lot more freedom than uncrowned checker pieces—they still must move diagonally on the black squares, but they may move forward or backward and can jump in either direction. Kings can be jumped and captured, however, in the same way as other pieces.

The game continues, with each player making moves in turn, until one player wins by capturing all the opponent's pieces or blocking him from making any more moves. The game is considered a tie if neither player can make any moves. If the players decide to play another game of Checkers, they may want to switch colors.

Checkers can become a very long game if the players take lots of time pondering each move. That's why it's a good idea to establish two rules: first, a player must move the first piece that she touches, and, second, moves must be made within a certain time limit—say 3 to 5 minutes. These rules, of course, may be relaxed or abandoned according to the players' wishes.

Whole books have been written on Checkers strategies, but there are a few basic rules of thumb to help novice players get off to a good start. First, players should try to keep

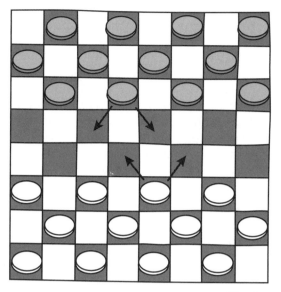

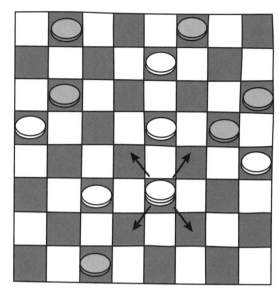

Checkers—moving

pieces toward the middle of the board rather than along the edges—this reduces the chance of being cornered and leaves pieces open to move more freely. Also, the pieces that advance first should be backed up by other pieces to prevent the opponent from jumping them. Finally, players should try to plan at least one move in advance—and also try to figure out the opponent's plan. The more developed the strategy is, the better the chance of winning.

French Checkers
Although it may be confusing at first, French Checkers, once mastered, can be a terrific challenge. As in regular Checkers, players try both to capture

Checkers—jumping

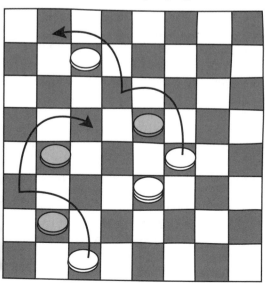

enemy checkers and to advance their pieces to their opponent's back row to become Kings. In this variation, these two goals are often at odds. That is because, although they may move forward, uncrowned checkers are not allowed to *jump* forward. They may only jump backward, once or multiple times. This rule can considerably lengthen a Checkers game. Only when a piece has become a King is it allowed to jump forward as well as backward. There is no huffing in French Checkers.

Giveaway Checkers
The object of Giveaway Checkers, also known as Losing Checkers, is the reverse of that of regular Checkers. In this variation, players try to be the first to have all their checkers captured or blocked. The checkers themselves move in the same way as in regular Checkers, but in this case players try to put their pieces in the path of their opponent, forcing their opponent to take their checkers. Players must make any possible jump. Kings are crowned the same way, but players should avoid getting Kings. Since Kings must also jump if the opportunity arises, savvy players will try to set up multiple jumps that an enemy King cannot avoid making. The first player either to lose all of his pieces or to be unable to make any more moves is the winner.

Italian Checkers
In this challenging Checkers variation, Kings cannot be captured by uncrowned checkers. Instead of placing the checkerboard so that each player has a dark square at the lower left, the board is turned so that a light square is in that position. Otherwise, the pieces are set up as in regular Checkers, with each player's pieces lined up on the dark squares of her first three rows.

The player with the dark pieces makes the first move. As the game proceeds, players must jump and capture whenever possible, and if two jumps can be made, they must choose the one that will yield more captures. If several captures are possible, but one is a King, the King must be taken (but only by another King). Players should remember these rules when formulating their strategies.

Spanish Checkers
Spanish Checkers is played in the same way as Italian Checkers, except that the Kings can move more than one space at a time without even jumping. They may move forward on the diagonal as many spaces as are vacant. They may also, along a diagonal, make "long jumps"—jumps that include empty spaces as well as spaces with checkers on them. At the end of such a jump, however, there must be an empty space where the King can land; if there is more than one such place, the player can choose which location to use. Only one checker can be captured in a single jump; that is, the King cannot jump over two checkers that are next to each other. Multiple jumps, over several checkers that have vacant spaces in between, are allowed.

German Checkers
German Checkers has the same rules as Spanish Checkers, with two exceptions. In this game, *all* the checkers (not just Kings) may move both forward and backward. Also, a piece can

be crowned King only if it ends its turn in the back row. If there are further jumps to be made in a backward direction, the piece must take them and forfeit becoming a King on that turn.

Russian Checkers

Russian Checkers follows the same rules as German Checkers except that the player with two jumping possibilities does *not* have to take the one with the most captures. Also, any piece that makes it to the opponent's back row is immediately crowned King. The piece can then continue its turn as a King if there are more possible jumps that it can make.

Dama

Dama, also called Turkish Checkers, is played on a standard checkerboard, but each player gets 16 pieces instead of 12. Checkers may be borrowed from another set, but buttons of different colors or coins of different denominations can be used as well.

To set up the game, players place their checkers on both the dark and light squares of their second and third rows. The back rows remain empty. The player with the dark pieces then begins by moving a checker one space forward. All subsequent moves, includ-

ing jumps, by uncrowned checkers must be forward or sideways (not backward or on a diagonal). As in Checkers, each player tries to advance pieces to the opponent's back row to become Kings. Kings may move one space forward, backward, or sideways, but never diagonally. And as in Spanish Checkers, they may also make "long jumps" (jumps that include empty spaces as well as spaces with checkers on them), but never diagonally. Players may decide to use huffing rules.

Diagonal Checkers

In this variation, the board is turned so that the point of a lighter corner faces each player. To set up the board, each player places her 12 checkers on the dark squares in her corner, with two in the first row, four in the second, and six in the third (see diagram). The player with the dark pieces goes first, moving a checker

forward on the diagonal to an adjacent empty space. All subsequent moves by uncrowned checkers, including jumps, must be forward. Players try to advance their checkers to the opponent's back row, but in this case the back row consists of only two squares. Kings may move backward as well as forward. There is no huffing in Diagonal Checkers.

Diagonal Checkers—starting position

Fox and Geese

Young children enjoy this simplified form of Checkers.

Players: 2

Ages: 6 to 11

Place: Table or other flat surface, with seating for both players

Equipment: Checkerboard; 5 checkers (4 light, 1 dark)

Fox and Geese, also called Box the Fox, is a hunt-and-capture game played on a checkerboard. It's a good way to introduce young children to one of the basic concepts of playing checkers—moving in turn on the diagonal—without having to deal with the complexity of the standard game. Only five checkers are used, with a dark "fox" trying to break through a line of four white "geese." This straightforward game requires a bit of

strategic thinking, but not nearly as much as regular Checkers.

First, players decide who gets the dark piece and who plays the light pieces. The player with the four light "geese" positions the pieces on the dark squares of his own back row. The player with the dark "fox" may place her piece on any of the black squares on the board; for maximum freedom of movement, the fox will probably not want to start alongside any of the edges of the board.

The player with the geese gets the first move. His object is to prevent the fox from getting past the line of geese to his back row. (Of course, the other player, with the fox, does everything she can to make it through.) The geese may move forward only on the diagonal, as in regular Checkers. The fox, however, may move forward *or* backward on the diagonal, like a King in checkers. There is no jumping in this game.

The player with the fox wins if she is able to get to the opponent's back row. The player with the geese wins if he surrounds and traps the fox so that it cannot make any more moves.

Wolf and Goats

In this version, which requires a total of 12 light pieces, a group of "goats" tries to block a lone "wolf," who is trying to get past them. The light pieces are positioned on the dark squares of the first three rows, just as in regular Checkers. The dark wolf starts at the dark square either farthest to the left or farthest to the right on the first row of the opposite end of the board. The play is similar to Fox and Geese, with the wolf striving to sneak past the goats to the other side. The important difference between this game and Fox and Geese is that, in Wolf and Goats, the wolf *is* allowed to jump the opponent's pieces and to remove them from the board. Goats, however, cannot jump.

Checkers Go-Moku

This challenging game is a cross between Checkers and Tic-Tac-Toe.

Players: 2

Ages: 7 to 14

Place: Table or other flat surface, with seating for both players

Equipment: Checkerboard; 24 checkers (12 light, 12 dark)

Checkers Go-Moku is an adaptation of the Japanese board game Go. It is played on a standard checkerboard. As in Checkers, the object of the game is to capture the opponent's pieces. To take an opponent's piece, it is necessary to get five pieces of the same color onto five adjacent squares. Go-Moku requires patience and strategic thinking, which children have usually developed by the age of 7 or 8.

First, players decide who gets the dark pieces and who the light. The player with the dark pieces always goes first, placing a checker on any square, light or dark, of the empty board. The other player then places a piece, and this goes on in turn until all 24 pieces are on the board. During this phase, a player should try to lay his pieces as close to one another as possible. His opponent should, when necessary, set down her own pieces in a way that prevents him from laying five (or four or three) pieces in a row. After all the checkers have been put down, players take turns moving any one of their pieces in any direction (including diagonally) to any empty adjacent square.

As the pieces are moved, the goal is to line up five checkers—horizontally, vertically, or diagonally—while simultaneously trying to block the opponent from doing the same. When a player does get five in a row, he may take any one of the opponent's checkers off the board. He then has to reposition each of the lined-up pieces before he can claim a new five-in-a-row combination.

The game ends when one of the players—the loser—has only four pieces left and cannot, therefore, place five in a row.

Chinese Checkers

Played on a colorful star-shaped board,
Chinese Checkers is a simple strategy game.

Players: 2 to 6

Ages: 6 to 14

Place: Table or other flat surface, with seating for all players

Equipment: Chinese Checkers set consisting of six-sided star-shaped board and 6 sets of 15 pegs or marbles

Chinese Checkers is a relatively modern game that features the jumping action of Checkers without the complicated strategy. Its simplicity, fast pace, and attractive board and pieces make Chinese Checkers a favorite of young children. More advanced game players, however, should not discount Chinese Checkers as a "baby game"—it can be quite challenging when played by clever thinkers.

The Chinese Checkers board is shaped like a star with six triangular points, each a different color (see diagram). (The six-sided middle area is yet another color.) On this board, instead of colored squares to mark the spaces (as in Checkers), there are shallow indentations or holes in which the game pieces nestle. Each triangle has 15 such indentations or holes (5 at its base near the middle area, then 4 above that, then 3, then 2, then 1 at the very point). More holes, evenly spaced, fill the middle area. Six sets of 15 pegs (or marbles), each set sporting a color that matches a different triangle, are included in store-bought Chinese Checkers kits.

When there are only two players in the contest, each starts with a full set of 15 pegs. They face off from opposite points, and each fills her whole triangle with her game pieces. In a game with three or more players, each uses only 10 pegs, leaving the bottom row of five holes uncovered. Three players set up at alternating points of the triangle; four players set up on two sets of opposing points; five players use any five points; and six players use all the points. No matter what the setup, over the course of the game, each player's object is to move all his pieces into the triangle directly opposite.

In Chinese Checkers, the youngest player usually goes first, beginning the game by moving a piece one space. The pieces may be moved backward, forward, or diagonally, as long as there is an empty adjacent space.

starting position

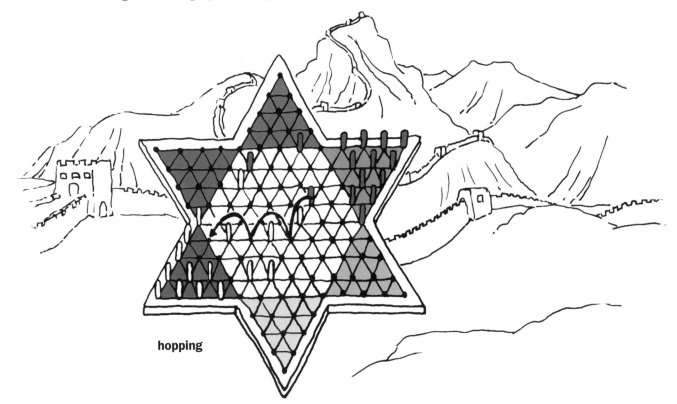

hopping

Pieces may also be jumped over other pieces—either those of an opponent or a player's own—as long as there is an empty space on the other side. On a single turn, a piece may make several consecutive jumps, as long as there are adjacent pieces to jump and open spaces beyond. Jumps in Chinese Checkers are simply a way of moving across the board; no pieces are captured or removed.

Play goes around to the left, with each player making one move per turn. Little by little, players move their pieces out of their triangles and into the middle, where they encounter enemy marbles. Savvy players try to arrange their up-front marbles in patterns that allow the marbles packed in the back to jump out into the open. The player who sets up the most multiple jumps (also known as "ladders"), while simultaneously denying his opponents the opportunity to do the same, is likely to be the player to move across the board most quickly. The first player to get all her pieces into the opposite point of the star—in the same four- or five-row configuration—is the winner.

Halma

This intriguing strategy game gets its name from a Greek word for "jump."

Players: 2 or 4

Ages: 8 to 14

Place: Table or other flat surface, with seating for all players

Equipment: Halma game board with 256 squares (4 standard checkerboards may be used); 2 sets of 19 pieces and 2 sets of 13 pieces, with each set a different color (checkers, buttons, coins, or commercial Halma pieces may be used); marker or masking tape (optional)

The inspiration for Chinese Checkers, Halma is a more complicated strategy game that was originally played on a checkerboard four times the size of a standard board (16 x 16 squares, or 256 total, as opposed to a standard board's 64). A bit more intricate than its descendant, Halma is a good challenge for older kids who have already mastered Chinese Checkers.

A Halma set can be bought at a store or easily improvised at home by either combining four standard checkerboards into a square or dividing each square on one checkerboard into four smaller squares (the color of the squares doesn't matter in this game). Depending on how many play-

ers are playing, a home base must be marked out in each of two or four corners. If there are only two players, the home bases consist of 19 squares each in opposite corners (see diagram on this page); if there are three or four players, the home bases consist of 13 squares each (see diagram on next page) in all four corners. These areas are now outlined with masking tape or a marker.

In a two-player game, Halma requires each player to have a set of 19 game pieces, with the sets in different colors. For homemade Halma that means at least two sets of standard checkers. In a three- or four-player game, each player must have a differently colored set of 13 pieces. For a homemade game, that means two more sets of standard checkers that don't match the other two in color—or a good collection of coins or buttons.

The game pieces are now laid in two, three, or four of the home bases, depending on the number of players. Over the course of the game, each player aims to move all of her pieces from her home base into the home base directly opposite her.

The basic rules of Halma are the same as those of Chinese

Checkers, although the board is very different. The youngest player usually goes first, beginning the game by moving a piece one space. The pieces may be moved backward, forward, or diagonally, as long as there is an empty adjacent space. Pieces may also jump over other pieces—either those of an opponent or a player's own—as long as there is an empty space on the other side. On a single turn, a piece may make several consecutive jumps, as long as there are adjacent pieces to jump and open spaces beyond. Jumps in Halma (as in Chinese Checkers) are simply a way of moving across the board; no pieces are captured or removed from the board.

Just as in Chinese Checkers, play goes around to the left, with each player making one move per turn. Little by little, players move their

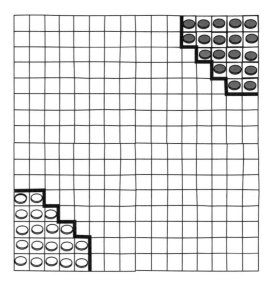

starting position (2 players)

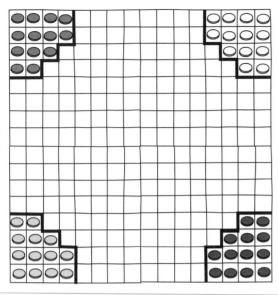

starting position (4 players)

pieces out of their home bases and into the middle, where they encounter enemy game pieces. Savvy Halma players, like skillful Chinese Checkers players, arrange their up-front pieces in patterns that allow the pieces packed in the back to jump into the middle arena. They also try to set up multiple jumps (or "ladders"), while keeping their opponents from doing the same, in order to move across the board quickly. Because the Halma board has more spaces than the Chinese Checkers board, and each player has more pieces, getting all the pieces from one corner to another is trickier, requiring quite a lot of planning.

The first player to get all his pieces into the opposite home base is declared the winner.

Pyramid

Playing Pyramid is like playing Chinese Checkers on a checkerboard.

Players: 2

Ages: 7 to 14

Place: Table or other flat surface, with seating for both players

Equipment: Checkerboard; 20 checkers (10 dark, 10 light)

Pyramid is a territory game that combines the object of Chinese Checkers with the moves of standard Checkers. Players compete to be the first to move all their checkers from their side to the opponent's side of the board. Pyramid is easier and faster-paced than Checkers, making it a good choice if time is tight or the players are young or inexperienced.

A standard checkerboard is used to play Pyramid. Players decide on their colors; then each arranges his ten pieces in a triangular (pyramid) shape on the dark squares on his side of the board (see diagram). The first row

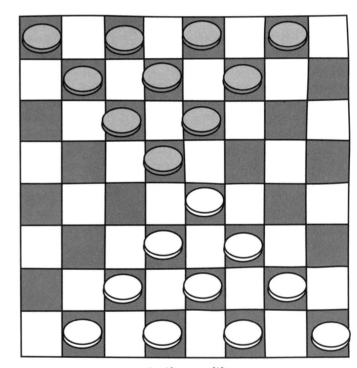

starting position

(the one closest to the player) gets four checkers, the second row three, the third row two, and the fourth row one. The points of the two triangles should touch diagonally.

The player with the dark pieces gets the first move. As in Checkers, pieces are moved one space forward diagonally on the dark squares. Pieces may not move backward. A player may jump over an opponent's piece if it is in an adjacent diagonal square and has a vacant space beyond it, but there is no capturing of pieces—the jumped checker stays in its place. As in Chinese Checkers, multiple jumps ("ladders") are permitted. Players may not jump over their own checkers.

The first player to get all her pieces to the opposite side of the board in the precise configuration of the opponent's original pyramid is the winner.

Reversi

The inspiration for a commercial game, Reversi is a strategy game of constant turnover.

Players: 2

Ages: 9 to 14

Place: Table or other flat surface, with seating for both players

Equipment: Checkerboard; 64 checkers or other markers (such as poker chips or coins); masking tape (optional)

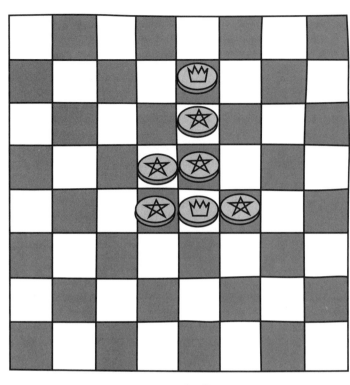

"trapping"

Reversi is a 100-year-old game that some people may remember as the commercial game Othello. A standard checkerboard and a set of 64 checkers or other markers with distinctive sides are all that is needed to play this intriguing game. Although it is played on a checkerboard, Reversi bears little resemblance to Checkers. The game begins with an empty board, and each player competes to have the most markers with her symbol on top at the end. Reversi is easy to learn to play but very difficult to master, making it an excellent game for both beginners and seasoned strategists.

Sixty-four markers with a different marking on each side are needed to play the game. Standard checkers pieces often have different symbols stamped on each side (usually a star and a crown). Alternatively, blank checkers or poker chips may be marked with a bit of masking tape on one side. Coins (with heads on one side, tails on the other) also make excellent Reversi pieces. Before beginning, players decide who will be assigned which of the two markings.

To start, players sit across from each other with the empty board between them. The first player lays down a marker in one of the four squares in the center of the board. The other player lays down a marker in another one of the four center squares. These squares must be filled first.

After the four center squares are filled, players take turns placing one marker at a time on the board. Both dark and light squares are used. Only moves that trap one or more of the opponent's markers are allowed. This means that any marker must be laid *next to* one of the opponent's pieces and *in line*—vertically, horizontally, or diagonally—with one of the player's own. This move "traps" one or more markers with one top symbol between two with the other.

When a player has a marker at each end of a line that contains one or more of the opponent's markers in the middle, the "trapped" piece or pieces are flipped over to match those on the ends. For example, if there is a crown checker and then two star checkers in a line, and the crown player now adds another crown at the far end of the line, on the other side of the stars (see diagram), all the checkers in the line are turned over so that crowns are on top. Although the markers are never moved off a square once they are put down, they may be flipped back and forth many times during the game.

The players continue to take turns laying down their markers, with the goal of turning as many markers as possible to their own side. If a piece closes off two lines of markers, both lines are turned over. If a player cannot lay down a marker next to an enemy marker and in line with one of his own, he forfeits his turn. He must continue to pass until he can play a piece.

It's good strategy to go for the corners. The four corner squares are prime Reversi territory because once a marker is placed there, it can never be flipped (no enemy marker can get on the other side of it). It's even worth passing up the chance for a large capture and instead taking a smaller one if it means gaining a corner position. The worst squares are one square in, diagonally, from the corners. Players should avoid these as long as possible and instead try to force the opponent into placing her pieces there.

In Reversi, the lead tends to flip back and forth as quickly as the markers. The game continues until all 64 squares are filled or until neither player can make another move. The player with the most markers on the board at the end of the game is the winner.

Seega

Popular in Africa, Seega challenges strategy enthusiasts.

Players: 2

Ages: 9 to 14

Place: Table or other flat surface, with seating for both players

Equipment: Paper; pencil; checkerboard and tape (optional); 24 checkers (12 dark, 12 light)

Seega, also called Senat, originated in Egypt 3,000 years ago and is now popular all over Africa. Played on a modified checkerboard with 25 squares, Seega is a strategic battle game in which each player competes to capture all of the opponent's pieces. Something of a cross between Checkers and Reversi, it is an excellent game for children who have mastered Checkers and some of its numerous variations.

There are two ways to make a Seega board, which consists of a grid of five squares by five squares. Either it can be drawn in a flash on a sheet of paper, or a checkerboard can be modified by using paper and tape to cover the last three rows on each of two adjacent sides. An X or other quickly recognizable design is drawn in the board's center square.

Each player receives 12 checkers, with one player taking the dark pieces and one taking the light. One player starts by placing two checkers anywhere on the board except the center square (both dark and light squares on a checkerboard are used). The remaining player does likewise. After each has made her first move, the players put down one checker per turn until all the pieces are laid out on the board. Because there are 24 checkers and 25 squares, this means that every square except the center one has a checker on it.

The player who places the last checker on the board then begins the next phase of the game, moving any one of his pieces one square over—in any direction except diagonally—into an empty square. At this point the center square can be used. If the player has nowhere to move on his first turn, he may move one of the opponent's checkers to free up a space and move immediately into it.

Players take turns moving and each time trying to trap one or more of the opponent's pieces in a line with their own pieces on both ends. For example, if there is a light checker with two darks lined up next to it and an empty space beyond the last dark checker, a light checker moved onto that space captures both the dark pieces. Captured checkers are removed from the board.

Captures *may not be made diagonally*, however, and any checker in the center square is safe from capture and protects other checkers in its line. If, for example, two light checkers are lined up and one is in the center square, even if the opponent moves a dark piece on either side of the line, both light checkers are safe.

If a player moves her checker into a position where it traps two lines of her opponent's checkers, she must decide which line to take; both captures may not be made. If a piece that makes one capture can make another capture in one more move, it may do so in the same turn. If a player moves his piece between two of his opponent's pieces, his checker is not captured. A capture must be made by a *move* of the capturing color.

Seega has three additional rules, designed to promote a fair game. First, if a player's pieces are all blocked, preventing any moves, the opponent must take an extra turn to free up a square. Second, players may not keep moving back and forth between two spaces; after a checker has been moved back and forth three times (that is, three total moves), the player must make a different move or forfeit the piece. Third, if a player who is surrounded by the opponent's pieces refuses to move (in order to protect other pieces), he forfeits the game.

The easiest Seega strategy is defensive. A player should try to position some of her pieces to form a barrier that protects the rest from attack, while trying to prevent her opponent from doing the same. Unfortunately, such a strategy often ends the game in a draw. For a livelier game, players should use an offensive strategy and try to control as many corners as possible; after all, no one can surround and therefore no one can capture a corner piece.

The first player to capture all the opponent's pieces wins the game. If the game ends in a stalemate, with both sides unable to make any moves, the player with the most checkers on the board is the winner. If both players end up with the same number of checkers, the game is declared a tie.

Lasca

Although played on a modified checker board, Lasca is a very different game from standard Checkers.

Players: 2

Ages: 9 to 14

Place: Table or other flat surface, with seating for both players

Equipment: Lasca board or modified checkerboard; 22 checkers (11 dark, 11 light); masking tape (optional); paper (optional)

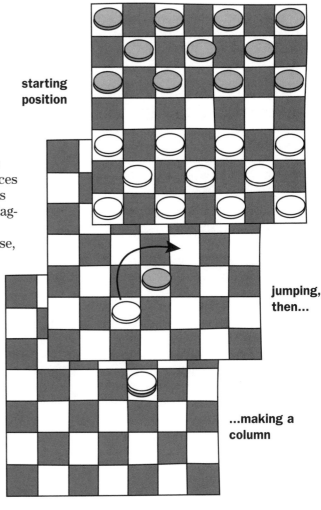

starting position

jumping, then...

...making a column

Like Checkers, Lasca is a strategic capture game, but it has a personality all its own. As in Checkers, the goal is to capture all the opponent's pieces or at least make it impossible for the opponent to make further moves. The moves in Lasca, however, are completely different from those in Checkers. Lasca should be taught only after Checkers is well understood because the rules, though similar, are more complicated.

A store-bought Lasca board has only 49 squares (7 rows of 7 squares), as opposed to the standard checkerboard of 64 squares (8 rows of 8). A checkerboard can be made into a Lasca board, however, by using taped-down paper to cover the last row of squares on each of two adjacent sides. Each of the checkers should have two distinct surfaces—most store-bought Checkers sets come with plastic checkers that have a star printed on one side and a crown on the other. If there is no difference between the sides, a distinguishing mark can be made with a bit of masking tape.

The players decide who will be which color, then line up their checkers with the unmarked side up on the *light* squares of their first three rows (see diagram). (If Checkers with stars and crowns are used, the star side goes up.) In Lasca, the player with the

light pieces goes first. At the start of the game, all the pieces are called "soldiers." Soldiers may move forward on the diagonal just like pieces in Checkers, except, of course, that in Lasca the pieces are moving on the light rather than the dark spaces. Players take turns moving their soldiers forward toward the opposite side of the board. Each player makes only one move per turn.

A piece may not be moved onto a square already occupied by another piece. But if, along a diagonal, one of the adjacent squares is occupied by an enemy piece and the square beyond that is empty, the player may jump over the opponent's piece to the square beyond. On a single turn, two or more pieces may be jumped if there is an empty space diagonally before and after each jumped-over piece. A player must make a jump if possible; if there is a choice of jumps, he may take whichever one he prefers.

If a soldier advances to the back row on the opponent's side, it is turned over and becomes an "officer." An officer may move like a King in Checkers—forward or backward diagonally (along the light squares in Lasca). Whenever one of a player's soldiers becomes an officer, her turn is over.

The rules regarding jumps are what make Lasca different, challenging, and fun. In Lasca, the jumped checker is not removed from the board but instead is placed beneath the piece that jumped it to begin a "column." The top piece of a column is called a

"guide." The guide's color shows which player the column belongs to, and the visible side shows whether it may move as a soldier or an officer. When a column is jumped, only the guide is taken, no matter how many pieces are beneath it. If the jumping piece is an officer and the new guide (top piece or remaining piece) in the column just jumped belongs to the opponent, the jumping piece may jump the column again (in the reverse direction) and pick up another piece, at which point the turn ends. Each captured piece is placed at the bottom of the column that captured it. Pieces retain their rank as soldiers or officers when they are captured, so that when they rise to the top of a column and become guides again, they move according to their old rank.

The game continues until one player's checkers have all been captured or all his moves are blocked. The other player wins the game.

Tangram

In this puzzle game, players race to reconstruct a cut-up shape.

Players: 3 or more, plus an adult or older child to supervise

Ages: 7 to 11

Place: Table or other flat surface, with seating for all players

Equipment: Sheets of cardboard and scissors for each player

In Tangram, loosely based on an old Chinese puzzle game, players create their own simple jigsaw puzzles. Participants then trade puzzles and race to put the pieces back together.

Each player starts with a cardboard rectangle (or square) of approximately the same size. (A standard piece of shirt cardboard can be nicely divided into two or more rectangles before the game begins.) With a pair of scissors, each now makes one straight cut in each direction across the shape, creating four smaller pieces. (If desired, the players can agree to cut their squares or rectangles into six pieces.) Although the cuts must be straight lines, they can be made on angles, resulting in pieces that are somewhat uneven.

The pieces are then scrambled and, at a signal from the supervising adult or older child, slid over to the player to the right.

At once, players begin quickly trying to reconstruct the pieces in front of them into their original rectangles. This task often is more difficult than it would seem. The minute a player succeeds, he calls out and play immediately comes to a halt. If his reconstruction is correct, he scores 10 points. (If his reconstruction is not correct, play resumes at once. The supervising adult or older child must be prepared to settle disputes.) The puzzles are scrambled anew and slid to the right for another round.

The game continues until each player has had a chance to grapple with every other player's puzzle. The player with the highest score at the end of the game is the winner. For an even more challenging game of Tangram, players can start with nonrectangular shapes, such as triangles, circles, and hexagons.

Sidewalk and Blacktop Games

The games in this chapter all have one thing in common: they need to be played on a hard, flat surface. Although these games have historically been played on city sidewalks and playground blacktops, many can be adapted for indoor fun by drawing the playing area on a large sheet of paper or cardboard and taping it securely to the floor. In many cases, a specific grid or court needs to be marked. All these games require some easy-to-find equipment, as noted, such as ropes, coins, cards, stones, jacks, marbles, or bottle caps. Most can be played on some level by any school-age child, but they do demand some skill and a lot of concentration.

Hopscotch

In this classic game players carefully hop their way to the end of a chalked-in board.

Players: 1 or more

Ages: 6 to 12

Place: Outdoors on pavement

Equipment: Chalk; marker for each player (old rubber shoe heel, flat stone, hockey puck, etc.)

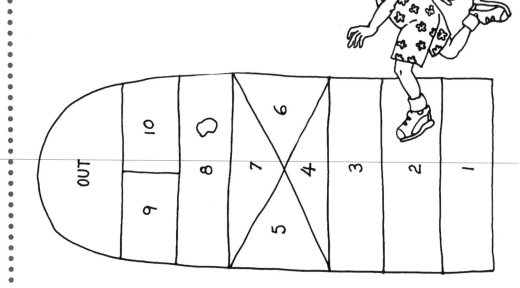

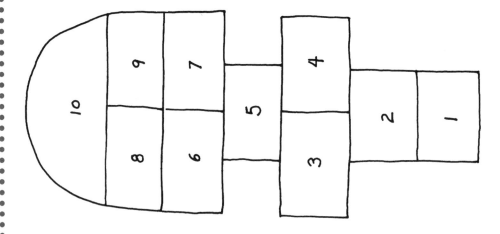

Hopscotch has been popular for hundreds of years and is played in some form on almost every continent. As varied as the versions are, they all involve hopping through a grid without stepping on the lines. Playing Hopscotch helps kids develop balance, agility, and good aim. Allowances—such as letting players hop the whole grid on both feet—can be made for younger children who want to participate.

First, the grid is drawn with chalk on the pavement. One basic American Hopscotch grid is a rectangle about 10 feet (3m) long by 4 feet (1.2m) wide, with a half circle attached to one end. Generally, the rectangle is divided into 10 spaces, which are numbered from 1 to 10; there are many possible ways to do this (see diagrams). In one version, the half-moon space at the top is marked "Out." Any flat, easy-to-throw object that will stay put when it lands can be used as a marker; old rubber shoe heels are probably best, but hockey pucks, flat stones, and empty metal shoe-polish containers (filled with sand or dirt) also work well. In a pinch, coins or bottle caps can be used too, though these tend to roll away very easily.

To begin, the first player stands behind the line at the end of the grid opposite the half-moon area and tries to toss her marker into square number 1. If she fails, the next player gets to go. If she succeeds, however, she begins to make her way square by square to the other end of the grid. First, she must jump completely over the square holding her marker. Then, she must hop from square to square on one foot, except if she encounters two squares (or, as in the case of numbers 5 and 6 in the top diagram, two triangles) side by side, in which case she sets one foot in each square. When she reaches the half-moon area, she must hop in, turn around with another hop (without putting her foot down), and head back. When she reaches the square *just before* the square in which her marker lies, she stoops over and picks the marker up, then hops into that square and completes the course.

If she does all this without stepping on a line, putting her other foot down when on a single square, falling, stepping into the square that contains the marker, or hopping more than once in either direction in any single square, she may go again. Now she stands at the starting line and tosses her marker into square number 2. This time, she'll have to hop over square 2.

left; three more are drawn to the left of the top square, and so on in the same pattern until all 19 squares are drawn (see diagram). The squares are not numbered, and no marker is used. The first player starts at one end and hops through the grid on one foot. Once she reaches the other end, she writes her initials inside any square of her choice. The other players on their turns must then avoid jumping on the initialed square. On her own later turns, however, the player who

Play continues in the same manner through all 10 or 11 spaces (including "Out") on the grid. A player can keep going until he fouls out. Then, on his next turn, the player starts with the number he fouled on.

The first player to complete the entire grid is the winner. For a longer game, the winner is the first player to complete the course up *and* back—from square 1 through 10 or "Out" and back to 1 again.

Japanese Hopscotch

Japanese Hopscotch, which should be played with two or three players, uses a board that is a snakelike trail of 19 blocks. Four 1-foot (30cm) squares are drawn side by side; two more are drawn on top of the square at the far

Japanese Hopscotch

1' (30cm)

1' (30cm)

initialed the square may land in it with both feet.

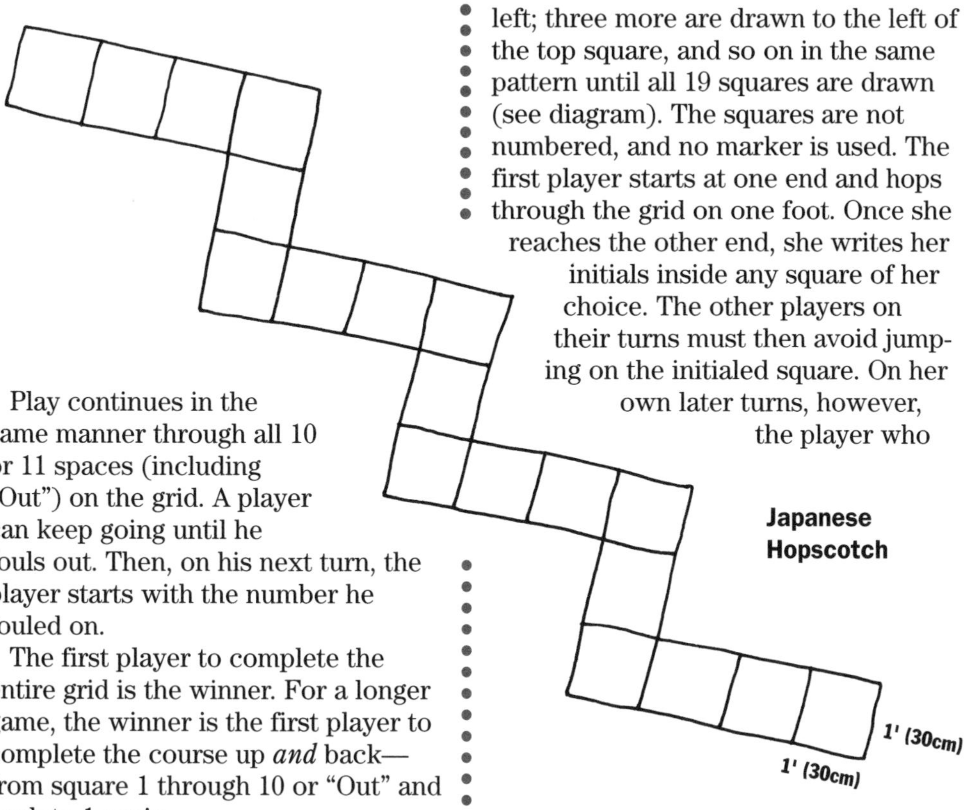

The game continues, with any player who makes it through initialing the square of his choice. A savvy player will initial two squares in a row, making a tough obstacle for oppo-

nents. The player who "owns" the most squares at the end of the game is the winner.

Window Hopscotch

Window Hopscotch, a game for no more than three players, uses a rectangle that is 3 by 7 feet (90cm by 2.1m) and divided into 21 one-foot (30cm) squares (see diagram). The squares are numbered from 1 to 21, beginning with the lower left square on the long side, moving up and down across the grid, and ending at the upper right square. Window Hopscotch is very similar to Japanese Hopscotch, except that in this game a marker, such as a flat stone or bottle cap, is used.

The first player throws his marker onto any square and hops on one foot through the numbers sequentially until he reaches that square. He then retrieves his marker and hops back to the beginning of the course. If the trip is successful, he initials the square into which he threw the marker. On later turns, the owner of the square may use this square as a rest stop, where he can put both feet down, but everyone else must jump over it. The player with the most initialed squares at the end of the game is the winner.

7' (2.1m)

3	4	9	10	15	16	21
2	5	8	11	14	17	20
1	6	7	12	13	18	19

3' (90cm)

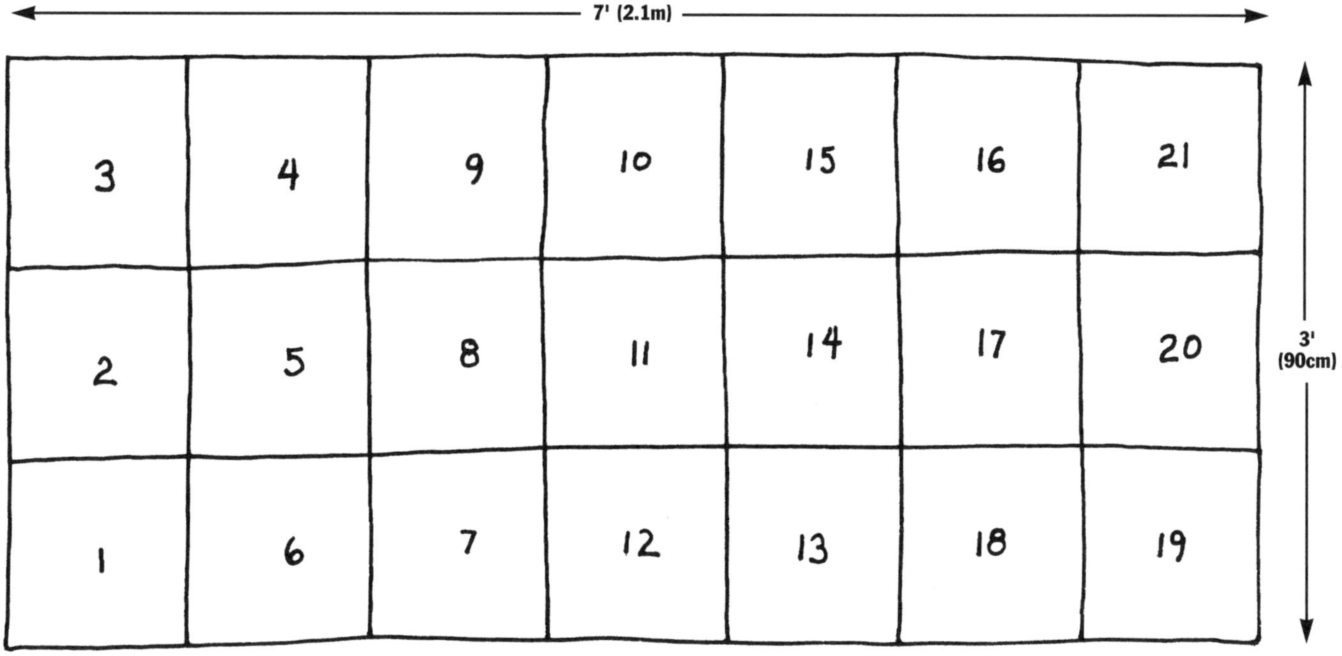

Window Hopscotch

Jump Rope

For Jump Rope a player needs nimble feet
to keep on hopping to the beat.

Players: 3 or more

Ages: 6 to 11

Place: Outdoors on pavement

Equipment: Jump rope or 10 to 15 feet (3m to 4.5m) of fabric (not plastic) clothesline; stick, stone, or ball (optional)

Jump Rope incorporates rhythm, memory, cooperation, and creativity into one of the best conditioning exercises around. The endless variations of this game have made it one of the most popular sidewalk and playground games for hundreds of years. Children all over the world jump rope, and the rhymes they chant while jumping mirror their cultures. The coordination and agility to jump rope are usually developed between the ages of about 6 and 8. Kids may want to refine their skills by practicing on their own before entering into competitive jumping.

For the most basic game of Jump Rope, two players stand apart and each hold one end of a jump rope or clothesline (knotted on each end). It's usually easiest if these two players are about the same height. The rope handlers then begin swinging the rope in a circle with an even rhythm so that the middle just skims the ground with each turn. At its height the rope should be at least high enough off the ground to clear the jumper's head.

The first jumper stands outside the swinging rope on the side where the rope moves away from him after touching the ground. When he is ready, he scurries to stand under the rope, usually turning to face one of the rope handlers. This is best done as soon as the rope touches the ground, so that the jumper has almost a full turn of the rope before it's necessary to hop over it. Once in, the jumper hops over the rope each time it swings underfoot. The best way to establish a good rhythm—and to extend endurance—is to take a second small hop in between jumps over the rope.

After a basic jumping rhythm has been established, both the turning and the jumping can be varied to make the game more interesting and challenging. The turners may shout "Salt!" and turn the rope slowly or yell "Pepper!" and speed it up. The jumper may be required to hop on one foot, rock from back foot to front foot, or jump high enough for the rope to pass under her twice before landing. (This last option requires some quick rope turning!) Really experienced jumpers may also bring a stick or a stone—which is alternately placed on the ground and picked up between jumps—or a ball to bounce.

As the jumper jumps, he counts each jump, until he misses. The jumper then becomes a turner and the next jumper runs in. The player with the most jumps after everyone has had a turn is the winner.

Counting Rhymes

Chants and rhymes are a perfect accompaniment to the thump-thump-thump of jumping the rope, and players will enjoy making up their own rhymes as they go along. Some established rhymes end with counting. Here are two of the most popular counting rhymes:

Cookies, candy in the dish,
How many pieces do you wish?
One, two, three, four . . .

Down in the valley where the green
grass grows,
There stands _____ (jumper's name),
pretty (or handsome) *as a rose.*
Along comes _____ (jumper's sweet
heart) and kisses her (or him) *on the*
cheek.
How many kisses did she (or he) *get*
this week?
One, two, three, four . . .

Ice Cream Soda

Many Jump Rope rhymes are said to predict the name of a sweetheart. Here's an old favorite:

Ice cream soda, lemonade, punch,
Tell me the name of your
honeybunch.
A, B, C, D . . .

The caller continues to go through the alphabet until the jumper misses. The letter she trips on is the first initial of the "honeybunch." The rhyme is repeated to find out the last initial—then the players try to figure out who the sweetheart could be.

Visiting

This Jump Rope game requires at least five players. The first player runs in and starts skipping. He then calls out for the other players to join in with a chant such as this:

I call in my very best friend,
And that is _____ (name of
  another player).
One, two, three!

At the count of "three," the person called jumps in and joins the original jumper. The two friends may now invite yet another friend in for a visit.

Teddy Bear

This favorite rhyme instructs the jumper to perform certain motions and stunts while jumping. In a competition, the first player to get through without any mistakes is the winner.

Teddy bear, teddy bear, turn around
  (jumper turns around),
Teddy bear, teddy bear, touch the
  ground (jumper touches the
  ground),
Teddy bear, teddy bear, tie your shoes
  (jumper touches shoes),
Teddy bear, teddy bear, read the news
  (jumper pretends to read the
  newspaper),
Teddy bear, teddy bear, go upstairs
  (jumper lifts knees to imitate
  walking up stairs),
Teddy bear, teddy bear, say your
  prayers (jumper puts hands
  together in prayer),
Teddy bear, teddy bear, turn out the
  light (jumper pretends to switch
  off a light),

Teddy bear, teddy bear, say "good
  night!" (jumper says "good night"
  and jumps out).

"A" My Name Is . . .

This game requires the jumper to think quickly on her feet. The first jumper begins with a chant involving the letter A:

A, my name is _____ (name
  that begins with the letter A, like
  Amy),
My husband's (wife's) *name is*
  _____ (another name that
  begins with A, like Albert),
We come from _____ (place that
  begins with A, like Alabama),
And we sell _____ (object that
  begins with A, like anchovies).

The player then runs out and the next jumper runs in. The second jumper must repeat the rhyme using the letter B: "B, my name is Bobby," for example, and so on. This goes on throughout the alphabet. If a player misses a jump or cannot think of a word to fill in the rhyme, her turn ends and another jumper gets a shot.

Follow the Leader

In this variation of standard Follow the Leader—meant for four or more players—one person runs into the

turning rope, does a stunt while jumping, and runs out. The jumper, for example, might hop on one foot, clap hands, or spin completely around. All the subsequent jumpers must imitate the original action. Any player who fails to perform the stunt correctly becomes a turner.

To make this game even more challenging, each player can be required to add a stunt of his own to the original stunt. All later players must complete the whole string of stunts before adding a new one.

Double Dutch

This jump rope variation uses two ropes. Each turner holds one end of each rope in a different hand; the two ropes shouldn't cross. The rope in the left hand is swung clockwise while the rope in the right hand is swung counterclockwise so that the two ropes alternately skim the ground. It may take a few tries for the turners to find the rhythm of turning both ropes at once. Once they do, the prospective jumpers are in for a challenge. With two ropes passing underfoot, a jumper has to leave the ground twice as often. Skilled Double Dutchers hop back and forth from one foot to another to stay alive. Many variations of the single-rope game can be played in this two-rope version.

Marbles

Taking careful aim, players shoot to
capture their opponents' marbles.

Players: 2 or more

Ages: 6 to 12

Place: Outdoors on pavement or dirt,
or indoors on carpeted, linoleum, or
vinyl floor

Equipment: 4 or more $^1/_2$-inch
(12.5mm) marbles for each player;
same-size or larger "shooter" marble
for each player; chalk, yarn, or sticks
for marking playing area

The game of Marbles has been
entertaining children for many
hundreds of years and can be
found in some form in almost every
country in the world. A forerunner of
such adult games as billiards, bowling,
and golf, Marbles requires good aim
and a steady hand to shoot the marble
toward its destination.

In years gone by, marbles—often
called "aggies"—were made of agate
(a semiprecious stone), and every
marble was unique, with distinctive
markings easily identifiable to its
owner. Today, marbles are mass-
produced and are largely indis-
tinguishable from one another.
That's why most kids are more
interested in the quantity of
marbles they amass than in the
specific qualities of each one.
A game of Marbles, however,
is just as much fun to play
with glass, plastic, steel,
clay, or stone marbles as
it was with the great
aggies of several genera-
tions ago.

In most Marbles
games the player
shoots a marble toward
an opponent's marble with the
aim of hitting and thereby capturing it. Before the game starts, players must decide if they are playing
for keeps. Either way, players should

make sure they know which marbles
belong to them and how many they
have coming into the game. To avoid a
lot of tears, parents may want to discourage kids from gambling away
their marbles.

The best place to play Marbles is on
a hard surface that is not perfectly
smooth. Concrete, blacktop, and
packed dirt are prime Marbles-playing
locations, but industrial carpeting and
textured vinyl flooring are good rainy-
day alternatives. Players draw or
mark out a large circle, 4 to 6 feet
(1.2m to 1.8m) across, in the playing
area. (Yarn does the trick on a carpeted floor.) Every participant should
have at least four $^1/_2$-inch (12.5mm)
marbles (usually made of glass or pol-
ished stone). Each player also needs a
"shooter." It's best to use a larger ($^3/_4$-
inch or 19mm) marble as the "shoot-
er," but a regular marble, as long as it
is easily identifiable, can also be used
for this purpose. Each player places

the same number of marbles—usually
four to six—anywhere inside the circle. One marble is reserved as the
shooter, but no other marbles are used
in the game.

To begin the game, the first player
kneels and sets down her shooter outside the circle. She then propels her
shooter toward the marbles within.
Novice players may shoot by simply
rolling the marble. The traditional way
to "pitch" a marble, however, is to
flick it with the thumb. If the player
hits another marble, she shoots again
(from the spot where her marble
comes to rest) and continues in this
way until she either misses altogether
or rolls her shooter out of the circle.
If at any time during her turn she manages to knock a marble out of the circle, she keeps that marble as booty
(even if her own marble goes out of
the circle on the shot) and it is eliminated from the game. After the first
player's turn ends, the next player
begins in the same fashion and tries to
hit the remaining marbles.

If a player's shooter is still inside the
circle when his turn rolls around
again, he starts his turn from that
spot. Otherwise, he starts his turn
from outside the circle. As a general
rule, a player should try to end his
turn with his shooter outside the
circle, because shooters in the
circle are fair game for other
players. Any player whose
shooter is knocked out of
the circle by another player
must give up all the marbles
she has won so far to that
player. She does, however,
get her shooter back so
she can keep on playing.

The game continues
with each player shoot-
ing in turn until there
are no more marbles
left in the circle. The
player with the most
marbles wins the match.

Pyramid

This variation calls
for just two players
and is best played
with at least six

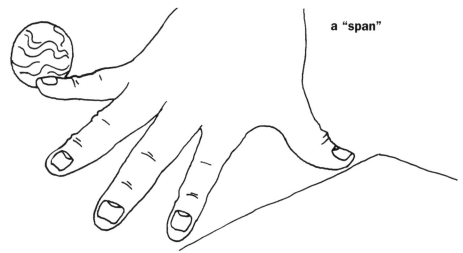

a "span"

marbles per player. To play Pyramid (also called Castle), players mark a circle about 2 feet (60cm) across. The first player sets three marbles close together inside the circle to form a base for a fourth marble, which rests on top. The second player then shoots a marble from outside the circle with the aim of knocking down the pyramid. If successful, he claims all four marbles. If not, he must forfeit one marble to the builder. To make the game more challenging, the shooter can be required to knock the pyramid marbles outside the circle on his shot. The players take turns building and shooting at pyramids. The first player to collect all the marbles is the winner.

Boss Out

Boss Out is a Marbles chase game for two players. The game starts when the first player throws his marble on the ground a few feet (1m or so) in front of him. The next player then crouches in the same spot from which the first player made his throw and shoots a marble with the aim of hitting the first one or landing within a "span" (the distance between the tip of the player's thumb and the tip of the pinkie with the fingers outstretched) of the first one. If the shooter succeeds in hitting or spanning the first marble, she wins both marbles. If not, the first player retrieves his marble and tries to hit or span the second

player's marble, which is still lying there. Once one player wins the other's marble, another round begins, with the loser of the previous round tossing out a marble. The game goes on until the players call it quits or one player wins all the marbles.

Knuckle Box

For this variation, players draw a square with 18-inch (45cm) sides and place an equal number of marbles anywhere inside the square. The first player shoots from a spot one "span" (measured from the tip of the player's thumb to the tip of the pinkie with the fingers outstretched) away from any side of the square. The goal is to knock marbles out of the square. The player gets to keep any marbles he knocks out, as long as his shooter also leaves the square. (No one gets any marbles knocked out of the square if the shooter stays inside the square.) If the shooter's marble stays in the square, the next player takes her turn and the shooter's marble becomes a target. If the shooter isn't hit, the first player may retrieve his shooter on the next turn. If the shooter is hit, the shooter's owner must turn over any marbles won so far during that game (though he does get his shooter back). Play continues until all the marbles have been knocked out of the square. At this point the player with the most marbles wins.

Shooting Gallery

In this variation, two lines are marked on the ground several feet (1m or so) apart. Setting up behind one line, the first player shoots a marble past the second line. (On the opening shot, if she doesn't make it to the other line, she goes again until she does.) The next player then tries to hit the first marble. If successful, he wins both marbles. If not, he must forfeit a marble (not in play) to his opponent and the next player may shoot at either marble behind the line. She may even try to hit both. The game continues until one player runs out of marbles. Or the game can end after a predetermined number of shots or time period, in which case the player with the most marbles is the winner.

Holey Bang

In this simple "hole" game, played outdoors on dirt and requiring at least six marbles per player, a shallow hole is dug in the earth and a line is drawn 6 to 20 feet (1.8m to 6m) away from the hole (depending on the age and skill of the players). Players take turns trying to shoot their marbles into the hole from behind the line. The first person to sink her marble collects all the marbles that missed the hole. Whoever ends up with the most marbles wins. Players may also choose to keep score—1 point for each hole in one. In that case, the player who has the most points at the end of the game is the winner.

shooting

Jacks

It takes a sharp eye and a quick hand to bounce the ball and scoop up the jacks.

Players: 1 or more

Ages: 6 to 14

Place: Outdoors on smooth pavement or indoors on uncarpeted floor

Equipment: Jacks set (10 metal jacks plus 2 extras and 1 small rubber ball)

Jacks has its origins in the ancient game of Knucklebones, which was played with sheep knuckles. Today's jacks are small, six-pronged metal objects that are just the right size and weight to fit comfortably in the hand. Jacks is a game of speed, agility, concentration, and (most of all) hand-eye coordination. Children can—and frequently do—spend years perfecting Jacks techniques, but the novice player can enjoy the game just as much as the expert. Kids bitten by the Jacks bug often spend hours alone honing their skills before competing with friends. The game should be played on a smooth, flat surface—a sidewalk that's in good repair or an uncarpeted floor serves nicely.

Jacks is generally played in a crouching position. To decide who will go first, each player takes a turn balancing all the jacks on the back of her hand, tossing them in the air, and trying to catch them in her palm. The player who catches the most jacks goes first.

The first player gently tosses a handful of ten jacks so that they spread out on the ground. He then throws the ball into the air, picks up one jack with his throwing hand, lets the ball bounce once, and catches the ball with the same hand. (Novice players can be allowed a double bounce.) It's a good idea to toss the ball straight up in the air so it doesn't land or bounce out of reach. A ball thrown too high, however, may be difficult to control.

The jack is then transferred to the other hand, and the process is repeated with each jack until all ten jacks have been retrieved. This round is called "Onesies."

If the first player successfully completes Onesies, he moves on to try Twosies. In this round the jacks are picked up two at a time. Next, for Threesies, three groups of three jacks must be snatched up, then one more

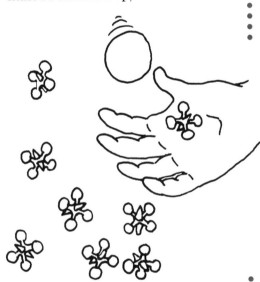

throw is required to grab the remaining jack. (Leftover jacks also occur in Foursies, Sixies, Sevensies, Eightsies, and Ninesies; each time they are all picked up on one toss.) The player continues in this way up to Tensies, when all ten jacks must be scooped up on one throw.

The whole sequence, of course, is usually not accomplished in one turn. When a player makes a mistake—fails to pick up the correct number of jacks, drops a jack, or doesn't catch the ball after one bounce—another player gets to go. Players begin their next turn with the number they failed on. The first player to make it through Tensies wins.

Eggs in a Basket

There are many variations of Jacks, and new ones are being invented all the time. For Eggs in a Basket, the jacks are scattered on the ground, and the hand that is not throwing the ball is placed on the ground with the palm cupped to create a "basket." The challenge is to toss the ball, pick up a jack, put it in the basket, and catch the ball on one bounce. The game continues in sequence from Onesies all the way through Tensies.

Crack the Eggs

This Jacks game is played like Eggs in the Basket, but in this variation each handful of jacks must be tapped on the floor before being placed in the basket.

Flying Dutchman

In this challenging variation, the player tosses the ball in the air, picks up a jack (or jacks) with the same hand, and then catches the ball *without* letting it bounce. To transfer the picked-up jacks out of the throwing hand, the ball must again be tossed in the air, the jacks moved to the other hand, and the ball caught after one bounce.

Sequences

In this variation, one jack is picked up on the first throw, two on the second, three on the third, and four on the fourth—at which point all ten jacks have been retrieved. The jacks are not transferred into the other hand after each pickup, so the challenge is to throw the ball and pick up jacks with a hand that is already holding jacks.

Once all the jacks are in the player's hand, she tosses the ball, spreads the jacks out on the floor again, and catches the ball after one bounce. The final and most challenging step in Sequences involves tossing the ball one last time and picking up all ten jacks on one bounce. Meeting that challenge means victory.

Skully

In this target contest, players compete to shoot markers through the nine bases of the Skully court.

Players: 2 to 6

Ages: 6 to 14

Place: Outdoors on pavement

Equipment: "Shooter" (bottle cap, poker chip, checker, smooth stone, etc.) for each player; chalk for marking court

Skully, also known as Skelly or Skellzies, is a classic inner-city target-shooting contest—a fixture of urban playgrounds and schoolyards. The rules of Skully have changed over its century-old history and geographical migrations. The version described here, currently the most popular, was refined by generations of New York City children.

To prepare for the game, a Skully court is drawn with chalk on a hard, flat surface (see diagram). The perimeter of the court is a square 4 feet (1.2m) on each side. In the middle of the square the "pit" is drawn: a 13½-inch square (34cm) crossed by two diagonal lines (representing the skull and crossbones for which the game was named). Next, eight 7-inch (17.5cm) squares are added—one inside each corner and one midway along each side. Finally, a 4-inch (10cm) square is drawn in the middle of the pit. The squares are numbered as shown in the diagram.

Each of the players should have his own "shooter." The traditional Skully shooter is a standard crown-rimmed bottle cap; it can be personalized with paint on the flat side and weighted with either melted wax or clay on the hollow side.

To begin, all players place their shooters on the start line, located outside the court behind the number 2

square. The order of players is decided, and taking turns, each player flicks her shooter across the court toward the number 1 square. The idea is to land the shooter completely inside the number 1 box without touching any lines and then to flick it, in order, into the number 2 box, the number 3 box, and so on. Landing in the correct numbered box immediately wins the player a free flick—and the shooter may be repositioned anywhere within that box to get the best possible vantage point for the next shot.

If a shooter lands inside the court but not in a numbered box, it remains where it landed while the other players take their turns. Any shooter that goes out of bounds (beyond the limits of the outer square)—either by being flicked too hard by its owner or being bumped out by an enemy shooter—must be placed at the spot where it went out before it is shot in the next turn. If a shooter goes out of bounds two turns in a row, it must be returned to the starting line and the player is forced to begin the whole sequence anew. (Otherwise players continue where they left off.) And beware the skull and crossbones: if a shooter lands in the pit, in the area around square 9, he loses three turns!

Besides landing inside a box, a player may advance by means of a "sweep," which is using the shooter to

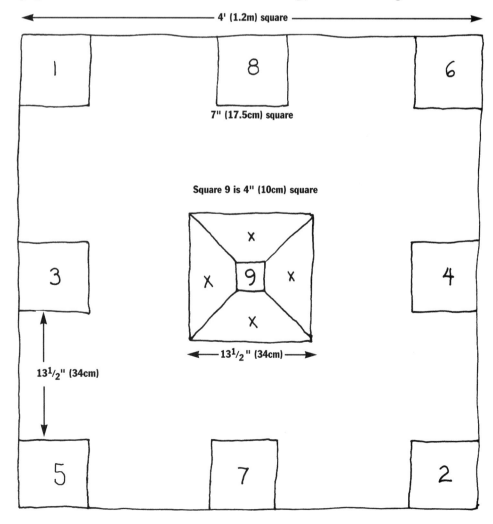

knock another player's cap off the court. A successful sweep allows the shooter to progress to the next box automatically and continue the shooting sequence.

When a shooter reaches the number 9 box, that player must turn around and complete the sequence in reverse to box number 1. Returning shooters are called "poison" because if a shooter belonging to a player who has not yet reached number 9 touches a poison shooter or is struck by one, that player is out of the game. A "poison" player can win the game even before making it all the way back to the starting line by eliminating all her opponents. Otherwise, the first player to return to the number 1 box and flick the shooter past the starting line is the winner.

Marble Boccie

In this mini-version of an Italian lawn-bowling game, players compete to shoot their marbles close to a target.

Players: 2 or more

Ages: 7 to 12

Place: Outdoors on packed dirt or pavement

Equipment: 6 same-color marbles for each player; large "target" marble; stick or chalk for marking playing area

Marble Boccie is a variation of Marbles that closely approximates the traditional Italian lawn-bowling game called *bocce*. Players shoot their marbles at another target marble, aiming to get as close to it as possible. As in all marble games, good aim, concentration, and a steady hand are keys to success. While regular marbles is best played on a hard, smooth surface that allows unrestricted rolling, Marble Boccie is best on hard, packed dirt, which offers more friction—and more control. But pavement can also be used.

First, a shooting line is drawn with a stick or chalk at one end of the playing area. Each player should have six marbles of one color so that it is easy to tell who owns each marble.

Standing behind the shooting line, the first player flicks a large marble—the "target"—into the field. Next, the same player shoots one of his six marbles, aiming to land it as close as possible to the target. Each of the other players then takes a shot in turn, and the play goes on until all the players have pitched their six marbles. There are no penalties for hitting other marbles or the target. In fact, the best strategy is to play aggressively, trying to knock other players' marbles out of the way.

After all the marbles are shot, the player whose marble is closest to the target scores 1 point for that marble; if any of her other marbles are closer to the target than any opponent's marble, she gets a point for each of them. No other points are scored. Succeeding rounds are played in the same way. The first player to score 21 points wins the game.

Wall Boccie

In this variation on Marble Boccie, the target marble is placed 6 inches (15cm) in front of a wall. Each shot must bounce against the wall before landing as close to the target as possible. If a marble stops before it hits the wall, it is removed from the game and may not be shot again in that round. Other rules and scoring remain the same as in Marble Boccie.

Hole in One

In Hole in One, players sink their shots by rolling a coin into a cup.

Players: 2 or more

Ages: 6 to 10

Place: Outdoors on pavement or indoors on uncarpeted floor

Equipment: Plastic cup and coin for each player

Hole in One is a simple game that can be played outdoors on pavement or indoors on an uncarpeted floor. Children compete to roll coins into a tipped-over cup—not as easy a task as it might seem. It's fun to experiment with different coins because the variations in size and weight make for different kinds of rolling challenges.

First, a plastic cup is laid on its side—this is the "hole" on the ground. Players sit or crouch on the ground about 5 or 6 feet (1.5m or 1.8m) away from the cup, and each takes a turn trying to roll his coin into the cup. Each "hole in one" counts for a point. The game goes on until one player reaches a predetermined score and wins the game.

Roll a Goal

Roll a Goal is played in the same way as Hole in One except that "goal posts" are used instead of a cup. Players roll coins through the goal marked by books, folded pieces of paper, candlesticks, standing cups, or any other upright objects. The goal posts may be placed farther apart for an easier game or closer together for a more challenging one.

Cover It

This coin- or card-tossing game requires just a bit of aim and lots of luck.

Players: 2 or more

Ages: 8 to 14

Place: Outdoors on pavement, near a wall

Equipment: Handful of pennies (or other same-size coins) or several playing cards for each player

Cover It is usually played as a coin-tossing game, but playing cards can also be used. Although the outcome depends almost entirely on luck, children greatly enjoy the game all the same. Cover It can be played on the spur of the moment and can fill as much or as little time as the players have.

To begin, the players stand about 5 feet (1.5m) in front of a wall, each holding a handful of coins or cards. The first player throws a coin or card against the wall and leaves it wherever it falls. The next player then tosses a coin or card against the wall, with the hope that when it rebounds it will touch or "cover" the other coin or card. If the second coin or card touches the first at all, the player who threw it collects both objects and puts them in her ammunition pile. If not, her coin or card is left where it fell. After the first toss, if the coin or card fails to hit the wall before it lands on the ground, it is retrieved and the player loses her turn.

Players take turns tossing. As more and more items accumulate on the ground, they are all up for grabs. The winner is the player with the most coins (or cards) after a predetermined amount of time, or the first player to reach a predetermined number of coins (or cards).

Touching the Mummy

In Touching the Mummy—also known as Hitting the Mummy—the first coin thrown is designated the "mummy," and the object is to cover only that coin. If a player throws a coin that does not touch the mummy, it is left where it fell. When a player does touch the mummy, he takes all the coins on the field *except* the mummy. Any player who picks up the mummy by mistake must pay one coin to each of the other players. Scoring is the same as in Cover It.

Brother Jonathan

Players must flip coins onto a board to score in this penny-pitching game.

Players: 2 or more

Ages: 8 to 14

Place: Outdoors on pavement

Equipment: Handful of pennies (or other same-size coins) for each player; chalk for drawing the board

Coins are more than just money—they're also essential game pieces in coin-tossing games. Although no money actually changes hands in Brother Jonathan, the coins certainly do fly. This 200-year-old game sharpens a child's aim and throws in a bit of a math lesson, too.

Before the game begins, a board must be drawn with chalk directly on the pavement (see diagram). First, a large rectangle about 5 by 8 feet (1.5m by 2.4m) is outlined, then a horizontal line is drawn about 2 feet (60cm) in from each short side of the rectangle. Next, the newly created box at one end is divided into five equal strips running across the box. Each strip is now divided into three or four small boxes of different sizes. A number from 1 to 20 is marked in each space, with the smaller spaces getting higher numbers and the larger spaces getting lower ones. No number may appear in more than one space. These numbers represent the point value of the space.

Each player should have the same number—and the same type—of coins. To play, participants stand behind the first line at the far end of the board (away from the small boxes) and take turns pitching their coins onto the numbered spaces, keeping track of their scores as they go along. A coin that lands on a dividing line or outside the scoring box does not earn any points.

The first player to reach a predetermined score (say, 100) is the winner. If no player has reached this score after the first handfuls of coins have been tossed, the players all retrieve the coins and continue the game.

Wall Jonathan

This game is played on the same board as Brother Jonathan, but the board is drawn in front of a wall. Players must throw the coins against the wall so that they rebound onto the board. Getting a coin into one of the small, high-scoring boxes takes a great deal of skill.

Crack Loo

The board for Crack Loo is slightly different from the one used in Brother Jonathan. Instead of a rectangle divided into numbered segments, it has a bunch of random lines drawn near one another to suggest cracks in the sidewalk or pavement. Each "crack" is numbered. A pitching line is marked a few feet (about 1m) from the area where the cracks are, and players stand behind it, aiming their coins at the cracks. Players score points for landing directly on a crack.

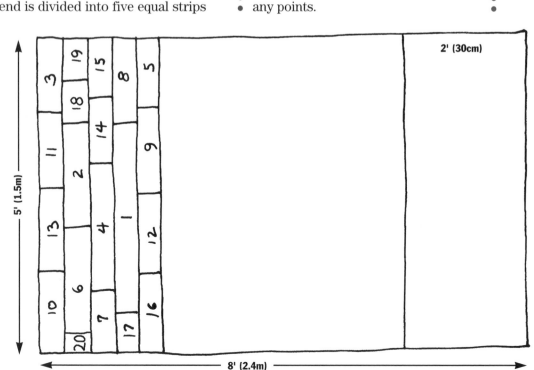

Fivestones

In this ancient game of skill, the challenge is to flip and catch stones.

Players: 1 or more

Ages: 8 to 14

Place: Outdoors on pavement or indoors on floor (away from breakable objects)

Equipment: 5 small rounded stones, dice, jacks, or packaged Fivestones cubes

Fivestones was originally called Knucklebones because it was played with the knucklebones of sheep. The game is a predecessor of Jacks and has been played in many parts of the world for more than 2,000 years. Unlike Jacks, Fivestones does not use a ball. Fivestones requires concentration and good hand-eye coordination, making it best for kids 8 years and up. They'll relish the challenge and variety this game offers.

Although Fivestones is an absorbing solo activity, competing with other players increases the excitement. To begin, a player crouches down with five small rounded stones (dice, jacks, or Fivestones cubes may also be used) in the palm of his hand. His goal is to do five intricate maneuvers with the stones—involving throwing the stones in the air, catching them, and picking them up off the ground—in succession. If he fails at any one of these maneuvers, his turn immediately ends and the next player gets a shot. On his next turn, the first player picks up where he left off.

The first Fivestones throw—called "Ones"—goes like this: The stones are tossed up into the air from the open palm all at once (see diagram). While the stones are in the air, the player turns her palm over and tries to catch the stones on the back of her hand. She then reverses the trick, tossing the stones from the back of her hand and

catching them in her palm.

If the player manages to catch all the stones, she immediately goes on to the next maneuver. If all five stones fall to the ground, the turn is over. If, however, four or fewer stones have fallen to the ground by the end of the basic throw, the turn goes on. With the fallen stones lying on the ground, the player transfers all but one of the caught stones into her nonthrowing hand. She then throws the single stone into the air and tries to pick up one of the fallen stones with her throwing hand while catching the tossed stone with the same hand. This action is repeated until all the stones have been picked up.

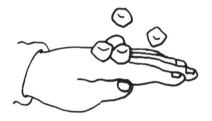

For the second toss ("Twos") the stones are scattered on the ground. A single stone is picked up and thrown into the air. While that stone is in the air, the player must pick up two of the stones on the ground and then catch the tossed stone with the same hand. After transferring the two stones to her nonthrowing hand, the action is then repeated to retrieve the other two stones.

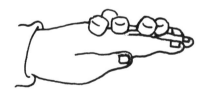

The third toss ("Threes") is played in the same way as Twos, except that only one stone is picked up when the single stone first goes airborne, but three are picked up the second time.

The fourth and final toss ("Fours") is played much like Twos and Threes, but this time when the single stone is thrown into the air, the four remaining stones are swept up together.

As the game progresses, players often have to try several times before succeeding at a toss. The first player to complete every toss through Fours is the winner.

London

Good aim is key in this "shooting" and drawing game.

Players: 2 or more

Ages: 8 to 14

Place: Outdoors on pavement

Equipment: Marker (stone, bottle cap, etc.) for each player; chalk

Skill and luck combine to make London a very absorbing game. It differs from other marker-shooting games in that instead of amassing points, players shoot for a chance to add to a drawing they must complete to win the game. Skillful marker-shooters will be successful in this game. But even those with less than perfect aim can luck into victory.

First, a rectangle 3 by 8 feet (90cm by 2.4m) is drawn with chalk on the sidewalk or blacktop (see diagram). The rectangle is divided into seven equal spaces by drawing six parallel lines crosswise. A half circle is attached to one end of the large rectangle, and the word "London" is written inside.

To begin, the first player stands or kneels at the base of the rectangle opposite the "London" zone and rolls, tosses, or slides a marker onto one of the interior spaces. The marker should be a small, hard object such as a stone, bottle cap, button, or coin. If the marker lands outside the grid or on a line, the player retrieves it and the next player takes a turn. If, however, the first player succeeds, he removes the marker and draws a circle in the space where the marker landed. This circle represents the head of a stick figure. the player then initials the head to identify it as his own. (Alternatively, each player can use a different color of chalk.)

All the players in turn do the same, shooting their markers and drawing the heads of stick figure in the spaces where their markers land. As the game continues, if a player's marker lands in a space where she has already drawn a head, she may add a stick body to this figure. When she later lands there again, she may add a leg; yet again, another leg. Once a figure has a head, a body, and two legs, it is complete. The next time the player lands in that same space, she begins another figure.

A player may build stick figures in any or all of the spaces. His goal, however, is to build three complete figures in a single space. He can get a little help from the "London" zone: any time the marker lands there, a player may add a body part to any of his figures on the grid or start a new figure in any of the zones.

When a player has three full figures in one space, he aims for that space—or the "London" zone—one more time. Once he hits it, the player draws a line through all three figures, creating "arms" to link them all together. The first player to link three figures wins the game.

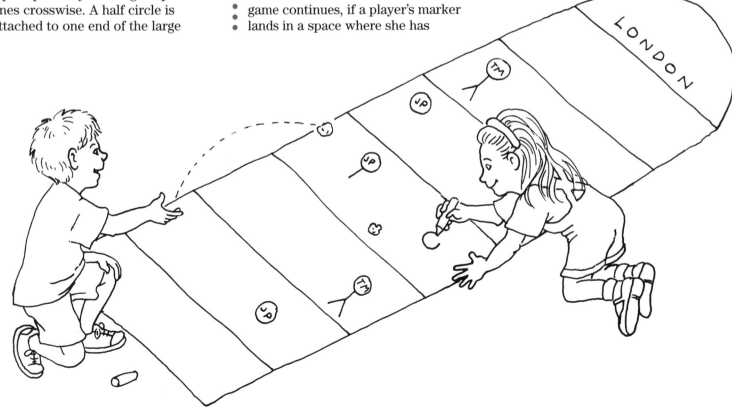

Card Flipping

Whether players are flipping for fun or profit, the outcome is all in the cards.

Players: 2

Ages: 8 to 14

Place: Outdoors on pavement, grass, or dirt or indoors in area away from breakable objects

Equipment: Players' own sports card collections (baseball, basketball, football, hockey, etc.) or other sorts of trading cards

Many American children amass sizable collections of sports cards. While the surest way to add to a collection is simply to buy more cards, winning cards in a flipping contest is *much* more fun (not to mention free). Of course, there's always the risk of losing, too. Card flipping is especially thrilling because of its element of risk—players have absolutely no control over what they win or lose. That's why prized cards that a child would never want to lose, such as a favorite player or a rare card, should be removed from the pile before playing this game.

To begin, the two players stand facing each other and holding their personal stacks of sports cards face up in their hands. The number of cards need not be exactly the same. The player whose top card has the lower series number—this can generally be found on the back in the upper right corner—starts the game.

The first player calls "Match!" or "Mismatch!" and each player flips the top card off his stack, grasping it by the corner and turning it over so that it falls to the ground or floor. If both cards fall face up or face down, the flip is a match. If one is face down and one is face up, the flip is a mismatch. If the caller predicted the correct outcome, he wins both cards. If not, the opponent gets them.

Players may decide to keep the same caller throughout the game or to take turns being the caller. There's no advantage either way since the outcome of the game is pure luck. Play continues until the players have had enough of the game or one player is out of cards.

Flipping for Distance

Another, perhaps more skilled, way to compete for cards is to flip for distance, with the player whose card travels the farthest winning the round. The card is held between the thumb and the forefinger; then the wrist is flicked to send the card sailing. For a big win, players may decide that whoever flips the card the farthest in five to ten rounds gets to take all the flipped cards.

Flicking for the Bowl

This variation, played with sports cards and a large bowl, is at its simplest with two players, but can be a blast with even two or three or more. It's a high-stakes contest in which players can win or lose large numbers of cards in one fell swoop.

To play, the bowl is set on the floor and each player stands about 8 feet (2.4m) away from the bowl, or closer if everyone agrees, with a pile of cards in his hands. The number of cards need not be exactly the same for each player. Taking turns, each player flicks one card, aiming to land the card in the bowl. A round ends when all players have flicked one card.

If no cards have landed in the bowl, play continues, with each player flicking another card in turn.

All cards that miss the bowl should remain on the floor untouched. If a single player has landed a card in the bowl, he collects all the flicked cards, including his own and all the cards that landed on the floor.

Sometimes, more than one player will land a card in the bowl. In this case, any player whose card missed the bowl, if any, is temporarily out of the game. The remaining players continue tossing, with any and all players who miss the bowl dropping out at the end of each round. Only once a round finishes with a single player having landed a card in the bowl are all the cards—those both in and out of the bowl—collected by the winner. The other players then rejoin the game. The winner has first flick in the next round.

The game continues in this fashion until one player loses all of his cards or until all players have had enough of the game. A predetermined number of rounds may also be set. The player who has won the most cards at the end of the game is Flicking champion.

Hunt and Hide-and-Seek Games

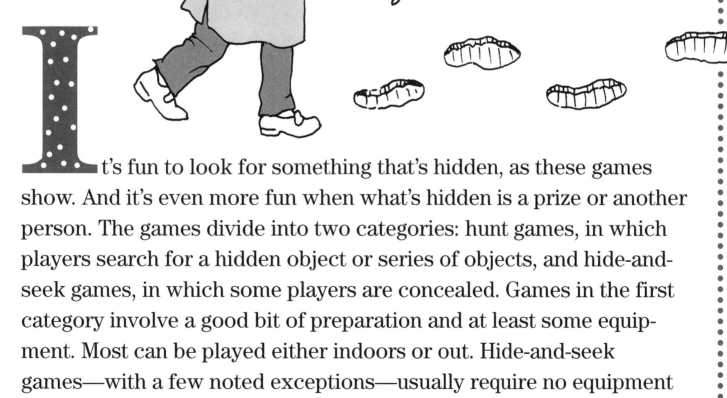

I t's fun to look for something that's hidden, as these games show. And it's even more fun when what's hidden is a prize or another person. The games divide into two categories: hunt games, in which players search for a hidden object or series of objects, and hide-and-seek games, in which some players are concealed. Games in the first category involve a good bit of preparation and at least some equipment. Most can be played either indoors or out. Hide-and-seek games—with a few noted exceptions—usually require no equipment and are best played outdoors, where there's room to run. This chapter includes games for a wide range of ages, from 4-year-olds to teens.

Hot and Cold

In this hunting game the temperature rises as players close in on a hidden object.

Players: 2 or more

Ages: 4 to 7

Place: Indoors or outdoors in area with good hiding places for objects

Equipment: Small object such as lollipop or small toy for each player

Hot and Cold is a hunting game for young children, and it is frequently played at parties. Kids seem to get a kick out of the game's central concept: that the hunter "warms up" as he gets closer to a hidden object and "grows colder" when he wanders away. Any small object can be hidden, but the best idea is to use a piece of candy or a small toy, which can then serve as the prize for the winner.

First, one player is sent from the room or somewhere out of sight and the others hide the object. If the game is being played outdoors, clear boundaries should be established for the hiding area.

When the searcher returns to the play area, the hunt begins. As the hunter looks for the object, the other players provide clues to its location by calling out, "You're getting warmer" if the searcher nears the prize, or "You're getting cooler" if he gets farther from it. The farther away the searcher goes, the more frigid his condition becomes—the hunter may go from being cool to cold to frosty to freezing. Likewise, as the searcher gets closer to the prize, the temperature may climb from slightly warm to warm to very hot—all the way to burning!

Eventually, the searcher discovers the object and is rewarded with the prize

he found. The game should then be repeated until every player has had a chance to be the searcher and collect his own prize.

Bean Hunt

This seek-and-collect game calls for sharp eyes and quick wits.

Players: 2 or more, plus an adult or older child to set up and supervise

Ages: 4 to 8

Place: Indoors in room with good hiding places for objects

Equipment: Sack of beans, peanuts, or several dozen other small objects; paper cup for each player

Bean Hunt and similar hunting games are often thought of as party games, but they also work as everyday indoor activities for a group of children. Besides being fun, Bean Hunt encourages children to practice their counting skills, and it promotes persistence by rewarding players who do a thorough search.

Before the game begins, an adult or older child hides peanuts, dried beans, pennies, or similar small objects in the nooks and crannies of a room. The objects can be hidden behind doors, under furniture or cushions, between books, on windowsills—anywhere that it's safe to search for them.

After all the beans have been hidden, each child is given a paper cup in which to collect the beans (or other objects) and the players are sent on a search-and-recover mission. Children are given 5 to 10 minutes to find as many beans as possible. Players should be told if any places are off-limits.

When the time is up, each child counts her beans. The player who collects the most wins.

Card Hunt

Two players or teams compete to find all the cards of a certain color.

Players: 2 or more (even number), plus an adult or older child to set up and supervise

Ages: 4 to 8

Place: Indoors in room with good hiding places for cards

Equipment: 2 standard decks of cards

Card Hunt is a search-and-recover game with a twist—players must find not just the hidden cards but specifically the ones that match those in their hands. This takes concentration, persistence, and the ability to keep a secret (no small challenge for 4- and 5-year-olds). The last thing any player wants to do is to give away the location of an opponent's card.

Before the game starts, the players stay out of sight while the supervising adult (or an older child) hides all 52 cards in one deck around the room. The supervisor then divides the players into two equal teams and separates the remaining deck into piles of red and black cards. Each member of one team is given a red card, and each member of the opposing team receives a black card.

Now, each player searches for the card that exactly matches, in number and suit (clubs, hearts, diamonds, spades), the one in her hand. If any other cards are discovered along the way, they should be left in place. When the player finds the matching card, she brings it to the adult, who then gives her another card from her team's pile.

Whenever a player uncovers a card that doesn't match the card he's holding but *is* his team's color, he should try to remember where it is. That way, if he is given this card to match on a later go-round, he'll know exactly where to find it.

The game continues in this fashion until all of the cards have been handed out. The first team to find all its cards is the winner.

Puzzle Hunt

Players hunt for the missing piece to complete their puzzles in this classic challenge.

Players: 3 or more, plus an adult or older child to set up and supervise

Ages: 5 to 9

Place: Indoors in room with good hiding places for objects

Equipment: Picture postcard for each player; scissors

This hunting game combines the fun of a search with the challenge of putting together a jigsaw puzzle. Children will enjoy creating their own puzzles and then searching for the missing pieces.

First, each player chooses a picture postcard (a magazine page glued to a piece of cardboard will also work) and cuts it into four jigsaw pieces. The pieces should have knobs and curves that fit together. If necessary, the adult or older child can demonstrate how to do this. To make the game more challenging, the pictures can be similar, the puzzles can be cut into six or eight pieces, or players can give each other the puzzles they make.

Next, the players are sent out of the room, each with only one piece of his puzzle. The adult or older child hides the rest of the pieces in nooks and crannies around the room. When the players

return, they must search for the other pieces to their puzzles.

The first player to find all her pieces and put her puzzle together is the winner.

Huckle, Buckle, Beanstalk

This hunting game calls for an eagle eye and a poker face.

Players: 5 or more

Ages: 6 to 10

Place: Indoors in room with good hiding places for objects

Equipment: Small object, such as a pencil, book, toy, or piece of fruit

Huckle, Buckle, Beanstalk delights parents and teachers because it encourages a large group of children to be quiet and sit still. Kids like it because the challenge is twofold: to spot a hidden object and at the same time not do anything that would clue the others in on where it is.

To begin, one player selects a small object, which he holds up for the others to see; then, while the rest close their eyes or leave the room, he hides the object and then sits down. The object—which can be anything from a pencil to a small book or piece of fruit—should be placed so that it is partially, but not completely, hidden from view. It should be visible from just about any spot in the room.

When the object has been hidden, the players open their eyes or return to the room and begin hunting for it. The twist here is that they must hunt with their eyes only—no moving around the room allowed—since the object is partially visible. Players may be told where to stand; they might, for example, form a ring in the middle of the room. The first player to spot the object says, "Huckle, Buckle, Beanstalk," and sits down, on the floor or on a chair. In this way the finder avoids letting other players know where the object is.

One by one, as the other players see the object, they say, "Huckle, Buckle, Beanstalk," then sit down. When all the players are sitting down (or after a period of a few minutes), the first one who saw the object whispers its whereabouts to the hider. If the hider confirms that the first spotter has in fact found the object, the object is retrieved from its hiding place and the first spotter takes a turn as hider. If by chance the first spotter is mistaken (or fibbing about having seen the object), the hider checks with the second spotter. If the second spotter can prove she knows where the object is, she gets a turn as hider.

Hunt the Key

By faking passes, players conspire to keep a hunter from tracking down a hidden key.

Players: 8 or more

Ages: 6 to 10

Place: Anywhere with seating in a circle for all players

Equipment: Key or other small object, such as a coin or marble

Hunt the Key is often played at parties because it requires a relatively large group of players. The more participants there are, the more challenging the game. This is a good exercise in cooperation, as the group works together to conceal the location of the key from the hunter.

All the players except one sit in a tight circle. The remaining player, who is the hunter, sits in the middle of the circle. The hunter closes her eyes and slowly counts to ten out loud. Meanwhile, the other players begin passing a key (or any other small object) around the circle, keeping it hidden in their hands. When she reaches ten, the hunter opens her eyes and—while the key continues to be passed—tries to figure out which player has it.

This task is not as easy as it sounds, because while one player actually passes the key, all the other players pretend to pass a key. The hunter watches and watches until she is ready to guess who has the key. When the hunter calls the suspect player's name, the passing immediately stops, and the suspect then opens his hands for all to see.

If the hunter is right, she is the winner and the player with the key becomes the hunter. If the hunter is wrong, she closes her eyes and starts counting to ten again. If she fails to find the key after three tries, another player takes over as hunter.

Hunt the Ring

The goal of Hunt the Ring is the same as Hunt the Key, but in this version players stand in a circle holding on to a piece of string that is long enough to go all the way around the circle—and the hunter seeks a small curtain ring (or other similar-size ring) instead of a key. The ring is threaded onto the string, and the ends of the string are tied together with a knot that is small enough to let the ring slide over it.

Each player in the circle holds the string in front with both hands. As in Hunt the Key, the hunter closes his eyes and counts to ten while the others begin passing the ring around the circle. The players keep their hands over the ring to hide it and make fake passes to confuse the hunter. In this game the hunter touches the hand of the player he suspects has the ring. If the hunter is right, they switch places; if not, the game goes on. All players should get a chance to be the hunter.

Treasure Hunt

On a voyage of discovery, players follow a series of clues to a hidden treasure.

Players: 2 or more, plus an adult or older child to set up and supervise

Ages: 7 to 12

Place: Indoors in large room or outdoors in yard or other play area

Equipment: Pencil and paper; tape; prize, such as candy or small toy

Kids love a Treasure Hunt because there's a prize at the end. It's also a wonderful game for helping them learn to decode riddles and clues. The difficulty of the hunt can be adjusted to the age of the players, with obvious clues for younger hunters and trickier ones for experienced explorers.

This game is best played outside, where the hunting area can be much larger, but it can also be played indoors on a smaller scale. To set up the game, an adult (or older child) plants a series of clues (in the form of written notes) taped on or next to or inside objects scattered across the hunting area. Each clue contains information that leads to the next clue in the sequence, and the final clue leads to a treasure. For example, in a backyard treasure hunt, the adult might plant a note on a doghouse that, when found, will lead the hunter to a garden hose, on which another clue will be found, sending the hunter to a swing for another clue (and so on). The first clue in the sequence is always given out at the beginning of the hunt.

What really makes the game fun is the challenge presented by the clues themselves. They don't have to be simple directions ("Take ten steps backward and look behind you"). Instead, they can take the form of riddles. For example, for a garden hose, the clue might be: "I'm full of water, but I don't get wet." For a swing, it could be: "I fly in the air, but I never go anywhere." It's up to the treasure hunters to decode these clues to find the next one. Players will appreciate as much creativity as possible in the clues—clever rhymes are especially welcome!

The person who sets up the hunt should make sure that the clues lead smoothly from one spot to the next, and that no clue is placed so close to the treasure that the prize could be found accidentally. The longer the game—that is, the more clues and objects along the way—the more delightful it is (although it's also more work for the person setting it up). No matter how many clues are used, the next-to-last object provides the clue to finding the hidden treasure: candy, a small toy, or a similar prize.

A treasure hunt can be noncompetitive, with players working through the clues together to find one large prize or several small prizes waiting at the end. Or the hunt can be played competitively with individuals or teams racing to discover the treasure. In that case, the adult needs to prepare a separate series of clues (containing the same number of clues) for each individual or team. Since this can be a bit time-consuming, it's a good idea (good for the adult) to form teams whenever there are more than three players. In the competitive version, the first individual or team to find the prize wins the hunt.

Scavenger Hunt

In this absorbing hunt game, players compete to find all the objects on a list.

Players: 2 or more, plus an adult or older child to set up and supervise

Ages: 7 to 14

Place: Indoors (throughout home) or outdoors in yard or other play area

Equipment: Piece of paper and plastic or paper sack for each player; pencil; timer; small items (coins, paper clips, pens, small toys, etc.) to hide (optional)

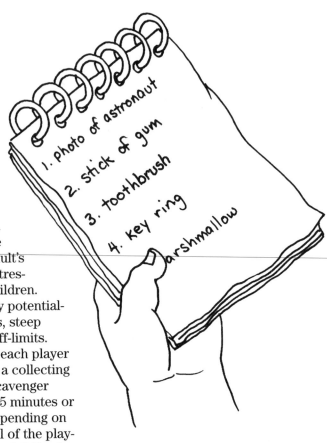

There are two ways to stage a Scavenger Hunt. In the first, usually played indoors, the players search for a list of items that can be found around the home. In the second, they hunt for familiar items that can be found outdoors. Both games are fun and challenging for any child old enough to read a list and persevere through a long search. Although usually thought of as a party game, a clever Scavenger Hunt delights children any day of the year.

If the Scavenger Hunt is held indoors, an adult or older child prepares a list of items for each player after making sure each item can be found in the home. Good ideas include small balls and toys, photographs, coins, paper clips, erasers, playing cards, and candies. For younger children, the list should simply be an inventory of items to find. For older kids, the list might instead contain more playful directions, such as "Find something that goes in your mouth." The item in question could be a piece of gum, a toothbrush, or a box of raisins.

If the hunt is planned for outdoors, the list should contain items that can be found in the neighborhood. In a suburban area, for example, the list might include a smooth rock, a forked stick, a brown leaf, and a seed. For a more challenging search, the list can be more specific: an earthworm, an evergreen leaf, a holly berry, and a piece of slate, for example. It's important to establish boundaries for the search. The best bet is to limit the hunt to the supervising adult's yard or property to avoid trespassing and wandering children. Also, be sure to define any potentially dangerous areas (ponds, steep inclines, etc.) as strictly off-limits.

At the start of the hunt, each player is given a copy of the list, a collecting bag, and a time limit. A Scavenger Hunt can last as little as 15 minutes or as long as a few hours, depending on the age and attention level of the players as well as the length and difficulty of the list.

Now the players set off to hunt for their booty. The player who's the first to find everything on her list or the one to find the most objects in the time allotted is the winner. A scavenger hunt can also be played in teams—with two groups competing to be the first to collect all the required items.

Magazine Scavenger Hunt

Generally played indoors, this version of Scavenger Hunt requires a stack of old magazines (or catalogs) and a pair of scissors for each player. The hunters try to find certain words or pictures in the magazines. To play the game, one player makes a list of things to hunt for, such as "a picture of a baby" or "an article with the word 'food' in the title." Each child then searches for those items and uses scissors—safety scissors are recommended for young children—to cut them from the magazines. The first player to collect everything on his list is the winner. Magazine searches can also be included as part of a standard Scavenger Hunt.

Personalized Scavenger Hunt

In this funny variation of Scavenger Hunt, the other players serve as the hunting ground! This version is more fun when it's played with teams. Participants are given a list of items that are likely to be found on or in the possession of the other players. The list might include keys, glasses, jewelry, pens, combs, hair clips, tissues, coins, or even articles of clothing. Each team (or player) tries to be the first to collect everything on the list, searching first on their own team members and then trading with other teams. The first team (or player) to locate everything on its list is declared the winner.

Hide-and-Seek

In this classic game, the hiders try to reach home base before the seeker.

> **Players:** 3 or more
>
> **Ages:** 5 to 12
>
> **Place:** Indoors or outdoors in area with good hiding places for kids
>
> **Equipment:** None

Children have been playing Hide-and-Seek for thousands of years. Champion Hide-and-Seek players are clever when choosing their cover, crafty when timing their escape, quick when running for home, and stealthy when they are "it." Whether the game is being played indoors or out, the boundaries of the hiding area should be established before the game begins, and kids should be warned about unsafe hiding places, such as empty refrigerators, crawl spaces, or abandoned buildings.

The first order of business for a game of Hide-and-Seek is to choose someone to be "it"—the player who will search for all the others after they have hidden themselves. If the game is being played outdoors, a home base is also established. This could be a tree, porch, patio, or part of the wall of a building.

When everyone is ready to begin, the player designated "it" closes her eyes and counts to 50 or 100 while the other players race to find hiding places. When "it" has finished counting, she yells, "Ready or not, here I come," and sets out to find the hidden players. Players who are found and tagged are out for the rest of the game.

If the game is played outdoors, the action can be taken up a notch. In this version, instead of tagging a player, the minute "it" sees a hider, she yells, "One, two, three on _____ [the player's name]!" Then, the two players race for home. If "it" reaches home first, the player is caught. If the hider wins the race, he shouts, "Home free!" or "Allie, Allie, oxen free!" and is safe. Players may also come out of hiding and try to sneak to home base when "it" isn't looking.

If "it" is staying so close to the base that no player can run home, the first player to be found can call, "Base sticking!" If this happens, "it" must move farther away from the base. In fact, it's a good idea to establish a zone of about 50 feet (15m) around the base where no player may hide. "It" is then required to venture out of that area to seek the hiders.

The game continues until everyone is caught or is home free. The first person to be caught is "it" in the next round. If the game is being played indoors without a base, the first person to be found is "it" in the next round.

I Spy

This version of Hide-and-Seek is played like the standard game, except that upon seeing a hider, "it" runs back to home base and yells out the hider's name and location: "I spy _____ [the player's name] under the steps!" for example. If "it" is correct about both the name and location, the hider is captured. To avoid this, a hider can try to run for home if she thinks she's been spotted. If she gets there before "it" can say, "I spy . . ." she's home free. I Spy is especially challenging when played at dusk.

Sheep and Wolf

In this version of Hide-and-Seek, the hiders and seekers change roles: the "wolf" hides while all the "sheep" close their eyes until the wolf howls. The sheep then look around for the wolf. When the wolf is spotted, the player who sees him yells, "I see a wolf!" The wolf then chases the sheep and tries to tag one before the sheep reaches home. If a sheep gets caught, he becomes the next wolf. If, however, no sheep are caught before making it back home, the wolf remains the wolf for the next round.

Cops and Robbers

In this hide-and-seek game, the robbers try to avoid being caught by the cops.

Players: 6 or more (even number)

Ages: 6 to 11

Place: Outdoors in area with good hiding places for kids

Equipment: None

Cooperation is key in this hide, seek, and chase game. Besides the thrill of the hunt and chase, Cops and Robbers offers the excitement of pitting the "good guys" against the "bad guys."

First, players divide into two equal teams and decide who will be the "cops" and who will be the "robbers." Next, a home base, or "jail," is selected. Trees, porches, patios, and stoops all

make good jails. The cops cluster around the home base, close their eyes, and count to 50 (or 100) while the robbers hide. The cops then set out to apprehend the criminals. Any robber a cop manages to find and tag is considered captured.

Captured robbers are brought back

to jail, and there they must remain unless another robber stages a "jail break." A jail break is set in motion when one of the uncaptured robbers sneaks up to the jail and tags it without being tagged by a cop. Immediately, all the jail inmates are freed, although they must sit out the rest of the game, until the cops have "arrested" all the robbers still at large.

At the end of a round, when all the robbers have been tagged, the players count the number of robbers still in jail. This could be the whole team of robbers if there were no successful jail breaks. Or it could be only one robber if there was a jail break right before the end of the round. Now the teams switch roles, with the robbers becoming cops and vice versa. Once the new cops have rounded up the new robbers, the jail population is again totaled. The team that captured the most criminals wins.

Kick the Can

This hide-and-seek game adds the risk of capture and the clank of an aluminum can.

Players: 3 or more

Ages: 6 to 12

Place: Outdoors in area with good hiding places for kids and away from windows

Equipment: Aluminum can

Kick the Can was historically played in the city, where the can made a satisfying clatter on the pavement. In this hunt-and-capture game the players band together

against "it," who is trying to find and imprison the bunch. Kick the Can is best played in a large outdoor play area where there is nothing (such as a house window) that could be damaged by a flying can.

Before beginning, a home base is established—it can be a stump, rock, manhole cover, garbage can lid, or circle drawn in the dirt—and the can is set beside it on the ground. One player is chosen to be "it." To begin the game, "it" kicks the can as far as possible and all the other players run and hide. "It" must retrieve the can (in

some versions of the game, "it" must touch the can only with his feet), place it next to home base, and then close his eyes and count to 50.

All the other players should have found hiding places by the time "it" finishes counting. At this point, he yells out, "Ready or not, here I come!" and starts searching for the hiders. When "it" finds someone, he runs to home base, bangs the can on the ground, and calls the hider's name, followed by "Kick the can, one, two, three!" The discovered player is now officially captured and must come and stand near home base. "It" goes back on the prowl, continuing to round up prisoners.

There is a way for prisoners to escape, and that is for one of the remaining hiders to make a dash for home base while "it" is out hunting and kick the can (at the same time shouting, "Home free"). The captives are then free to rush off and hide again, and "it" must retrieve the can and return it to home base before looking for hiders again. But if "it" happens to spot the brave rescuer heading for the can and manages to touch home base before she kicks it, then the prisoners are stuck where they are. And "it" can now call the

rescuer's name, bang the can on the ground, and send her to jail.

The game goes on until all the hiders have been captured. The next "it" is the first player captured since the last "Home free." If the game goes on too long because of too many "Home frees," players may decide that the first player to be captured three times becomes "it."

Ghost in the Graveyard

This spooky twilight game combines features of Tag and Hide-and-Seek.

Players: 3 or more

Ages: 8 to 14

Place: Outdoors in large area with good hiding places for kids

Equipment: None

Ghost in the Graveyard takes advantage of the cover of growing darkness to create a special kind of run-and-chase contest. In a reversal of the usual hide-and-seek roles, the player who is "it" hides while the others count. But the biggest difference is that instead of waiting to be found, the "ghost" actually stalks the seekers. Kids will find it deliciously spooky to run around while waiting for an apparition to pop up and try to grab them.

Choose a nice, big area to set up the game. All that's needed is a tree, porch, or other large, stationary object to serve as home base. Since the game is played at dusk, make sure the playing area is safe and free of things like sprinklers, tree roots, or anything else that could trip up a night-blind ghoul.

First, one player is chosen to be the ghost. While all the other players close their eyes and count to 50 (or 100) at home base, the ghost hides. Next, the players set out on a ghost-hunting mission. As they search for the ghost, the ghost tries to take them by surprise and to tag as many players as possible

before they make it back to home base. It's bad form to stay too close to home base, and older children may want to make a rule that no one is allowed to stay within a certain distance of the base. Any player who spots the ghost yells to warn the others to dash home. Those tagged by the ghost are out until the end of the round, which comes when all the players are either tagged or have reached home safely.

At the end of each round, the players who have reached the base safely close their eyes and count to 50 (or 100) again. All the players who were tagged in previous rounds become ghosts and team up with the original ghoul to chase down the remaining players. The last player to remain "alive" is the winner.

Sardines

In this hiding game, players end up packed together like sardines in a can.

Players: 6 or more

Ages: 7 to 12

Place: Indoors or outdoors in area with good hiding places for kids

Equipment: None

In this game full of wiggles and giggles, the biggest challenge is to keep from giving the hiding place away by laughing. Instead of one "it" searching for all the other players, each player seeks to *join* the others in one hiding spot. Sardines is most fun when played in an area with lots of safe places to hide.

To begin, all players except one close their eyes. The open-eyed player hides while the others count to 100.

The hiding space should be just roomy enough for several children, but not too big. Good choices are behind a curtain, under a large bed, in a closet, behind a leafy bush, or under a slide.

When the counting is finished, a second player searches for the first while the others keep their eyes closed and count to 100 again. If the first player is found, the second joins him in the hiding place. If not, the seeker is out of the game. Play continues in this manner until each child has had a chance to be the seeker.

The game is over when all the players have had their turn to seek. All the sardines packed in the hiding spot are winners.

Ring-a-Levio

Older children enjoy teaming up for this game involving prisoners, borders, and guards.

Players: 10 or more (even number)

Ages: 7 to 13

Place: Outdoors in large yard or other play area

Equipment: Stones or sticks for marking borders

Ring-a-Levio is team hide-and-seek raised to a high level. Instead of just a home base, this game has a "den" and a "danger area," which are marked out and patrolled by a guard. To play, kids need to understand the concept of imaginary borders and must be interested in cooperative play.

Before the game begins, participants divide into two equal teams. Next, a den is designated in the center of the playing area. The den should be about 5 feet (1.5m) square, with its corners marked with stones or sticks. Players then mark out a danger area, which should be a 30-foot (9m) square, with the den at its center; this larger square should also be marked off with stones or sticks.

Each team chooses a "den warden," or guard to watch over the den. All the members of one team stand inside the den with their eyes closed while the other team runs and hides. When everyone on the hiding team has found a hiding place, the hiders' den warden yells, "Ready!" At that signal, the players on the search team quickly fan out to try to capture their opponents. When a hider is found, she is brought back to the den and kept there as a prisoner.

The searchers' den warden stays near the den and guards the inmates, and he may not wander outside the danger area. The prisoners can escape only if one of their teammates sneaks past the den warden, gets both feet inside the den, and shouts, "Ring-a-Levio!" As the inmates run out, the den warden can try to recapture them—but he may do so only within the danger area. If they make it past that border, they are free.

The game continues until all of the hiders have been captured—or until the players tire out. The hiders and the seekers switch roles for the next round of play.

Races and Relays

Nothing is quite as exhilarating as running a race—
except possibly winning one. The races in this chapter are as varied
as the children who will run, walk, creep, or hop in them. Included
are passing races, races of skill, races of timing, and races of balance.
Some of the races are run by individuals, and some are relay races
that require team participation. Many make great party games,
although they are by no means limited to party play. A number
require some props or equipment, as noted in the entries. The entries
also indicate whether a race is best conducted indoors or outdoors.
All these races and relays require adult supervision to make sure no
one gets injured.

Obstacle Course

Players compete to navigate the Obstacle Course in the shortest period of time.

Players: 2 or more, plus an adult to set up and supervise

Ages: 3 and up

Place: Outdoors in yard, park, or field

Equipment: Obstacles to create the course (such as lawn furniture, playground equipment, garden hose, string, sprinkler, hula hoops, empty crates, beach ball, paper plates, water balloons); stopwatch or other timer; pencil and paper for scoring; balls or other props (optional)

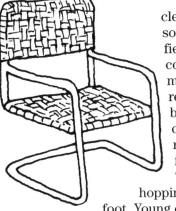

An Obstacle Course is endlessly enjoyable because it is never the same race twice. The goal is to complete a series of physical challenges faster than anyone else. The difficulty of the course depends on the skill level of the participants—the course can be modified for children of different ages, from 3 years on up.

This game definitely requires an adult to supervise the course's construction and to make sure no one gets hurt. Children have a tendency to try to perform feats that are too difficult for them. Also, there should be absolutely no running with sharp objects or anything that could be

harmful if fallen on. Only one child should be allowed on the course at a time. Setting up the course is half the fun, however, so children should be allowed to contribute their ideas—and their energy—to the task.

An Obstacle Course can be set up in a yard, a park, or any similar play area. A backyard course might include lawn furniture: chairs and chaise lounges are perfect for climbing over and slithering under. A garden hose or rope can be twisted into a tortuous track that players walk or hop along with one foot on either side. Or they can do a "tightrope walk" along a hose that curves around and doubles back on itself. Hula hoops can be laid on the ground for players to hop through. Kids might also jump over a row of strategically placed sticks or weave between trees. A large cardboard box with the ends cut off can serve as a tunnel. In hot weather, a moving sprinkler adds water-dodging fun. The possibilities are endless. Swing sets, jungle gyms, slides, and other playground equipment can also be included if the course is for children over 6.

To liven things up, the children might be required to maneuver the course holding a beach ball or balancing a table tennis ball on a paper plate. When that gets too easy, they can try carrying an armful of water balloons. Another "handicap" is wearing a large hat while running the course—if it comes off, it's back to the starting line.

Running the course properly can also be made to involve silly rules, like jumping up and down three times after completing an obsta-

cle or singing a song at a specified point in the course. Players might be required to bark like dogs, crow like roosters, or flap their "wings" while hopping on one foot. Young children in particular delight in such zany stunts.

Once the course is laid out, the adult who's supervising the game should walk the players through it and demonstrate what to do at each of the

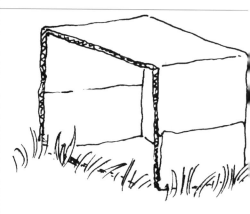

obstacles. Players then take turns running the course while being timed. For each child, the adult calls out, "Ready, set, go!" and then starts the stopwatch (or other timer). If an obstacle is not navigated correctly, the onlookers yell out to the runner and he must run back and keep trying that obstacle until he gets it right. Each player's time is marked on a scoresheet. The player who completes the course in the shortest amount of time is the winner.

A variation on this theme is Obstacle Course Follow the Leader, which requires the child to remember what the last runner did at each point in the course and then to imitate it.

Toesies

Rolling across the carpet (or grass) toe-to-toe is the aim of this game.

Players: 2 or more (even number), plus an adult to supervise

Ages: 3 to 8

Place: Indoors in large room with carpet or mats (cleared of furniture and breakable objects), or outdoors on grass on warm day

Equipment: None

This simple contest is amusing for young children. The idea of joining toes and rolling along the ground seems easy enough, but players who try their feet at Toesies usually get hilarious results. This is a game of cooperation not competition.

To begin, two players lie down feet to feet on a mat, cushy carpet, or lawn. Toesies should be played in a warm place because the participants must be barefoot. At a signal, the two players try to roll across the ground together, keeping their toes touching all the while.

If four or more players are participating—and the playing area is wide enough—teams may have a Toesies race. The first pair to cross the finish line without ever losing touch with each other's toes is the winner.

Apple on a String

In this Halloween favorite, players race to consume apples suspended from strings.

Players: 2 or more, plus an adult to set up and supervise

Ages: 4 to 10

Place: Outdoors or indoors, anywhere string can be hung from a height and eating is allowed

Equipment: Apple or cookie for each player; string; darning needle (for adult use only) and buttons (optional); clothesline (optional)

The Apple on a String race is a Halloween standard that is also popular for birthday parties. It takes a bit of preparation to set up the game, but young children will appreciate the effort. This is a good contest for mixed ages.

First, an adult must manage to suspend an apple from a string for each player. The classic way to do this is to thread a darning needle with a string that has a large button knotted at the end and then to pass the needle through the apple so that the button rests on the bottom and the needle comes out on top. (The string may also be tied to the apple's stem, if the stem is secure.) Cookies may be used in place of apples—they're easier to string up and also easier to eat. The apples or cookies should be hung so that they hang down to the level of the players' chins. Stringing a clothesline across the playing area and then hanging the apples from it is one effective way to do this.

Each child stands in front of his treat with his hands behind his back. At the start signal, each tries to take a bite out of the apple (or cookie). If the players' efforts are futile, they may be given the hint to swing the apple back and forth—by pushing it with a cheek or forehead—and then to try to bite the apple on the backswing. The first player to eat her apple down to the core, or the one who has eaten the most after a specified time, is the winner.

Red Light, Green Light

Players must obey the rules of the road as they race toward the "light."

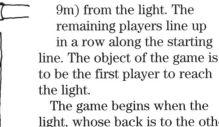

Players: 4 or more, plus an adult to supervise

Ages: 5 to 10

Place: Outdoors on grass or pavement

Equipment: Stones, sticks, or chalk for marking line

Red Light, Green Light is a classic racing game. One of the reasons it has remained popular through so many generations may be that it's a very good game for a group with mixed ages. In Red Light, Green Light, the ability to follow directions and stop and start on command is just as important as speed. The player who moves the *least* over the course of the game may actually win the race.

First, one player is chosen to be the "light." The light stands facing a tree or wall. A starting line is marked on the ground about 20 to 30 feet (6 to 9m) from the light. The remaining players line up in a row along the starting line. The object of the game is to be the first player to reach the light.

The game begins when the light, whose back is to the other players, calls, "Green light!" That's the signal for the runners to move forward as quickly as possible. At any moment, usually quite quickly, the light calls, "Red light!" and whips around to face the players. As soon as "Red light" is called, the runners must stop in their tracks. If the light sees anyone moving a muscle, that player is sent back to the starting line.

After the light is satisfied that all traffic offenders have been caught, she turns around again and calls, "Green light!" The game continues in the same manner. The first player to reach and tag the light is the winner and becomes the next light.

Mother, May I?

Children must follow "Mother's" directions to reach the finish line.

Players: 4 or more, plus an adult to supervise

Ages: 6 to 12

Place: Outdoors on grass or pavement

Equipment: Stones, sticks, or chalk for marking lines

In Mother, May I? the maternal figure is a powerful rule setter who can play favorites with her "children" if she likes. So it's not hard to understand why being "Mother" is the coveted role in this game. What child doesn't love the chance to give orders and be in complete control? Luckily, it's fun (if challenging) to be one of the racing "children," too, and the best game is one in which every player gets a chance to play both roles.

First, starting and finish lines are marked about 25 feet (7.5m) apart, and one player—a girl or a boy—is chosen to be Mother. Mother stands at the finish line facing the other players, who line up in a row on the starting line.

Each player in turn must ask Mother for permission to move ahead. The first might ask, "Mother, may I take three giant steps?" Mother responds in any way she sees fit. She may, for example, answer, "No, but you may take ten baby steps," or "No, but you may take three hops." This instruction is not enough, however, to allow the player to move. The player must again beg permission by asking, "Mother, may I?" If Mother says, "Yes, you may," the player moves forward as directed. But Mother may reconsider: if Mother says, "No, you may not," the player is not allowed to move.

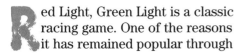

If the player forgets to ask permission to move ahead or moves in the wrong way, he must go back to the starting line. Each player in turn makes his request of Mother, and Mother continues to lay down the law.

The game continues in this manner until one player—of Mother's choosing, of course—crosses the finish line and is declared the winner.

Classic Relay

Smooth teamwork and swift feet are the basic elements in this race.

Players: 6 or more (divisible into equal teams), plus an adult to supervise

Ages: 5 to 14

Place: Outdoors on grass or pavement

Equipment: Baton (or stick); stones, sticks, or chalk for marking lines

The Classic Relay is an ancient competition that was as much a mainstay of the ancient Greek Olympics as it is of the modern Olympic Games. Although relays have been varied and modified almost beyond recognition, the classic running relay is the perfect combination of teamwork, timing, and speed.

Players divide into two or more equal teams of three to five players. Depending on the ages of the runners and the sizes of the teams, the finish line may be marked on the ground 40 to 100 yards (roughly 40 to 100m) away from the starting line. Runners are placed at equal intervals along the course—for example, if each team has four runners and the course is 100 yards or meters long, runners would be positioned at the starting line, the 25-yard (25m) line, the 50-yard (50m) line, and the 75-yard (75m) line.

The first runner on each team carries a baton—a smooth stick of wood 1 to 2 feet (30 to 60cm) long will do nicely. Once everyone is in position, the adult who's supervising the race shouts, "Ready, set, go!" The first runner on each team dashes to the second runner and hands her the baton. The second runner does the same with the third runner, and so on, until the last runner has the baton. He runs with it to the finish line. During the race, no runner may move until she is holding the baton. The team whose last runner crosses the finish line first, without dropping the baton, is the winner.

An alternative way to set up a Classic Relay is to mark a starting and a turning line about 30 to 50 feet (9 to 15m) apart. Each team lines up single file behind the starting line, with the runner in front holding the baton. At the signal "Go!," the runner at the head of each line races to the turning line, turns around, and sprints back to the starting line. The baton is passed to the next team member in line, and the finished runner goes to the back of the line. This is repeated until every player has had a chance to run the relay. The first team to have all their runners complete the course is named the winner.

Bunny Hop Relay

In this bouncy rabbit race, teams hop their way to the finish line.

Players: 8 to 30 (divisible into equal teams), plus an adult to supervise

Ages: 4 to 8

Place: Outdoors on grass or pavement

Equipment: Stones, sticks, and chalk for marking lines

Bunny Hop Relay is a fun twist on a classic relay for very young contestants. Small children love bouncing around the yard like lively little bunnies.

Before beginning, two lines are

marked on the ground at least 15 feet (4.5m) apart; these are the starting and turning lines. The children are divided into two or more equal teams of four or five players, and the teams line up single file behind the starting line.

Once everyone's in position, the adult who's supervising the race calls out, "Ready, set, go!" The first player on each team races to the turning line hopping like a bunny (squatting, with arms around his knees, and jumping along). The racer rounds the turning line and heads back to the start. The next player in line may go only when the first has crossed the starting line. The first team to have all its hoppers make it out and back is the winner.

Kangaroo Relay

In this variation, which can be enjoyed by kids up to 10, players jump rather than run. The "kangaroos" stand upright on both feet and jump as far as possible, keeping both feet together. They must rely on the spring in their knees and heels and strong leg muscles to propel them. The setup and rules are the same as in the Bunny Hop Relay, except that the starting and turning lines are set farther apart—about 30 feet (9m). This race may require a bit more strength and coordination than the Bunny Hop.

Newspaper Walk

In this race each runner stays on top of the news by keeping a newspaper under their feet.

Players: 2 or more, plus an adult to supervise

Ages: 5 to 10

Place: Indoors in large room with smooth floor (cleared of furniture and breakable objects)

Equipment: 2 sheets of newsprint paper for each player; masking tape or chalk for marking lines (optional)

A more fitting name for Newspaper Walk might well be Newspaper Shuffle, because that's the motion of this race. Run individually or as a relay, this party race is a great change of pace because it allows the slower runners a chance for victory. This game should be played indoors on a smooth floor. It's best to use sheets of newsprint paper (available at art supply stores), rather than actual newspapers, because newspa-per ink may leave stains and is messy to clean up.

The race may be run from wall to wall, or starting and finish lines can be marked on the ground about 20 to 30 feet (6 to 9m) apart. To begin, players take off their shoes and each participant or team is given two sheets of newsprint. The players line up at the starting line—if teams are competing, they line up single file. An adult—or an older child or extra player (if there are teams)— acts as the starter.

Once everyone's in position, the starter signals, "Ready, set, go!" and the runners place a sheet of paper under each foot and start off toward the finish line. Feet must stay on the paper sheets at all times—if any part of a foot touches the floor, the player must return to the starting line and begin again. Runners try to achieve a smooth, gliding shuffle to speed their progress. A player whose paper tears must continue gliding on whatever scrap she has left.

If Newspaper Walk is being run as a straight race, the first player to cross the finish line is the winner. The race may be run in groups of a few children at a time if there's not enough room for everyone to participate at once. The winners from each group can then face off.

If the game is being played as a relay race, each player travels to the far wall (or turning line) and back, then steps off the sheets of paper. The next team member then steps onto the paper and runs the course. If the paper tears, team members must continue with whatever morsel is left. The first team to have all its members make it to the far wall and back is the winner.

One-Foot Relay

In this challenging race, players must hop the course on one foot.

Players: 6 or more (divisible into equal teams), plus an adult to supervise

Ages: 6 to 12

Place: Outdoors on grass or pavement

Equipment: Stones, sticks, or chalk for marking lines

The One-Foot Relay is true to its name—the object of the game is to "run" the entire race while hopping on one foot. Because children develop at different rates, it is important to find out whether everyone knows how to hop. Most children are able to hop distances by about age 6.

First, two lines are marked on the ground 20 to 30 feet (6 to 9m) apart; these are the starting and turning lines. Then, the players divide into two or more equal teams of at least three players, and each team picks a captain. The teams line up single file behind their captains at the starting line.

Once everyone's in position, the adult who's supervising the game cries, "Ready, set, go!" and the first child on each team hops to the turning line on one foot. If the other foot touches the ground, the player must return to the starting line and begin again. At the turning line, the hopper switches feet, hops back to the team, and tags the next player. Each member of the team hops the course in this manner.

The first team to have all its hoppers complete the course is declared the winner.

Mixed Relay

Variety is the spice of the Mixed Relay, in which every player moves in a different way.

Players: 6 or more (divisible into equal teams), plus an adult to supervise

Ages: 6 to 14

Place: Outdoors on grass or pavement

Equipment: Stones, sticks, or chalk for marking lines; ball for each team (optional)

A Mixed Relay is a creative sort of race. Each runner on a team must traverse the course moving in a different way, and there's no end to the variety of methods to choose from: skipping, cartwheeling, moon-walking, marching, or just about anything else. Balls add even more novelty to the race—older players can add rolling, bouncing, dribbling, and catching to their repertories.

First, two lines are marked on the ground 30 to 50 feet apart (9 to 15m); these are the starting and turning lines. Next, the players divide into two or more equal teams of three to five players, and each team lines up single file behind the starting line. All the players together then decide how each player in line will run the race. The first players on each team might, for example, be required to hop; the second players might be required to run backward; the third players to walk toe to heel; and the fourth players to race pigeon-toed.

Once these decisions have been made and everyone's in position, the adult who's supervising yells, "Ready, set, go!" and the first runner from each team sets off as quickly as possible—in the prescribed manner—to the turning line and back again. As soon as the first player has crossed back over the starting line, the next runner journeys in the predetermined style to the turning line and back. This continues until each team member has had a chance to race.

The first team to have all its runners complete the course is the winner. For a longer race, each player is required to run the course with every motion, so the players must run as many times as there are members of the team (four turns each for four players, for example). In this version, all the players, in turn, use the first motion; then each, in turn, does the second; and so on, until the last player finishes with the last motion.

Three-Legged Race

Cooperation is key in the Three-Legged Race, since players are literally tied to their partners.

Players: 4 or more (even number), plus an adult to supervise

Ages: 6 to 14

Place: Outdoors on grass

Equipment: Large scarf or bandanna for each pair of players or each team; stones or sticks for marking lines

Players get up close and personal in the Three-Legged Race, a classic picnic game in which partners' legs are tied together. To keep falling to a minimum, pairs should be composed of children of similar heights. A soft surface is a must for this hobbling race—there are sure to be lots of spills and thrills.

The Three-Legged Race can be run as either an individual race or a relay. First, starting and finish lines are marked off on the ground about 30 to 50 feet (9 to 15m) apart. Then, whether it's an individual race or a relay, every player must find a partner. The two partners in each pair stand side by side, with one arm each around the other's shoulder and their inside legs tied together (loosely, please!) with a bandanna or scarf. If the race is being run as a relay, the pairs are divided into two equal teams. The couples or the teams of couples (lined up in *double* file) then stand together behind the starting line.

When everyone's in position, the supervisor yells, "Ready, set, go!" and the couples—or the first couple on each team—run toward the finish line. It takes a while for couples to establish a smooth motion together. If a couple falls, they must maneuver themselves back into an upright position and continue the race. If the race is a relay, the pair turns at the finish line and races back to tag the next couple on their team. Each couple completes the course in turn.

The first couple to cross the finish line, or the first team to have all its couples complete the course, is the winner.

Back-to-Back Race

Running back-to-back isn't easy, so it takes a lot of cooperation to win this race.

Players: 4 or more (even number), plus an adult to supervise

Ages: 6 to 11

Place: Outdoors on grass

Equipment: Stones, sticks, or chalk for marking lines

The Back-to-Back Race may be played as either a straight race or a relay. This contest takes some real coordination, so it's not appropriate for preschoolers. Kids are sure to be entertained by the awkwardness of this exercise. This race requires an even number of players, since it is run in pairs.

To begin, two lines are marked on the ground 20 feet (6m) or more apart; these are the starting and turning lines. If the race is run as a straight race, each player stands back-to-back with her partner and hooks elbows. The pairs line up at the starting line. When everyone is in position, the adult supervising the race yells, "Ready, set, go!" and the pairs move toward the turning line—running in whatever fashion they find quickest and most efficient. Usually one player moves forward and the other back-

ward, but they're permitted to both run sideways or switch to different methods as they move. They may not, however, unlink elbows at any time during the race. On reaching the turning line, they turn around and head back to the starting line. The first pair to make it all the way out and back wins.

If the race is run as a relay, each team forms a line of pairs behind the starting line. The first pair on a team takes off, racing to the turning line and back. Only when the first pair has returned and crossed the starting line may the team's second pair begin its segment of the race. Relay teams may have as many pairs as necessary to give every child a chance to participate. The first team to have all its pairs cross the finish line is declared the winner.

Leapfrog

Leapfroggers hop over each other's backs in a bouncy race to the finish line.

Players: 6 or more (divisible into equal teams), plus an adult to supervise

Ages: 7 to 12

Place: Outdoors, preferably on grass

Equipment: Stones or sticks for marking lines

This hopping good time should be in every child's repertory of games. Its appeal lies in the gleeful fun of hopping over a friend's back with legs flying and the fact that a game of Leapfrog can be played almost anywhere outdoors (preferably on grass) with almost any number of kids.

First, a starting line and a finish line are marked on the ground anywhere from 50 to 100 feet (15 to 30m) apart, and the players divide into two or more equal teams. The first player on each team then squats down at the starting line with her palms flat on the ground and her chin tucked into her chest. The other players line up behind her.

When everyone is in position, the adult supervisor cries, "Ready, set, go!" and the second player on each team runs up to his squatting teammate, places his hands on the stooped player's shoulders, and vaults over her with legs spread apart. After "leapfrogging" over the first player, the second player squats down in the same way on the spot where she landed. The third player then leaps over both of the others, one at a time, toward the finish line.

When all the players on a team have leaped and are squatting in a line, the child at the end stands up and leapfrogs down the line. The pattern repeats itself as each player gets up and leapfrogs as soon as she is hopped over. The first team to get all of its members over the finish line is named the winner.

Crab Relay

Players don't have to be "crabby" to run this race, but they do need to know how to crawl like a crab.

Players: 8 to 30 (divisible into equal teams), plus an adult to supervise

Ages: 7 to 12

Place: Outdoors on grass

Equipment: Stones, sticks, or chalk for marking lines

This variation of the traditional relay race is quite challenging because the participants must travel the course crawling sideways like crabs! To get into the "crab" position, the runner lies on her back and then props herself up on arms and legs—it's a good idea to have an experienced "crab" demonstrate this position and the sideways crab motion, to uninitiated crustaceans.

First, two lines are marked on the ground 15 to 20 feet (4.5 to 6m) apart; these are the starting and turning lines. (The race can be longer for older children, but not too long, since it's not easy to do the crab crawl.) The participants are divided into two or more equal teams of four or five players.

When the adult who's supervising the race shouts, "Ready, set, go!" the first player on each team sets out for the turning line scurrying like a crab—sideways. Each crab races to the turning line, then returns to the starting line. Once he's crossed the starting line, the next player on his team may go. Each player travels the course in turn. The first team to have all their crab crawlers complete the course is the winner.

Sack Race

In this old-fashioned picnic race, players hop in sacks to the finish line.

Players: 2 or more, plus an adult to supervise

Ages: 7 to 12

Place: Outdoors on grass or sand

Equipment: Burlap sack or old pillowcase for each player or team; stones or sticks for marking lines

The Sack Race is so much fun because it's such an unusual challenge. After all, it isn't every day that kids get to hop around in a sack or pillowcase. This race also involves a lot of falling down, providing some hearty laughs for the players who remain upright. Because of all the tumbles, the Sack Race should be run on a soft, forgiving surface, such as a grassy lawn or a sandy beach.

This game may be run as either an individual race or a relay. If run individually, each player receives a sack or pillowcase and lines up along a starting line. A finish line is marked about 30 feet (9m) away. The course may be shortened or lengthened depending on the age and skill of the participants.

When everyone is in position, the adult who's supervising the game cries, "Ready, set, go!" and each player climbs into his sack, holds it up around his body, and hops or hobbles toward the finish line. Novice sack racers quickly learn that trying to run in the sack results in tangled feet and a belly-flop onto the grass. The best way to move is with a series of long, smooth broad jumps. A player who falls must get back up and continue the race without taking her feet out of the sack. The first player to cross the finish line wins the race.

If the Sack Race is run as a relay, players divide into two or more equal teams and each team lines up single file behind the starting line. When the starter shouts the word, "go!" the first player in each line climbs into her team's sack and sets off. When she reaches the far boundary, she turns around and heads back to the starting line, where she gets out of the sack and passes it to the next player in line, who climbs into the sack and runs the course. The race continues until all the members of the team have had a turn in the sack. The first team to have all its racers complete the course is the winner.

Piggyback Race

One player carries the burden while the other gets a free ride in the Piggyback Race.

Players: 4 or more (even number), plus an adult to supervise

Ages: 8 to 12

Place: Outdoors on grass or sand

Equipment: Stones or sticks for marking lines

Kids seem to delight in carrying each other piggyback for no reason at all, so what could be more fun than a Piggyback Race? Children under 8 should not be carriers in this race—they don't have the strength or balance. Older children of about the same size can compete, or larger children may be permanent carriers and younger ones only riders. This race should be run on a soft

surface, such as grass or sand, to avoid injuries from the inevitable falls.

This race may be run by individual pairs or as a relay. Either way, two lines should be marked on the ground about 30 feet (9m) apart; these are the starting and turning lines. Players then divide into pairs or two or more equal teams of at least three pairs. Each pair or team then lines up behind the starting line.

As soon as everyone's in position, the adult who's supervising the race signals, "Ready, set, go!"—at which point one player from each pair (or from the first pair on a team) climbs up on her partner's back and wraps her arms loosely around the carrier's shoulders and her legs around the carrier's waist. The carrier, holding on to the rider's legs, then runs to the turning line, sets the rider down, and climbs onto the former rider's back. (Skip this step if players are not the same size.) The pair then races back to the start.

If the race is being run as a relay, the next pair runs the course after the first has returned, and so on down the line. The first pair or the first team to complete the course is the winner.

Wheelbarrow Race

In this funny race, human "wheelbarrows" are pushed toward the finish line.

Players: 4 or more (even number), plus an adult to supervise

Ages: 8 to 12

Place: Outdoors on grass or sand

Equipment: Stones or sticks for marking lines

The Wheelbarrow Race is another classic picnic race that must be run on a soft surface to avoid injury. Teamwork is a high priority in this race, as partners struggle to drive their human wheelbarrows as quickly as possible. Look for some dirty hands after this game. It's a good idea to have soap and water handy nearby.

The Wheelbarrow Race can be run as either an individual race or a relay. Either way, every player must have a partner. Starting and finish lines are marked on the ground about 30 feet (9m) apart. The pairs line up along the starting line. For a relay race, the players divide into two or more equal teams, whose members line up double file behind the starting line. Next, the pairs (or the first couples on the teams) get ready to adopt the wheel-

barrow position—one player gets down on hands and knees (or face down, flat on the ground) and the other stands behind.

When everyone's in position, the adult who's supervising the race shouts, "Ready, set, go!" and the standing player of each pair picks up his partner's legs and holds them by the ankles at waist height. The "driver" then proceeds to push the "wheelbarrow" toward the finish line as the wheelbarrow walks on her hands. Falls and mishaps are inevitable, and broken-down wheelbarrows must be picked up from the point where they collapsed.

In a relay race, the pairs travel to the far boundary and then they switch roles and race back to the start, tagging the next couple in line as they cross the starting line. This continues until all the pairs have run the race.

The first pair to cross the finish line or the first team to have all its pairs complete the course is the winner.

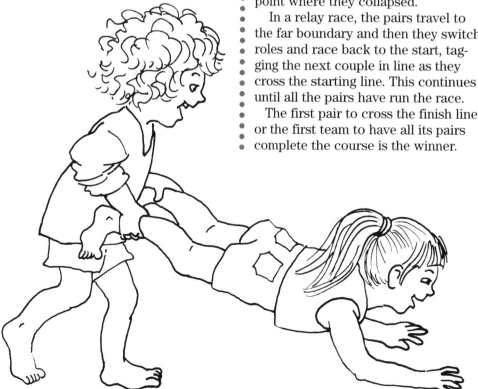

Dizzy Izzy

In this dizzying race, players try to make it to the finish line without swerving or falling.

Players: 2 to 20, plus an adult to supervise and additional adults or older children as spotters (if needed)

Ages: 8 to 12

Place: Outdoors on grass or pavement

Equipment: Baseball bat, broom handle, or yardstick for each player or team; stones, sticks, or chalk for marking lines; blindfolds (optional)

Dizzy Izzy lives up to its name—it's a race that players run only after spinning themselves around in circles. The discombobulated racers then compete to be the first to make it across the finish line. If Dizzy Izzy is played as an individual race, blindfolds may be added to make the contest even more difficult. If it's run as a relay, blindfolds are not used.

Before beginning, a starting and a finish line are marked off on the ground about 15 to 20 feet (4.5 to 6m) apart. For the individual race, all the players line up along the starting line. Each player holds a "stick"—a bat, yardstick, or broom handle. If the participants are blindfolded, there should be several spotters on hand to steer players clear of obstacles.

When all the contestants are in position, the adult who's supervising calls out, "Ready, set, go!" and each player places the bottom end of her stick on the ground and grips the top end with both hands. She then places her forehead on top of her hands and proceeds to spin her whole body around the stick three times. The players then stand up straight, drop the stick, and race to the finish line. Needless to say, with all the prior spinning, there's a lot of stumbling and bumbling, swerving and curving going on. And if the players are blindfolded, the confusion grows and the fun increases as players try to get their bearings. The first player to cross the finish line wins.

If Dizzy Izzy is played as a relay race, two or more equal teams line up single file behind the starting line, with a turning line marked on the ground 15 to 20 feet (4.5 to 6m) away. The first player on each team races to the turning line, where the sticks are waiting. He then rotates three times around the stick and returns dizzily to the starting line, where he tags the next player. Each succeeding player repeats the action in turn. The first team to have all its runners complete the course is the winner.

Pick and Cup

Players compete to pass an assortment of objects down the line in this easy party race.

Players: 8 or more (even number), plus an adult to supervise

Ages: 3 to 6

Place: Indoors in large room or outdoors on grass or pavement

Equipment: 2 identical piles of about 10 small objects (such as coins, beans, buttons, marbles, or candies)

Pick and Cup, which can be played equally well indoors or outdoors, is an simple passing race that is perfect for preschoolers.

Players are divided into two equal teams. The members of each team sit side by side in a line on the floor or ground facing the opposing team. A pile of ten or so objects is placed beside the first player in each line. Anything small enough to fit in the players' cupped hands may be used—coins, candies, buttons, beans, marbles, thimbles, and grapes are some examples. (But be sure kids know not to put these in their mouths.) Both teams should be given the same kind of objects so that the level of difficulty is exactly the same.

When everything is ready, the adult who's supervising the game shouts, "Ready, set, go!" and each line's leader picks up an object from his pile and drops it into the cupped hands of the next player. The third player then picks the object out of the second player's hands and deposits it into the cupped hands of the fourth child. This continues down the line until the object reaches the last player, who then places it on the floor. It doesn't matter if the last person in the line is a cupper or a picker. The first player must wait until the first object is all the way down the line before picking up the second object from his pile. Any player who drops the object must retrieve it and pick up where he left off. The first team to pass all the objects down the line is the winner.

Ring-on-a-String Relay

The speediest ring wins in this sit-down passing race.

Players: 8 or more (even number), plus an adult to supervise

Ages: 3 to 8

Place: Indoors in large room or outdoors on grass or pavement

Equipment: 2 rings; roll of string; scissors

The Ring-on-a-String Relay is a passing race that is suitable for very young children. The great thing about this party game is that there are no piles of objects or loose pieces to keep track of—everything is neatly self-contained. Players remain in one place for this race, so it can be played indoors or outdoors.

First, players divide into two equal teams. Next, two pieces of string of equal length are cut; each should be several feet long—2 feet (60cm) or so for each team player. A ring (washers or empty spools can also be used) is threaded onto each string; the ends of each string are tied together to form a circle. The two teams then sit or stand in two separate circles, and each team member holds on to her team's loop of string. One player on each team holds the ring. Players should step far enough back so that the string is pulled taut.

When everything is ready, the adult who's supervising the game calls out, "Ready, set, go!" and both teams begin passing the ring around the circle to the right as quickly as possible. A lot of excited action is generated as each player tries to get rid of the ring as hastily as she can, usually by flinging it along the string to the player next to him. The first team to pass the ring around the circle three times wins.

Doughnut-on-a-String

This game is played in the same way as Ring-on-a-String, with one small exception—a doughnut is used instead of a ring. This makes the game much more challenging (and sticky), as a doughnut can crumble if it is handled too roughly. (Obviously, if the game is played indoors, a crumb-tolerant spot is needed.) If a team's doughnut falls apart, that team automatically loses the game. Each member of the winning team gets a fresh doughnut for a prize—the losers get doughnut holes, of course!

Double Pass

There's no running in this sit-down passing race, but there's still plenty of action.

Players: 8 to 20 (even number), plus an adult or older child to supervise

Ages: 4 to 8

Place: Indoors in large room or outdoors on grass or pavement

Equipment: Deck of 52 cards or pile of about 50 small objects (marbles, small wrapped candies, pennies, etc.)

The Double Pass is a simple but challenging party race for young children. The game is most appropriate for indoor play because the players will be sitting on the floor with a pile of small objects or playing cards. (Cards shouldn't be used if the game is played outdoors—they're sure to blow away.)

First, the players divide into two equal teams, which each choose a captain. The members of each team sit in a line to the left of their captain. The two lines should be facing one another. A pile of cards or objects is placed next to each captain.

Once everything's ready, the person who's supervising the race yells, "Ready, set, go!" and the captains start passing the objects down the lines, one by one. The players pass the objects in front of them using only their *right* hands. When an object reaches the last player in line, that player transfers the object to his *left* hand and it is now passed back down the line behind the players' backs, using only left hands. As the objects return to the head of the line, the captain begins piling them up neatly in a second pile beside her. The captain must be careful not to put the returning objects back into the first pile.

Players continue simultaneously passing objects in both directions until all the objects have made it back to the captain. The first team to return all its objects to the captain is the winner.

Peanut Race

Nimble noses are necessary to propel peanuts in this riotous race.

Players: 2 or more, plus an adult to supervise

Ages: 5 to 12

Place: Indoors in large room with soft carpet (cleared of furniture and breakable objects)

Equipment: Peanut in its shell for each player; masking tape for marking lines

The Peanut Race is a party favorite because it's such a silly sight. Watching players race to the finish line pushing peanuts with their noses is enough to crack up even the most party-shy child. This game is best played indoors on a soft carpet.

Before beginning, starting and finish lines are marked off on the floor about 15 feet (4.5m) apart. Each player is given a peanut in the shell and lines up at the starting line.

Once everyone's in place, the adult supervisor yells, "Ready, set, go!" and the runners put their peanuts on the floor and begin to push them toward the finish line with their noses. Players may crawl on hands and knees, slither along the floor like snakes, or propel themselves in any other fashion as long as only their noses make contact with the peanuts. If any part of the body other than the nose touches the peanut, the player must return to the starting line. The first player to push her peanut across the finish line is the winner.

If the race is being run as a relay, participants divide up into equal teams and line up single file behind the starting line. At the end of the "Ready, set, go!" signal, the first player in each line pushes his peanut toward the far boundary, crosses it, turns around, and pushes his peanut back to the starting line. There, the next player on his team takes charge of the peanut. Each player repeats the same action. The first team to have all its members complete the course wins the game.

Flying Fish Relay

In this funny race, players frantically fan their fish to the finish.

Players: 6 to 20 (divisible into equal teams), plus an adult to supervise

Ages: 5 to 9

Place: Indoors in large room (cleared of furniture and breakable objects)

Equipment: Construction paper; pencil; crayons or colored markers (optional); scissors; newspaper or magazine and paper or plastic plate for each team

The Flying Fish Relay, known as Kippers in England, takes a bit of preparation—the kids can make the fish themselves as a pre-race art activity. Young children have a wonderful time fanning their fish around the room during this novelty race.

The first order of business is creating the fish. Fish shapes about 10 inches (25cm) long should be drawn with a pencil on colored construction paper and cut out with scissors. If the players make the fish themselves, they may also want to decorate them, using crayons or colored markers, for example. Each player gets one fish, and each team receives a rolled-up newspaper or magazine.

Two or more equal teams of three to five players line up single file at one end of the room. A paper or plastic plate is placed opposite each team on the floor at the other end of the room (or at a closer finish line, if that seems too far).

The adult supervisor now calls out, "Ready, set, go!" The first player on each team immediately places her fish on the floor and tries to fan it across the room and onto the plate by flapping her newspaper (or magazine) enough to create a strong breeze. This is a tricky operation, and the fish are sure to fly in quite a few different directions before they make it to their proper destination.

As soon as the fish lands on the plate, the racer runs back to her team and hands the newspaper to the next player, who lays his fish on the floor and starts fanning. Each player in turn fans a fish onto the plate. It doesn't matter if a fish is accidentally fanned off the plate.

The first team to fill its plate with fish is the winner.

Pass the Orange

Players race to pass the orange down the line using only their feet or their chins.

Players: 8 or more (even number), plus an adult to supervise

Ages: 6 to 10

Place: Indoors in large room (cleared of furniture and breakable objects) or outdoors on grass, pavement, or even sand

Equipment: 2 firm oranges

Pass the Orange is a classic party race in which the children compete to pass the fruit without ever touching it with their hands. Instead, players use their feet or their chins. (No tangerines, please—they're too small to handle.) This game is played just as easily indoors (in a large room) as outdoors.

Before beginning, the players divide up into two equal teams. In one version of Pass the Orange, the members of each team take off their shoes and sit side by side on the floor or ground in a line facing the other team. Legs are held together, sticking straight out in front, toes pointed. The first player in each line is given an orange, which is placed on top of her feet.

When everyone is in position, the supervising adult calls out, "Ready, set, go!" and the player with the orange tries to pass it down the line, balancing the fruit on her toes and gently dropping or rolling it onto the outstretched toes of the next player. If the orange drops to the floor before it is on top of the second player's feet, the first player must pick it up with her feet and try again. The orange is passed down the line in this manner.

An alternate version has the players stand side by side. The orange is tucked under the chin of the first player. To pass it along, he must nuzzle the orange under the chin of the second player. If the orange drops or if a player touches it with his hands as it is being passed down the line, it is returned to the beginning of the line.

Whichever passing method is chosen, the first team that passes the orange to the end of the line is named the winner.

Dress Me

In this hilarious race, teams pull an extra layer of clothing on and off two players who are holding hands.

Players: 8 or more (divisible into equal teams), plus an adult to supervise

Ages: 6 to 12

Place: Indoors in large room (cleared of furniture and breakable objects) or outdoors on grass or pavement

Equipment: Extra-large old short-sleeved shirt for each team

The challenge in Dress Me is to be the first team to remove an over-sized shirt from one player and put it on another while the two hold hands! Sound impossible? It's not, but it's no easy task, either. This topsy-turvy race delights kids with its silliness while teaching them cooperation and teamwork.

First, the participants divide up into two or more teams of four or five players. Each team is given a large shirt—either a T-shirt or a short-sleeved button-front shirt with all the buttons buttoned except for the one at the neck. One player on each team pulls the shirt on over his clothes and then joins hands with a teammate.

When everything's ready, the adult who's supervising cries, "Ready, set, go!" and the others on each team try to transfer the shirt from the first player to the second. The two players must continue to hold hands until the shirt has been transferred. Eventually children figure out that the only way to accomplish this is to pull the shirt over the head of the first player, then slide it over the two players' linked arms and onto the second player, inside out. When the second player is wearing the shirt, a third player on the team takes her hands, the first player becomes a dresser, and the task begins anew.

The race continues until all of the players have worn the shirt. The first team that gets the shirt onto its last player is the winner.

Tunnel Relay

The goal of this race is to keep the ball rolling through a tunnel of legs.

Players: 10 or more (divisible into equal teams), plus an adult to supervise

Ages: 6 to 12

Place: Outdoors on grass or pavement

Equipment: Playground ball for each team; stones, sticks, or chalk for marking lines

The Tunnel Relay is a playground race that should be played on a firm surface so that the ball can roll easily. This unusual race has a bit of complicated choreography, but once players get the hang of the motion, they're sure to enjoy it.

First, starting and finish lines are drawn on the ground about 30 to 50 feet (9 to 15m) apart, and the players divide into two or more equal teams of at least five players each. One player on each team stands on the starting line facing the finish line with his legs spread apart. The rest of the team lines up behind that player in single file about a yard (1m) apart. These players too should have their legs spread wide apart and should all be facing the finish line. The player at the front of each of the lines holds the ball.

When everyone is in position, the adult who's supervising the race signals, "Ready, set, go!" and the player with the ball rolls it through his own legs and back through the "tunnel" created by all the other players' legs. The other players are free to help the ball through the tunnel. When the ball reaches the last player in line, she snatches up the ball and then runs to the front of the line, where the action starts over again. In this manner, the whole line moves slowly toward the finish line. If the ball escapes from the tunnel, it is retrieved and rolled again from the place it escaped.

The team that makes it over the finish line first is the winner.

Balloon Tunnel Relay

The Tunnel Relay can be adapted for indoor play by using balloons instead of balls. In this version of the game, the balloon is passed from one player's hands to the next player's hands between the legs, and the finish line is at the opposite end of the room. Other aspects of play remain the same.

Hurry, Waiter!

In Hurry, Waiter! players try to serve up victory without dropping the ball.

Players: 10 or more (divisible into equal teams), plus an adult to supervise

Ages: 6 to 11

Place: Indoors in large room (cleared of furniture and breakable objects) or outdoors on grass or pavement

Equipment: Table tennis ball and plastic plate for each team

This hilarious party race allows players to try their hands at being waiters. In this case, though, the "meal" is a table tennis ball and the goal is speed rather than style. This game can certainly be played outdoors, but it is one of those races that is particularly suited for indoor play because it doesn't require too much space.

First, participants divide into two or more equal teams of at least five players, and each team chooses a captain. The teams line up single file behind their captains, with each team member leaving a foot or two (.3 to 6m) of space between herself and her teammates front and back. The captains are given a table tennis ball on a plastic plate. (Paper plates are too flimsy for this game.)

When the captains all have their plates and everyone is in position, the adult who's supervising the game calls out, "Ready, set, go!" At this signal, each "waiter"—holding the plate with one hand and balancing the ball atop it—turns to face his lined-up teammates and proceeds to weave in and out among them without dropping the ball or the plate. If either is dropped, the runner must pick it up and go back to the beginning of the line and start again.

When the waiter reaches the end of the line, he runs straight back to the head of the line and hands the ball and plate to the next player, saying, "Here is your breakfast, Sir [or Madam]." The first player then rushes back to stand at the end of the line, while the new waiter starts weaving down the line. This goes on until every member of the team has had a turn being the waiter. The first team to finish is the winner.

For an extra challenge, players can be required to hold the plate on an open palm at shoulder level, like real waiters. For this, it is essential that the plates be unbreakable.

Firefighter's Race

In this wet and wild relay, "firefighters" race
to get their water where it belongs.

Players: 6 or more (divisible into equal teams), plus an adult to supervise

Ages: 6 to 11

Place: Outdoors on grass, pavement, or sand

Equipment: Paper cup for each team; 2 buckets or large bowls (not glass) for each team; stones, sticks, or chalk for marking lines

Firefighter's Race is a fun summer party race that allows participants to be sprinkled without getting drenched. Children will enjoy the challenge of running with a cup full of water—a forbidden activity in everyday life. Needless to say, this game should be played outdoors.

A starting line and a finish line are drawn on the ground about 30 feet (9m) apart. The participants divide into two or more equal teams of at least three players, and the teams line up single file behind the starting line. A bucket or bowl filled with about 6 cups of water is placed on the starting line in front of each team, and an empty bowl for each team is placed on the finish line. It's important that the starting amounts of water for each team be as equal as possible.

The first runner on each team is given a paper cup. When everyone's in position, the adult who's supervising yells, "Ready, set, go!" and the first child on each team scoops a cupful of water out of his team's full bowl and runs to the finish line, trying to move as quickly as possible while spilling as little as possible. On reaching the finish line, the runner pours the water into the empty bowl and dashes back to his teammates. As he crosses the line, he hands the cup to the next player, who takes it and repeats the action. As the initial bowl empties out, players may tip it up or lift it to pour the water out into their cups.

The team that is first to transfer all its water to its bowl is the winner. The other teams should keep going until they've transferred all their water, too—because if the first team has spilled a significant amount and the water in its final bowl is noticeably less than in the other teams' bowls, the first team is disqualified and the next team to transfer all its water becomes the winner.

Straws and Beans Race

Even though no running is involved, players may be out of breath at the end of this passing race.

Players: 8 or more (even number), plus an adult to supervise

Ages: 6 to 11

Place: Indoors in large room with floor seating for all players

Equipment: Drinking straw for each player; 12 large dried beans; 4 saucers

In the Straws and Beans Race, teams compete to transfer a plateful of beans down the line using only drinking straws and their breath. To play this game successfully and with-out frustration, children should be old enough to understand how to pick up an object with one end of a straw by sucking on the other end and how to let it go. Obviously, the straws should be narrow enough and the beans wide enough that there is no chance of a child sucking a bean up through the straw and into his mouth (kidney beans work well). Participants should also, of course, be past the age where they might be tempted to place small objects in their mouths.

First, the participants divide into two teams. The members of each team sit side by side in a row on the floor facing the opposing team. A saucer filled with six large dried beans is placed at one end of each line, and an empty saucer is placed at the other end. Each player is given a drinking straw.

When everything is ready, the adult supervising the game signals, "Ready, set, go!" and the player closest to the beans on each team picks up a bean by placing one end of the straw against the bean and drawing in her breath. Holding her breath to keep the bean in place, the first player turns to the next, who holds one hand cupped directly in front of him. Positioning the straw above this player's hand, the first player exhales. The bean should now drop into the second player's hand. The second player immediately uses his straw to "pick" the bean up from his hands and then passes the bean to the next teammate. The bean is passed down the line in this manner and placed into the empty saucer. No player may move her hand when a bean is in it. If a bean drops at any point along the way, it is returned to the beginning of the line.

The first team to pass all six beans down the line is the winner.

Clothespin Relay

In this challenging relay, participants race to build a stack of clothespins that won't topple.

Players: 16 to 30 (divisible into equal teams), plus an adult to supervise

Ages: 7 to 11

Place: Indoors in large room (cleared of furniture and breakable objects) or outdoors on pavement

Equipment: 10 clothespins (or beanbags, building blocks, or other stackable objects) for each team

Clothespin Relay—a passing and building race—doesn't involve any running. This contest is especially good for a large group stuck indoors, because relatively little space is needed to play. After all, the racers aren't going anywhere.

First, players divide into two or more equal teams. Each team forms a single-file line, and a pile of ten clothespins is placed at the feet of the last child in each line. Any objects that can be stacked—with a little bit of difficulty—can be substituted for the clothespins. (Building blocks make good substitutes.)

When everyone's ready, the person who's supervising the race yells, "Ready, set, go!" and the last child in each line begins passing the clothespins, one at a time, toward the front of the line as quickly as possible. No one can hold more than one clothespin at a time.

The players at the heads of the lines have the task of stacking the clothespins so that only the bottom one touches the ground. This is not easy. If the stack topples, it must be rebuilt, and clothespin passing is temporarily halted. The first team to stack up all the clothespins wins the round.

The first team to win three rounds wins the game. Different players should be at the front and back of the line in each round.

Potato Relay

This potato-retrieving relay calls for a seamless combination of speed and balance.

Players: 6 or more (divisible into equal teams), plus an adult to supervise

Ages: 7 to 12

Place: Indoors in large room (cleared of furniture and breakable objects) or outdoors on grass or pavement

Equipment: Potato for each player; large spoon for each team; stones, sticks, chalk, or masking tape for marking lines

The Potato Relay is similar to the Egg and Spoon Relay. But this version is not as messy. Teams compete by running the course with a potato on a spoon. This is no easy task, especially since touching the potato with hands or feet is forbidden (though this rule can be suspended for younger kids).

Players divide into two or more equal teams of at least three children. Two lines are marked on the ground 20 to 50 feet (6 to 15m) apart (or less if the relay is inside); these are the starting and turning lines. Teams line up single file behind the starting line, and the first player in each line is given a large spoon. A pile of potatoes equal to the number of players on each team is placed on the turning line across from each team.

When everything's in place, the adult who's supervising the contest yells, "Ready, set, go!" and the first player in each line runs to his team's potato pile and picks up a potato using only his spoon. After picking up the potato, he hurries back to the start with the potato balanced on the spoon. If the potato drops, it must be picked up again with the spoon. The runner puts the potato down to the side of his team after crossing the finish line and passes the spoon to the next team member, who races off to retrieve another potato in the same fashion. Each player retrieves a potato in turn. The first team to bring all its potatoes back to the starting line is the winner.

Egg and Spoon Relay

In this popular relay, runners carry precious—and breakable—cargo.

Players: 8 to 30 (divisible into equal teams), plus an adult to supervise

Ages: 8 to 12

Place: Outdoors on grass or pavement

Equipment: Metal spoon for each player; hard-boiled egg (or several raw eggs) for each team; stones, sticks, or chalk for marking lines

The Egg and Spoon Relay is a party and field-day classic. In this twist on the traditional relay race, players carry eggs on spoons held in one hand. One itty-bitty trip-up produces a big splat! But never fear: in a friendly contest no one ends up with egg on his face.

To begin, two lines are marked off on the ground about 15 feet (4.5m) apart; these are the starting and turning lines. Players divide into two or more equal teams of four or five players, and the teams line up single file behind the starting line. The lead player on each team holds a spoon with one hand. The eggs may be hard-boiled or raw—either way, this race should definitely be run outdoors. If raw eggs are used, the adult supervising the race needs to keep several extra eggs on hand to replace the ones that shatter. It's best in this case if players are wearing old clothes that can withstand gooey slip-ups.

Once everyone is in position, the supervisor signals, "Ready, set, go!" and the first runner on each team races to the turning line and back with the egg on the spoon. If the egg drops, it is picked up or—if it's raw and breaks—it's replaced on the spot by the person supervising the race. When the first runner returns to the starting line, she removes her egg by hand and sets it on the spoon of the next runner in line, and the course is repeated. This goes on until everyone has had a turn to run.

The first team to have all its players complete the course is the winner. If raw eggs were used, it's a good idea to have water and a towel handy to clean up any sticky mishaps.

Suitcase Relay

In this suitcase-packing race, speed, rather than neatness, counts.

Players: 6 or more (divisible into equal teams), plus an adult to supervise

Ages: 8 to 12

Place: Outdoors on grass or pavement

Equipment: Small old suitcase or large paper bag for each team; assortment of old clothes; stones, sticks, or chalk for marking lines

For some reason, children who have never so much as put their socks in a drawer—much less packed a suitcase—find this race wildly entertaining. It just goes to show that the fun of an activity is all in the presentation. It's best to use old suitcases and clothes as props for this race to remove any danger that good things will get broken or soiled.

To set up the race, two lines are marked on the ground about 50 feet (15m) apart; these are the starting and turning lines. Participants divide into two or more equal teams of at least three players. The teams line up single file at the starting line. An assortment of old clothes (T-shirts, socks, pajamas, jeans, etc.) is folded and placed in a small suitcase or large paper bag for each team. This step guarantees that all the clothes will fit in their container. The number and type of items in each suitcase should be similar. One suitcase is placed at the front of each line and opened; then the contents are removed and set in a pile next to the suitcase.

When everything's ready, the adult who's supervising the contest yells, "Ready, set, go!" and the first player on each team packs the suitcase, closes and latches or zips it, picks it up, runs with it to the turning line and back, and then unpacks it. The next player again packs up the suitcase, closes it, dashes back and forth, and

finally unpacks. The action continues in the same way down the line. The first team to have all its players pack, run, and unpack is the winner.

Players are not permitted simply to dump the clothes on the ground when they unpack or to stuff them back in when they pack. They must at least attempt to keep the clothes neatly folded as they are put in and taken out of the suitcase. This may well be the greatest challenge of the race.

Here's a good way to run the Suitcase Relay with a large number of players: Instead of having each player pack, run, and then unpack at the starting line, half of each team starts out at the starting line, and the other half at the turning line. The suitcases

begin on the starting line fully packed.

After the signal "Ready, set, go!" the first player on each team opens his suitcase, puts on the contents, and runs with the empty suitcase to the turning line. Clothes should be put on properly (no shirts tied around the waist!), but it's not essential that buttons be buttoned. The player then quickly takes off the clothes, and the first runner at the turning line packs them back into the suitcase. When the case is packed, that runner sprints with it back to the starting line, gives it to the next player, and then joins the back of the group at the starting line. The actions are repeated, in turn, and this back-and-forth action continues until each player has been *both* packer and dresser. The first team to finish is the winner.

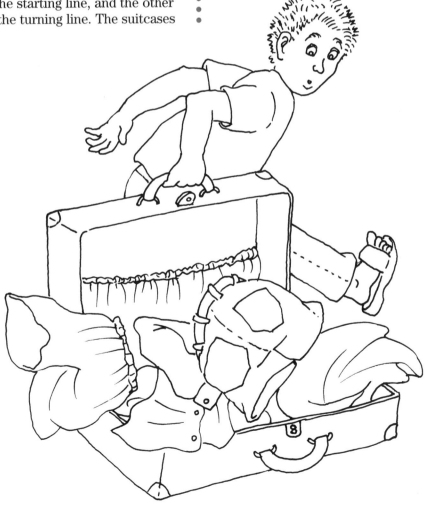

Gossip Relay

In this cross between Telephone and Classic Relay, everyone gets the message.

Players: 8 or more (divisible into equal teams), plus an adult to supervise

Ages: 8 to 14

Place: Outdoors on grass or pavement

Equipment: Stones, sticks, or chalk for marking lines

Instead of passing a baton, in Gossip Relay, the players pass a message. And it's a lot harder to keep a message intact as it travels from player to player than it is to hand off a stick. Gossip Relay is like the popular game Telephone, but it has an added element of speed that makes it even more challenging. Kids of all ages delight in the way the words and messages get garbled as they make their way down the line.

Before beginning, two lines are marked off on the ground 30 to 50 feet (9 to 15m) apart; these are the starting and turning lines. Players divide into two or more equal teams of at least four players. The teams line up single file at the starting line. Next, the adult who's supervising the contest whispers the same message to the first person in each line. The message can be anything from a three-word tongue-twister like "Silly Sammy Slick" to a complete sentence such as "Susie rode her bike to the store to buy a head of cabbage."

When each of the front runners has been given the message and every-one's in position, the supervisor shouts, "Ready, set, go!" and the first players in each line race to the turning line and back. When the panting runner returns to the starting line, he whispers the phrase (or what he *thinks* is the phrase) to the next player in line. That player in turn runs the course and then whispers the phrase to the next team member.

This goes on until the last player on one of the teams crosses the finish line and yells out the message. If the message is perfectly correct—if it's exactly the same message that the starter gave out before the race began—that team is named the winner. If the message is repeated incorrectly (say, as "Susie told Mike and a boar to buy a bed of luggage"), the next runner to cross the finish line calls out her version of the message. The first team whose runner crosses the finish line *and* says the message correctly is the winner. If no one gets it right, no team wins, and the race is run again—with a different message to remember correctly.

Two-Minute Walk

Timing is everything in this indoor race, as players try to navigate the course in exactly 2 minutes.

Players: 2 or more, plus an adult to supervise and keep time

Ages: 7 to 12

Place: Indoors in large room (cleared of furniture and breakable objects)

Equipment: Stopwatch or other timer

The Two-Minute Walk is a rather unusual race because the child who finishes first is not necessarily the winner. Since the goal of the game is to time the walk as close to 2 minutes as possible, players must possess an impeccable sense of timing to figure out when exactly that amount of time has passed. Practice indeed makes perfect in this contest.

The Two-Minute Walk is usually played indoors, where players start by lining up against a wall, with a time-keeper at the opposite wall. When the timekeeper gives the signal "Ready, set, go!" the racers begin meandering across the room. Without looking at any clock or watch, each player tries to time her arrival at the opposite wall at exactly 2 minutes. As the players begin touching the wall, the timekeeper takes note of who reaches the wall in an amount of time that's closest to 2 minutes (whether under, over, or exactly at the two-minute mark).

When the last player reaches the wall, the timekeeper announces the winner—the player whose walk was the closest to 2 minutes.

Tag and Chase Games

Children find it thrilling both to chase one another and to be chased, and the games in this chapter are all versions of these time-honored pastimes. From simple circle games to blindfold games and intricate stalk-and-capture games, there's a tag game for children of almost every age and physical ability. In general, though, it's best if the players are relatively close in age, or at least running ability, to give both the taggers and the chasers a chance. Most of these games are best played outdoors, although all can be moved into a gym or similar large, empty room. Some, as noted, call for a course to be marked on the ground. Others require some equipment, such as small objects to be "captured." All the tag and chase games are the most fun when a large number of players participate.

Follow the Leader

It takes imagination and physical prowess to be the leader in this noncompetitive game of imitation.

Players: 3 or more, plus an adult or older child to supervise

Ages: 3 to 8

Place: Outdoors in yard, playground, or field

Equipment: None

The point of Follow the Leader is for all the players to imitate the actions of a leader as exactly as possible. For each player, this becomes an individual challenge, although the game can be played competitively, as an elimination contest.

The best place to play Follow the Leader is at a playground or similar area where there are lots of obstacles and equipment to jump over, crawl under, run around, and slither through.

First, one player is chosen to be the leader, and all the other players line up behind him. Then, the leader sets off on a varied course and the other players follow, trying to keep up with the leader while imitating all of his actions as closely as possible. For example, on a playground, the leader might run for 50 yards (about 50m), then climb up on a stump and jump off, race up a slide and whiz down on his stomach, crawl under the slide, whirl around a swing post three times, hop 10 steps on one foot, travel hand over hand across several monkey bars, drop to the ground, walk backward 20 paces, and then do a somersault on grass.

The leader should be careful not to do anything dangerous or too difficult for the other players. Clearly, the course and actions chosen for a group of 3-year-olds should be much easier than one for 7- or 8-year-olds.

If the game is being played competitively, players drop out when they fail to follow one of the leader's stunts. The last player remaining (other than the leader) is the winner and becomes the new leader. If the game is being played just for fun, the players stay in the line and keep up as best they can. Every 5 minutes or so a new leader should be chosen.

Tag

Tag's magic lies in the thrill of the chase and the equally thrilling satisfaction of outrunning—or outwitting—"it."

Players: 5 or more, plus an adult or older child to supervise

Ages: 3 to 14

Place: Outdoors on grass or pavement

Equipment: None

Tag is an ancient game that is beautiful in its simplicity: one player chases the others, who try to avoid being tagged. There are, of course, infinite variations on this theme. Children of all ages can play at any time and on almost any surface. All that's needed is boundless energy—which children possess—and an open area where kids can run.

Before beginning the game, someone must be designated "it" (the chaser). "It" closes her eyes and counts to ten while the other players disperse.

The action begins when "it" starts chasing the other players, who try to avoid being tagged. The first person to be tagged becomes "it," and the game continues without a break.

Tag may also be played as an elimination game, in which each person who is tagged must drop out, and the original "it" remains in that role throughout the game. The last untagged player is then the winner and becomes "it" in the next game.

Stoop Tag

Stoop Tag is played the same way as standard Tag, except that anyone in the squatting position (crouched down with knees bent and backside close to the ground) is safe from capture and "it" must stay at least 5 feet (1.5m) away. If a stooped player stays down for longer than the count of three, however, she is considered tagged and becomes the new "it."

Reverse Tag

Reverse Tag, best for kids at least 5 years old, is played like standard Tag, except that everyone, including "it," runs backward! To make the game even more challenging, each "it" who follows the first "it" can be required to keep one hand on the place on his body where he was tagged.

Tree Tag

In Tree Tag, a player is safe from being tagged if she is touching a tree. She may not touch a tree, however, if "it" is 10 feet (3m) or more away from her. In a related version, Touch Wood Tag, players agree that anyone touching wood (or another material, like iron or stone) cannot be tagged.

Chain Tag

Also known as Bronco Tag and Hook-On Tag, this variation is the most fun when played by a large group. The first child tagged must join hands with "it," and the two then pursue the other players while joined together. Each player who is tagged hooks on to become another link in the chain. As the chain grows, only

the players on the two ends may make a tag. The last person to remain outside the chain is the winner of the game.

Flashlight Tag

This game, which requires a flashlight, is played at twilight, and care should be taken that the play area is free of "hard-to-see" obstacles. Instead of tagging by touching another player, "it" catches the others by shining a flashlight beam on them. Players are eliminated when captured, and "it" continues in his role until all but one player is caught.

Shadow Tag

Instead of tagging a player physically, "it" steps on a player's shadow. This game is best played in the late afternoon, when shadows lengthen as the sun begins to set.

Freeze Tag

In this version, a player who has been tagged must "freeze" in the position and spot she was in when tagged. She must stand perfectly still until another player sneaks up and tags her, setting her free. Since the only way "it" can win is by freezing all the players, he has both to chase down and tag the unfrozen players and to guard the frozen ones.

Cross Tag

In this cooperative version of Tag, "it" begins the game by calling out the name of another player and running after her. "It" must continue chasing only that player until another player crosses in between the two of them. "It" must then chase the crossing player. The players should work together to try to help each other stay safe from "it."

Carry Tag

In Carry Tag, an object such as a ball, hat, or shoe is passed from player to player. "It" may chase and tag only the player who is holding the object (which must always be in sight). The players, of course, are constantly trying to hand off the carried object to someone else; this they do simply by touching another player with the object. If a player is tagged while carrying the object, he passes the object to "it," and he becomes the new "it." The new "it" must count to three, giving the old "it" a chance to get away, before beginning the chase. Any player who drops the object automatically becomes "it."

Skip Tag

Skip Tag is played like standard Tag, except that all the players must skip rather than run. Close cousins to this game are Hop Tag, in which players must hop on one foot, and Walk Tag, in which they must walk.

Floating Tag

Also called Hang Tag, Floating Tag must be played in an area where there are things to climb; it is best played with children 5 or older. In this version, a player is safe from being tagged if both her feet are off the ground. Players may climb trees, a jungle gym, fences, or anything else that enables them to "float" in space and have their feet off the ground. A player may not float if "it" is farther than 15 feet (4.5m) away.

Duck, Duck, Goose

In this classic preschool tag game, the last one around the circle is a silly goose.

Players: 8 or more, plus an adult or older child to supervise

Ages: 3 to 6

Place: Indoors in large room (cleared of furniture and breakable objects) or outdoors on grass or pavement

Equipment: None

Duck, Duck, Goose is a childhood favorite because it's easy to learn and fun to play. Preschoolers never tire of chasing each other around in a circle, and for some reason, they find a lot of humor in the words "duck" and "goose."

To begin, all the players except one sit cross-legged in a large circle. The remaining player is "it." "It" walks around the outside of the circle saying, "Duck!" as she taps each player on the head.

This continues until "it" suddenly taps a player and says, "Goose!" The "goose" must jump up and chase "it" around the circle. If "it" makes her way back to the goose's sitting spot without being tagged, the goose becomes the new "it." If "it" is caught, the goose returns to his place and "it" must start tapping again.

Drop the Handkerchief

Players must pay attention to where the handkerchief falls or risk becoming "it" in this circle chase game.

Players: 8 or more, plus an adult or older child to supervise

Ages: 3 to 7

Place: Indoors in large room (cleared of furniture and breakable objects) or outdoors on grass or pavement

Equipment: Handkerchief or small piece of paper

Drop the Handkerchief is a good tag game for very young children because it's played in a circle, with only two players running around

at any given time. Besides the thrill of the chase, this game offers the suspense of never knowing just when or where the handkerchief is going to fall.

To begin, all the players except one stand in a ring holding hands. The remaining player is "it." He walks slowly around the outside of the ring holding a handkerchief or small piece of paper and begins singing the classic rhyme: *A tisket, a tasket, / a green and yellow basket. / I wrote a letter to my love / and on the way I dropped it. / A little child picked it up / and put it in his pocket.* At any time during the song, "it" secretly drops the handkerchief behind one of the players but keeps on singing.

The players in the circle, meanwhile, keep an eye on "it," and most will be able to tell quickly when he's dropped the handkerchief. A few moments may pass, however, before the player "it" has chosen realizes the handkerchief has been dropped behind her. When she does, she sets off in pursuit of "it." "It" races around the circle, trying to get back to the chosen player's space in the ring before being tagged. When dropping the handkerchief, "it" should try to play it cool and perhaps stroll along a few steps before tearing off around the ring. The more time that passes before the chosen player realizes that she must give chase, the farther ahead "it" will be.

If "it" is caught before reaching the empty spot in the circle, he remains "it" and must drop the handkerchief again. But if "it" gets all the way around the circle, the pursuing player becomes the new "it."

Run For Your Supper

In this suspenseful game, two players race around the outside of the circle in pursuit of one free spot.

Players: 10 or more, plus an adult or older child to supervise

Ages: 4 to 8

Place: Indoors in large room (cleared of furniture and breakable objects) or outdoors on grass or pavement

Equipment: None

Run for Your Supper is a good circle tag game to play with a large group of young children. Little kids savor the suspense of waiting to see who will have to run for his "supper" (the empty spot in the circle) and appreciate the fact that there are no distinct winner or losers.

To begin, all the players except one join hands and form a circle. The remaining player is "it" and stands outside the circle. "It" walks slowly around the circle. Then, when the others least expect it, she pulls two players' hands apart and shouts, "Run for your supper!"

"It" takes one of the vacated places. The two separated players run in opposite directions around the outside of the circle, racing for the other empty spot. The first one to make it around the circle and slap "its" outstretched palm ("give her five") joins the circle. The remaining player is the new "it."

Cat and Mouse

In this circle tag game, players join forces to prevent the "cat" from catching the "mouse."

Players: 8 or more, plus an adult or older child to supervise

Ages: 5 to 10

Place: Indoors in large room (cleared of furniture and breakable objects) or outdoors on grass or pavement

Equipment: None

Cat and Mouse is a simple circle game for young children. Everybody cooperates to help protect the underdog mouse, but—in contrast to the cartoons—the crafty cat usually triumphs in the end. This somewhat offbeat game can entertain a large group of kids who are tired of the same old activities.

To begin, all the players except two join hands and form a ring. One of the remaining players is the "mouse" and stands inside the circle. The other—the "cat"—remains just outside. The mouse starts the game by dashing under the linked hands of any two players in the ring and running around outside the ring, while trying to avoid being tagged by the cat. To escape the cat, the mouse may at any time dart into the circle, while the cat must always remain outside. But the mouse must never stop moving, and she may not stay in the circle for more than a few moments.

The players in the circle try to help the mouse escape the cat's paws. They may raise their arms so that the mouse can easily get back inside the circle to safety. And they may block any attempts by the cat to reach inside the circle to tag the mouse. (Reaching inside is a perfectly acceptable move for the cat, if he can manage it. The cat is not, however, allowed to put even one foot inside.)

The game continues until the mouse is tagged. The mouse then becomes the cat, the cat joins the circle, and another player is chosen to be the mouse.

Sewing Up the Gap

A runner weaves in and out to "sew up" the circle and avoid being tagged.

Players: 10 or more, plus an adult or older child to supervise

Ages: 5 to 10

Place: Indoors in large room (cleared of furniture and breakable objects) or outdoors on grass or pavement

Equipment: None

Sewing Up the Gap is a simple circle tag game with an interesting twist: the pursued player must run in and out of the circle, "sewing up" all the gaps, without being tagged. The more players there are, the more fun—and challenging—the game is.

First, all the players but two form a ring, standing about an arm's length apart, with their arms at their sides at first. One of the remaining players is "it" and the other is the runner. They start the game standing outside the circle on opposite sides.

To begin, "it" starts chasing the runner. As he scampers out of the reach of "it," the runner tries to weave in and out of the circle of players. Each time the runner passes from the outside to the inside of the circle (but *not* when he runs from the inside to the outside), the two players he runs between must join hands to "sew up the gap." The runner does not have to sew up the gaps in any particular sequence; he can dart in and out of the circle at will and around the circle in whatever direction he pleases. But once he has sewn up a gap, he may neither enter nor exit the circle through that gap. The whole time, "it" must remain outside the ring while trying to catch the runner.

If the runner can close all the gaps before being tagged, he is safe inside the circle and wins the game. If the runner is tagged, however, he becomes "it." The former "it" joins the circle, exchanging places with another player, who now becomes the runner.

Fox and Geese Chase

This circle tag game is best played in the snow or on the sand, where it's easy to mark out the course.

Players: 8 or more, plus an adult or older child to supervise

Ages: 6 to 12

Place: Outdoors on pavement, sand, or snow

Equipment: Chalk, shovel, or stick for marking the course

Fox and Geese Chase is played *on* a circle rather than in one. It's a great game for the beach or the snow, where there's no problem marking a circular course in the playing area.

To prepare for the game, an adult or older child should mark a circle at least 30 feet (9m) in diameter with eight to ten spokes, evenly spaced, running from the center to the circle's edge. On snow-covered ground, the circle can be drawn with the back of a snow shovel. A stick or the edge of a shovel works nicely in sand or dirt. Chalk works equally well on a blacktop playground .

One player is chosen to be the "fox" and stands in the middle of the circle. The others are "geese," and each takes a place at any point along the rim and spokes of the wheel.

At a signal, the fox starts chasing the geese. All the players—hunter and hunted—must stay on the lines at all times as they run hither and thither. Should two geese meet, they may maneuver carefully around each other, as long as they don't step off the lines. When the fox catches up with a goose, she tags the goose, who then joins the fox in hunting the other geese. The last goose left is the winner and becomes the fox for the next round.

Octopus

In this tag game, the "fish" must stay out of the reach of the tentacles of the "octopus."

Players: 8 or more, plus an adult or older child to supervise

Ages: 4 to 10

Place: Outdoors on grass or pavement

Equipment: Stones, sticks, or chalk for marking boundaries

In this tag game with a marine-life theme, the little "fish" try to swim away from the big, bad "octopus." Little kids enjoy pretending to be fish or octopuses—making swimming motions and fish faces or becoming waving "tentacles."

First, a playing area is designated as the "ocean." The area does not have to have side boundaries, but it must have two clearly marked ends. One player is then chosen to be the octopus (the equivalent of "it" in other tag games). The other players—the fish—gather at one end of the ocean. When the octopus yells, "Cross!" the fish must try to "swim" across the ocean without being tagged by the octopus.

Any fish who makes it to the ocean's other boundary is safe. The fish who are tagged become the octopus' "tentacles" and help the octopus try to catch more fish on the next crossing. (The tentacles may move around by themselves, or they may hold hands with the octopus and with one another—making the octopus grow larger and larger with each crossing.)

The fish continue swimming across the ocean, back and forth, until all but one have been tagged. The surviving fish is the winner and becomes the next octopus.

Pom Pom Pullaway

In this variation, one player is "it" and stands in the middle of a clearly marked 25-foot (7.5m) square. The other players line up along one side of the square. When "it" calls out, "Pom Pom Pullaway, if you don't come, I'll pull you away" (or "Pom Pom Pullaway, run away, catch away"), the other players try to run to the opposite side of the square. Any player who is tagged by "it," or who runs out of the boundaries, must join "it" in the center. The "its" then call out the Pom Pom Pullaway rhyme in unison and try to catch the remaining players, who continue to run back and forth each time the rhyme is repeated. This goes on until only one untagged player is left. That player is the winner.

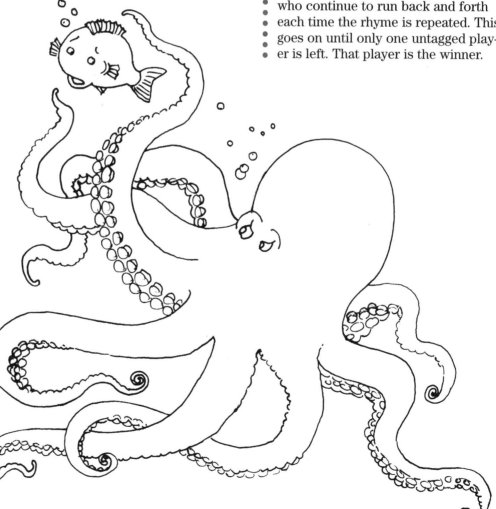

Rabbit

There are no winners or losers in this spirited chase game, just a lot of rabbits on the run.

Players: 6 or more (divisible into 3 equal groups), plus 2 extra players and an adult or older child to supervise

Ages: 5 to 10

Place: Outdoors on grass or pavement

Equipment: None

Rabbit differs from other tag games in that players "switch off" acting as the hunter's quarry. Each little "rabbit" is safe in her hutch until a homeless bunny takes refuge there and sends the original inhabitant on the run. Kids who are ready to advance beyond the simplest circle tag games enjoy the freedom of Rabbit.

First, one player is chosen to be the "hunter" (or "it"), and another is chosen to be the first "rabbit." The rest of the players divide up into groups of three, two of whom join hands to form a "rabbit hutch." The third player in each group becomes the rabbit hiding inside the hutch.

To begin, the hunter starts chasing the homeless rabbit. When that rabbit gets tired, he may trade places with one of the rabbits hiding in a hutch. The ousted rabbit now becomes the object of the chase, until she decides to take refuge in one of the hutches.

If a rabbit is caught, he becomes the hunter and the hunter turns into a rabbit. At this point, the rabbits hiding inside hutches should change places with players serving as part of a hutch; this way, everyone has the chance to run and to rest. Then the hunt begins anew. The game continues for as long as the rabbits keep running.

Steal the Bacon

Teams compete to snatch up a slab of "bacon" in this game of speed and suspense.

Players: 9 or more, plus an adult or older child to supervise

Ages: 6 to 12

Place: Outdoors on grass or pavement

Equipment: Hat, handkerchief, ball, or other small object to serve as the "bacon"; stones, sticks, or chalk for marking boundaries

In this team tag game, only one player from each side is actively competing at any given time. Players count off and are assigned numbers but do not get involved until their numbers are called. This is a good game for a wide variety of ages because, though it's easy to learn, its element of suspense keeps it interesting—any player's number may be called at any moment. Steal the Bacon is a contained game that can be played in a small yard or driveway.

First, two boundary lines are drawn about 20 feet (6m) apart, and the "bacon" (a hat, ball, handkerchief, or some other object) is placed in the middle of the space in between. Next, players divide into two equal teams, with one person left over to act as the referee. If there is an even number of players, the adult or older child supervising may serve as referee.

Team members line up along their team's boundary line, facing the other team. Next, each side counts off so that each player has a number. Each player should be standing directly across from the player with the same number on the opposing team.

The game begins when the referee calls out a number. The two players assigned that number must now dash into the middle and try to grab the bacon. The one who makes the grab must now make it back to her own boundary line without being tagged by the baconless player.

A player who successfully brings home the bacon scores 1 point for his team. If the "thief" is tagged, no points are scored. The two stealers often duck and bluff to try to catch their opponent off guard before making a move to pick up the bacon. The first team to score a predetermined number of points (usually 21) wins the game.

Hopping Bases

In this team tag game, players hop rather than run after their opponents.

Players: 11 or more (preferably odd number), plus an adult or older child to supervise

Ages: 6 to 12

Place: Outdoors on grass or pavement

Equipment: Stones, sticks, or chalk for marking boundaries

Hopping Bases is an organized team game of tag with a twist—instead of running after one another, players chase their opponents by hopping on one foot. To play the game, children must have the balance and coordination to hop on one foot for relatively long periods of time. It's a hoot to be a spectator at a Hopping Bases match, but it's even more fun to be a participant.

First, a playing field at least 60 feet (18m) long and 15 feet (4.5m) wide is marked off. Boundaries can be marked with stones, sticks, or chalk, depending on the playing surface. Next, a circle about 6 feet (1.8m) in diameter is drawn in the middle of the field. The players divide into two equal teams, with one player left over as "it." If there is an even number of participants, one must sit out each round.

Both teams line up behind their boundary lines at opposite ends of the field. "It" stands in the center of the circle. When "it" gives the signal to start, all the other players begin hopping on one foot from one end of the field to the other. As long as "it" stays in the center, he may stand on both feet. But when "it" emerges from the circle, he must also hop. "It" tries to tag as many players as possible as they attempt to cross the field. Tagged players are "out" and must leave the field.

Except for "it," any player who puts her other (nonhopping) foot down is also out of the game and must join the spectators at the sidelines. If "it" puts his other foot down, he must return to the center before hopping out again to tag. Any player who reaches the opposing boundary line is safe and may stand on both feet.

The team with the most players to make it safely to the other side is the winner of the game.

Red Lion

Players taunt rather than hide from "it" in this hunt, chase, and capture game.

Players: 8 or more, plus an adult or older child to supervise

Ages: 7 to 12

Place: Outdoors on grass or pavement

Equipment: None

Red Lion is a tag game that dates back to colonial days, when it was called Red Line—a reference to the British troops in their infamous red coats. Since then, the game has evolved into more of a "circus": the hungry lion, guarded by a keeper, waits in its den hoping for the chance to capture taunting onlookers. Since physical restraint is an important element of this game, players should be relatively evenly matched both in size and strength.

First, one player is chosen to be the "lion" ("it") and another to be the "keeper." The lion chooses a "den," a spot on which he stands. The keeper stays nearby.

To begin, all the other players stand around the den chanting, "Red Lion, Red Lion, come out of your den! Anybody you catch will be one of your men." At the moment of her choice, the keeper abruptly shouts, "Loose!" and the lion charges out of the den in pursuit of the other players.

The lion chases the players until he catches someone. The captive tries to

escape the lion's grip, but if the lion can roar "Red Lion" three times before the prisoner pulls loose, the tagged player becomes a lion too. The two big cats then return to the den, and the game continues as before.

Once there are several lions in the den, the keeper can make the game more interesting by calling out special instructions immediately after letting the lion loose. If she yells, "Cow catcher!" players can be caught only if two lions join both hands and trap the captive between their linked arms. If the keeper calls, "Tight!" all the lions have to join hands and try to surround someone. If the keeper calls, "Doubles!" the lions must link arms and hunt together in pairs, but they need not trap a captive between them, as with "Cow catcher!"

The last player to avoid becoming a lion is the winner. The first two players captured become the lion and keeper in the next game.

Poison

The first player to step into the circle becomes the "poison" from whom the others flee.

Players: 8 or more, plus an adult or older child to supervise

Ages: 7 to 12

Place: Outdoors on grass, dirt, or sand

Equipment: Sticks for marking circle

Poison is a tag game with a unique way of determining who's "it"— and a few other special rules, too. Before play begins, a circle just a few feet (about 1m) in diameter is drawn on the ground. (It should be small enough for two players to stand with arms linked around it.) If the game is being played on dirt or sand,

the circle can be drawn with a stick; on grass it can be outlined with sticks. Because Poison is a rough-and-tumble game, a "soft" surface, such as sand, is ideal. It's also a good idea for the players to be relatively equally matched in both size and strength.

All the players now link arms at the elbow and form a ring around the circle. Together, they choose a material that will be considered "safe" for the upcoming round of play. When touched or held by a player, this "safe" material offers protection from being tagged. The chosen material should be readily at hand, in easy running distance of the circle—for example, wood, cloth, stone, or water. Any object or surface made of that material is "safe."

The action begins as soon as the adult or older child supervising the game gives an agreed-upon signal. The players, arms still linked, wriggle and shake and push and pull their neighbors with the intention of forcing someone to step into or on the circle in the middle. (No ganging up on one player allowed!) The first player forced into the circle becomes "it." At

that instant, all the other players yell, "Poison!" and dash off—in search of some "safe" material. More than one player may use the same material. If, for example, the "safe" material is water, any number of players can rush to a nearby birdbath.

"It" immediately heads after them. If all the players manage to get to "safe" material without being tagged, the round ends, and "it" is out of the game. If, however, "it" can tag some-

one before she reaches "safe" material, then the tagged player is out of the game. With that, the ring forms anew, a different "safe" material is chosen, and another round begins. (If a new "it" is needed, the players again battle to force someone into the circle.)

The game goes on until there are only two players left. These two battle at the circle—linking arms and trying to push one another in. The last one to remain outside is the winner.

Streets and Alleys

The playing course is constantly changing in this challenging chase game.

Players: 15 or more, plus an adult or older child to supervise

Ages: 7 to 12

Place: Outdoors on grass or pavement

Equipment: None

Because at least 15 players are required to play Streets and Alleys, it's a particularly good game for school or camp groups or for a large party. Children enjoy its fast-paced excitement and the unexpected changes of direction that complicate the chase.

To create the course, all the players except three divide up into three groups of equal size (or as nearly equal as possible). The members of each group join hands with arms outstretched to create three parallel rows. If there are 15 players total, for example, there will be 4 children in each row, with 3 others (for the moment) standing to the side. The players in each row face in the same direction with about 5 feet (1.5m) of space between the rows. These spaces are the "streets."

The three remaining players are the

runner, the chaser, and the caller. The runner starts at the end of one street; the chaser at first stands in front of the rows and then pursues the runner through the course. The caller, who also stands in front of the rows, gives

the signal to begin. At the caller's signal, the runner tears off down the streets with the chaser in hot pursuit.

At any moment, the caller may shout, "Alleys!" When this happens, the players in the rows immediately drop hands, turn to the right, and join hands with their new neighbors (in the 15-player game, there will now be four rows of 3 players each). The aisles between the new rows are the "alleys." The runner and chaser must now quickly change directions and resume the chase.

STREETS!

The runner and the chaser must confine their chase to the streets and alleys—they may not duck under the other players' clasped hands. The caller continues to call "Streets!" and "Alleys!" at random intervals, and the chaser and runner continue running through the lines of players until the runner is caught. Players begin each round in the street formation, with a new runner, chaser, and caller.

Running Up the Alleys

In this simpler version of Streets and Alleys, the players making up the course don't change direction, so no caller is necessary. Players form rows of four or five children each, and the chaser pursues the runner up and down these alleys. Once the rows are formed, they do not change. When the runner gets to the end of an alley, he and the chaser must run around the last person and into the next alley. Play continues until the runner is tagged. A new runner and chaser are chosen for the next round.

Capture the Flag

Quick and stealthy runners have the advantage in this race to capture "flags" from behind enemy lines.

Players: 8 or more (even number), plus an adult or older child to supervise

Ages: 8 to 14

Place: Outdoors in large grassy area

Equipment: Handkerchief, bandanna, or square of cloth for each player (preferably with distinctive colors for each team); stones, sticks, parking cones, strips of cloth, or long piece of rope for marking playing area

apture the Flag is a team game in which players try to retrieve handkerchiefs ("flags") from the opposing team's territory without being tagged. Some children develop intricate offensive and defensive tactics; others play the game as a wild free-for-all. Either way, Capture the Flag is loads of fun for children old enough to follow the rules.

First, a playing area at least 30 feet (9m) in length (or much more, if desired) is designated and a dividing line marked at the center. Next, players divide into two equal teams. Each player lays a handkerchief just inside the far boundary of her territory. If possible, the handkerchiefs should be of two different colors, one for each team. Largish squares of cloth—torn from old sheets, for example—work just as well and may be given distin-guishing marks for each team. Once the flags are laid down, players take a place behind their team's side of the dividing line and wait for the supervising adult or older child to give the signal to begin.

The object of the game is for one team to capture all the other team's flags. The only way to capture a flag is to dash into enemy territory and snatch one before being tagged by a player on the opposing team. If a player manages to grab a flag, she may walk freely back into her own territory and place the stolen flag back behind her boundary line as booty.

If she gets tagged before grabbing a flag, however, she's in trouble. She becomes a prisoner of war and must now stand behind the enemy's boundary line. The only way she can escape is if another player on her team runs back and tags her, without himself getting caught in the process. A player may free as many of his fellow teammates from captivity as he can tag without getting caught. But once he's freed prisoners, he may not go after the flag—he has to return to his own territory first. And he's fair game until he gets there. A freed prisoner may return to her own territory without risk of recapture, but she too has to wait until she gets there before turning around and setting off on any further flag-capturing (or prisoner-rescuing) missions.

It's common in this game for teams to launch raiding parties. Several players run across at once with the hope that at least one of them will make it to capture a flag (or to liberate any prisoners). Other players try deception, standing innocently on their side of the dividing line—then unexpectedly rushing to grab a flag.

The first team to capture all of the opponents' flags is the winner. The game may also be played with a time limit. In this case, the team with the most flags at game's end wins.

A slightly more involved version of this game can be played on any vast plot of land—even one with hills and trees and streams. In this case, outside boundaries do not even need to be marked; only the dividing line must be perfectly clear. Parking cones,

pieces of cloth tied to trees, or a long piece of rope laid on the ground will do the trick.

In this version, there is only one flag per team, which is set far back in that team's territory. Each team conspires to steal the other's flag (and protect its own). A flag guard is usually assigned to stay nearby at all times. In this game, it's not enough to reach the flag without being tagged; a player must pick it up and evade capture on

her way back to her own territory, too. If she succeeds, her team wins. If not, the flag is laid down on the spot where she was tagged, and the foiled flag stealer is hauled off to jail.

The jail is generally a tree or the side of a house or some other distinct site, and a captive must stay there until rescued. Any would-be rescuer has to make it all the way to the jail itself to free his fellow teammates. If there are several captives, they may hold hands to form a human chain, with one end touching the jail. Any rescuer need only touch the last figure in the chain to free them all. Like the flag, the jail should also have a full-time guard. When one team successfully nabs the other team's flag and bring it "home," victory is declared.

Blind Man's Bluff

In this circle game, a blindfolded player tries to identify others using only the sense of touch.

but today's game is quite harmless. Blind Man's Bluff can be enjoyed by players of all ages—the more, the merrier. It's a great party game, which can be played in several different ways.

In the most common form of Blind Man's Bluff, an adult who's supervising the game blindfolds one player

Players: 6 or more, plus an adult to supervise and put on blindfolds

Ages: 4 to 12

Place: Indoors in large room (cleared of furniture and breakable objects) or outdoors on grass or pavement

Equipment: Blindfold (bandanna or scarf)

Blind Man's Bluff, which dates back to ancient Greece, went through several permutations to become the present-day game of blindfolded circle tag. Some of the earlier versions involved hitting other players with branches or poking them with long sticks,

with a bandanna or scarf and then guides this player to stand in the middle of a circle formed by the others. The players in the circle hold hands and walk around in one direction until the "blind man" claps three times. At this signal, the circle stops moving and the blind man points randomly (without peeking) toward a player in the ring. The designated player must now approach the blind man and stand still while the blind man tries to identify the "captive" by touching his face, hair, and clothes. The blind man gets one or two guesses to identify the player.

If the blind man guesses correctly, the identified player takes a turn in the center. If the guess is wrong, the blind man remains blindfolded for another round.

The game can also be played without forming a circle. In this version, players scatter around the playing area but must remain in one spot after the blind man's three hand claps. The blind man then turns around three times before heading off, usually with

hands stretched out front, in search of the others. (With younger players especially, the supervising adult may need to offer gentle guidance should the blind man wander too far astray, and of course the play area should be free of any obstacles that might trip up the searcher.) The first player to be found and identified takes the blind man's role on the next round.

Squeal, Pig, Squeal

In this version, the sense of hearing rather than the sense of touch is used to identify other players. As in Blind Man's Bluff, participants circle around a blindfolded player. While the circle moves, the players also sing a song like "Ring Around the Rosey" or "Here We Go Round the Mulberry Bush." At the end of the song, the blind man points to one player and commands her to make a sound (or the blindfolded player makes a sound that the others must imitate). The command could be to squeal like a pig, quack like a duck, cry like a baby, or drip like a faucet. The "squealing" player

may try to disguise her voice to fool the blind man. If the blind man can guess the player's identity in one or two tries, they switch places. The blind man must continue guessing until he correctly identifies a squealer.

Colin Maillard

Colin Maillard (named after a blind Belgian soldier who lived a thousand years ago) requires chairs for all but one player. Players sit in the chairs facing inward in a circle around the blindfolded child, who is standing in the center. When ready, after a signal from the supervising adult, the blind man—Colin Maillard (pronounced "MY-yar")—moves toward a player and sits on his lap. Then Colin Maillard must identify the player on whose lap she is sitting without touching any other part of his body. Stifled giggles often give the identity away! If his identity is guessed correctly in one try, the sat-on player becomes Colin Maillard in the next round. After he's been blindfolded, all the other players switch seats.

Thieves

A blindfold makes it challenging to nab the raiding "thieves."

Players: 5 or more, plus an adult to supervise and put on blindfolds

Ages: 5 to 10

Place: Indoors in large room (cleared of furniture and breakable objects) or outdoors on grass or pavement

Equipment: Blindfold (bandanna or scarf); newspaper; toys, candy, costume jewelry, coins, or other prizes to serve as "loot"

Thieves is a game of cunning and stealth, as well as a good test of reaction time. A blindfolded player must act swiftly to apprehend the

other players, who are trying to sneak up and steal her booty. This is a great party game because the prizes are built in if kids are allowed to keep their spoils—just make sure everyone has an equal chance to be a thief.

One player is blindfolded by the supervising adult and given a rolled-up newspaper to guard a pile of "treasure"— candy, toys, costume jewelry, coins, or other prizes—that is placed in front of her. It's best if the blindfolded player sits down on the floor or ground. The other players make a wide circle around the blindfolded child.

The players in the circle take turns trying to sneak up and snatch as many

items as possible from the treasure pile. They must do this as quietly as possible so as not to be heard by the blindfolded player. If the blindfolded player hears a thief, she calls, "Thief, thief!" and tries to tag the robber with the newspaper without getting up and leaving her post as guard.

If the thief is tagged, he must return to the circle empty-handed—and another player gives it a try. The round ends after each player has paid one visit to the booty pile. The thief who has collected the most loot wins. If, by chance, the blindfolded player has managed to prevent any loot from being stolen, she is the winner.

Ball Games

Because the number of games that can be played with a ball is limitless, this chapter merely skims the surface of the play possibilities. Its sampling of ball games covers all age groups: circle games for preschoolers, throwing and catching games for slightly older kids, and sports-related games for those who are ready for more sophisticated play. Many of the games are played with a "playground ball"—a large, soft rubber ball. Tennis balls, basketballs, handballs, footballs, and even Frisbees also play prominent roles. Some of the ball games require other equipment, as noted in the entries. Almost all are meant to be played outdoors, for the most part in an area safely distant from traffic, pedestrians, and windows or other breakable objects. Games that involve kids throwing balls at one another should always be closely supervised by an adult.

Around Ball

Fancy passing makes for creative competition
in this basic circle game.

Players: 10 or more (even number),
plus an adult to supervise

Ages: 3 to 8

Place: Outdoors on grass or pavement, or indoors in gym or similar room

Equipment: 2 playground balls

In its most basic form Around Ball is a circle ball-passing game for young children. It's played by two teams arranged in rings. Each team aims to be the first to move the ball around the circle five times. Adding difficult passing methods and stunts makes the game much more challenging. Children hone their passing and catching skills during this game; they also learn quite a bit about teamwork and cooperation.

First, the players divide into two equal teams and choose a captain for each. Each team then forms a separate circle, with the distance between the players in the circles ranging from 3 to 6 feet (.9 to 1.8m), depending on their passing and catching skills. Each captain holds a playground ball.

At the signal "Ready, set, go!" the game begins with each captain throwing the ball to the player on his right.

Players continue to pass the ball to the right as quickly as possible. When the ball has made a full trip around the circle and is back in the captain's hands, he shouts, "One!" and keeps on passing the ball. The captains count each round. If the ball is dropped, it is returned to the captain and the round starts over.

Players who have basic throwing and catching down pat may want to add a bit of variety to the game by passing the ball in a special way. Passing the ball between the legs, behind the back, or with a single bounce from one player to the next–these are just a few ways to spice things up. As in the basic game, a dropped ball goes back to the captain and the round is begun again.

The first team to finish five rounds is the winner. When the ball finishes its fifth circuit, the captain holds it high over his head and yells "Five!" to announce the victory.

Astride Ball

Budding goalies can hone their blocking
skills in this circle game.

Players: 8 or more

Ages: 4 to 10

Place: Outdoors on grass or pavement

Equipment: Playground ball or soccer ball

Although Astride Ball is a rather simple circle game for young children, it becomes quite challenging when played at top speed. Players in the circle test their reaction time as they try to keep a rolling ball from passing between their legs.

First, all the children except one form a circle and stand about 3 feet (90cm) apart with their legs spread and hands on their knees. This is the "astride stance." The remaining player stands in the center of the circle.

The game begins when the player in the middle starts rolling the ball along the ground with his hands, with a sort of bowling motion, in an effort to pass the ball through the legs of any player in the circle. The roll may be fast or slow, but it should not leave the ground. The other players may block the ball with their hands or by snapping their legs together. When not threatened with the ball, however, all players in the circle must maintain the astride stance.

When the player in the middle scores a goal, he joins the circle and the player who let the ball pass between her legs goes into the center. The game goes on for as long as the participants want to play.

Call Ball

This fast-paced game requires players to respond quickly when their nicknames are called.

Players: 5 or more, plus an adult to supervise

Ages: 6 to 11

Place: Outdoors on pavement

Equipment: Tennis ball

Call Ball is a noisy game in which a player must run to catch the ball when the nickname or number that has been assigned to him is called. This game develops speed, agility, catching skill, and reaction time. It has the added bonus of reinforcing memory by requiring each player to recall both her own nickname and those of her opponents. Call Ball should be played on pavement or another hard surface that allows the ball to bounce well—and the ball should be in good condition to ensure high bounces.

Before the game starts, each player is given a nickname for the purpose of the game. The names may be days of the week, months of the year, names of animals or flowers, and so on. Be creative! For very large groups, the players may be assigned numbers.

To begin, one player bounces the ball as high into the air as possible and calls out the nickname of another player. As soon as the ball leaves the bouncer's hand, the other players run away—all except the player who has been called, who must try to catch the ball before it hits the ground again. If successful in catching the ball, that player then bounces the ball and calls out the name of another player, who must rush back to try to catch the ball before it hits the ground again. This goes on until someone fails to catch the ball.

If a called player does not catch the ball, he loses 1 point and calls out, "Stop!" as soon as he has retrieved the ball. At that point, the other players must freeze wherever they are. The player who missed then throws the ball at any other player—below the neck only, please!—except the one who called his nickname. If a player is hit, she loses a point and gains possession of the ball. If the thrower misses, however, he loses another point and the player who originally called him gets the ball again. The game continues in this manner, with each player who takes possession of the ball bouncing it as high as possible and calling out the nickname of another player.

Any player who loses 3 points is eliminated from the game. The last player remaining in the game is the winner.

Center Ball

Center Ball has something for everyone—it's a circle game, tag game, and ball game rolled into one.

Players: 10 or more, plus an adult to supervise

Ages: 7 to 12

Place: Outdoors on grass or pavement

Equipment: Playground ball, basketball, or volleyball

In spite of its circle format, Center Ball is not for preschoolers. Instead, it's a rather complicated but thoroughly delightful game, which develops speed, passing, and catching skills in young athletes.

Center Ball can be played on either grass or pavement. To set up, all the players except one form a ring. They should be positioned far enough from one other so that when they stretch out their arms, their fingertips just touch those of their neighbors. The remaining player stands in the middle of the circle, holding the ball.

The game begins when the player in the center throws the ball at any player and then runs past that player outside the circle. If the thrower's target catches the ball thrown at her, the catcher immediately rushes to the center of the circle, puts the ball down on that spot, and takes off after thrower. Her aim is now to tag the thrower before he can find a way back into the circle and touch the ball. If she can do so, he's stuck as the thrower again. If not, she becomes the thrower, and the thrower takes her place in the ring. If by chance the thrower's target failed to catch that original throw, there is no running and chasing; she simply takes her place in the center of the circle immediately and becomes the thrower.

The game can go on for as long as participants wish to play.

Monkey in the Middle

Two players play a fast game of catch, trying to keep the ball away from the "monkey" between them.

Players: 3
Ages: 6 to 12
Place: Outdoors on grass or pavement
Equipment: Playground ball

There are no winners or losers in Monkey in the Middle, just an ever-changing contest of two against one. The sole object of the game is for two players to keep the ball away from the "monkey" by using fancy throwing and catching moves or simply speedy exchanges. Kids seem to revel in the lighthearted teasing and "ganging up" that this game allows. To keep the contest on an even keel, it's best if the players are fairly equal in size and athletic ability.

To begin, two players stand about 10 feet (3m) apart and the remaining player stands between them. The outside players start playing a game of catch, with the goal of keeping the ball away from the monkey. Meanwhile, the monkey tries to intercept the ball any way she can, including picking it up after one of the other players has dropped it. It's not

unusual to see the monkey running, jumping, and scrambling all over the other players in an attempt to gain possession of the ball.

The player who has last touched the ball before the monkey snatches it becomes the new monkey. The game keeps going for as long as the participants wish to play.

Keep Away

Keep Away, best played with 8 to 20 kids, is a team game that operates on the same principle as Monkey in the Middle: the goal is to keep the ball away from the opponent. This game is played on a large playing field. Players divide into two loosely even teams. Because the two teams mix on the field, one team should wear something, such as hats or bandannas, to distinguish it from the other team.

One team starts with the ball and passes it from player to player, trying to keep it away from members of the other team. The other team tries to intercept the ball in any way possible—except that tripping, hitting, or other rough play is not allowed. There is no beginning or end; the game stops when the players are exhausted. The winning team may be judged as the one that kept possession the longest—although that's often a point of dispute.

Spud

In this rowdy tossing and catching game, players try to avoid being hit by the ball.

Players: 4 or more, plus an adult to supervise

Ages: 6 to 12

Place: Outdoors on grass or pavement in large open area, away from traffic, pedestrians, and windows

Equipment: Playground ball

Spud is an extremely popular ball game that can be played on grass or pavement with players of almost any age. A noisy game that includes lots of calling out, Spud requires catching skills and a good aim. The ability to run fast is also a benefit. Although the ball is soft, children should be reminded to keep their throws aimed below the neck.

To begin, one player holds the ball and the rest cluster around her. The child with the ball then throws it high into the air while calling out the name of another player. As that player runs to catch the ball, the rest dash away from him as fast as they can. If the player is able to catch the ball before it bounces, he may immediately throw it up again and call out another player's name. If not, he must pick up the bouncing ball and, at the top of his lungs, yell, "Spud!" With that, all the running players must immediately freeze. The player who picked up the ball must also freeze on the spot.

The player with the ball then chooses an opponent to hit with the ball. He is allowed to take four giant steps toward his intended victim, and as he takes them, he calls out the letters S, P, U, and D. He then throws the ball toward his target. If the target is hit, she is assigned the letter S. If the targeted player catches the ball, however, or the thrower misses altogether, the thrower gets an S. The penalized player starts the next round by throwing the ball up and calling out another player's name.

The game goes on, with players being assigned S then P then U then D. A player who gets all four letters, spelling "S-P-U-D," is eliminated from the game. The game can end there, or it can continue until only one player—the Spud champion—is left.

Baby in the Air

The rules for Baby in the Air are similar to those for Spud, but each player is assigned a number before the game begins. Instead of calling out a player's name, the player tossing the ball into the air calls out a number, and the player whose number was called scrambles for the ball. In this variation, the thrower may take three giant steps toward her target. And in this variation, the penalty letters don't spell "S-P-U-D"—they spell "B-A-B-Y."

Catch the Ball

Players build passing and interception skills in this challenging circle game.

Players: 12 or more, plus an adult to supervise

Ages: 7 to 14

Place: Outdoors on grass or pavement

Equipment: Playground ball, basketball, or football

Catch the Ball is a great game for a large group with a limited amount of playing space. Because it's played in a circle, the game is contained, but it is no less action-packed than many games played on bigger fields. Players must be nimble and speedy as they try to intercept a ball as it is tossed across the circle. Younger kids can start out with a large, soft playground ball; older ones relish the challenge of playing with a basketball or football. Catch the Ball can be played equally well on pavement or grass.

First, all players except one form a large ring. The remaining player starts out in the middle of the circle. The game begins when the players in the circle start passing the ball to one another. The ball may be thrown to any other player in the circle at any speed. The player in the middle tries to intercept or block the pass or knock the ball out of the hands of another player. (Caution: this can get rough!) The players in the circle quickly figure out that they should get the ball out of their hands as quickly as possible.

If the player in the middle succeeds in disrupting the ball movement, she trades places with the last person to have touched the ball. If a player in the circle drops the ball or makes a wild, uncatchable throw, he takes a turn in the middle. Play goes on for as long as the participants wish.

Dodge Ball

No matter how the players in this game are arranged, the object is to dodge the bombarding ball.

Players: 10 or more (even number), plus an adult to supervise

Ages: 6 to 12

Place: Outdoors in large open area or indoors in gym

Equipment: Playground ball; stones, sticks, chalk, or masking tape for marking the court

Dodge Ball is one of those classic games that almost no North American gets through childhood without playing. Kids can work off their excess energy on the Dodge Ball court: attacking an "enemy" is perfectly acceptable in the context of the game. Dodge Ball also promotes speed, agility, aim, and fun. Children should be warned not to throw the ball too hard or at anyone's head or neck, and games should always be supervised by an adult.

The basic Dodge Ball game is played on a court about 30 feet (9m) square. The boundaries are marked off with sticks, stones, chalk, or the like; then the court is divided by a center line. Players divide into two equal teams, which stand on opposite sides of the center line.

The game begins when one player throws the ball at a player on the other team. A player who is hit by the ball is eliminated from the game. If the target manages to catch the ball, however, the thrower is out. If the ball bounces before it hits anyone, no one is out. Whether the ball hits someone or not, the player who retrieves it takes possession and immediately uses it to try to hit someone on the opposing team. If the ball rolls or bounces out of bounds, a player on the receiving team gets to bring it back into play.

The game continues with the ball being thrown back and forth and players catching or being hit by the ball. Any player who steps over the center line or out of the court while trying to dodge the ball is out.

The first team to eliminate all the players on the opposing team is declared the winner.

Prison Dodge Ball

Prison Dodge Ball is played in the same way as basic Dodge Ball, except

that players who are eliminated are not necessarily out for the entire game. Instead, a player who is hit by the ball or steps out of bounds is in "prison" and must stand in a line of players to the side of the court. If a player catches a ball, the thrower is sent to prison and the catcher's first teammate in prison rejoins the game. This goes on, with players moving in and out of prison each time the ball is caught. If players decide to stop the game before one team is completely eliminated, the team with the most players left on the court is the winner. Prison Dodge Ball is best with 20 or more players, and it may be played with several balls at once for a faster-moving game.

Greek Dodge Ball

This variation is similar to Prison Dodge Ball, except that the prisoners line up along the back boundary of the opposing team's side of the court, facing their own team. And they are very much active participants, even from prison. If a ball manages to bounce or roll through the enemy ranks back to them, or if one of their own teammates throws the ball up and over the enemy and back to them, the prisoners can use it to strike the enemy from behind. If a prisoner does hit an opposing player, the prisoner is freed and the unlucky dodger is sent to the other prison.

Bombardment

Bombardment is played in much the same way as regular Dodge Ball, but when a player is hit by the ball, he must go and stand among the players on the opposing team's side of the court. From there, the player tries to catch balls that are thrown by his teammates or dodged by the opposition. A player who catches one of his teammates' throws before it touches the ground may rejoin his own team. Players try to rebuild their team by throwing the ball to teammates on the other side. But players must take care: any soft pass meant for a teammate may be easy to intercept.

Crossover Dodge Ball

This variation is like regular Dodge Ball, except that it is played with four balls for every ten players. The balls are divided equally between the teams at the beginning of the game and are played simultaneously. A player who is hit by a ball is not eliminated but instead crosses over to the other team. The game goes on until all the players end up on one side—or until everyone is exhausted.

Firing Squad Dodge Ball

Instead of being played on a two-sided court, Firing Squad Dodge Ball is played against a windowless wall. One team lines up along the wall, facing out. The "firing squad" lines up facing the enemy about 15 feet (4.5m) in front of the wall. There should be about 2 or 3 feet (60 or 90cm) in between each player in both lines.

Members of the firing squad team take turns throwing the ball at any player against the wall. The targeted players may dodge the throw, of course, but they must stay within 2 or 3 feet (60 or 90cm) of the wall at all times. A player who is hit is out. If the ball is caught, the thrower is eliminated. The team with the last remaining player is the winner.

Circle Dodge Ball

Players inside a ring of children must dodge the flying ball in this schoolyard classic.

Players: 10 or more (even number), plus an adult to supervise

Ages: 6 to 10

Place: Outdoors in large open area or indoors in gym

Equipment: Playground ball

As its name suggests, this game is Dodge Ball played in a circle. As in all Dodge Ball games, the goal is to avoid being hit with the ball. Since this version is so contained, however, it is even more challenging. Players should be reminded not to fire hard at close range and to aim below the neck. Circle Dodge Ball helps kids develop aim and agility. It may be played outdoors on pavement or grass or indoors in a gym.

First, players divide into two equal teams. One team forms a large, loose circle, and the members of the other team stand inside this circle.

The game begins when the players forming the circle throw the ball into the middle with the aim of hitting players from the opposing team. The players in the middle dodge the ball to avoid being hit. Anyone who is hit by the ball joins the circle and becomes a thrower. A hit does not count, however, if it bounces before making contact with a dodger. It also does not count if the dodger manages to catch the thrown ball. If more than one player is hit by the same throw, only the first one hit joins the outer circle. If the ball comes to a halt within the circle or if it is caught by a dodger, it is rolled back out to the players who form the ring.

The game continues until only one player is left in the middle—the Circle Dodge Ball champ. For the next round, the dodgers form the circle and the throwers are in the middle.

Hunter and Rabbits

This cross between Dodge Ball and tag has some elements of basketball, too.

Players: 8 or more, plus an adult to supervise

Ages: 6 to 11

Place: Outdoors on pavement or indoors in gym

Equipment: Playground ball

Hunter and Rabbits is a fast-paced playground game that is great for large groups of children. As the name of the game suggests, a "hunter" tries to catch "rabbits" by hitting them with the ball. Hunter and Rabbits requires the speed and stamina of tag, the agility and aim of Dodge Ball, and the dribbling and passing skills of basketball. It should be played on a hard surface that allows for good ball bouncing.

Although Hunter and Rabbits is not played on a marked-out court, the boundaries of the playing area should be established so the rabbits do not run too far afield. One player is designated as the hunter and the rest are rabbits. The hunter has possession of the ball.

The hunter's goal is to hit as many rabbits as possible by throwing the ball (below the neck only!) at them. The hunter may chase the rabbits but may not carry the ball while running. Instead, the ball must be dribbled (continuously bounced up and down) any time the hunter moves with it. If the hunter hits a rabbit on the feet, legs, bottom, chest, or shoulders, that rabbit is caught. Heads, however, are strictly off-limits. If the hunter hits a rabbit's hands or arms, it doesn't count, so rabbits may try to block a ball thrown at them. Whatever happens, the hunter has to fetch the ball after he's thrown it.

When a rabbit is caught, she becomes another hunter. The former rabbit joins the original hunter in trying to hit the remaining rabbits. When there is more than one hunter, the ball is no longer dribbled; instead, the hunters now pass the ball back and forth to each other as they try to get closer to the rabbits. A hunter may only move his feet when he is dribbling the ball.

The game goes on until there is only one rabbit left. The surviving rabbit becomes the hunter for the next round.

Battleball

In this Dodge Ball game, players battle one on one to score points for their teams.

Players: 11 or more (preferably odd number), plus an adult to supervise

Ages: 8 to 14

Place: Outdoors on grass or pavement

Equipment: Playground ball; stones, sticks, or chalk for marking boundaries

Battleball is a team Dodge Ball game, but players battle out the rounds in one-on-one competition. As a result, the game, while action-packed, is not particularly fast-moving. From the sidelines, the players who are not doing battle cheer their teammates on, and those in the ring know that the success of their respective teams rests on their shoulders—a lesson in team spirit for all.

Before play begins, a large square playing court is marked with chalk, stones, or sticks, depending on the playing surface. A 20-by-20-feet (6-by-6m) square works well for ten players, but the court should be expanded for larger groups. The ball is placed precisely in the center of the playing area. Next, all the players except one divide into two equal teams. The remaining player serves as the referee. (If there is an even number of players, the supervising adult becomes the referee.) Each team counts off from one, so each team member has a number. The teams then line up in order along opposite sides of the square, with each player facing the player on the other team who has the same number.

The game begins when the referee calls out a number. The two players with that number race onto the court and try to grab the ball. The first one to reach the ball picks it up and remains on that spot. His task is now to hit the other player with it. The other player, of course, wants to avoid being hit, so she scoots away from the thrower. She can't go far, though; she has to stay inside the square.

If the thrower manages to hit the

dodger with the ball or if the dodger steps outside the square, the thrower's team scores a point and the turn is over. If the dodger manages to catch a thrown ball before it touches the ground, her team scores a point and the turn is over. If the thrower misses the dodger completely and the ball lands outside the square, no points are scored, and the turn is over.

If, however, the ball bounces inside the square before either hitting or being caught by the dodger, or before going outside the square, no points are scored—but the turn is not over. Instead, the dodger must toss the ball back to the thrower, who gets to keep trying.

Once the turn is over, the ball is put back in the center, the referee calls a new number, and play progresses. The referee need not call

out the numbers in order but should use up all the numbers before repeating any, so each person has a chance

to play the game.

The first team to score 21 points is the winner.

Bounce Ball

This tricky dodging game is played with a tennis ball in a narrowly confined area.

Players: 4 or more, plus an adult to supervise

Ages: 8 to 14

Place: Outdoors on pavement away from traffic, pedestrians, and windows

Equipment: Tennis ball; chalk for marking the court

It's not easy to dodge the bouncing ball in Bounce Ball because players must stay inside the boundaries of the court. This fast-paced game is a lot of fun for older children who may be bored with more conventional Dodge Ball games. It calls for speed, agility, and the ability to catch a tennis ball on the run. Because a good bouncing surface is necessary for the game, Bounce Ball should be played

on pavement. The game should not be played near houses, windows, cars, or passing pedestrians because the ball is sometimes hard to control.

Before play starts, a court is outlined with chalk. For four players, a 30 by 30 feet (9 by 9m) square works well. The size of the court should be increased if more players participate. All the players must stand within the boundaries.

The game begins when one player throws the ball as high into the air as possible. Everyone tries to grab the ball on its way down. The player who manages to nab the ball immediately tries to hit an opponent by bouncing the ball off the pavement toward another player. The players are free to run, jump, and duck to avoid being hit; but they may not set foot outside the boundaries. If the ball hits someone after bouncing once, the hit player is eliminated and must leave the court. If no one is hit, or if the ball is caught on the bounce, everyone is safe for the

moment. After two bounces, or whenever the ball goes out of bounds, it is fair game for anyone to grab and bring back into play. If the ball is thrown and hits another player before it bounces, both the thrower and the player who was hit are out.

Before an eliminated player leaves the court, she restarts the game by throwing the ball into the air again. The game goes on, with players trying to avoid being hit by the bouncing ball, until only a single player is left: the Bounce Ball champion.

Big Black Bug

Chanting a rhyme that has been passed down through generations enlivens a simple bouncing game.

Players: 1 or more

Ages: 4 to 10

Place: Outdoors on pavement or indoors in gym or similar room

Equipment: Playground ball

For as long as children have been bouncing balls, they have been chanting songs and rhymes to accompany the steady "thump-thump-thump" of the ball hitting the pavement. Besides adding interest, these rhymes challenge the bouncers to perform varied stunts. Big Black Bug, an old favorite, is fun to play alone, but like all bouncing-ball rhyme games, it's even more challenging with a companion to compete against.

There are many ways to bounce a ball, especially when playing alone, and the more bounces a child knows, the more fun a rhyme game is. The ball may be simply bounced up and down. It can be bounced while clapping, stamping, or twirling around. The ball can also be bounced against a windowless wall in many different ways— thrown overhand, underhand, or under the leg, for example. It can be bounced before it hits the wall or made to bounce after. A player can throw it behind his back—then turn around to catch it. The ball may be caught with one or two hands.

In Big Black Bug, the player starts with the basic bounce, then must do seven different kinds of bounces, without dropping the ball, while chanting this rhyme:

Big black bug
Sitting on a rug,
I one it,
I two it,
I three it,
I four it,
I five it,
I six it,
I seven it,
You ate it!

Players decide for themselves how each bounce is to be performed. In a

competition, the first player to make it all the way through with no mistakes is the winner.

Charlie Chaplin

The rhyme in this variation runs:

Charlie Chaplin went to France
To teach the ladies how to dance.
This is what he taught them:
Heel, toe, and over you go!
Heel, toe, and over you go!
Heel, toe, and over you go!

The ball is bounced up and down for the first three lines. On "heel," the bouncer taps the ground with one heel. On "toe," she taps a toe. On "over you go," she passes the ball under a leg.

Oliver Twist

In this variation, players take turns bouncing the ball with one hand and carrying out particular actions or pantomimes. The first to finish without any mistakes is the winner. As always, the players start with basic bouncing before the real funny business starts.

Oliver-Oliver-Oliver Twist,
Bet you a dollar you can't do this:
Number one—touch your tongue,
Number two—touch your shoe,
Number three—touch your knee,
Number four—touch the floor,
Number five—be alive (wildly wave arms),
Number six—pick up sticks (pantomime),
Number seven—jump to heaven,
Number eight—shut the gate (pantomime)
Number nine—walk the line,
Number ten—start again.

O'Leary

O'Leary is a challenging bouncing-ball rhyme that may be played alone or as a competition.

Players: 1 or more

Ages: 6 to 10

Place: Outdoors on pavement near windowless wall

Equipment: Tennis ball or handball for each player

In O'Leary each player must bounce a ball off a wall and perform a series of motions while simultaneously chanting a rhyme. This is not easy to do, especially if a player is trying to be speedy enough to finish before an opponent. A windowless wall and a paved surface are necessary to play the game. The rhyme, sung to a tune similar to "Ten Little Indians," is easy to learn:

One, two, three, O'Leary,
Four, five, six, O'Leary,
Seven, eight, nine, O'Leary,
Ten, O'Leary, postman.

Players stand just a few feet (1m) away from the wall, and each holds a tennis ball or a handball. The following eight motions are performed while chanting the rhyme. It's amazing how quickly kids commit them to memory.

1. Throw the ball under a raised right leg so that it bounces against the wall once, then catch it in the air.

2. Throw the ball under a raised left leg so that it bounces against the wall once, then catch it in the air.

3. Bounce the ball off the ground against the wall and catch it in the air under a raised right leg.

4. Bounce the ball off the ground against the wall and catch it in the air under a raised left leg.

5. Bounce the ball off the ground against the wall and catch it in the air on a circle formed by joining the right thumb and index finger at the tips.

6. Bounce the ball off the ground against the wall and catch it in the air on a circle formed by joining the left thumb and index finger at the tips.

7. Throw the ball against the wall, twirl around once to the right, and catch it in the air.

8. Throw the ball against the wall, twirl around once to the left, and catch it in the air.

O'Leary is fun to play alone. It's also a good game to play against one opponent—both perform the motions at the same time and the one who finishes first without mistakes is the winner. If there are more than two players, they can compete to see who can get farthest through the rhyme without any mistakes in one turn.

Four Square

This ball-bouncing game, played on a chalk-marked court, is a schoolyard standard.

Players: 4 or more

Ages: 6 to 11

Place: Outdoors on pavement

Equipment: Playground ball; chalk for marking the court

Along with Hopscotch, Jump Rope, and Dodge Ball, Four Square is one of the games most likely to be played on an elementary school playground. Many schoolyards actually have Four Square courts painted onto the blacktop. The game is well-suited to school-age kids because it is cooperative yet competitive and can be played at a pace to match the skill level of the participants. The open-handed ball batting used in Four Square is also an excellent practice for volleyball, handball, and even tennis.

To make a Four Square court, a 16 (4.8m) to 20-foot (6m) square is drawn and divided into four boxes of equal size (see diagram). The boxes are labeled A, B, C, and D clockwise from the upper left, and a diagonal serving line is drawn in square A (the server's square) from upper right to lower left .

Four players play Four Square at a time—with one standing in each square. Throughout the game, players try to spend as much time in square A as possible. The best square to start in, then, is square A. The worst is square D. One way to determine the starting order is for kids to do Eeny, Meeny, Miney, Mo or One Potato, Two Potato (see Pre-Game Show on page 17) to decide who gets to start the game in square A.

The game begins when the player in square A serves the ball from behind the service line. She bounces the ball once on the ground, then bats it underhand with one or both open palms into any other player's square. The ball must bounce once in the square before the second player hits it. The second player, in turn, tries to hit the ball into another player's square, also underhand with one or both open palms. Again, it must bounce once in the new square, then that square's inhabitant tries to hit it into another. The ball keeps moving in this way until a player makes an "out." There are quite a few ways to do this: hitting the ball onto a line between squares or on the edge of the court; hitting the ball out of the court altogether; hitting the ball with a fist or an overhand motion; hitting the ball with any part of the body other than the hands; failing to return a ball after it has bounced once; or stepping over the serving line while serving.

An out changes the players' square assignments, but just how it changes them depends on who makes the out. If there are players waiting to join in the game, the player who makes the out must leave the court and go to the end of the waiting line. In any case, the player who makes the out or his replacement always gets sent to square D—the end of the line, so to speak. If the server makes the out, she moves into square D, D moves into C, C moves into B, and B moves into A—and becomes the server. If the player in square B makes the out, he moves to square D, D moves into C, and C moves into B; but the server stays put. If C makes the out, she and D switch places. If D makes the out, everyone remains in place.

There is no scoring system or distinct winner in Four Square. Players simply try to spend the most time serving (and if there are more than four players, the most time in the game). Players may also take pride in making the fewest mistakes.

Stoopball

Stoopball challenges players to catch a ball bounced off the steps of a stoop.

Players: 1 or 2

Ages: 8 to 14

Place: Outdoors on pavement near a stoop or set of steps

Equipment: Tennis ball or handball

Although Stoopball originated on urban streets, the game may be played against any set of outdoor steps, from those on a farmhouse porch to those behind a suburban school. If no steps are handy, the ball may be bounced against a curb (in a modified version of the game)—provided there is no traffic.

Stoopball can be enjoyed as a solitary challenge or as a competitive game. A good aim is required.

In Stoopball, each player stands about 4 feet (1.2m) from the stoop (a greater distance for expert players) and throws the ball at the steps. The object is to catch the ball after it bounces off the steps—not an easy task, considering the unusual angles at which balls often ricochet. To score a point, a player must make the ball bounce off the top of one step and rebound off the front of the next step up (the riser) so that it comes back to the player—who then has to catch it. Alternatively, the player may try to bounce the ball off the sharp front edge of a step and catch it on the rebound; that tricky maneuver is worth 10 points. If a player fails to catch the ball or to bounce it correctly, he loses a point.

When playing alone, players often set a point goal (usually 100 points) for themselves and then see how quickly they can achieve it. Another way to play alone is to see how many points can be scored in a specific period of time. In competitive Stoopball, players take turns trying to rack up points, with the first to reach a predetermined total taking the Stoopball crown. Whenever one player makes a mistake, the other player gets to go.

Five-Ten Stoopball

This version of Stoopball requires more space and is really meant to be played solo. The player stands about 10 feet (3m) in front of the stoop and tosses the ball against the steps. If, on the rebound, the ball is caught before bouncing on the pavement, 10 points are scored; balls caught after one bounce are worth 5 points. If the ball bounces more than once, the player's whole score is erased and she starts back at 0.

Sidewalk Tennis

This modified version of tennis is perfect for driveways or playgrounds.

Players: 2

Ages: 7 to 14

Place: Outdoors on pavement, away from pedestrians and windows

Equipment: Tennis ball; chalk for marking the court

Sidewalk Tennis, sometimes called Two-Square, is a great game for tennis aficionados who lack a tennis court. This game follows the basic rules of tennis, but rackets and a net are not necessary. Children need speed, agility, and excellent hand-eye coordination to play Sidewalk Tennis, which is an excellent preparatory drill for the real sport.

To make the court, a rectangle 12 feet (3.6m) long by 6 feet (1.8m) wide is drawn and divided into two equal squares. The center line serves as the net, and players face each other from opposite sides of the court.

After deciding who will serve first, the players begin the game. The first server stands anywhere on his half of the court and serves the ball by bouncing it once and hitting it with an open palm. The ball must go over the

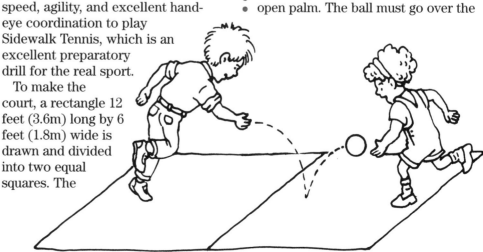

"net" and bounce once within the boundaries of the opponent's court before it is returned. The players volley the ball back and forth in this manner until someone loses the volley by missing the ball, not getting it over the net, or hitting it out of bounds.

If the server loses the volley, the other player gets to serve, but no one wins any points. If the nonserver loses the volley, the server gets a point—and gets to serve another time. A player can score *only* when he's serving.

The first player to score 11 points is the winner; however, the game must be won by at least 2 points. Thus, if the score is 11–10, play continues until someone has a 2-point lead.

Handball

This street version of Handball requires only one wall and a tennis ball.

Players: 2

Ages: 4 to 8

Place: Outdoors on pavement next to a windowless wall

Equipment: Handball or tennis ball; chalk for marking the court

Handball is a sport enjoyed by both adults and children. Kids don't need a fancy health club with a four-walled court to play the game—they can have just as much fun hitting a tennis ball against a playground wall. Handball is great exercise and develops agility and hand-eye coordination. It is best played by kids at least 9 years old, as younger kids may have trouble keeping up with the fast pace. Handball should be played on pavement adjacent to a solid wall (no windows, please!).

A regulation Handball court is 20 feet (6m) wide and 34 feet (10.2m) deep. The serving line is 16 feet (4.8m) from the wall and runs the width of the court. When devising their own courts, players may use these dimensions or alter them to fit the space available. Either way, the boundaries should be marked with chalk before beginning the game.

Singles Handball is played with two players. Both players start in the middle of the court, facing the wall. The first server stands behind the serving line and serves the ball by bouncing it on the ground once and then hitting it against the wall with an open palm. The ball must rebound off the wall and bounce back over the serving line to be in play. The server gets two tries to make a fair serve. If she fails, her opponent takes over the serve.

Once the served ball falls fair, the nonserving player must hit it back against the wall before it can bounce a second time. The players then alternate trying to hit the ball against the wall. After the serve is hit, the ball may be hit either after one bounce or before it bounces at all. Once hit, however, the ball must reach the wall directly, without bouncing off the ground first.

If a player commits an error—allowing the ball to bounce twice before she returns it or allowing her own return to bounce before reaching the wall—she loses the volley. She also loses if she hits a ball that flies off the court, either before reaching the wall or afterward (before it bounces). If a player loses a volley when she is serving, her opponent takes over the serve. If she loses a volley when her opponent is serving, the opponent scores a point and keeps serving. (In other words, a player can score points *only* when she is serving.)

A player may not interfere, intentionally or unintentionally, with her opponent when he is trying to hit the ball. This counts as a "foul." If the server fouls, the serve goes to the other player; if the other player fouls, the serve is repeated.

The first player to score 21 points is the winner.

Doubles Handball
This variation is played with two teams of two players. When the ball is in play, the teams (like individual players in Single Handball) take turns hitting the ball, but teammates themselves don't have to alternate. The nearest team member may always return the ball. When a team is serving, however, the nonserving member of the team must get off the court. She can run back on as soon as the serve is complete. The serving partner continues to serve until his team loses the serve; when the team regains the serve, the other partner serves.

Handball Tennis

This game of tennis without rackets is not for the tender-handed.

Players: 8 or more (even number)

Ages: 9 to 14

Place: Outdoors on pavement, away from traffic, pedestrians, and windows

Equipment: Handball or tennis ball; chalk for marking the court

The only racket in Handball Tennis is the noise that the two teams are likely to create as the game heats up. Played on a homemade court with a handball or tennis ball, this game requires speed, good hand-eye coordination, and cooperation among team members. Older kids who can stick to a relatively structured set of rules are sure to enjoy this fast-paced street or playground game.

First, a court measuring approximately 50 by 25 feet (15 by 7.5m) is outlined in chalk, and a line is drawn across the center of the court to divide it in half. Players divide into two equal teams, each team occupying one side of the court. Players on each team count off to determine the order of the serve. The team members—including the first server—spread themselves across their team's side of the court.

The first server serves the ball by bouncing it on the ground once and then hitting it with the palm of his hand into the opponents' side of the court. The server gets two chances to do this. If he doesn't succeed, the other team takes over the serve. Once a ball is served fairly, the receiving team tries to return it to the other side. The players on the receiving team may let the ball bounce on their side as many times as they want before returning it, but once the ball is hit, it must travel directly to the other side, without bouncing. The ball continues to be volleyed back and forth in this manner.

If a team's players fail to return the bouncing ball across the center line, they lose the volley. They also lose the volley if the ball rolls off their side of the court after bouncing once, if it comes to a stop on their side, or if they hit the ball off the court. If they happen to be serving when they lose a volley, they must turn the serve over to the opposing team. If the opposing team is serving, however, that team scores a point—and gets to keep serving. (In other words, a team can score *only* when it is serving.)

When a team regains the serve after losing it, a different player gets to be the server. That player continues to serve the ball until the team loses the serve again.

The first team to score 21 points is the winner.

Kickball

This popular field game might be described as baseball for the feet.

Players: 6 or more (even number), plus an adult to supervise

Ages: 6 to 12

Place: Outdoors on baseball diamond or large grassy field, away from traffic, pedestrians, and windows

Equipment: Playground ball; store-bought bases, T-shirts, or similar objects to serve as bases; stick or similar tool for marking "pitcher's mound"

Played with roughly the same rules as baseball, Kickball can be enjoyed by children in a wider age range. Because the ball is large and slow and is kicked rather than hit with a bat, it is much easier to handle and control. A good, well-organized game of Kickball can enjoyably fill a long afternoon. The kicking, running, fielding, and throwing skills developed while playing Kickball translate well into future soccer and baseball expertise. The rules outlined here cannot begin to cover every quirk of the game, any more than baseball could be described in a few short paragraphs. But they should be more than enough to get started.

Before play begins, a Kickball diamond must be created. The four sides of the diamond should be 20 to 30 feet (6 to 9m) long, and the corners marked as home plate, then (going counterclockwise) first base, second base, and third base. Opposite home plate, in the field beyond the diamond, there should be plenty of room for kids to run around. In the center of the diamond, a line should be drawn in the ground with a stick or otherwise marked to indicate the "pitcher's mound"; the pitcher must stand behind this line when pitching to the batter at home plate.

Participants divide into two equal teams. One team starts in the field, with one of its players serving as the pitcher. Another player should stand near first base, with the others scattered about near the bases or out in the area beyond the diamond. If there are enough players to cover the field, a team can send one member to stand behind home plate as the catcher. (Otherwise, the other team can provide a catcher.)

The other team is "at bat." They either count off to determine the batting order or a captain sets the order. The game begins when one player from the batting team steps up to home plate and the pitcher rolls the ball to her. He can roll it hard or soft, bumpy or smooth. But he should aim to get it over home plate. The job of the player at bat is to kick the ball as far into the field as possible.

If she tries to kick the ball but misses, this is considered a "strike." If she misses three times on her turn at bat, she is "out" and must give way to the next player in the batting order. (Strikeouts, however, are rare in

Kickball.) If she kicks the ball and it lands outside the adjacent right or left edges of the diamond, this is considered a "foul." Four fouls are counted as an out.

A batter doesn't have to try to kick every ball the pitcher rolls her way; she can wait for one she likes. If, however, she lets a ball pass and it goes over home plate, that counts as a strike. If she lets it pass and it doesn't go over the plate, this counts as a "ball." Four balls allow the batter to go to first base—on a "walk."

If the player kicks the ball—in the air or on the ground—into either the infield (inside the diamond) or the outfield (outside the diamond but between first base on the right and third base on the left), it is a "fair ball." She then heads off toward first base. If a "fly ball" (kicked up in the air) is caught before it touches the ground, the kicker is out, which means she must rejoin her team near home plate. If the ball is not caught in the air, the players in the field scramble to pick up the ball and try to put the kicker out in one of three ways:

throwing the ball to the first baseman before she can get there, tagging her with the ball, or hitting her with a thrown ball (no hits on the head allowed!). Depending on how far she kicks the ball (or how well the other team fields it), she may continue running from base to base, stopping only when she thinks she can't go any farther without getting caught. If she kicks the ball really well, she may make it all the way around—for a "home run." If not, she stays on the base she's reached and runs when the next player at bat kicks the ball. At that point the fielders can try to put both her and the second kicker out. A run is scored when a player makes it safely around all the bases and reaches home plate.

Players continue coming up to bat until their team has three outs. The teams then switch positions and the batting team takes the field. When each team has had a turn to bat and a turn to field, one inning is completed. The game usually continues for five innings. The team with the most runs at the end of the game is the winner.

Beat Ball

In Beat Ball the only way to score is with a home run. If a player doesn't make it around all the bases and back to home plate without getting caught, he's out. This sounds tough for the kickers, but there is a twist to make this game tough on the fielders too. Whenever a fielder chases down a kicked ball, she must initially throw it to the first baseman—even if the runner has already passed first base. Then it must go to the second baseman—even if the runner has already passed second base. The same holds with third base and home. Only if the team can do this and still get the ball to a base before the runner gets there is the runner out. There's no tagging or throwing the ball at the player in this version.

Batter's Choice

This Kickball variation is played much like Beat Ball, except that instead of kicking the ball, the batter throws the ball wherever he wishes on the field. There is no pitcher in Batter's Choice.

Newcomb

Newcomb is a simplified version of volleyball, in which players throw and catch rather than volley.

Players: 8 or more (even number)

Ages: 7 to 12

Place: Outdoors on pavement, grass, or sand

Equipment: Volleyball; volleyball or tennis net (or rope or clothesline); stones, sticks, or chalk for marking the court

In Newcomb the court, the ball, and the configuration of players are exactly the same as in volleyball. The action of the game, however, is very different. Instead of the ball

being hit from player to player, it is thrown over the net and caught on the other side. This makes Newcomb a much slower game—perfect for children who are not quite skilled enough for volleyball. Because the ball never needs to bounce, Newcomb can be played on grass or even sand, as well as on pavement.

First, players divide into two equal teams and mark out a court, using stones, sticks, or chalk. The court can be anywhere from 20 by 40 feet (6 by 12m) to 30 by 60 feet (9 by 18m), depending on the number of players and their ages. A net is stretched across the middle of the court. A standard 7-foot (2.1m) high volleyball net may be used (and lowered according to the players' abilities). A tennis net will also do, as will a rope or clothesline tied between two trees.

The teams spread out on opposite sides of the net, arranging themselves in two or three rows, depending on how many players are participating. The game begins when one player—standing anywhere inside his team's section of the court—"serves" by throwing the ball over the net. The other team tries to catch the ball after it flies over the net. If it is caught, it is then thrown back over the net. The throw can be high or low, hard or soft, so long as it makes it to the other team's side of the court.

The teams continue throwing the ball back and forth over the net, hoping that the other team will miss or drop it. The ball may not be passed from player to player on the same team—the person who catches the ball must throw it back.

The "volley" ends when one team drops the ball, fails to get it over the net, or throws it out of bounds. If the serving team commits the error, the opposing team gets to serve. If the nonserving team commits the error, however, the serving team scores a point. (In other words, *only* the serving team can score points.)

Whenever a team regains the serve, a new team member should serve, until everyone has had a chance to serve. The first team to score 21 points is the winner, but the game must be won by a difference of at least 2 points. Thus, if the score is 21–20, play continues until one team gains a 2-point lead.

Indian Kickball

The ancient game of Indian Kickball more closely resembles road races and soccer than it does traditional Kickball.

Players: 6 to 12 (even number)

Ages: 8 to 14

Place: Outdoors in large open area or along trail

Equipment: Different-colored tennis ball for each team; sticks or stones for marking course

Indian Kickball is considered to be a spiritual game by the Indians of Mexico and the southwestern United States. Traditional Native American athletes often perform sacred rituals before setting out with teammates to kick a wooden or stone ball barefoot (ouch!) along a course of 20 to 40 miles (32 to 64m). The version of Indian Kickball given here also requires stamina and fancy footwork, but the course has been reduced to a mile (1.5km) or less in the interest of young players. Tennis balls have been substituted for wood and stone balls, and sneakers or running shoes are recommended to protect tender feet.

Played as a contest between two teams, Indian Kickball is run as a race from one point to another. Teammates work together to move their ball along the course with their feet. First, players divide into two teams of three to six players each. Each team should have a different-colored tennis ball. A course for the race is then marked with sticks or stones. The course may be anywhere from 100 yards (90m) to a mile (1.5km) long, depending on the stamina of the players and the time available. Hills, curves, and rough terrain make the course more interesting. But it should be wide enough for at least three or four kids to be jostling about in the same general area at any one time.

Each team stands grouped around its ball several yards apart at the starting line. Someone is chosen to be the starter and gives the signal "Ready, set, go!" Immediately, one player on each team kicks the ball along the course and the other teammates set off after it. Working together, teammates continue to kick their ball along the course as quickly as possible. Players should try to strike a good balance in their kicks—very long kicks may move the ball forward quickly, but they tend to go out of control (and off course). The straighter the course the ball travels, the more quickly it will get from point to point.

The first team whose ball crosses the finish line is the winner.

Punt and Catch

This goal-kicking game is good practice for future football players.

Players: 10 or more (even number)

Ages: 8 to 12

Place: Outdoors in large grassy or paved area, away from traffic, pedestrians, and windows

Equipment: Playground ball, soccer ball, or football; stones, sticks, or chalk for marking goal lines

Kids can perfect their kicking, running, and catching skills as they play Punt and Catch. The game may be played with a playground ball, soccer ball, or football, depending on the abilities and interests of the players.

Before the game starts, two goal lines are set up 30 to 50 feet (9 to 15m) apart. Players divide into two equal teams. Each team then spreads out along one of the goal lines.

The game begins when a player from the first team punts the ball from behind her goal line toward the other team. A punt is a special kind of kick: instead of placing the ball on the ground, the kicker drops the ball from her hands and kicks it up into the air with the top of her foot. Her aim is to kick the ball over the heads of the other team's players so that it lands past the opposite goal line. If she's able to do this, her team gets a point. If, however, her kick doesn't make it to the opposite goal line, the other team scores a point. The other team also gets a point if a player on that team is able to catch a punt before or after it sails over the goal line.

After the first kicker's turn, a player from the opposing team tries to punt from his goal line. The kick alternates in this way between the teams until each player has had a chance to punt.

The team with the highest score is the winner.

Errors

Errors is a one-on-one game that helps players hone their baseball fielding skills.

Players: 2

Ages: 5 to 8

Place: Outdoors on pavement

Equipment: Playground ball

Although it is played with a playground ball, the action in Errors is similar to a baseball fielding drill. In this game each player tries to score points by forcing her opponent to make an error. This is an excellent game for young children who are interested in learning baseball rules but are not ready for a baseball and glove. Errors should be played on pavement, where the ball can roll quickly and smoothly.

To play, opponents stand 20 to 30 feet (6 to 9m) apart and take turns rolling the ball to each other. The player fielding the ball must pick up the ball and immediately roll it back.

If the fielder misses the ball, bobbles it, or rolls it back in a wild manner, this counts as an "error"; when one player commits an error, the other player scores a point.

The players continuously alternate in the roles of thrower (or, rather, roller) and fielder, with the roller trying to force the fielder into making an error. This is accomplished by rolling the ball hard and fast or putting a spin or curve on it.

The first player to score 21 points is the winner.

One Old Cat

One Old Cat is a two-base game that's great practice for baseball.

> **Players:** 8 to 12 (or up to 20 for team game)
>
> **Ages:** 7 to 11
>
> **Place:** Outdoors on baseball diamond or grassy field, away from traffic, pedestrians, and windows
>
> **Equipment:** Softball and bat; store-bought bases, T-shirts or similar objects to serve as bases; stone or stick to mark "pitcher's mound"

One Old Cat is a baseball-type game that can be played in a limited amount of space. Because there are only two bases, the game requires much less in the way of fielding and ball-handling skills than does regular baseball. Players do, however, need to be able to hit a pitched ball, a skill that is sure to improve with the practice this game provides. One Old Cat is usually scored individually, but it may also be played as a team game with anywhere from 12 to 20 players divided into equal teams.

First, two bases—home plate and first base—are marked about 30 to 40 feet (9 to 12m) apart. First base is not directly in front of home plate but set diagonally to the right, in the position that first base would be on a regular baseball diamond. With a stick or stone, a "pitcher's mound" is marked on the ground about 20 feet (6m) in front of home plate. One player is chosen to be the pitcher and stands at the pitcher's mound. Another is the catcher, who stands behind home plate, and a third is the batter. The rest of the players spread out in the field.

The game begins when the batter steps up to the plate. The ball is pitched underhand. The batter swings at the first pitch she chooses. If she misses the ball entirely or tips it to the side or behind her, that counts as a "strike." If she gets three strikes, she's "out" (though the third strike counts only if it's a clean miss, not a tip.) Then the batter goes out into the field. The catcher becomes the batter, the pitcher now becomes the catcher, and one of the fielders takes over the pitcher's spot.

If the ball is hit, however, the batter tries to run to first base and home again. The players in the field, meanwhile, scramble for the ball. If one of them catches it in the air, the batter is out. It's also an out if the ball is picked up off the ground and thrown to the catcher (who must have his foot on home plate) before the batter can make it back to home. But if the batter makes it, she scores a run and gets to bat again.

The game continues until every player has had a chance to bat. The player who has scored the most runs at the end of the game is the winner.

Pickle

Players try to run between the bases without being tagged or caught in a "pickle."

Players: 3

Ages: 7 to 14

Place: Outdoors on grass

Equipment: Playground ball or baseball and gloves for 2 players; store-bought bases, T-shirts or similar objects to serve as bases

Pickle, also known as Running Bases, re-creates a baseball game's rundown, or "pickle"—a situation in which a runner is caught between two bases, with fielders on either side trying to tag him out. Younger kids can play the game with a playground ball; older ones enjoy the challenge of using a baseball and glove to mimic a real baseball pickle. Either way, children find this game wildly exciting and great fun.

First, two bases are set up approximately 30 feet (9m) apart (if a playground ball is used) or up to 50 feet (15m) apart (if a baseball is used). Two players are fielders and stand on the bases. The remaining player is the runner, who starts the game standing on one of the bases.

The two fielders begin the game by tossing the ball between them. during this game of catch the aim of the runner is to run from one base to the other, thereby scoring a "hit." The problem is, if she is tagged off base by a fielder holding the ball, she's out—and must trade places with the fielder who tagged her. So she may want to wait until one of the fielders drops, overthrows, or mishandles the ball and then take off. Or she may simply decide to dash into the middle and take her chances.

Sometimes, just the pressure of having to tag the runner will cause the fielders to fumble the ball. Often, however, the runner will get trapped in a pickle, with the fielders closing in from both sides. The fielders continue to throw the ball back and forth over her head. If they're really good, the fielders will eventually succeed in tagging the runner.

If the fielders lose control of the ball, or if the runner is especially tricky or quick, she may scramble past a fielder to a safe base. She may not, however, run outside the "base-path," the loosely defined strip of territory between the two bases. If the fielders drop the ball, she can keep on running from base to base, scoring hit after hit, until they track it down again. If, however, she has to back-track to the base where she started, she doesn't score—although she is free to try again.

The runner scores a "run" for every four hits. When her turn ends, she keeps all the runs she has scored. Any extra hits are erased, however; they do not carry over to her next turn as runner. The player with the most runs after a specified time is the winner.

Bat Ball

Players compete to score runs by batting the ball with their hands in this base-running game.

Players: 8 to 20 (even number)

Ages: 7 to 11

Place: Outdoors on grass or pavement, away from traffic, pedestrians, and windows

Equipment: Playground ball; T-shirts or similar objects to serve as bases

Equipment: Stones, sticks, or chalk for marking lines

Bat Ball has its roots in baseball, but no bat is actually used in this game. Instead, players bat the ball with their fists or palms and then try to run the bases before they are tagged "out." This game requires speed and hand-eye coordination, as well as good aim. Bat Ball is a good introduction to baseball skills and rules for young children and an exciting game in its own right for slightly older ones.

First, two bases are marked approximately 30 to 40 feet (9 to 12m) apart; one is the home plate and the other, called the long base, is in the field. T-shirts, trees, or any similar marker can serve as bases. Players divide into two equal teams. One team starts out on defense, standing here and there in the field behind the long base. The other team starts out on offense and lines up behind the home plate to take turns at bat.

Play begins when the first batter steps up to the plate, tosses the ball into the air, and smacks it out into the field with his fist or palm. (The batter gets only one chance to smack the ball.) The batter may hit—or try to hit—the ball anywhere, so long as it's in front of home plate. He may hit it high in the air, on the ground, or any other way he pleases. The batter then sets off running, trying to make it to the long base and back again.

The players in the field, meanwhile, go after the ball. If one of them manages to catch it in the air, the batter is out and goes to the end of the batting line. If a fielder scoops the ball off the ground, she must tag the batter with the ball before he makes it to the long base and back. She may also throw the ball to a teammate who is closer to the batter, so that her teammate can make the tag. The tag itself must be made by touching the batter below the waist with the ball; throwing the ball at the batter is not permitted. If the fielding team does tag the batter, he's out. But if he makes it home, his team scores one run.

The first team continues batting until it has three outs. The teams then switch positions. The team with the highest score after four innings wins.

Punchball

In this modified baseball game, the players' own fists serve as bats.

Players: 6 or more (even number)

Ages: 8 to 14

Place: Outdoors on pavement, away from traffic, pedestrians, and windows

Equipment: Handball or tennis ball; store-bought bases, T-shirts or similar objects to serve as bases

Punchball, also called Triangle Ball, is a version of baseball that has been modified for street play. Because the ball should be able to bounce, the game must be played on pavement. Punchball is not an easy game to play. It requires speed, good catching and throwing skills, and excellent hand-eye coordination. Older kids in particular relish the challenge. The game should be played well away from traffic, pedestrians, and breakable objects like windows. The rules outlined here do not cover every quirk of the game, any more than baseball could be described in a few short paragraphs. But they should be more than enough to get started.

Before play begins, a triangular field is laid out, with home plate at one point and bases at the two others. (Think of a regular baseball diamond with second base cut off.) The two bases should be no more than 25 feet (7.5m) apart, but the distance between each base and home plate can be from 25 to 40 feet (7.5 to 12m). The bases can be indicated with store-bought bases or with T-shirts, or similar objects. The "outfield," the area beyond the bases and opposite home plate, should have plenty of room for kids to run around.

Players divide into two equal teams. One team spreads out in the field, with one player standing near first base. (The other base is usually called third base instead of second base because it's where third base would be on a regular baseball diamond.) The other team is "at bat." These players either count off to determine the batting order or choose a captain to set the order. The game begins when one player from the batting team steps up to home plate with the ball in hand, tosses the ball into the air, and then tries to hit it, using his fist instead of a bat. (The game may also be played with the fielding team providing a pitcher, who pitches to the batter in such a way that the ball reaches him after making one bounce.)

As in regular baseball, if the batter misses the ball entirely or tips it to the side or behind him, that counts as a "strike." If he gets three strikes, he's

"out" (although a third strike counts only if it's a clean miss, not a tip). In that case, the next player in the batting order takes a turn.

If the ball is successfully hit into the field, however, the batter heads toward first base. If the ball is caught in the air, the batter is out. Otherwise, the fielders scramble to pick the ball up and put the batter out in one of two ways: by throwing it to the first baseman (who must have a foot on the base) before the batter gets there or by tagging the batter with the ball before he reaches first base. (Throwing at the runner is not allowed, though!)

Depending on how far he's punched the ball or how well it's been fielded, the batter may continue running from first to third, stopping there if he thinks he can't go any farther without getting caught. If he punches the ball really hard, he may even make it all the way home—for a "home run." If not, he stays on the base he's reached and runs when the next player punches the ball. Each time a player makes it home, his team scores a run.

Players continue coming up to bat until a team has three outs. Then the teams switch positions and the batting team takes the field. When each team has batted and fielded once, one inning is completed. The game usually goes on for five innings. The team with the most runs at the end of the game is the winner. If there is a tie, extra innings are an option.

Stickball

This simplified version of baseball originated on city streets but can be played on almost any paved surface.

Players: 6 or more (even number)

Ages: 7 to 14

Place: Outdoors on pavement, away from traffic, pedestrians, and windows

Equipment: Tennis ball or handball; baseball bat or cut-down broom handle to serve as the stick; T-shirts or similar objects to serve as bases (optional)

Although baseball may be America's favorite pastime, Stickball has been the game of choice for generations of city kids. Played on sandlots and playgrounds, as well as other paved areas, Stickball is often a child's first introduction to baseball. Although the rules are looser and the field (and usually the teams) smaller than in baseball, the spirit of the game and the skills necessary to play it are much the same. Still, the rules outlined here do not cover every wrinkle in the game, which, like baseball, has many elaborate rules. But they should be more than enough to get started.

Before play begins, a stickball diamond must be created. The sides of the diamond should be 50 to 75 feet (15 to 22.5m) apart, if possible, and the corners marked in some way as home plate, first base, second base, and third base. In traditional city stickball, players often improvise in creating their diamond. Home plate may be a manhole cover, first base a fire hydrant, second base a telephone pole, and third base a stoop. In any case, it's helpful to have a windowless wall behind home plate so overthrown balls won't fly too far. And there should be plenty of room beyond the diamond opposite home plate for kids to run around.

Players divide into two equal teams. One team starts out in the field with one player acting as pitcher, standing in the middle of the diamond. Another player stands near first base, with the others scattered near the bases. If there are enough players, a second baseman, third baseman, shortstop (between second and third), and catcher (behind home plate) can be assigned, with the others stationed in the outfield.

The other team is "at bat." The players either count off to determine the batting order or choose a captain to set the order.

To begin the game, the batting team's first player stands at home plate, while the fielding team's pitcher throws the ball overhand so that it bounces once and then over home plate. (The players may decide to dispense with the pitcher and have the batter throw the ball up into the air himself.) If the fielding team does not have a catcher, a member of the batting team may assume this role and return missed balls to the pitcher.

If a batter swings and misses the ball, that counts as a "strike." Three strikes equal an "out," and the player must give way to the next player in the batting order. If the batter hits the ball so that it lands behind him or outside the diamond to the right of first base or to the left of third base, this is considered a "foul." A foul counts as a strike unless the batter already has two strikes. A batter does not have to swing at every pitch; he can wait for one he likes. But a player who fails to swing at a pitch that could be hit is likely to be teased by the other team. In Stickball there are no "balls" or "walks" awarded for bad pitches.

If the batter hits a ball—in the air or on the ground—either into the infield (inside the lines of the diamond) or out into the outfield (outside the diamond but between first base on the right and third base on the left), it's a "fair ball." He

immediately drops the bat and runs toward first base. If a "fly ball" (one hit high in the air) is caught before landing, the batter is out. Otherwise, players in the field scurry to retrieve the ball and try to put the batter out by either touching first base before he gets there or throwing it to a teammate who will. They may also tag the batter directly to put him out, but they are not allowed to throw the ball at him and tag him that way.

Depending on how far he hits the ball or how quickly the other team retrieves it, the batter may keep running from base to base, stopping only when he thinks he can't go any farther without being tagged. (Once he's

passed first base, the only way to get a batter out is by tagging him before he's reached the next base.) When a batter has stopped on a base, he remains there and tries to advance when the next batter hits the ball. A "run" is scored whenever a player makes it back to home plate.

If there are only three players per side and all are on base, a "ghost runner" is said to be on third base and the runner who would otherwise be there comes home to bat. If the hit is fair and the runners advance, the ghost runner scores a run.

Stickball has one rule that's *very* different from baseball: if a ball is hit "out of the park" (to a place way, way

out of the field), it is *not* a home run. Instead, the player who hit it is out and is expected to go get the ball. In Stickball, it's simply bad form to hit the ball too far.

When the batting team collects three outs, the teams switch places. After each team has had a chance to bat and field, an inning is completed. The team with the most runs after a predetermined number of innings (say, 9) is the winner. If the score is tied, then extra (full) innings are played until the tie is broken.

Speedball

Speedball is like baseball on the fast track—the innings are quick and to the point.

Players: 10 to 20 (even number), plus an adult or older child to serve as umpire (optional)

Ages: 8 to 14

Place: Outdoors on baseball diamond or large grassy area, away from traffic, pedestrians, and windows

Equipment: Softball or tennis ball; bat; glove for each player (optional); store-bought bases, T-shirts or similar objects to serve as bases; stones or sticks to mark "pitcher's mound"

Speedball is a game for kids who have places to be and people to see. As its name suggests, it's a speedy version of baseball. In Speedball only four players get a chance to bat before the next team is "up," so the game time is a lot shorter than in baseball.

Speedball—the rules of which are a bit more relaxed than those of baseball—can be played on a regulation baseball field with nine or ten players per team. It can also be enjoyed in an ordinary backyard with T-shirts for bases and only enough players to cover the infield. If a tennis ball is used, there's no need for gloves. Softballs, however, call for protective gear. As in any baseball-type game, running, throwing, catching, and hitting skills are the most valuable. The rules outlined here do not cover every quirk of the game, which can be as complicated as baseball. But they should be enough to get started.

An umpire isn't strictly necessary in an informal game, but having one can ensure fairness. An adult or older child can serve as ump, or if there's an odd number of players, someone can volunteer for this role, perhaps trading off with another player after a few innings.

If the game is not being played on a regular baseball or softball field, a Speedball diamond must be created. The sides of the diamond should be 20 to 30 feet (6 to 9m) long, and the corners marked as home plate, first base, second base, and third base. The field beyond the diamond opposite home plate should have plenty of room for kids to run around. In the center of the diamond, a line is marked on the ground with a stone or stick as the "pitcher's mound." The pitcher must stand behind this line when pitching to a batter at home plate.

Players divide into two equal teams. One team starts the game in the field with one player acting as the pitcher. Another should stand near first base, with the others scattered about near the bases or out in the area beyond the diamond. If there are enough players, a second baseman, third baseman, shortstop (between second and third), and catcher (behind home plate) can be assigned, with the others in the outfield. The umpire, if there is one, stands behind the catcher.

The other team is "at bat." These players should either count off to determine the batting order or choose a captain to set the order.

The game begins when the first batter steps up to the plate and the pitcher throws the ball underhand. If the batter swings at the ball and misses, this is considered a "strike." If she does this three times before hitting a fair ball, she is "out" and must give way to the next player in the batting order. If she hits the ball so that it lands behind her or outside the diamond to the right of first base or to the left of third base, this is considered a "foul." A foul counts as a strike unless a batter already has two strikes.

A batter does not have to swing at every ball the pitcher throws. She can wait for one she likes. If, however, she lets a ball that can be hit pass, that counts as a strike. If she lets a ball pass that cannot be hit, that counts as a "ball." Four balls automatically allow the batter to go to first base—a "walk." It is up to the umpire (or the catcher, if there is no umpire) to honestly call balls and strikes.

If the batter hits the ball—in the air or on the ground—either into the infield (inside the lines of the diamond) or into the outfield (outside the diamond but between first base on the right and third base on the left), it is a "fair ball." She now sets off for first base. If a "fly ball" (one hit up in the air) is caught before landing, the batter is out. Otherwise, the players in the field scramble to pick up the ball and try to put the player out either by throwing the ball to the first baseman (who must have his foot on first base) before the batter gets there or by tagging the batter directly. (No throwing the ball at the player is allowed!)

Depending on how far she hits the ball or how quickly the other team retrieves it, the batter may keep running from base to base, stopping when she thinks she can't go any farther without being tagged out. If she hits the ball really hard, she might make it all the way around the bases for a "home run." If not, she stays on the base she's reached and tries to advance as far as possible when the next batter hits the ball.

A "run" is scored whenever a player makes it back to home plate. In Speedball, as in baseball, a side is retired after three outs; when each team has batted and fielded once, an inning has been played. In Speedball, however, only four players per team may bat each inning. So even if three outs have not been made, a team's inning is over after the fourth batter bats. There is one exception to the four-batter rule: a player who is walked does not count as one of the four batters. The team with the most runs after five innings is the winner.

Playground Rounders

This compact base-and-ball game is a simplified version of an English game.

Players: 8 or more (even number)

Ages: 8 to 12

Place: Outdoors on pavement, away from traffic, pedestrians, and windows

Equipment: Tennis ball; chalk for marking bases and boundaries

Rounders originated in England, even though it is sometimes called Danish Rounders. The adult version, which uses a bat, resembles baseball. In this simplified version, however, no bat is used—instead, a tennis ball is hit with the hand. Rounders makes a good playground game because only a relatively small diamond is needed. It is usually played on pavement, since distinct baselines must be drawn. The game itself calls for speed, dexterity, good catching and throwing skills, and the ability to make contact with a pitched ball. The rules outlined here do not by any means cover every aspect of this game, which has many of the same elaborate wrinkles as baseball. But this description should be more than enough to get started.

To set up, a playing diamond with sides 15 to 20 feet (4.5 to 6m) long sides is drawn with chalk on the pavement. Boxes are drawn in the corners to represent home plate, first base, second base, and third base. A large circle is drawn in the middle of the diamond to serve as the "pitcher's mound."

The players divide into two equal teams. One team starts in the field. This team should designate a pitcher to stand on the pitcher's mound and a catcher to stand behind home plate. The remaining fielders spread out beyond the diamond, opposite home plate. All other fielders are outfielders—there are no base players.

The other team is "at bat." These players either count off to determine the batting order or choose a captain to set the order.

The batting team's first player stands behind the plate to begin the game. The pitcher throws the ball underhand over home plate above the head of the batter, who must swat it with his hand and then run to first base. A batter need not swat at any ball pitched to him; he can wait for one he likes. But he is allowed only one swat. If he misses or hits it poorly, he must still run toward the base.

If the batter hits a "fly ball" (one that goes up in the air) and it is caught before landing, he is "out" and must rejoin his team near home plate. Otherwise, the players in the field scramble to pick the ball up and quickly throw it to the pitcher. Even if the batter misses the ball, the catcher scurries to chase it down and throw it to the pitcher. When the pitcher catches the ball, she touches it to the ground inside the pitcher's mound and yells, "Down!" If the batter is not on base when the pitcher calls "Down!," he is out.

Depending on how far he hits the

ball or how quickly the other team retrieves it, the batter may continue running from base to base. If he hits the ball well enough, he may even be able to make it all the way back to home plate. But if he is not on a base when the pitcher "downs" the ball, he's out. Once the player has stopped at a base and the ball has been downed, he waits there until the next player hits, at which point he can advance.

Runs are scored when players make it safely around all three bases and

back to home plate. Unlike in baseball, any number of players may be on any one base at any given moment. A player does not *have* to advance when another batter hits the ball. Runners may wait as long as they like to make a move, keeping in mind that they can't score if they don't reach home plate.

The batting order does not remain the same throughout the game. Instead, the order changes according to the order in which the players

return home or are put out. As soon as a player scores a run or is out, she joins the end of the batting line. If there is only one player left who is not on base, he keeps batting until another player returns home.

When the batting team has three outs, the teams switch places. When each team has had a turn batting and fielding, one inning has been played. The team with the most runs after an agreed-on number of innings is the winner.

Around the World

Players try to sink shots from seven spots around the basket in this game.

Players: 2 or more

Ages: 8 to 14

Place: Driveway or other area with basketball hoop, or one end of basketball court

Equipment: Basketball; chalk, masking tape, or stones for marking shooting spots

A round the World is a basketball game that offers both novice and experienced players great practice in shooting free throws. Because shots are taken in turn, there is no offense, defense, or contact involved. The goal is to be the first to get a basket from every spot on the course. A basketball hoop, a ball, and something to mark the shooting spots are all that players need.

First, seven spots are marked with chalk, masking tape, or stones in a semicircle around the basket. The shooting marks can be closer to the basket for young players and farther away for older ones.

To begin, the first player stands on the first spot and tries to shoot a bas-

ket. If successful, she moves to the next spot and shoots again. As soon as the player misses a shot, the ball goes to the second player, who starts shooting from the first spot. Each player takes a turn and gets as far "around the world" as he can before missing. For the second round, play-

ers start at the spot from which they last missed.

The first player to make it through the course—from the first to the seventh spot and back again—is the winner.

Steal the Dribble

This basketball drill tests players' ball-handling skills.

Players: 2

Ages: 8 to 14

Place: Basketball court, or driveway or other paved area; chalk or masking tape for marking boundaries (optional)

Equipment: Basketball

While most basketball games test shooting skills, Steal the Dribble concentrates on ball dribbling, intercepting, and defending skills. An enjoyable one-on-one game to play after a long afternoon of shooting baskets, Steal the Dribble requires a good measure of agility and coordination. The tallest player has no natural advantage, for a change.

The game is best played on a basketball court. If played on ordinary pavement, a free-throw line (a few feet [1m] long) and a small circle (about 2 feet [60cm] across) need to be marked there with chalk or masking tape about 15 feet (4.5m) apart. The circle represents the spot right under the basket on a real court.

The two players decide who will have possession of the ball first. Starting from the free-throw line, that player then dribbles the ball, bouncing it up and down with one hand at a time, to the point just below the basket. (There is no shooting in this game.) This dribbling feat would not be hard if the other player wasn't trying to steal the ball or knock it away. The dribbler can proceed in a straight line or a winding one; she may double back or fake one direction and go another, but she must continue dribbling without interruption the whole time. Neither player may make physical contact with each other.

If the dribbler makes it to the basket without having the ball knocked away or stolen by her opponent and without making any mistakes, such as putting two hands on the ball or holding it for a moment, she scores a point. Even if she is touched or otherwise jostled by the defender, as long as she makes it intact, she scores a point. If, however, the dribbler errs or loses control of the ball, the defender scores a point. When a point is scored, the players switch roles.

The winner is the player with the most points after a predetermined amount of time (say, 10 minutes) or the first player to reach a certain number of points (say 5).

Twenty-one

To play this basketball game, players must master both free throws and layups.

Players: 2

Ages: 8 to 14

Place: Driveway or other area with basketball hoop, or one end of basketball court

Equipment: Basketball; chalk or masking tape for marking free-throw line

Twenty-one is probably the most popular basketball-shooting contest. It gives a player the opportunity to perfect her foul-shooting and layup techniques while engaging in hot competition with her opponent. The risk of going over 21 points and having to start all over again adds to the excitement of the game.

A regulation basketball hoop is hung 10 feet (3m) above the ground. The height can be modified for younger players if the hoop is on an adjustable pole. For this game, a free-throw line is marked with chalk or masking tape about 15 feet (4.5m) in front of the basket. One player stands under the basket while the other shoots from behind this line. If the shooter makes a basket, she scores 2 points and gets to keep shooting until she misses.

When a shot is missed, the player under the basket scrambles to recover the ball, dribbles (that is, bounces the ball with one hand at a time) back to the basket, and shoots a layup, trying to bounce the ball off the backboard so that it goes through the hoop. If he makes the basket, he earns 1 point and gets to take his turn at the free-throw line. If he misses the layup, however, the first player gets the ball again.

The first player to reach exactly 21 points wins. If, however, a player's point total goes over 21, her entire score is wiped out and she must begin again. This means that a player with 20 points does *not* want to make a free throw. Instead, if she's at the free-throw line, she'll have to miss intentionally and hope to score her final point off a miss by her opponent. Of course, it's always risky to give an opponent a chance to pick up points. A savvy player might start calculating early and try to arrange her moves so that she'll eventually be at the free-throw line with 19 points.

Shootout

This basketball-shooting contest is a great way to hone hoop skills.

Players: 2 or more

Ages: 8 to 14

Place: Driveway or other area with basketball hoop, or one end of basketball court

Equipment: Basketball; stopwatch or watch with second hand; chalk or masking tape for marking the court; pencil and paper for keeping score (optional)

Shootout is a combination of several basketball contests that help players improve their skills. These competitions may be played separately, as games in their own right, or together, as part of a hoop-shooting tournament. Players should be divided according to age or skill so they can compete with others at their level. Shootout can be played on a driveway or playground with a standard basketball hoop, 10 feet (3m) high, as well as at one end of an indoor basketball court.

The following contests can be played one at a time or as one game:

Bounce and shoot: Participants take turns shooting as many baskets as they can in 1 minute. The shots may be made from anywhere on the court, and the ball must bounce one time between shots (including shots that go in). The player gets 1 point for each basket.

Speed shoot: Chalk or masking tape is used to mark out a half-circle with a 3-foot (90cm) radius directly in front of the basket. All shots must be taken from behind the half-circle mark. Each player in turn then shoots as many baskets as possible during the course of 1 minute. The player quickly retrieves the ball after each shot, whether or not the ball goes in the basket. Each contestant receives 1 point for a good shot.

Free throw: Chalk or masking tape is used to mark a free-throw line about 15 feet (4.5m) in front of the basket (or closer for younger players or if space is limited). Each player takes 20 "free throws," shooting without interference from behind the line; another player stands under the basket retrieving balls and throwing them back to the shooter. One point is scored for each basket.

Layup: This contest tests dribbling and layup skills from three different starting points. First, players must dribble the ball, continuously bouncing it up and down with one hand at a time, right up to the basket. There, they must execute a successful layup, shooting so that the ball bounces off the backboard and through the hoop. The starting points can be marked with chalk or bits of tape. The first spot is 20 feet (6m) directly in front of the basket. If the player misses the layup after dribbling in, he's eliminated right away. If successful, though, the player goes on to the next spot, which is 20 feet (6m) from the basket on the left side. If that layup is made, the player dribbles in from a point 20 feet (6m) from the basket on the right. And if that shot is made, he starts again, continuing until he misses, when it's the next player's turn. A player scores 1 point for each basket.

Deadeye Dick: In this contest for medium- and long-range shooting, each player takes three shots from each of five shooting spots on the court. The spots can be marked with chalk or bits of tape. The first shooting spot is the free-throw line, and each basket from there is worth 2 points. The second spot, from which baskets are worth 3 points each, is 3 feet (90cm) behind the free-throw line. The third spot is 12 feet (3.6cm) to the left of the second spot, and the fourth spot is 12 feet (3.6cm) to the right of the second spot; from both, baskets are worth 4 points each. The fifth spot is 9 feet (2.7m) behind the free-throw line (or 6 feet [1.8m] behind the second spot); from there a basket is worth 5 points. A perfect score is 54.

If Shootout is being played as a tournament, the player with the highest score after completing all the events is the winner.

Horse

In this basketball shooting game, no one wants to be the H-O-R-S-E.

Players: 2 or more

Ages: 9 to 14

Place: Driveway or other area with basketball hoop, or one end of basketball court

Equipment: Basketball

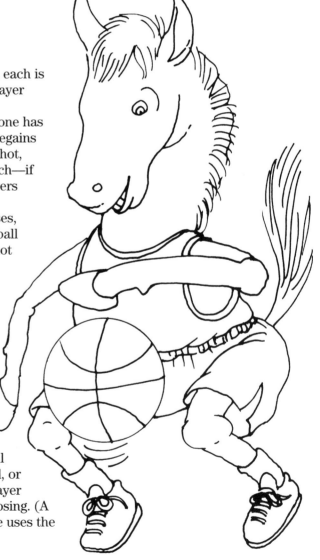

Horse is probably the most popular basketball shooting duel played on driveways and playgrounds across the country—and it can even be played with several people at once. Sort of a follow-the-leader basketball game, Horse is most fun if the players are equally matched in shooting skills. The game gains momentum as the letters of the word "H-O-R-S-E" are assigned to players who miss a shot.

Before beginning, players establish a shooting order. To start, the first player tries to shoot a basket from anywhere on the court. The lead shooter can use any type of shot he wants—underhand, overhand, hook shot, or layup. If the ball goes through the basket, the next player in line must attempt the exact same shot from the exact same spot.

If the second player or any later player fails to sink the shot, each is assigned the letter H. If a player makes the shot, no letter is assigned to her. After everyone has had a turn, the first player regains the ball and takes another shot, different from the first, which—if he makes it—the other players must again try to imitate.

Once the first player misses, the second player gets the ball and a chance to take the shot of her choice. If she makes it, the others must try to copy that shot. If she doesn't, the next player in line has a chance to initiate a shot.

Play continues in this manner, with players trying to imitate each other's shots and misses being penalized with the letters H-O-R-S-E. The game can go on until all but one player is eliminated, or it can end when the first player becomes a horse, thereby losing. (A shorter version of this game uses the word "P-I-G.")

One-Goal Basketball

A ball and one hoop are all that are needed to play this simple version of basketball.

Players: 2 or more (even number)

Ages: 9 and up

Place: Driveway or other area with basketball hoop and backboard, or one end of basketball court

Equipment: Basketball; chalk or masking tape for marking free-throw line, if needed

On driveways and playgrounds all across North America, the thump-thump-thump of One-Goal Basketball can be heard anytime the weather gets warm (and sometimes even when it's not). Basketball is an action-packed game that requires skill and stamina, and once they begin playing, kids get hooked. One-Goal Basketball is great because there's no need for a gym or ten players, and—in this version in particular—the rules are fewer in number and simpler than in real basketball. The game can be played in an area as small as 20 feet (6m) square with anywhere from two to ten players. Kids become skilled at handling a basketball around age 9 or 10, but even younger children may enjoy practicing their skills in this loosely organized game.

A regulation basketball hoop is hung 10 feet (3m) above the ground. The height can be modified for younger players if the hoop is on an adjustable pole. If played on a regular basketball court, the boundaries of the court underneath the basket and to each side can serve as the boundaries for One-Goal Basketball. The territory behind the free-throw line is the "backcourt." If the game is being played in a driveway or similar place,

a free-throw line should be marked with chalk or masking tape about 15 feet (4.5m) in front of the basket. The edge of the pavement can serve just fine as the boundary.

Players divide into two equal teams. The game begins with one team taking possession of the ball in the backcourt. The object of the game is to score points by shooting the ball through the basket while trying to prevent the other team from doing the same. Players may shoot the ball from anywhere on the court, and when a basket is sunk, 2 points are scored.

As players look to shoot, the ball may be passed from player to player on the same team. Players must dribble the ball, bouncing it up and down using one hand at a time, if they wish to move with it. Meanwhile, opposing players may try to steal a ball that is being dribbled or to intercept a ball that is being passed. If a ball is dropped or knocked off the court, the team that did *not* touch it last gains possession at the point where the ball went out of bounds.

Whenever a basket is scored, the other team gets possession of the ball, again in the backcourt. Whenever a shot is missed, however, both teams may scramble for the ball as it rebounds off the rim or backboard. If the team that didn't shoot manages to control the rebound, the ball must be passed or dribbled to the backcourt before it may be shot again. If the shooting team snatches the rebound, it is permitted to shoot again without returning to the backcourt.

When trying to steal the ball or prevent an easy shot, players may not bump or push the player with the ball. This is called a "foul." There are many

different ways to deal with fouls in One-Goal Basketball, but here's a simple and fair approach: When a player with the ball is fouled, play stops and he is allowed to take a shot without interference from the free-throw line. If he makes it, the basket is worth 1 point. But whether he makes it or not, his team retains possession of the ball, starting in the backcourt. When an offensive player is responsible for excessive jostling, the fouled player simply takes possession of the ball in the backcourt.

There are also several violations that require a team to give possession of the ball to the other team: moving with the ball without dribbling ("traveling"); dribbling, stopping and holding the ball, then dribbling again ("double-dribbling"); dribbling with two hands at the same time (also "double-dribbling"); stepping over the free-throw line when attempting a free throw; failing to pass or shoot the ball within 5 seconds (an optional rule); hitting the ball with feet or fists; and jumping to make a shot without releasing the ball. With no referee, players must monitor themselves.

The team with the highest score after a specified period of time is the winner. Alternatively, players may decide to play to a predetermined number of points (usually 21); in this case, the first team to reach that score is the winner.

One Man Out

In this game, played with four or more players, one player acts as a guard against all the others. The offensive players try to shoot the ball and score, while the guard tries to intercept the ball and prevent the others from making baskets. When a player makes a basket, she scores 2 points. But if she misses the shot, she becomes the new guard. If the guard intercepts the ball, the last offensive player to touch it becomes the guard. This game is every person for himself—whoever scores 10 points first wins

Flying Saucer Golf

This adaptation of miniature golf tests
players' skill at throwing a flying disk.

Players: 2 to 4

Ages: 8 to 14

Place: Outdoors in park or large yard
with plenty of possible targets

Equipment: 1 or 2 plastic flying disks
(such as Frisbees); pencil and paper
for keeping score

In Flying Saucer Golf, players compete to throw their flying disks through a course of their own making. Depending on the participants' creativity and the playing area, the course can be made simple and straightforward or ingenious and complex. To play, kids should have pretty good control in throwing a flying disk. An open area like a park or large yard is the best place to play.

First, the "golf course" must be created. Most Flying Saucer Golf games consist of 9 "holes" (although there can be 18 if the time and space are available). Each "hole" is a target at which the disk is aimed. Trees, fences, playground equipment, and water fountains make good targets for holes; parked cars, flower beds, and people do not! The course can be mapped out in advance or made up as the players go along. Either way, the holes should be 50 to 100 feet (15 to 30m) apart. A really great Flying Saucer Golf course also includes some "hazards." These may be anything from a puddle or a row of bushes that the disk must sail over to a gap in a fence that it must pass through. Besides deciding the location of each hole, players must decide how each hole will be played—that is, whether the disk is required to hit it, go through it, skim over it, or whatever. They must also choose "teeing-off" sites for each hole.

The first player starts by throwing the disk at the first hole from its appropriate "teeing-off" site. If he doesn't reach the hole on his first shot, he keeps trying from the point at which the disk the lands. Once he makes it to the hole, he writes down the number of throws it took. Each of the other players plays the first hole in turn and records her score. The participants then move on to the second hole.

The game continues with players playing the holes in sequence. When everyone has completed the course, the scores are totaled. As in real golf, the player with the *lowest* score is the winner of the game.

Ultimate

Ultimate is an action-packed game that combines
elements of football, soccer, and hockey.

Players: 6 or more (even number)

Ages: 8 to 14

Place: Outdoors on large grassy field,
away from traffic, pedestrians, and
windows

Equipment: Plastic flying disk (such as
a Frisbee); stones or sticks for marking boundaries

In Ultimate, much as in football, soccer, and hockey, the aim is to move the "ball" down the field and across the opposing team's goal line. In this case, the ball is a flying disk, which is thrown from player to player. Because the disk is likely to soar high and far, the game is very fast-paced. Kids should be relatively proficient at throwing and catching a flying disk or the game won't be much fun.

To set up the game, stones or sticks are used to mark out a rectangular playing field about 180 feet (54m) long and 90 feet (27m) wide (the size may be adjusted according to the size of the playing area and the skill of the players). The short ends of the field are the goal lines and the long ends the boundary lines. Next, the players divide into two equal teams and decide who will receive first.

To start the game, each team lines up along its own goal line. One team throws the disk toward the other (receiving) team. Members of the receiving team try to catch the disk or let it fall to the ground without being touched and then pick it up. Either way, the receiving team now moves the disk down the field by throwing it from one player to another, with an eye toward getting it into the hands of a team member who is over the opposition goal line.

Of course, the opposing team puts its energy into stopping the advance of the team with the disk and gaining possession of the disk. If it intercepts or knocks down a pass, it gets the disk. But no tackling or physical contact with other players is allowed.

The only permissible way for the advancing team to move the disk is to pass it through the air. It can be sent forward, backward, or sideways—high or low. A player may not run while holding the disk, but he may pivot on one foot as he searches for a teammate to pass it to. The other

team members are allowed to run around as much as they like, trying to find an open receiving spot.

If the advancing team allows the flying disk to land on the ground or if a team member takes a step while holding the disk, the other team immediately takes possession, on the spot where the error occurred. If the disk flies out of bounds, the other team takes possession by throwing it back onto the field from where it landed.

A goal is scored when one team member throws the disk over the opposition's goal line and it is caught by a teammate located on the far side. Each goal is worth 1 point. After a goal, the teams again line up along their goal lines, the scoring team throws the disk toward the opposi-

tion, and play resumes. The team with the highest score after a specified period of time, or the first team to reach a predetermined score (usually 11 points), is the winner.

Playground Soccer

Speed, endurance, and fancy footwork make for champions in this fast-paced kicking game.

Players: 4 to 22 (even number)

Ages: 7 to 14

Place: Outdoors on large grassy or paved area, away from traffic, pedestrians, and windows

Equipment: Soccer ball or playground ball; stones, sticks, or chalk for marking boundaries; 4 sticks about 4 feet (1.2m) long, broom handles, trash cans, or similar objects for goal posts; watch or other timer (optional)

Soccer, probably the most popular ball game in the world, is played in about 150 countries. In Great Britain and many other places, it is called "football," but it is very different from the U.S. game of football. Soccer players are constantly on the move, often racing up and down the field, as each team tries to score by kicking the ball into the other team's goal. Unlike most ball games, soccer does not involve throwing or catching skills; players (except for the goalie) are not even allowed to touch the ball with their hands or arms while it is in play. Instead, soccer players must perfect their kicking skills—kicking not just with their feet but also with their legs, hips, even their stomachs and chests. Older, more experienced players may even learn to "kick" with their heads.

The basic game of Playground Soccer is easy to learn, although the rules outlined here cannot possibly cover all the ins and outs of the game. This description, however, should be more than enough to get started.

Before play begins, a rectangular field about 70 to 80 yards (63 to 72m) wide and 100 to 110 (90 to 99m) yards long should be marked with chalk, stones, sticks, or similar markers, depending on the playing surface. (These measurements may be reduced some if space is tight.) In the center of each endline (each short side of the rectangle), a goal should be defined by two goal posts about 15 feet (4.5m) apart. Two long sticks or broom handles set upright in the ground or two overturned trash cans work well as goal posts.

The players divide into two equal teams, preferably evenly matched in skill. The two teams then determine which goal each will defend and who gets the ball first. If there are more than two players on a team, each team selects one player—the goalie—to protect its goal.

To begin the game, each team spreads out on the half of the field nearest its goal. The ball is placed in the center of the field for a "kickoff" by a player on the starting team. The members of the opposing team must be about 10 yards (9m) away from this centerpoint. The kicker now tries to kick the ball to a teammate. Once he kicks it, the opposing team may rush in to try to gain control of the ball. The kicker is not allowed to touch the ball again until another player (either a teammate or an opponent) has had a turn.

Each team now battles for possession of the ball. When a player gets the ball, she tries to move it toward her opponents' goal. She may "dribble" it, kicking it short distances in front of her as she runs toward the goal, or she may work closely with her teammates, passing the ball back and forth to other players, as they advance together toward the goal.

At any point an advancing player may try to kick the ball into the goal, but to score a point, she has to get the ball past the goalie so that it enters the goal between the goal posts, either on the ground or at a height below the goalie's upraised arms. In defending the goal, the goalie may pick up or catch the ball with his hands or use any other part of his body to block a shot. If the goalie manages to stop the shot, he may pick up the ball, walk a few feet (1m) in front of the goal, and kick the ball out of the area, toward one of his own teammates. If, however, a goal is scored, play starts again in the center of the field, with a kickoff by the nonscoring team.

Part of what makes soccer so exciting is that the opposing team is always trying to steal the ball away from the team that has it. To intercept a player's dribble, the opponent may stand in front, blocking the dribbler's path and ready to make a play for the ball the minute it is kicked. Or the opponent may come from the side, hooking her foot in to sneak the ball away. In making the attack, however, players are not allowed to shove or trip each other. If a player breaks this rule, the opposing team gets a free kick at the spot where the "foul" occurred. A free kick is also awarded to the opposing team any time a player (other than the goalie) puts his hands on the ball.

There is, however, one situation in which a player is permitted to use his hands. If one team kicks the ball outside the side boundary lines, a player from the opposing

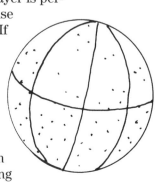

team picks up the ball and throws it in, over his head, from the spot where it went out. If the attacking team sends the ball out of bounds at the endline, the goalie gets to kick it into play from about 20 feet (6m) in front of the goal. But if the defending team accidentally kicks it out at its own endline, the attackers get the opportunity to kick the ball in from one of the endline corners.

Playground Soccer may be played against the clock, with two halves of, say, 15 or 20 minutes each. Players then get a chance to catch their breath during the halftime break. If they want, the teams can switch goals for the second half. At the end of the game, the team with the most goals wins. If no one wants to keep track of the time, though, Playground Soccer may be played until one team wins by being the first to achieve an agreed-upon number of goals.

Soccer Keep Away

Players must keep their hands off the ball in this soccer practice game.

Players: 10 or more (even number), plus an adult to supervise

Ages: 6 to 10

Place: Outdoors in large open area or indoors in gym

Equipment: Playground ball

As in Monkey in the Middle, the object here is to prevent the player in the center from getting hold of the ball. But in Soccer Keep Away players must pass, stop, or intercept the ball without using their hands or arms at all. This game is a fun way to develop kicking skills and to sharpen a player's ability to "trap" the ball—to stop or "catch" it without using the hands or arms.

To get ready for the game, one player stands in the middle of a circle or a square formed by the other players. (If there are only three players, the center player is in between the other two.) The outside players may not move into the center space during the course of the game. There should be at least 10 to 15 feet (3 to 4.5m) between each player on the outside.

One of the outside players starts the game by kicking the ball in the air to another outside player, with the goal of keeping the ball away from the center player. At the same time the center player scurries to intercept the ball, using any body part except the hands or arms. If the center player succeeds in intercepting and gaining control of the ball, he trades places with the last outside player to have kicked it, and that outside player is stuck with a penalty point.

To make the game more challenging, it can be decided that, after the kick, the ball may bounce only once before being trapped by a receiving player. If the receiver misses, she gets a penalty point. In this case, however, there is no trading of positions; the receiver simply retrieves the ball (without hands!) and kicks it to another player.

The game continues for as long as the players want. The player with the *fewest* points at the end is the winner.

Dribble Keep Away

This variation uses only three players. It is best played in a long rectangular area, about 50 to 60 feet (15 to 18m) long and 12 to 15 feet (3.6 to 4.5m) wide. One player is in the middle, and the other two try to maneuver the ball around him, either by passing it with a ground kick or dribbling it, using short forward kicks. Kicking the ball more than a foot (30cm) or so off the ground is not allowed in this game. If the middle player manages to get the ball, he replaces the player who last had it. This game is great for developing players' dribbling and "tackling," or ball-stealing, skills. There is no scoring and thus no winners or losers in this soccer workout.

Crab Soccer

This funny-looking game provides lots of laughs while strengthening all the basic soccer skills.

Players: 2 or more (even number)

Ages: 7 to 14

Place: Outdoors on grass, away from traffic, pedestrians, and windows

Equipment: Soccer ball or playground ball; 4 sticks for goal posts; additional sticks or stone for marking boundaries (optional); watch or other timer (optional)

Scurrying around upside-down on all fours, the players of Crab Soccer may look silly, but they're bound to be improving their kicking, passing, and ball-trapping skills. The object of this game, as in regular soccer, is to score a point by kicking the ball into the goal area. Because players are propped up on their hands, they are forced to use their legs and feet if they want to move the ball. Obviously this game requires a lot of arm and leg strength. To avoid tiring out, players should take frequent rests, with a 2-minute break every 5 minutes or so.

Crab Soccer is best played on a soft field of grass because players move about, in part, on their hands. The playing area should be about 10 feet (3m) square. The game may be played informally, without strict boundaries, or sticks or stones may be used to designate boundary lines. Either way two goals need to be established at opposite ends of the field. Each goal may be marked by placing two sticks about 5 feet (1.5m) apart in the center area of the endline.

If there are more than two players, they should divide into equal teams. The players decide who will start with the ball. Play begins in the center of the field, with each team (or player) on the side of its goal. First, however, the players must get into the crab (or spider) position. They sit down with their knees up and their hands on the ground by their hips; then they push up, with their backs toward the ground, so they can "walk" on their hands and feet. They must try to stay in this position throughout the game—if a player gets tired, she may lie down for a quick break, but she may not touch the ball in any way during the break.

The starting player may dribble the ball, kicking it slightly forward or to the side, or pass it to a teammate. An opponent must wait until the ball has been kicked, but then he may move in (on all fours) and try to steal the ball. No pushing or kicking at the other player is allowed. And, of course, players must stay in the crab position. If they try to use their hands to get the ball, they'll simply fall down!

Kids may find it hard not to laugh as they struggle to gain control of the ball from the crab position. But the smart player saves her breath for the task of maneuvering the ball toward and into the goal. If the player scores a goal, kicking the ball in between the goal posts, she scores 1 point and play begins again at the center, with her opponent starting off. If she misses and the ball goes out of bounds, her opponent takes possession of the ball at one end of the endline.

If side boundaries are used, the team or player who did not touch the ball last gains possession at the point it went out. Also, if a player commits a "foul" by touching his opponent, the opponent gets the ball at the point where the foul occurred.

Crab Soccer can be played against the clock, with the team or player with the highest score at the end of two 5-minute periods winning. Alternatively, the first player or team to gain an agreed-upon number of points may be declared the winner.

Sweep Hockey

Whatever the temperature, kids can practice basic hockey skills without any fancy equipment.

Players: 2 or more (even number), plus an adult to supervise

Ages: 8 to 14

Place: Outdoors on large paved area, away from traffic, pedestrians, and windows

Equipment: Plastic cup or container lid (not too hard) to serve as "puck" or "ball"; stiff household broom for each player; chalk or sticks for marking boundaries and goals; 4 trash cans (optional); watch or other timer (optional)

Armed with brooms for sticks, players in this game try literally to sweep the "puck" into the opponent's goal. Played on pavement, rather than on ice or grass, this hockey game is a fast-paced thrill, with players zipping up and down the field. Players must be sure, though, to follow all the safety rules, and it's a good idea to have an adult on hand to ensure this. When running, a player must hold her broom upright, out of the way of other players, and she must take care never to touch another player with her broom. No pushing or shoving of any kind is allowed. The champions in this hockey game are the ones who are most adept at handling the puck.

Before play begins, the playing field and the two goals should be marked with chalk or sticks. The dimensions may vary, depending on the space available, but the playing area should be a long rectangle—say, 70 to 100 yards (63 to 90m) long and 25 to 35 yards (23 to 32m) wide. Two goals should be marked at opposite ends, each about 6 feet (1.8m) wide and set in the center of the endline. Each goal may be marked with chalk or sticks, or two trash cans turned upside down can serve as the boundaries.

Each player should be equipped with a stiff household broom. A plastic cup or container lid is used as a "puck" or "ball"; the plastic should not be too thick or hard, so it doesn't hurt if a player accidentally gets zinged. If there are more than two players, they divide into two equal teams. The opponents then choose which goal they will defend. If there are more than two players on a team, each team selects one player—the goalie—to protect its goal. The supervising adult should serve as a referee.

To position themselves for the game, each team spreads out on the half of the field nearest its goal. The game starts with a "face-off": two opposing players face each other in the center of the field, standing about 5 feet (1.5m) apart on their respective sides of the field. The puck is placed in between the two players, who put their brooms on either side. At an agreed-upon signal from the supervising adult, the players vie to gain control of the puck. If there are only two players, one may try to sweep it to the side and nip past his opponent. In team play it may be easiest to whisk the puck to a teammate.

Brushing with his broom, each player now tries to move the puck down

the field toward and eventually into the opponent's goal. Kids soon figure out numerous dodges and feints to keep the puck under their control and away from their opponents. There's no stopping and resting with the puck, though; at all times the puck must be kept in motion (slow motion counts). Moreover, only the broom may be used to move the puck—no sneak kicks with the feet (or any other body part) allowed. The same rule applies to stealing the puck: only the broom may be used. When nabbing the puck, players must be careful not to trip the opponent. If a player breaks this or any other rule, it's a "penalty"; the opponent is then given the puck on

the spot where the error occurred, and no player from the opposing team may be within 10 feet (3m) of the puck when play resumes.

To score a goal, a player must shoot the puck past the goal line and into the "net." If she is successful, she (or her team) gains a point and there's a new face-off in the center. (It's a good

idea to take a few minutes for a rest break at this point.) If, however, the player misses and the puck goes out of bounds, the opposing player or team puts the puck into play from one of the corners at that end of the field. Any other time the puck goes out of bounds, the team or player who did not touch the puck last gains possession at the point it went out.

Play continues in this fashion until one player or team wins by scoring an agreed-upon number of points. Alternatively, Sweep Hockey may be played against the clock, with two halves of 10 to 15 minutes each. In that case, the player or team with the higher score at the end wins.

Strength and Wrestling Games

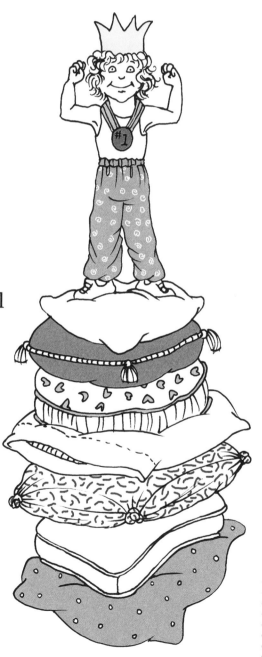

The games in this chapter are contests of strength, endurance, balance, physical coordination, or determination. Some pit individual against individual; others require cooperation and teamwork. All involve some physical aggression, and most must be closely supervised by an adult. It's very important to make sure that kids competing against each other are as closely matched as possible in size, strength, and coordination. Most of these games involve little or no equipment and can be played indoors or outdoors as noted.

Tug-of-War

This raucous contest is the ultimate test of team strength.

Players: 6 or more, plus an adult to supervise

Ages: 8 to 14

Place: Outdoors on grass or sand

Equipment: Long, sturdy rope; stick; rag, bandanna, or dark tape (optional)

Tug-of-War is a contest of strength, coordination, and teamwork that is played all over the world. In some ancient cultures, the two teams tugging the opposite ends of the rope represented two forces of nature—rain and drought, for example, or summer and winter weather—battling each other for dominance. Today, children love Tug-of-War because it's lots of fun and especially satisfying to see their opponents fall flat.

Players divide into two teams, which should be as equal as possible in size and strength. The center of the rope may be marked with a rag, bandanna, or piece of dark tape and positioned over a center line marked on the ground with a stick. The members of each team then line up, one behind the other, at opposite ends of the rope, leaving about 3 or 4 feet (90cm to 1.2m) of clear rope in the middle. Participants then pick up the rope. The player on each end may act as an anchor by looping the rope loosely around his waist. The anchor should be the strongest member of the team.

Once the teams are in position, the adult who's supervising the contest shouts, "Ready, set, go!" and immediately both teams begin pulling on the rope with all their might, trying to drag the opposing team over the center line. If the first member of a team crosses the center line or a team drops the rope, then the opposing team is the winner.

Tug-of-War can be played on any soft surface, such as grass or sand, but it's especially fun when played on opposite sides of a mud puddle or small stream. The supervising adult should make sure, though, that kids avoid a creek that's too deep or a site with a steep slope or any place with anything sharp on the bottom; after all, the losing team is going to fall into the mess at the end of the match. This game usually ends in hilarity with a pile of wet or muddy children.

Children's Tug-of-War

This version of Tug-of-War, played by children in Korea, does not require a rope. The members of each team clasp their hands around the waist of the player in front of them, and the two team captains—the players at the head of each line—hold hands or grasp wrists tightly. At a signal, each team tries to pull the other over a mark drawn between them on the ground. The captains may not let go until one or the other has been forced to cross the center mark.

Triangular Tug-of-War

This indoor Tug-of-War contest goes three ways—and the strongest corner wins!

Players: 3, plus an adult to supervise

Ages: 5 to 10

Place: Indoors on carpeted floor in large area (cleared of furniture and breakable objects) or outdoors on any soft surface, such as grass, dirt, or sand

Equipment: Rope or strong clothesline approximately 3 yards (3m) long; 3 handkerchiefs

Triangular Tug-of-War is a strength contest on a much smaller scale than classic Tug-of-War. It makes a great party game for school-age kids. It's also a good indoor diversion because it lets children blow off steam in a contained area (the game, of course, can be played outdoors, too). Contestants should be of similar size and physical ability, or there won't be much of a contest.

First, about 3 yards (3m) of rope or strong clothesline is tied into a circle with a secure knot. Next, the three players each pick up the rope with one hand, stretching it taut so that it forms a triangle. The children should be facing outward and holding the rope behind them with one hand. The supervising adult then places three handkerchiefs on the floor—carefully locating one in front of each player so that it is just out of the reach of each of the player's.

At the starting signal, all three contestants try to pick up their handkerchiefs without letting go of the rope. Players should try to use the weight of their whole bodies to pull forward rather than trying to pull just with their arms.

The first player to succeed in picking up his handkerchief (without letting go of the rope, of course) is declared the winner.

Red Rover

In this contest of strength, players try to break through a human chain.

Players: 10 or more (even number), plus an adult to supervise

Ages: 5 to 10

Place: Outdoors on grass or pavement

Equipment: None

Red Rover is not a game for the faint of heart. This intensely physical contest definitely favors the biggest and strongest players. Kids seem to find it exhilarating to slam into each other's clasped hands. Still, an adult should stay close by to make sure nobody gets hurt.

First, players divide into two equal teams and each team chooses a leader. Next, the two teams line up parallel to each other with about 15 feet (4.5m) in between. All the members of each team join hands. (To make an even more solid line, players may grasp their neighbors' wrists.)

The game begins when the leader of the first team selects one of the opposing players (let's call her Marya) and calls, "Red Rover, Red Rover, let Marya come over!" The player who has been called (in this case, Marya) runs across to the opposing line and, in an effort to break through the chain, throws herself against any pair of clasped hands. If the player manages to break through, she gets to choose a member of the opposing team to bring back to her line. If the player does not break the chain, she must join the opposing team.

Now it is the second team's turn to call "Red Rover!" The best strategy is for a team to call over the smallest, weakest members of the other team first, hoping to add them as reinforcements to its own line.

The game goes on until one team has captured all but one of the other team's players and wins the game. The game may also be called after a predetermined amount of time. In this case, the team with the most players at the end is the winner.

Bull in the Ring

The goal of Bull in the Ring is the same as that of Red Rover: to break through a chain of hands. This game, however, is played by joining hands in a circle, with one player in the middle. That player is the "bull," whose aim is to charge out of the circle. When the bull finally breaks through, a game of tag immediately begins, with all the other players dashing off in pursuit of the escaped bull. The first one to tag the bull is the winner and becomes the bull in the next round.

King of the Hill

The monarch in this game uses pushing and shoving techniques to defend her kingdom.

Players: 3 or more, plus an adult to supervise

Ages: 5 to 10

Place: Indoors on carpeted floor in large area (cleared of furniture and breakable objects) or outdoors on dirt, sand, or snow

Equipment: Sofa cushions or similar sturdy pillows if played indoors; none if played outdoors

King (or Queen) of the Hill is an age-old struggle to protect one's territory. Even though the "king" in this game might be only a 6-year-old perched on a stack of sofa cushions, he must have a strong desire to defend his domain. This is not a game for children who are bothered at all by physical contact—it can sometimes get a bit rough and rowdy.

When playing outdoors, it's best to choose a play area that has a hill or mound that the king or queen can defend. This is a great game for the snow or the beach, where a big mound can be built in short order. Indoors, a pile of big pillows in the middle of a rug is a good option. Avoid making the hill so high that someone falling down it might get hurt. Furniture, swing sets, and trees do *not* make good hills.

One player is designated as king or queen and ascends the hill to guard it from attackers. The other players try to dethrone the ruler by clambering up, then pushing and pulling her down the hill. Players should understand that hitting, hair pulling, biting, kicking, and the like are foul play and are not allowed. The pushing and shoving should be gentle—and should stop immediately if a player complains. To avoid accidents, it's important for the adult supervisor to call for "time out" whenever the game starts getting too rough.

The invaders continue their attack on the castle until the king or queen is forced off the hill. Whoever scrambles up to the top first immediately takes over.

Shove Winter Out

This game is an organized shoving match between the symbolic forces of summer and winter.

Players: 8 or more, plus an adult to supervise

Ages: 6 to 12

Place: Indoors on large wrestling mat (in area cleared of furniture and breakable objects) or outdoors on snow or sand

Equipment: Hats, scarves, or other markers for half the players; chalk or masking tape (optional)

Shove Winter Out can best be described as a kids' version of Japanese sumo wrestling. The game combines elements of physical strength, endurance, balance, and coordination. It originated in Tierra del Fuego, a group of islands at the southernmost tip of South America, where the harsh winter months predominate. As the native children wait for the return of summer, they amuse themselves with the fantasy of being able to "shove winter out" whenever they want.

Although Shove Winter Out can be played indoors on a large wrestling mat, playing it outdoors, especially in deep snow, is much more in the spirit of the game (winter clothing acts as a cushioning shield against bumps and bruises). A sandy beach is another good place to play.

First, players are divided into two equal teams, one representing winter, the other representing summer. If there's an odd number of players, the extra child can join the summer team or sit out and serve as referee. The members of each team should be easily identifiable. For instance, the winter team might all wear hats or scarves, while the summer team does not. (Natives of Tierra del Fuego use charcoal to mark the foreheads of winter children.)

A circle of about 12 to 15 feet (3.6m to 4.5m) across is stamped into the snow (or otherwise marked, perhaps with chalk or masking tape indoors, on the playing area). The winter players start the game inside the circle; summer players remain outside. All contestants fold their arms across their chests and keep them there throughout the game. Anyone caught violating this rule must drop out.

At a signal from the adult supervisor, the summer players enter the circle. Their object is to shove the winter kids out of the circle by using *only* their backs, buttocks, and shoulders. Absolutely no hand gripping or leg tripping; no head butts, biting, or spitting; and no knee rams or elbow jams!

As the winter players are forced outside the circle, they join forces with the summer team in trying to expel the remaining winter survivors. (The expelled winter players should remove distinctive clothing, like hats, to prevent confusion.) The game goes on until all the winter children have been pushed out of the circle. At the end of the round, summer and winter players reverse roles and start the game anew.

Stork Fight

In this contest of balance and wills, players try to force the opposing "stork" to stand on both feet.

Players: 2, plus an adult to supervise

Ages: 6 to 12

Place: Indoors on carpeted floor or wrestling mat (in large area cleared of furniture and breakable objects) or outdoors on grass or sand

Equipment: Scarf

Stork Fight is as much a contest of balance and coordination as it is a contest of strength. It's quite common for the smaller of two contestants to triumph because his center of gravity is lower, which makes him much steadier overall.

The two players stand side by side, facing each other, with their left feet touching. Their left ankles are tied loosely together with a scarf; each foot should still be able to wiggle about independently. At a signal, the contestants lift their attached left feet and begin hopping about on their right feet.

Each player's delicate mission is now to force the opponent to touch her left foot to the ground without his own foot doing so. With ankles connected, this is no easy task, but it can be done. Players shake and swing their left legs to knock the opponent off balance, but they don't want to swing too hard or they may knock themselves off balance, too. Opponents may not touch one another at any time.

Whenever a player's foot touches the ground, his opponent scores a point. The feet come up again immediately and the contest continues. The player with the most points at the end of a predetermined time (2 minutes, for example) is the winner.

Cockfighting

Players try to knock each other off balance in this game inspired by battling roosters.

Players: 2, plus an adult to supervise

Ages: 8 to 13

Place: Indoors on carpeted floor or wrestling mat (in large area cleared of furniture and breakable objects) or outdoors on grass or sand

Equipment: Plastic yardstick (1m ruler) for each player

This contest of strength and balance was inspired by a popular gambling tradition in Mexico and other countries, which pits two roosters against each other. In this game, players imitate relatively gentle chickens, rather than aggressive cocks, as they waddle about trying to bump each other off balance. Children will get a laugh out of watching their friends compete in this silly-looking game.

The two players squat down facing each other, bending forward over their knees. Each clasps his knees with his arms, and an adult slides a yardstick (1m ruler) behind each player's knees and in front of his elbows, locking him into position.

At a signal, the two players start waddling about, trying to knock each other over. Shoving, leaning, and butting are all fair game. The first player to succeed in tipping over her opponent is the winner. A player who lets the yardstick (1m ruler) fall automatically loses.

Hand Wrestling

This hand-to-hand battle tests opponents' strength and balance.

Players: 2, plus an adult to supervise

Ages: 9 to 14

Place: Indoors on carpeted floor or wrestling mat (in large area cleared of furniture and breakable objects) or outdoors on grass or sand

Equipment: None

In spite of its name, Hand Wrestling, sometimes called Indian Hand Wrestling, actually requires players to muster all the strength in their bodies. Opponents stand facing each other, with their right feet touching and their left feet planted firmly behind for support. They grasp each other's right hand in either a hand-shake or hand clasp grip.

At a signal, the players begin pushing and pulling on their opponent's hand in an effort to get her to lose her balance. The players may shake and yank from side to side or up and down. A player may not, however, make contact with the other player with her left hand. The first player who lifts a foot off the ground or touches the ground with any part of her body other than her feet loses the match.

One-Legged Wrestling

This variation is like Hand Wrestling on one foot. The opponents face each other, each holding his left foot off the ground with his left hand. The players clasp right hands and, at a signal, try to force each other off balance. The players may hop about as they shake and rattle their opponent. The first player to let go of his left foot or touch the ground with any part of his body other than the right foot loses the contest. This contest of human flamingos usually ends quickly and decisively.

Arm Wrestling

Contestants try to outmuscle each other
in this classic tabletop competition.

Players: 2

Ages: 9 to 14

Place: Table, with seating for both
players

Equipment: None

Arm Wrestling, like many small-scale wrestling games, originated as a contest of strength between wagering adults. But it has been taken up over the years by children who expect no payoff except fun. As in most wrestling and strength games, the enjoyment—and safety—of the contest is lost if the opponents are not fairly equally matched in both size and strength.

For an Arm Wrestling competition, the two opponents sit facing each other across a table. Each places his right elbow (left, if both players are left-handed) on the table, and the opponents clasp hands. Arm Wrestling doesn't really work with different-handed opponents.

At a count of three, each wrestler tries to push the other's hand backward onto the table, and the first player to do so is the winner. Elbows must be kept on the table at all times. Players may not lean or otherwise use the weight of their bodies to assist in pushing, and they may not use their free hands to grab the table (or anything else) for leverage. Arm Wrestling is often played as a best-of-three or best-of-five match.

Thumb Wrestling

Thumb Wrestling is a modification of Arm Wrestling that can be played by any two people, regardless of size and strength. The two opponents sit facing one another on opposite sides or on the same side of a table. With their right forearms flat on the table and thumbs facing upward, they curl their fingers and lock right hands. Pinkies rest on the table. The opponents' thumbs rest beside each other atop the interlocked fists.

The match begins with a count of "one, two, three": On "one," the players lift their thumbs and put them back down again; on "two," they switch their thumbs' places, each moving to the other side of the opponent's thumb; on "three," they switch their thumbs back and immediately lift them to begin the match. The first player to pin her opponent's thumb to her opponent's hand for a count of three is the winner. Hands must remain clasped throughout the entire match. Thumbs tend to do a lot of wriggling, ducking, and squirming about as they try to get a good angle in this contest. This game is usually played as a best-of-five or best-of-seven series.

Indian Wrestling

In this contest of strength and stamina, the winner takes victory lying down.

Players: 2, plus an adult to supervise

Ages: 10 to 14

Place: Indoors on carpeted floor or wrestling mat (in large area cleared of furniture and breakable objects)

Equipment: None

Indian Wrestling is an intensely physical contest that appeals to kids interested in real wrestling. It is not a game for the faint-hearted or for those who don't like to be grabbed and pushed. Kids should be as evenly matched as possible in size and strength. Same-gender matches are also a good idea.

To begin, the two opponents lie side by side on their backs with the tops of their heads pointing in opposite directions. Their right legs should be alongside each other but not quite touching. Players hook their right arms together at the elbow and, counting out loud, lift their right legs so that their legs point straight up in the air once . . . twice . . . three times. On the third lift,

the two players lock their legs behind the knees and at once begin pushing and pulling with their legs in an effort to force the opponent to raise his back off the floor. The first player whose back comes off the floor loses the match.

The wrestlers look like a big human pretzel as they writhe and squirm. The players must stay locked together throughout the contest, and they may use their left arms only for balance.

Party Games

Almost any game can be played at a party. Choose from the exciting games in this chapter—but don't forget the fun-filled possibilities in other chapters. Most of the games in this chapter are mildly competitive, active without being wild, and may be played by almost any size group. Some of these games appeal to children of all ages, but the focus is on younger kids. Many party games require some type of equipment, as noted in the entries. Balloons and music—guaranteed to add fun to any party—are put to good use.

A note about prizes: It's a good idea to prepare treats or small prizes to hand out to players when they are eliminated from a game. This helps avoid unhappiness and tears. The winner should, of course, get a special reward.

Farmer in the Dell

This noncompetitive singing game is merry entertainment for a group of young children.

Players: 6 or more

Ages: 3 to 7

Place: Indoors in large room or outdoors on grass or pavement

Equipment: None

Farmer in the Dell is more an activity than a game, but it's included here because it is such a good way to entertain a big group of little kids. Children relish singing the famous song about the farmer and all the people and animals that inhabit his farm. Preschoolers, of course, will need more help, direction, and singing support than slightly older players.

To begin, all players but one form a ring and join hands. The remaining player, the "farmer," stands in the middle of the ring. The players in the ring then begin moving in a clockwise direction, and everyone starts singing the lively chorus of "The Farmer in the Dell":

The farmer in the dell,
The farmer in the dell,
Hi-ho, the dairy-o,
The farmer in the dell.

As the singers move into the second verse, the farmer points to a player from the ring to join him (or her) in the middle as the "wife" (or the "husband"):

The farmer takes a wife (or husband),
The farmer takes a wife (or husband),
Hi-ho, the dairy-o,
The farmer takes a wife (or husband).

The ring then closes and the song starts up again. For each further round, the last player who entered the circle chooses another to come in. This goes on, round after round, with the words of the song changing with each round:

The wife takes a child . . .
The child takes a nurse . . .
The nurse takes a dog . . .
The dog takes a cat . . .
The cat takes a rat . . .
The rat takes the cheese . . .

Eventually, there will be more players inside than outside the ring. When the middle is too full for the players outside to hold hands, they continue to circle around the others anyway.

Other people and animals may take the place of these more traditional figures; in fact, kids can take turns starting off the chant with the character of their choice. But the last verse, when only one player is left on the outside, should always be "The rat takes the cheese . . ." As the last player enters the middle, the others reform a ring around her and sing:

The cheese stands alone,
The cheese stands alone,
Hi-ho, the dairy-o,
The cheese stands alone!

After finishing the last verse, the ring breaks up and the children cheer and clap. The cheese then becomes the farmer to start the next game.

Mulberry Bush

This noncompetitive musical game is a wonderful way to introduce young children to the chores of everyday life.

Players: 4 or more

Ages: 3 to 6

Place: Indoors in large room or outdoors on grass or pavement

Equipment: None

Mulberry Bush is the perfect party game for the youngest children. Even those who are just learning to talk will enjoy performing the actions and providing their own rendition of the song. A medieval nursery rhyme, "Mulberry Bush" was probably sung to keep small children entertained as parents went about their chores. There are no winners or losers in this game.

Players join hands to form a ring and walk around in a circle singing this song:

Here we go round the mulberry bush,
The mulberry bush, the mulberry bush,
Here we go round the mulberry bush,
So early in the morning.

The first chore is described in the next verse:

This is the way we wash our clothes,
Wash our clothes, wash our clothes,
This is the way we wash our clothes,
So early in the morning.

As they sing about washing their clothes, the players act it out in pantomime while continuing to move in a circle. With each subsequent verse, the players act the chore that they're singing about:

This is the way we iron our clothes . . .
This is the way we mend our clothes . . .
This is the way we sweep the floor . . .
This is the way we brush our teeth . . .
This is the way we wash our hair . . .
This is the way we comb our hair . . .

Children enjoy making up their own verses and actions. Players may want to try some modern ones, like these:

This is the way we drive the car . . .
This is the way we vacuum the floor . . .

The game can go on for as long as the players continue adding verses.

Ring Around the Rosey

This noncompetitive circle game can be played by the tiniest of partygoers.

Players: 4 or more

Ages: 3 to 5

Place: Indoors in carpeted room (cleared of furniture and breakable objects) or outdoors on grass

Equipment: None

More an activity than an actual game, Ring Around the Rosey is a cheerful circle sing-along. It's not easy to organize and entertain a bunch of 2-year-olds; the simplest circle games are all they can handle. The good news is that children this age are delightfully easy to please—the group thud at the end of the song is enough to send them into peals of laughter. (And they need never know that the lyrics originally described the plight of bubonic plague victims during the Middle Ages.)

To play, children join hands and form a ring. They begin to circle around and around, singing the classic words:

Ring around the rosey,
A pocket full of posies,
Ashes, ashes,
We all fall down.

On the word "down," the children abruptly plop down on the floor or ground all together. When they're ready, they stand up again and begin the chant anew. With each new round they can change their means of loco-motion—running, hopping, skipping, or galloping "around the rosey." There's also a fun verse for children to sing when they have fallen down, and it includes several lines that call on the players to perform certain actions:

The cows are in the meadow
Huddled all together (players hug a neighbor);
Thunder, lightning (players pound on the floor and wave their arms in the air),
We all stand up (players stand).

Once the children are standing, of course, they can continue with "Ring around the rosey." The game can go on as long as the children want.

London Bridge

In this musical game, players try to avoid being caught as they pass under a human bridge.

Players: 8 or more

Ages: 3 to 7

Place: Indoors in carpeted room (cleared of furniture and breakable objects) or outdoors on grass

Equipment: None

Playing London Bridge is as much fun today as it was 500 years ago. But the version that most grown-ups remember from nursery school days is actually only a fragment of the complete game; the unabridged version ends with a mock tug-of-war. London Bridge provides just the right balance of action, organization, and fun for any party of young children.

Two players face each other and join hands to form an arch above their heads. This is London Bridge, and the two players are the bridge's towers. These two players then secretly decide which of them will be the "gold" tower and which will be the "silver" tower.

The remaining players line up single file on one side of the bridge, and as they begin marching one by one under the bridge, everyone sings:

London Bridge is falling down,
Falling down, falling down,
London Bridge is falling down,
My fair lady.

At the words "My fair lady," the arms that form the arch are abruptly lowered, and the player who happens to be passing underneath at that moment is taken "prisoner." The prisoner must

then choose whether to go to the gold tower or the silver tower. Of course, she doesn't know which player is which, but she whispers her choice to the two towers (making sure only they hear her). The towers then send her to stand on the gold or silver side of the bridge, according to her choice.

The other players then start filing under the bridge again and strike up the song—although now the words of the song change a bit:

Build it up with iron bars,
iron bars, iron bars,
Build it up with iron bars,
My fair lady.

On the last line, another prisoner is captured and sent to one of the towers. The game continues, round after round, and the words of the song change with each round:

Build it up with steel and stone . . .
Steel and stone will bend and break . . .
Build it up with silver and gold . . .
Gold and silver, I have none . . .
Get a man to watch all night . . .

Suppose the man should fall asleep? . . .
Get a dog to bark all night . . .
Suppose the dog should find a bone? . . .

Of course, if there are fewer players than verses, the later verses can be eliminated. (If there are more players, they can come up with verses of their own or repeat the earlier verses.) When only one player is left, the final verse is sung:

Off to prison he (she) *must go,*
He (she) *must go, he* (she) *must go,*
Off to prison he (she) *must go,*
My fair lady.

After the last prisoner is captured and chooses a side, the gold and silver teams line up behind their respective halves of the bridge. The sizes of the teams may be very unequal, since the prisoners chose which tower they were sent to practically at random. Each player clasps his hands around the waist of the player in front, and—at the head of both lines—the two original towers firmly grasp each other's hands. The teams then pull and tug until one of the teams falls down. The team left standing wins the game.

Musical Chairs

Round and round the chairs the players go, and when the music stops, there's no seat for the slow.

Players: 6 or more, plus adult or older child to act as disc jockey

Ages: 3 to 10

Place: Indoors in large room (cleared of furniture and breakable objects)

Equipment: Chairs (1 fewer than number of players); music source that can be stopped and started easily (such as a cassette player, CD player, or radio)

If there were a children's party game hall of fame, Musical Chairs would be in it as one of the most popular honorees, right up there with Pin the Tail on the Donkey, Piñata, and the Limbo Contest. Its European origins date back hundreds of years, when the game poked fun at the plight of harried coach travelers scrambling for empty seats. Musical chairs is the perfect party icebreaker. Expect plenty of bumping, screaming, and giggling (but very little chivalry!).

To prepare, the chairs are arranged side by side in a straight line with every other chair facing the opposite direction. If space is limited, the chairs can be lined up back to back in two even rows. An adult or older child serves as the disc jockey (DJ), in charge of operating the music source.

Players then position themselves evenly in a loose ring around the line of chairs. When all are ready, the DJ starts the music and the players march around the chairs without touching them. After a few bars, the music is stopped without warning. At that moment, each player scrambles to find an empty seat and sits down as quickly as possible. The player stranded without a chair is eliminated.

One chair is then removed before the next round begins. The players stand up, the music starts, the players march, the music unexpectedly stops, and the first-come, first-served scramble for seating is repeated. With each successive round, one player and one chair are eliminated, until only two finalists are left standing. The climactic duel for the last chair decides which player is the winner!

Musical Bumps

This is Musical Chairs without the chairs! Players dance (or march or jump or hop) to the music, and when the music stops, everyone sits down on the floor as quickly as possible. The last person to sit down is out, and the game goes on.

Ownership Musical Chairs

In this variation of Musical Chairs, which requires a piece of cardboard for each player and a marker and a roll of tape, there is an equal number of chairs and players. To prepare for the game, each player uses tape to attach a sign with her name on it to an empty seat. Everybody now "owns" his own chair. When the music starts, the players parade around the chairs in the same direction. When the music stops, the players rush to their own chairs and sit down. The last player to sit is out of the game but remains seated. After all the rounds are completed, the last person standing is the winner.

Musical Hodgepodge

In this variation, players race for objects (numbering one fewer than the number of players) instead of chairs. Before the game begins, several nonbreakable objects, such as toys, blocks, stuffed animals, balls, pillows, and plastic cups, are scattered loosely in a pile in the center of the room. There should be no sharp or pointed objects, of course. The larger the objects, the easier they will be to pick up.

When the music begins, the children dance (or hop, skip, or jump) around the pile. When the music stops, each player hastily grabs one article from the floor. The child left empty-handed is out, and the game continues with one object being removed from the floor after every round. The last child holding an object when the music stops wins.

Musical Islands

This variation requires large sheets of paper (numbering, as usual, one fewer than the number of players in the game). These are scattered here and there around the room. When the music plays, players roam the room between the paper "islands," scrambling to stand on one when the music stops. More than one player may stand on an island; a player is eliminated only if he cannot fit his entire self on dry land. (No pushing or shoving allowed!) Whether a player is eliminated or not, one sheet of paper is removed after each round. As the game goes on, it gets harder and harder to squeeze all the players onto fewer and fewer sheets. When the game gets down to a single sheet of paper, all the players who manage to find themselves a place on the last island are declared the winners.

Musical Statues

This melodious game has a twist of its own: when the music stops, everyone stands still as a stone.

Players: 4 or more, plus adult or older child to act as disc jockey

Ages: 4 to 10

Place: Indoors in carpeted room (cleared of furniture and breakable objects) or outdoors on grass

Equipment: Music source that can be stopped and started easily (such as cassette player, CD player, or radio)

Musical Statues is another game in the Musical Chairs family. This one, however, requires nothing more than a music source to play. An adult or older child serves as the disc jockey (DJ) and is in charge of operating the music source.

Players arrange themselves throughout the room, and when the DJ turns on the music, they start dancing or otherwise moving to the music's rhythm. They may also sing, whistle, hum, or howl. Abruptly, then, the DJ

shuts off the music; at once all the players must freeze into "statues." As long as the music is off, the players hold their poses. Anyone who moves or makes a sound is immediately eliminated from the game. After a few moments, the music restarts and the statues come back to life.

Musical statues is actually much more difficult than it may seem. As many a parent knows, it's no easy task for a kid to hold still, even for a few moments. Playing faster music makes it harder still—inevitably it leads players to contort themselves into poses that, once the music stops, they find impossible to hold. Eliminated players may make life tough for the remaining statues, telling jokes and making faces in hopes of getting a statue to laugh or crack a smile.

The game goes on, with the music stopping and starting, and the players freezing and unfreezing until only one statue is left standing. This remaining player is the Musical Statues champion.

Statues

Statues is like Musical Statues without the music.

Players: 4 or more, plus an adult or older child to supervise

Ages: 5 to 12

Place: Indoors in large carpeted room (cleared of furniture and breakable objects) or outdoors on grass

Equipment: None

Statues is a game that actually challenges players to stand still. In this contest, players must strike a pose and hold it for as long as possible. Statues is best played in a large, open area that allows for maximum sculpting space.

First, one player is chosen to be "it" and act as the sculptor. The sculptor takes a player by the hand or wrist, swings her around three times (not too fast!), and lets go. As soon as she

is released, the twirled player freezes into a "statue" of any form.

Each player is twirled into a statue. All must pose without making a sound or moving a muscle. A sneeze or a scratch means instant elimination. When all the sculptures are complete, the sculptor wanders among them, trying to make them laugh or move. He may readjust limbs, tell jokes, or even tickle, but no hitting or poking is allowed. The statues are required to hold their positions for as long as they can. The supervisor should watch for any statue who moves and eliminate offenders from the game.

The last unmoving statue is declared the winner and becomes the sculptor in the next round.

Gods and Goddesses

Gods and Goddesses is a musical party game of grace and balance.

Players: 3 or more, plus adult or older child to act as disc jockey

Ages: 6 to 12

Place: Indoors in large room, either uncarpeted or with a low carpet (cleared of furniture and breakable objects)

Equipment: Hardcover book for each player; music source that can be stopped and started easily (such as a cassette player, CD player, or radio)

Like Musical Chairs, Gods and Goddesses is a game in which players take their cues from the sound of music. But its leisurely pace is quite different from the scrambling action of Musical Chairs. Gods and Goddesses is, in fact, a perfect game for calming a party down. As in Musical Chairs, an adult or older child should serve as the disc jockey (DJ) and take charge of operating the music source.

Before the action gets under way, each player is given a hardcover book of similar size and weight. The players spread out across the room and carefully balance the books on the tops of their heads.

When everyone is ready, the DJ starts the music (for this game, soft and slow music is best). At once the players begin walking around the room, stepping very deliberately so that the book will not drop. This can be quite an amusing sight. Players continue to move as long as the music plays. No one may use her hands to hold the book in place.

Every once in a while, the DJ abruptly stops the music. When he does, all the book-topped players come to a halt and gingerly go down on one knee. They hold that position until the music restarts, then rise and continue their graceful gliding.

Whether it happens while walking or kneeling, any player whose book slides off his head is immediately eliminated. Book balancing can be tricky, so it may not be long before most players are out. The last player with a book on her head wins.

Kitty Wants a Corner

In this outdoor version of Musical Chairs, the kitty without a corner is one forlorn feline.

Players: 5 or more

Ages: 3 to 7

Place: Outdoors on grass or pavement

Equipment: None

Kitty Wants a Corner is a simple racing game that appeals to young children. The game is played on the same principle as Musical Chairs—there are not enough "corners" for all the players—but there's no elimination and so there are no real winners or losers.

First, one player is chosen to be the kitty and stands in the middle of the playing area. Various objects, such as trees, playground equipment, corners of buildings, and fences, are designated as "corners." The number of corners should be one fewer than the number of players. Each of the players (except the kitty) starts the game at one of these landmarks.

The game begins when the kitty meows and calls, "Kitty wants a corner!" Each player must leave his corner and race toward another one. The kitty also dashes to a corner. The player who doesn't find a corner is the next kitty.

Pass the Present

The player who unwraps the last layer of paper gets to keep the prize in this circle game.

Players: 4 or more, plus adult or older child to prepare the present and act as disc jockey

Ages: 3 to 8

Place: Indoors in room with floor seating for all players

Equipment: Small toy, piece of candy, or similar item to serve as the present; wrapping paper and tape; music source that can be stopped and started easily (such as cassette player, CD player, or radio)

In Pass the Present, a secret gift, wrapped under layers of paper, is passed from hand to hand while music plays. But when the music stops, the players remove the wrapping one layer at a time—until one lucky player ends up with a treat. What delightful frustration this is, especially for young children. Pass the Present is also a terrific game for calming down a group of kids revved up from races, chase games, or other active competitions. In this game, an adult or older child serves as the disc jockey (DJ) and switches the music on and off.

The mystery gift must be prepared by an adult or older child well before the game. A small toy or some other treat is wrapped in ten or more layers of paper. Ideally, several different colors and designs of paper are used for the layers. Each layer is taped securely in place.

To play, participants sit in a ring on the floor, with one player holding the package. When all are ready, the DJ turns on the music, and the players begin passing the package around the ring in a clockwise direction. This continues until, abruptly, the DJ stops the music. The present-passing comes to an immediate halt,

and whoever is holding the package now gently removes the outermost layer of wrapping. The player must be very careful not to strip off any layer besides the top one.

Then the music resumes and the present is passed around anew. As the music stops and starts, one by one the layers of wrapping come off. The player who is fortunate enough to remove the final layer of wrapping gets to keep the prize.

Pass the Present may also be played as an elimination game everybody wins. Instead of wrapping one present ten times, the game preparer wraps as many presents as there are players in just one layer of paper each. (One of the presents should be slightly better than the rest and should be set aside.) The first present is passed around while the music plays.

When the music stops, the player holding the package unwraps and keeps it, but he has to leave the game. Then another package is given to the players, and the music starts anew. The last remaining player is awarded the best prize.

Mystery Parcel

In this variation, meant for children ages 6 to 8, the prize is wrapped in many layers, just as in regular Pass the Present. But there is a new twist: a message is written on each layer of wrapping paper directing the player holding the package when the music ends to give the package to someone else to open. The message, for example, might say, "Pass the parcel to the player with the longest hair" or "Pass the parcel to the player on your right." When the music stops, the player who is holding the package reads the message and then passes the package to the appropriate person. That player then unwraps the layer of paper before the music starts again. As in Pass the Present, the player who unwraps the last layer of paper gets to keep the present.

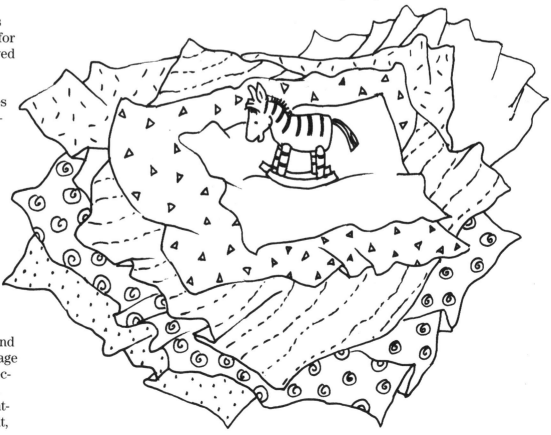

Spider Web

Players unravel a tangled mass of string to claim their prizes in this cooperative game.

Players: 3 or more, plus adult to set up and supervise

Ages: 5 to 11

Place: Indoors in large room full of furniture (but cleared of breakable objects) or outdoors in defined area

Equipment: Piece of string, yarn, or thread at least 10 to 20 feet (3m to 6m) long (and preferably a different color) for each player; name tag for each player; small wrapped gift or goodie bag for each player; scissors

Spider Web is an engrossing game that promises a reward for every player. Players work together, trying to unsnarl a "spider web" made of yarn or thread. Each strand leads to a prize, but depending on the state of the tangle, it may take quite some time to reach it. Younger children, of course, should be presented with a relatively uncomplicated web to avoid frustration. For older kids—who will enjoy a more difficult challenge—thread should be used rather than string or yarn. Spider Web can be played in a large room full of furniture (but cleared of breakable objects) or outside in a defined space, such as a backyard.

The web for this game must be set up well in advance by an adult. This takes a bit of effort but is well worth it. Step one is to prepare a treat for each player. A bag of candy or a small toy, wrapped in colored paper or packed in a little bag, is a nice option. Each treat is then tucked away in a hidden corner of the playing area, and the end of a piece of string, yarn, or thread tied to it. If possible, each gift should have a different color of string.

One by one, then, each strand of the web is rolled out. The strands are strung over, under, and around any stationary objects that happen to be around such as sofas, tables, and coatracks or (if the game is outside) trees, swing sets, and fences. The strands are also intertwined. When a strand is about 10 to 20 feet (3m to 6m) long, it is cut. A name tag is attached to the cut end by punching a hole in the tag, running the string through, and tying a knot. By the time all the strands have been strung, the playing area is one big network of strings.

When the players are ready, each child is lead to his name tag. The adult signals "Go!" and all the players start untangling and gathering their individual strands, winding them up as they go. players will discover they need to work together to free one another's lines.

The first player to reach her prize is the winner, but the game isn't over until all of the string is untangled and each child claims a prize. Sooner or later, everyone should make it. But scissors and help from the supervisor may come in handy if the game goes on for too long.

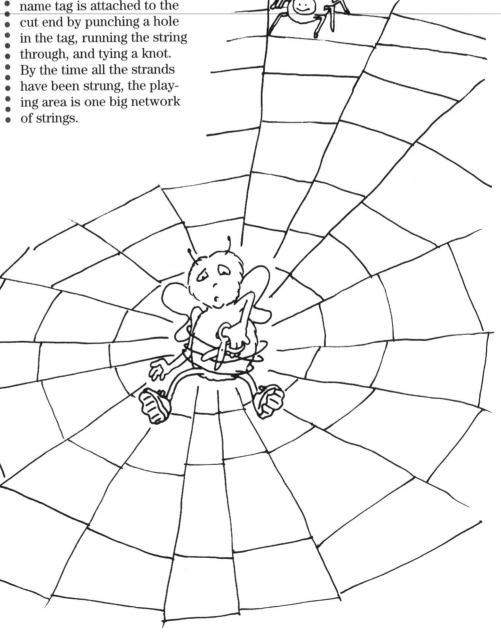

Telephone

In this game of mixed messages, players try to pass along a whispered phrase without getting it garbled.

Players: 6 or more

Ages: 6 to 14

Place: Anywhere with seating in a circle for all the players

Equipment: None

Telephone—also appropriately called Gossip, Rumors, and Whisper Down the Lane—is a great party icebreaker because it gets kids talking to one another. Once kids are old enough to control the volume of their voices and keep a secret, they are sure to love this game of mischievous whispers.

To play, participants sit in a circle on the floor or ground. One player is chosen to start, and it is his job to come up with (but not say out loud) a brief message of absolutely any sort. It might be "Johnny fell in the muddy lake" or "My answering machine has a fly on it" or even something completely nonsensical like "The math test is made of fudge." It doesn't matter. (To kick-start the game for very young children, phrases can be provided.) Whatever the message, the first player then whispers it into the ear of the player to his right. That player then whispers the message to the player on her right, and so on until the message makes it all the way back around to the player on the first player's left.

A player should speak as clearly as possible when whispering to his neighbor, but even if his neighbor doesn't hear him well, a player may not repeat the message. The neighbor has to pass along what she thinks she heard. In short order, the message is likely to be mixed up almost beyond recognition.

Just how mixed up becomes evident when the last player declares what she thinks the message is—and the first player announces what it really is. By that time, "My answering machine has a fly on it" might well be "Miami Beach has a very nice climate." The game continues on until every player has had a chance to send out a message. Mischievous players, very much in the spirit of the game, will choose messages with words that are likely to be misheard.

There are no losers in Telephone, only winners, because everyone will get a big laugh out of the unintentionally garbled words that spill out at the end of the telephone wire.

Taste Test

This game is for the tongue and mind—tasting goodies completely blind.

Players: 3 or more, plus adult to set up and supervise

Ages: 3 to 10

Place: Indoors or outdoors, at table

Equipment: 5 to 15 different foods with utensils and cups as needed to serve a portion to each player; blindfold (scarf or bandanna); pencil and paper for scoring

Taste Test asks players to identify different foods by taste, smell, and texture alone. (They aren't allowed to see or touch the foods.) This is a good pre–ice cream and cake activity, when hungry taste buds are at their sharpest.

It is up to an adult to set the stage for the Taste Test. Well before play begins, she should gather portions of 5 to 15 foods (including beverages)—enough for each player to have a small sampling of each food—and set everything out on a table.

Food selection is an important element in this game, and adults should feel free to use their imaginations. It's often a good idea to serve up a wide variety of textures and tastes, from saltines, chocolate, and carrots to raisins, gummy worms, hard-boiled eggs, and pudding. Another approach is to collect a range of similar items, like fruits, vegetables, or even hard candies. The subtle taste differences make this a good option for older kids. Milk, juice and other beverages are also welcome additions to the Taste Test. Whatever the choice, the adult should find out if any player has food allergies before finalizing the Taste Test selections.

The players should start in a room or area separate from the one in which the foods are being set up. When the buffet is ready, the players are blindfolded and led one by one by the adult to the tasting table. The adult gives each player one taste of each food. After swallowing, the player tries to guess the food's identity; the adult keeps track of right and wrong answers on a score sheet.

When everyone has taken a turn, scores are tallied and the player with the highest score wins the Golden Tongue award. After the winner is chosen, everyone eats the leftovers.

Limbo Contest

This body-bending contest challenges players' agility as they try to pass under the ever-lower Limbo stick.

Players: 4 or more

Ages: 3 to 14

Place: Indoors in carpeted room or outdoors on grass or sand

Equipment: Broom handle or stick of similar length

The Limbo is actually a dance that originated in the West Indies, where real experts can shimmy under a stick held only a few inches above the ground. Played with or without accompanying music, a Limbo Contest calls upon players' flexibility and balance as they take turns trying to pass under the stick. This is also a wonderful contest for mixed age groups because it's one of the few games in which the smaller children have the advantage.

Two people start by holding a long, straight stick, such as a broom handle, between them at about chest height.

The players line up single file and begin taking turns trying to shimmy under the stick without touching it. In the classic Limbo shimmy, the head and back arch backward while the arms are held out at the sides for balance. The feet shuffle forward either one at a time or both at the same time in a low hop. The head must be the last part of the body to pass under the

stick. (This rule can be relaxed a bit for very young players.)

After each player has had a turn to go under the stick, everybody lines up again, the stick is lowered a bit, and the whole process is repeated. Needless to say, as the game goes on, getting under the stick grows harder and harder.

One by one, players discover they simply can't make it. Either they bump the stick with their heads, or they fall on their bottoms trying to get lower. In either case, the player is eliminated.

The last player remaining in the game after everyone else has been eliminated is named the Limbo Contest champion.

Simon Says

Simple Simon? No way! This active party game requires players to listen closely and follow directions.

Players: 3 or more

Ages: 4 to 10

Place: Indoors in large room (cleared of furniture) or outdoors on grass or pavement

Equipment: None

Simon Says—sometimes called O'Grady Says—originated hundreds of years ago in southern Europe as a question-and-answer drill aimed at reinforcing proper behavior. Players are supposed to follow the directions that the leader of the game calls out, but only if the leader says "Simon says." Although the rules are simple enough for 4-year-olds to understand, even an astute 10-year-old can be outsmarted by a fast-talking "Simon." Besides being a lot of fun, Simon Says develops concentration and listening skills.

One player (or an adult) is selected to be "Simon," and the rest of the players line up facing him. When everyone is ready, Simon starts issuing commands to the group, telling them, for example, to clap their hands, put their fingers on their noses, or jump up and down. Simon must also perform whatever action he orders.

Whenever Simon issues an order that begins with the words "Simon says"—as in "Simon says, 'Hop on one foot'"—the other players must obey. If an order does not begin with those words, however, the others are forbidden to obey. Any player who fails to follow a command starting with "Simon says" or anyone who does follow a command made without "Simon says" is immediately eliminated from the game.

Throughout the game, Simon tries to think of ways to trip up the other players, who in turn try to avoid being out-smarted. The trick to being a great Simon is the ability to give commands quickly and rhythmically, demonstrating the actions without hesitation. That way, when there's no "Simon says," the players are more likely to follow along without stopping to listen for permission. One good strategy is to give the same command five or six times before suddenly switching to a new command without including "Simon says."

The game continues with players dropping out one by one. The last player to remain in the game is the winner. If another round is played, he becomes the next Simon.

Do This, Do That

This game is played in much the same way as Simon Says, except that the leader does not specify the action she is ordering; she just demonstrates it. In other words, instead of telling the players to pat their bellies, she simply pats her own belly. Just as she starts to perform an action, the leader says either, "Do this," or "Do that." If she says, "Do this," everyone must obey the order; if she says, "Do that," all the players must ignore it. Any player who makes a mistake is eliminated at once.

Pin the Tail on the Donkey

In this party classic, blindfolded players take turns trying to give a donkey its missing tail.

Players: 4 or more, plus adult to set up and spin players

Ages: 4 to 8

Place: Indoors in large room with free wall or outdoors near tree or wall

Equipment: Large sheet of cardboard or paper; paper tail for each player; markers or paint; scissors; pushpins, thumbtacks, or tape; blindfold (scarf or bandanna)

Pin the Tail on the Donkey is one of the most popular children's games of all time. It's been a winner for many generations because it combines luck, skill, suspense, humor, and a good dose of dizziness. Pin the Tail can be played indoors or out, but the playing area should be cleared of anything that could be damaged by the prick of a pin (and that includes people). Before beginning the game, it's important to make sure that players, especially very young ones, feel comfortable with being blindfolded and spun around.

Practically all toy and party supply stores sell ready-made Pin the Tail on the Donkey sets complete with a donkey target and dozens of tails. It's much more fun, however, to create the setup at home. Here's how: A picture of a donkey is drawn on a large sheet of cardboard and colored in with markers or paint. (Other animals work fine, too.) The donkey should be shown in side view (see diagram). Just as important, it must be drawn missing its tail. A narrow strip of paper several inches (cm) long is then cut out for every player, and the child's name or initials written on it. A pushpin or thumbtack is inserted near one end so that the strip dangles from the pin. (Tape can be used instead, to avoid all danger of pinpricks.) These strips are all donkey tails.

The donkey-bearing cardboard is then fastened to a wall or tree at the children's eye level, and each is given her initialed tail. She should be shown how to hold it to avoid pricking herself once the action starts.

One at a time, then, each player is blindfolded, spun around three times by the adult (this step can be eliminated for the youngest players), and pointed in the direction of the donkey. The player wobbles toward the drawing and blindly tries to place his tail as close as possible to the proper spot on the donkey's anatomy.

After everyone has taken a turn, the player whose tail is the closest to where a donkey's tail should be found is the winner.

Pin the Airplane on the Map

This variation of Pin the Tail on the Donkey—played with a big map of the world and cutouts of airplanes—is fun for slightly older children (6 to 10). Blindfolded pilots take turns trying to navigate their planes toward a pre-marked destination on the map. The player whose plane lands closest to this spot is the winner.

Piñata

Players take turns trying to break the piñata and shower the party with treats.

Players: 4 or more, plus adult to set up and spin players

Ages: 5 to 12

Place: Indoors in large room (away from breakable objects), on porch, or outdoors on grass or pavement

Equipment: Store-bought piñata or materials for making one (2 paper grocery bags, newspaper, string, markers or paint, crepe paper, tape, candy and nonbreakable trinkets for prizes); stick or bat; blindfold (scarf or bandanna)

In this traditional Mexican Christmas game, blindfolded children take turns trying to break open a decorated container filled with candy and toys. Beautiful animal-shaped piñatas can be bought at the store, but kids will enjoy playing with a homemade one just as much (more, maybe, because it isn't as difficult to break). Piñata-making can even be included in the party activities. Either way, breaking open a piñata is a wonderful grand finale for any children's party.

To make a piñata, place one paper grocery bag inside another, fill it with treats—such as candy or other wrapped snacks and small nonbreakable toys—and stuff the leftover space with crumpled newspaper. Gather the bag together at the top and tie it shut with string. Finally, use markers, paint, and crepe paper streamers to decorate it. (A funny face is especially appropriate on a piñata of this kind.)

The store-bought or homemade piñata is hung from a hook or similar fixture on the ceiling (if playing indoors) or from a tree branch (if playing outdoors). It should be just above the level of the players' heads, but within reach of a stick or bat.

Players line up to take turns trying to break the piñata. Each is blindfolded, given the stick, and spun around three times. The player then gets one chance to swing at the piñata and try to burst it. If he is unsuccessful, the next player takes a turn.

This continues until someone gives the piñata a good, solid whack and breaks it open, showering candy and prizes on all the participants. Everybody scrambles to snatch up as many treats as possible. Everyone is a winner in this game, but the player who breaks the piñata may be given a special prize.

Bubble Blow

These soap-bubble contests are great fun at an outdoor party for young children.

Players: 4 or more (even number)

Ages: 4 to 7

Place: Outdoors on grass or pavement

Equipment: Container of bubble solution (commercial or homemade) and wand for each child; sticks or chalk for marking playing area

Soap bubbles provide endless fascination for young children. Simply watching bubbles float and shimmer in the air is enough to entertain (well-supervised) toddlers. Slightly older partygoers will enjoy something a little more competitive. Bubble Blow challenges players not only to blow impressive bubbles but also to propel them across a playing field. One warning: this game definitely does not work well on a windy day.

It's easiest if each child is given her own bottle of bubble solution. The bottles of bubbles are inexpensive and provide each child with both a container and a bubble wand. An alternative is to prepare a homemade solution using water and dishwashing liquid, plus a bit of glycerin—a common lubricant, which can be found in drugstores—to ensure that the bubbles don't stick together. Mix 1 gallon (4l) of water, $\frac{1}{4}$ cup (65ml) of dishwashing liquid, and $\frac{1}{2}$ to 1 teaspoon (2.5ml to 5ml) of glycerin for a nice quantity to distribute to players. The homemade solution may be placed in a single tub, and participants can use either store-bought bubble wands or a piece of wire twisted into a loop for the bubble blowing.

To set up the playing field, three parallel lines at least 10 feet (3m) long are marked on the ground, with about 3 feet (90cm) between them. The players divide into two even teams and line up facing each other on either side of the center line. The line behind each team is its goal line. To start, a player on one team blows one bubble (for a good bubble, blow slowly!). As it rises into the air, the two teams start blowing on the bubble to send it past or over the heads of the other team and across the opposing goal line.

Players may cross the center line and pursue the bubble wherever it goes in order to help it along or to keep it from passing their goal line. But they are not allowed to use their hands, noses, or any other parts of the body to move the bubble—it would burst on impact anyway. They're not even allowed to flap their hands to stir up a wind. All they can do is blow. Moving a bubble over the opposing goal line earns the team a point. Once one team scores a goal, or if the bubble bursts before a goal is scored, the teams reassemble at the center line and try again.

Teams alternate blowing bubbles. The team with the most points after everyone has had a chance to blow a bubble—or after a predetermined amount of time (say, 10 minutes)—wins the match.

Avenue Goals

Teams compete to score goals by pushing a balloon down the "avenue."

Players: 6 or more (even number)

Ages: 4 to 8

Place: Indoors in large room (cleared of furniture and breakable objects) or outdoors on grass or pavement

Equipment: Air-filled balloon or lightweight ball

Balloon games are a hallmark of parties for young children—after all, nothing says "Happy Birthday" quite like a balloon. Avenue Goals is a sitting-down goal-scoring game that works best with an air-filled (not helium-filled!) balloon, although a lightweight ball works, too. Young children will enjoy the excitement of trying to score goals with a balloon, which isn't likely to travel in a straight line for long.

Players first divide into two equal groups (which are not the teams), and the two groups sit opposite each other on the floor or ground. In between the two lines of players, there should be 2 to 5 feet (60cm to 1.5m) of space. This space is the "avenue." Players then form two teams by counting off from one end—the odd-numbered players on one side are on the same team as the even-numbered players on the other side. One end of the avenue is one team's goal, and the opposite end is the other team's goal.

To begin, the balloon is placed in the middle of the avenue, and, at a count of three, each team tries to score by patting it toward the opposite team's goal and to keep it from passing through its own goal. (As in football or soccer, a team scores by crossing the opposing team's goal; if children don't understand this concept, they can simply be told which goal they should aim for.) The balloon may not be held or thrown, only pushed with an open palm. Players must remain seated throughout the game. When the balloon goes past the end of the avenue, the scoring team gets a point and the balloon is returned to the middle.

The team with the most points after a predetermined period of time is the winner. Or the teams can compete to be first to reach a certain score.

Overhead Goals

In this variation, the two rows of players are opposing teams. The teams should sit 2 to 4 feet (60cm to 1.2m) apart. As in Avenue Goals, the balloon is placed in the center, but now the participants try to bat it past the other team. A goal is scored when the balloon falls to the floor (or ground) behind the opposing team. Players can tap the balloon high or low, hard or soft, between opposing players or over their heads. Players may reach or even lean back as far as they want to prevent the balloon from landing behind them, but no player may leave his position on the floor. The team with the most points at the end of the game wins.

Balloon Flights

The child whose balloon makes the longest "flight" wins this funny party race.

Players: 2 or more, plus adult or older child to serve as starter

Ages: 5 to 8

Place: Indoors in large room (cleared of furniture and breakable objects)

Equipment: Air-filled balloon (preferably of different color) for each player; felt-tipped marker (optional)

Balloon Flights calls for good coordination and nimble fingers. It's a wonderful game for an enclosed space, since the balloons tend to travel about unpredictably in every direction.

To begin, each child is given a different-color balloon (if there are not enough different colors, players' initials may be marked on the balloons with a felt-tipped marker). Balloons should be filled with air—not helium. All the contestants then line up on one side of the room. Each child balances his balloon on an open palm.

At a signal from the game starter, the players flick the balloons off their palms with the thumb and forefinger of the opposite hand. The object is to keep the balloon in the air as long as possible. The balloons must only be flicked, never batted with a palm or fist. Any player whose balloon touches the floor (or pops) is eliminated. The last player with a balloon in the air is the winner.

Balloon Volleyball

In this version of volleyball, players hit a balloon back and forth over a piece of string.

Players: 6 or more (even number)

Ages: 5 to 10

Place: Indoors in large room (cleared of furniture and breakable objects)

Equipment: Air-filled balloon; string at least 9 feet (2.7m) in length; 2 sturdy chairs

Balloon Volleyball is a novel indoor take on a classic game, with the rules considerably simplified. This version, of course, is played with a balloon, making it much easier and slower-paced than its outdoor counterpart. There should be ample space to play, however, since players can get quite active in the excitement of the game.

To set up the "net," two players or helpers (both about the same height) stand on sturdy chairs (not folding chairs) about 8 feet (2.4m) apart, holding a length of string between them.

(If they can find a place to do so, the players should tie the string about 5 to 6 feet [1.5m to 1.8m] off the ground instead of holding it.) The remaining players are divided into two equal teams, which spread out facing each other on opposite sides of the net.

To start the contest, one player tries to smack the balloon over the net from anywhere on her side of the net. If it doesn't quite make it to the net, any other player on her team may give it another whack. In fact, as long as no player hits the balloon twice in a row and the balloon does not touch the floor, the players on the team may continue to whack it until it goes over the net.

If and when the balloon makes it over, the other team must return it before it hits the floor. Again, they're allowed as many hits as they need to get it back over. The teams continue hitting the balloon back and forth over the net, trying to make a shot the other team cannot return. The

volley ends when one team allows the balloon to fall to the floor or hits it under the net (or when a single player goofs by hitting it twice in a row). When this happens, the other team scores a point and continues, or takes over, the serve. A different player should serve each time a team regains the serve.

The first team to score a predetermined number of points (say, 15) is the winner.

Blow Volleyball

This variation is played in the same way as Balloon Volleyball, except that the balloon is blown, rather than hit, over the net. The string is held at a lower level for this game—holders stand on the floor rather than on chairs—and the members of each team arrange themselves closer to the net. To serve the balloon, a player places it on his palm, takes a deep breath, and blows it away. (The balloon may also be served by batting it off the palm with the other hand.) In the heat of the action, extremely enthusiastic players have been known to dive on their backs under the balloon to give it an upward breeze and keep it in play. Players should be warned, however, not to let themselves get too winded.

Balloon Basketball

Players try to hit a balloon to the other team's goal in this indoor basketball game.

Players: 6 to 10 (even number)

Ages: 6 to 10

Place: Indoors in large room (cleared of furniture and breakable objects)

Equipment: Air-filled balloon; 2 large sheets of paper; tape

Balloon Basketball is a goal-scoring party game that will be a hit with kids age 6 and up. Challenging and action-packed, this game of basketball is played by hitting a balloon in the air toward a paper "basket." A large, empty room is necessary for the court.

To set up, two sheets of paper are taped flat to the walls on opposite sides of the room; these serve as the

baskets, though they are really more targets than actual baskets. The baskets should be "hung" at about the height of the players' heads.

Next, the participants divide into two equal teams. They then arrange themselves anywhere they want in the room.

To begin the game, a player from each team comes to the middle of the court for a "jump ball." The balloon is smacked high into the air by a third person (from either team), and the two opposing players jump up and try to hit it to a teammate.

Throughout the game, each team's aim is to bat the balloon so it touches the opposing team's basket. Teammates work together, passing the balloon back and forth in an effort to advance it down the court. At no time may a player hold onto the balloon; it may only be slapped, flicked, or batted. The opposing team, meanwhile, tries to steal the balloon in the air and send it back in the other direction. If at any time during the game the ball touches the floor, it is returned to the center for another jump ball.

A team scores a point every time it hits the balloon onto the opposition's sheet of paper. The team with the most points after a predetermined amount of time wins the game.

Bobbing for Apples

This classic Halloween game provides wet, wild fun any time of the year.

Players: 2 or more, plus adult to set up and supervise

Ages: 5 to 12

Place: Porch; outdoors on grass or pavement; or indoors on linoleum or vinyl floor

Equipment: Apples (at least 1 per player); large metal or plastic tub; towel; timer with a second hand (optional)

Bobbing for Apples, also called Apple Ducking, is a Halloween party standard, probably because apples are so plentiful at that time of year. Children will delight, however, in trying to retrieve an apple from a tub of water with their teeth at any time of year. This game is especially refreshing on a hot summer day. Kids of any age can play, as long as they don't mind getting their faces wet.

To prepare, a large metal or plastic washtub is filled with cold water, and a bunch of apples (at least one for each player) are set afloat within. With their hands clasped behind their backs, players take turns trying to fish an apple out of the tub using only their teeth. If there are only a few participants and the tub is large enough, they may all bob at the same time.

Catching an apple is not easy. Although the apples float on top of the water, they usually plunge beneath at the slightest touch. As champion apple bobbers know, a good strategy is to stick the whole head underwater and then corner an apple against the side to get a tooth-hold. (A towel should be on hand for any player who gets too wet.)

If players are bobbing together, the first one to fish out an apple is declared the winner. If the players are taking turns, the player who retrieves an apple in the shortest amount of time wins. (A timer with a second hand comes in handy here.) While the winner should get something special, in this game everybody gets a scrumptious prize: an apple, of course!

Hot Potato

In this suspenseful circle game, players hurry to get rid of the scalding spud.

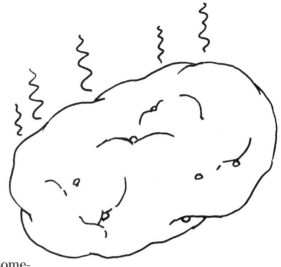

Players: 6 or more

Ages: 4 to 10

Place: Indoors in room with floor seating for all players (away from breakable objects) or outdoors on grass or pavement

Equipment: Potato, tennis ball, or beanbag

Hot Potato is a classic party game in which players try to pass a "hot" potato to someone else before they get burned. Quick reflexes, along with good throwing and catching skills, are a must for this fast-paced contest. Playing this game at the beginning of a party will rev the kids up. Hot Potato can be played with a genuine (but unheated) potato, or a tennis ball or beanbag can serve as a stand-in.

The players all sit on the floor (or ground) in a ring, with one child (or an adult) in the center holding the potato. The game begins when the leader closes his eyes and tosses the potato to one of the players in the circle. Immediately, this player throws the potato to someone else, who in turn throws it to someone else, and so on. The idea here is to get rid of the potato as quickly as possible, as if it were red hot.

At some point, the player in the center (eyes still closed) calls out, "Hot!" Potato movement stops at once and the player caught holding the potato (or, if it's in the air, the last person to touch the potato) must leave the circle. The potato then goes back to the center player, who closes his eyes again and sets the potato off on a new round. If the potato drops to the floor at any time, the nearest player should pick it up and put it back into play.

The game continues until all players except one have been eliminated. The last remaining player is the winner.

Musical Hot Potato

This variation calls for a music source that can be stopped and started easily (such as a cassette player, CD player, or radio) and an adult or older child to serve as the disc jockey (DJ). The children sit in a ring, and one player starts with the potato. When the DJ starts the music, the potato tossing begins. At a time of her choosing, the DJ abruptly stops the music—and the player holding the potato is out. This goes on until there is only one survivor.

Beanbag Toss

This target game challenges younger and older players alike.

Players: 2 or more

Ages: 5 to 12

Place: Indoors in large room (cleared of furniture and breakable objects) or outdoors on pavement

Equipment: Beanbag; paper, marker, and tape (for indoor target) or chalk (for outdoor target)

In Beanbag Toss players take turns trying to hit a target with a beanbag. A versatile game, it can be played indoors or out, and the target can be tailored to the players' ages and abilities.

For an indoor game, the target should be drawn with a marker on a large sheet of paper and taped to the floor. If the party is outdoors, it can be marked onto the pavement with chalk. Either way, the target should be round—it may be divided into concentric circles like an archery target or drawn with wedge-shaped segments (like pie pieces) around a center bull's-eye, like a dart board (see diagram on next page). The sections of the target should be big enough for a beanbag to fit easily without touching any lines. A point value ranging from 5 to 25 points is written in each section. If the target consists of concentric circles, the numbers should be highest in the center and lowest near the rim. If it's a pie design, the point values can be set up randomly, although the center section should have the top value.

A throwing line is marked about 4 to

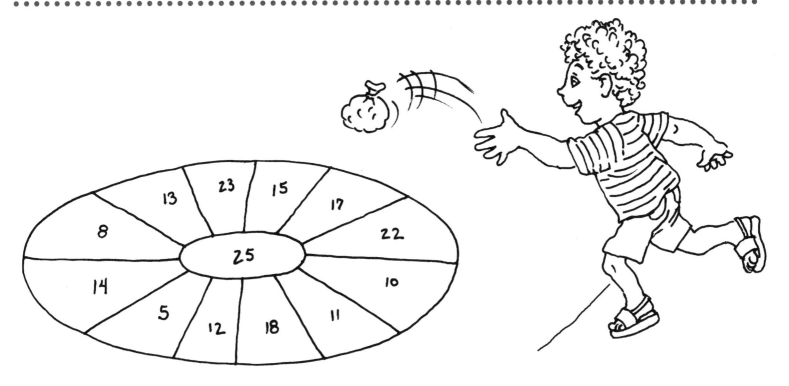

6 feet (1.2m to 1.8m) from the target. One at a time, players toss the beanbag onto the target from behind the throwing line. Points are scored if the beanbag falls completely within a sec-tion—but no points are given for a beanbag that touches a line.

There are two ways to determine the Beanbag Toss winner. Either the player with the highest score after everyone has had a set number of throws can be declared champion, or the first person to reach a predeter-mined score (like 100) can be given the crown.

Holey Board Game

Players compete for high scores by throwing balls through holes in a board.

Players: 2 or more, plus adult to pre-pare board

Ages: 5 to 12

Place: Indoors in large room or outdoors on grass or pavement

Equipment: Large piece of stiff card-board; scissors or utility knife; marker; table tennis ball or beanbag

The Holey Board Game is, as the name suggests, a game played with a board full of holes. This game of skill develops aiming and throwing skills as children try to toss a table tennis ball through the holes. The game works best for a small party because only one player can throw at a time, meaning that children have to wait for turns.

To prepare for the game, a "holey board" must be made (see diagram on next page). A stiff sheet of cardboard, such as the side of a large cardboard box, works well. Into this board are cut six to ten holes of different sizes, with the smallest holes a little bigger than the diameter of a table tennis ball. A more permanent board can be crafted from a sheet of plywood using a jigsaw, but such a project should be carried out by grown-ups only.

During the game, players try to throw a table tennis ball through the holes, and they score points when they succeed. Since the biggest holes are the easiest for scoring points, they should be worth fewer points than the smaller, more difficult, holes. With this in mind, a point value is marked next to each hole on the board, start-ing with 5 for the largest and going up in increments of 5.

Before play begins, the board should be propped up against a wall (not too close!) or table leg—or it can be held up by an accommodating adult. Players stand about 6 feet (2m) away from the board and take turns with the ball, trying to score as many points as possible on each toss. Three rounds of three throws for each play-er makes for a good game, but that may be modified depending on the size of the group and the time avail-able—as well as the players' interest in the game.

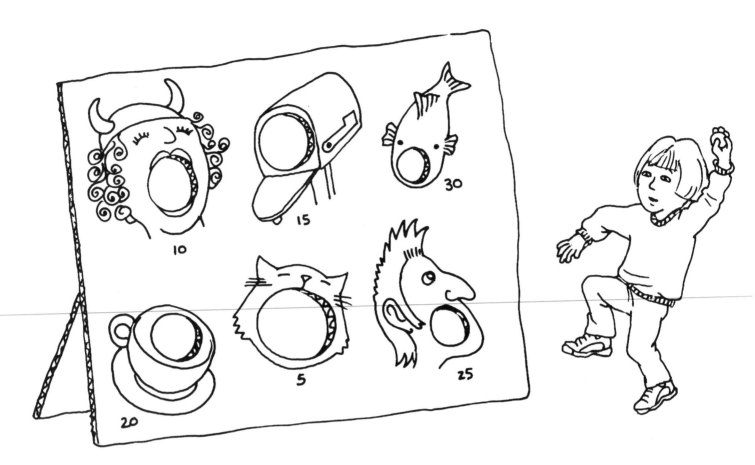

Each player keeps track of his own score in his head or players can draw up a scoring sheet. The player with the highest score at the end of the game is declared the winner.

Holey Board Game can also be played with a beanbag, and in fact this is probably a better bet for young kids. In that case, though, the holes in the board must be made a lot bigger—beanbag size—to accommodate the larger beanbags.

Egg Toss

Players compete to throw an egg as far as possible without breaking it.

Players: 4 or more (even number), plus adult or older child to serve as starter

Ages: 8 to 14

Place: Outdoors on grass or pavement

Equipment: Raw egg for every pair of players; smock for every player (optional); towel (optional)

This game combines skill, suspense, and an explosive ending. Egg Toss is a classic party contest for older children who are adept at throwing and catching a small object. Players team up to toss a raw egg back and forth until it breaks—and too bad if it happens in somebody's hands. Needless to say, Egg Toss is an outdoor game. Players should wear old clothes or smocks so they don't have to worry about getting their clothes dirty. Bare feet or washable shoes are also a good idea, as is a towel for cleaning up.

Players divide up into pairs. The participants then stand in two rows, facing each other about 3 feet (90cm) apart, with each player directly opposite his partner. Every player in one of the rows is given a raw egg.

At a signal from the game starter, the players with the eggs toss the fragile bundles to their empty-handed partners. The partner's job is, first of all, to catch the egg. This takes not only coordination, but some very gentle care. A clumsy catcher is likely to end up messy. After the first toss has been caught, the partner takes one full step backward and sends the egg flying back to the original thrower. This interchange goes on, back and forth, with each member of the pair catching the egg, stepping back, and throwing it. With each toss, a successful pass becomes a trickier proposition. Any pair whose egg breaks—whether in their hands or on the ground—is automatically eliminated from the contest.

The last pair with an unscrambled egg is the winner. These players should continue tossing and widening the distance between them to see just how far they can go before breaking the egg.

Water Balloon Toss

Based on the same principle as Egg Toss, this game substitutes water-filled balloons for the eggs. Partners toss the balloons, widening the distance between them until inevitably the balloons go splat. Bathing suits are the attire of choice for Water Balloon Toss. This is also a good game to play after Egg Toss—to clean things up.

Bottle Fishing

In this game of skill, players compete to snare bottles masquerading as "fish."

Players: 2 or more, plus adult or older child to serve as starter

Ages: 6 to 10

Place: Indoors in uncarpeted room (away from breakable items)

Equipment: Plastic soda bottle, string a few feet (1m) long, and 1-inch (2.5cm) diameter rubber washer for each player

Bottle Fishing is a contest that is likely to keep children occupied for quite a while. The challenge is to lift a bottle by its neck off the floor with a fishing line fashioned from string and a rubber washer.

The fishing lines should be prepared ahead of time. A piece of string a few feet (about 1m) long is tied to a simple rubber washer, which can be found in most hardware stores. The holes in the washers should be just wide enough to fit easily over the neck of a standard plastic soda bottle—

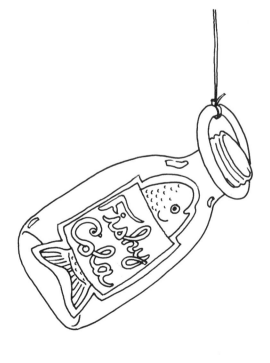

about 1 inch (2.5cm) across. The lines are distributed to the players, who stand in a row, each with an empty plastic bottle (no glass, please!) lying on its side on the floor at his feet.

At a signal from the game starter, the contestants try to "catch" a bottle by slipping the washer ring around the bottle's neck and pulling on the string to lift the bottle waist-high. This is a difficult and tricky task as the light-weight bottles have a lot of "fight" in them. Players must remain standing throughout the game. The first player to "reel in" a bottle is the winner.

Water Games

The games in this chapter share one prerequisite: they must be played in water. Water games supply endless summer fun for kids of all ages, swimmers and nonswimmers alike. Some inspire young children to "get their feet wet" and gain confidence in the water. Others offer seasoned swimmers a chance to strut their stuff. Whether kids pick a race, a tag game, or a sports-inspired game, playing it in a different element introduces new challenges and sensations—besides allowing everyone to cool off. The games here are best played in a swimming pool, although many could just as easily work in the shallow part of a lake or pond. As wonderful as water games are, however, they should all be played with caution and should *always* supervised by an adult with life-saving skills.

How Many Ways to Get There?

The swimmer with the most imagination triumphs in this version of Follow the Leader.

Players: 2 or more, plus an adult to supervise

Ages: 5 to 12

Place: Swimming pool

Equipment: None

How Many Ways to Get There? challenges players to come up with—and demonstrate—a wide range of ways to cross a pool. Played in shallow water, this is a great game to encourage young children to get wet and enjoy the water.

Players start in the water, lined up along one side of the pool. One player is selected to start, and she makes her way across the pool in any manner she chooses. If she can swim, she may choose a basic stroke like the crawl, backstroke, breaststroke, sidestroke, or elementary backstroke. Or she may choose to walk on tiptoe, hop, walk on her hands, somersault, dog-paddle, or glide across the pool. The possibilities are (almost) endless! The next player selects a different crossing method, and so on down the line.

Players may not repeat the method of any player who has gone before them, and the supervising adult should make sure no child stretches his swimming ability too far. The game continues back and forth across the pool, as long as imaginations don't run dry.

Any player who can't think of a novel way of "getting there" is eliminated from the game. The last player to cross the pool using an original movement is the winner.

Water Follow the Leader

In this wet version of the classic game, players imitate the actions of the leader.

Players: 3 or more, plus an adult to supervise

Ages: 5 to 10

Place: Swimming pool

Equipment: None

Follow the Leader is a lively activity that allows children to use their imagination, whether it's played on land or in the water. Since the followers must imitate the leader's actions, care should be taken to keep the stunts simple enough for even the weakest swimmer in the group to do. Nonswimmers can enjoy shallow-end Follow the Leader, in which no swimming ability is necessary.

First, one player is chosen to be the leader and the rest of the participants line up behind her. The leader begins moving through the water in any way she chooses, performing different stunts and motions along the way. Depending on the other players' skill levels, the leader may try swimming different strokes, somersaulting, walking on her hands, bobbing up and down, blowing bubbles, or floating on her back. The leader may also get out of the pool and jump back in with the others following behind. (No running in the pool area, though!)

There are no winners or losers in this game. After a predetermined amount of time, the leader goes to the end of the line and the next player in line becomes the new leader. The game continues until everyone has had a chance to lead.

Still Pond

In this game, swimmers try to make it across the pool without being caught in the act.

Players: 4 or more, plus an adult to supervise

Ages: 6 to 12

Place: Swimming pool

Equipment: None

The fastest swimmer does not always win the race in Still Pond. That's because the ability to stop suddenly and freeze in place is just as important as speed in this game. Still Pond is definitely more challenging if

played by good swimmers in deep water, but even nonswimmers can play in the shallow end.

First, one player is designated "it," and the rest of the participants spread out along one side of the pool in the water. "It" stays on the opposite side of the pool, closes his eyes, and begins to count to ten out loud. At this point, the other players start swimming across the pool (if they're in the shallow end, they can run or hop). At the count of ten, "it" shouts, "Still pond!" and opens his eyes.

Immediately, all the other players must freeze. If "it" catches anyone moving forward (treading water, of course, is allowed), the offending player must return to the starting line. "It" then closes his eyes and the counting and sneaking resume. This continues until one player makes it to the other side and wins the game. If it's too easy for the swimmers to cross the pool by the count of ten, the count can be reduced to five.

Sharks and Minnows

In this tag game, the "minnows" try to avoid being caught by the "shark."

Players: 5 or more, plus an adult to supervise

Ages: 6 to 12

Place: Swimming pool

Equipment: None

Sharks and Minnows is a water game that combines elements of Tag with elements of Red Rover. When the "shark" calls the "minnows" to cross the pool, they try to make it to the other side without being tagged. Depending on the swimming skills of the players, Sharks and

Minnows can be played in either the deep or the shallow end of the pool.

One player is chosen to be the shark. The others are the minnows and line up along one edge of the pool in the water. The shark stands (or treads water) in the middle and invites the minnows to come swimming. The minnows must then try to make their way across the "shark-infested" waters to the other side without being caught by the shark. Those who make it line up again on the opposite edge of the pool for the next round. Those who don't, however, must join the shark in trying to catch the survivors in the next round.

The last remaining minnow is the winner and gets to be the next shark.

Fisherman

In this variation, one player is designated the "fisherman" and the remaining players are "fish." The fisherman stands (or treads water) in the middle of the pool, while the fish line up along one side. The game begins when the fisherman yells, "Let's go fishing!" At this signal, all the fish must try to swim across the pool without being tagged. The fisherman, in turn, tries to "hook" (tag) as many fish as possible. Players who are tagged must join the fisherman in the next round.

When there are two or more tagged players in the center, the caught fish join hands to make a "net." The fisherman continues to swim around trying to catch fish, while the players who make up the net try to block fish as they swim by, slowing their progress long enough for the fisherman to tag them.

Whale and Herring

In this race and chase game, the "herring" conspire to outswim the "whale."

Players: 5 or more, plus an adult to supervise

Ages: 6 to 10

Place: Swimming pool

Equipment: None

Whale and Herring is a water tag game with a difference. In this game, the pursued "herring" must stay attached to one another while trying to maneuver their way clear of the "whale." The game is best played in waist-deep water since it would be too easy to devour herring swimming in shallow water.

One player is chosen to be the whale, and she takes her place along one wall of the pool. The remaining players—the herring—line up along the wall opposite the whale; they stand one behind the other with their hands on the shoulders of the player in front, so their sides are to the wall. The game begins when the whale starts to chase the line of herring, trying to tag the one on the back end. The herring, meanwhile, leave the wall and try to avoid the whale by twisting and turning the line without letting go of one another. It's no use for the herring to try to swim away from the whale, but if they keep the line slithering fast enough, it will be difficult for the big fiend to tag the fish on the end.

When the whale succeeds in tagging the end herring, she latches on to the end of the line and the player at the front of the line becomes the new whale. The game continues until everyone has had the opportunity to be the whale at least once. There are no winners or losers in this game.

White Whale

In this tag game, swimmers are taken by surprise by the predatory "white whale."

Players: 4 or more, plus an adult to supervise

Ages: 6 to 12

Place: Swimming pool

Equipment: None

White Whale is an exciting game for young players because of its element of surprise. Swimmers circle the innocent "black whale," never knowing when it will change into a ferocious "white whale" and give chase. Nonswimmers can play this game in shallow water, but it's much faster and more fun when the "fish" must really swim for their lives!

One player is chosen to be the whale and takes his place floating in the middle of the pool. The others circle around him, several feet (about 1m) away. At first this seems to be a peaceful scene, but the whale is just waiting for the right moment to attack. Whenever he's ready, the whale abruptly shouts out, "Thar she blows!" and starts off after one or more of the nearby players. The players all speed for the edges of the pool. The first swimmer who gets caught before reaching the edge must take the whale's place.

If everyone makes it to safety without being tagged, the whale returns to the center and calls out, "Black whale!" to invite the swimmers back. Until the whale "blows" and turns "white" and mean, swimmers have to move at least 5 feet (1.5m) away from the wall.

Marco Polo

In this "blind" version of water tag, Marco seeks his prey by sound alone.

Players: 3 or more, plus an adult to supervise

Ages: 6 to 14

Place: Swimming pool

Equipment: None

Marco Polo, named (for some reason) after the famous 15th-century Italian explorer, is probably the best-known and most-loved water game of all. In this tag game, "it" (known here as "Marco") must keep his eyes shut as he swims about hunting for his prey, tracking them down by the sound of their shouts. The game is not only extremely challenging and fast-paced but—adding to the fun—it's loud. As in all water tag games, strong swimmers may play Marco Polo in deep water, but others should stick to the shallow end. Since Marco has his eyes closed in this game, it is up to the other players (and the adult supervisor) to make sure that he doesn't bump into anything hard.

The players spread out in the pool, and the designated Marco clamps his eyes shut (peeking is not in the spirit of the game). As the others scatter, Marco begins stalking them blindly. He may splash about, hoping to catch players by chance. But to make his mission easier, he may, at any time, yell out the word "Marco!" The other players, wherever they are (unless they're underwater and can't hear him), must loudly respond with the word "Polo!" Marco can then follow the voices. However, Marco's potential victims need not stay in one place; they can swim quickly wherever they wish to stay out of his reach.

Although the players must respond to Marco's calls right away, they are free to try to confuse the game by yelling "Polo" at random times. One common trick for throwing Marco off the trail is to call out "Polo" a few times in succession and then to splash away just as Marco swims up to make a tag.

Marco Polo generally features a rule that players may not leave the pool at any time. Another version allows players to climb out and jump back in as much as they like. However, if the "blind" Marco suspects that someone has left the pool, he may call out, "Fish out of water!" and open his eyes. Any dry fish is considered tagged.

A player who is tagged drops out of the game. The last untagged player is the winner and becomes the next Marco.

Underwater Tag

Good lungs are an advantage in this game of tag—anyone who is underwater is safe from capture.

Players: 4 or more, plus an adult to supervise

Ages: 6 to 14 (at least novice swimmers)

Place: Swimming pool

Equipment: None

Underwater Tag is a chase game with a special aquatic twist: as long as players are completely submerged, they cannot be tagged. Strong swimmers will want to play Underwater Tag in the deep end, while beginning swimmers can play in shallow water. An adult should supervise carefully: kids sometimes overestimate their breath-holding ability.

One player is chosen to be "it," and the others spread out in the pool, as far away from "it" as possible. When everyone is ready, "it" gives a signal and begins his chase, swimming and splashing and darting about in an effort to tag another player. The others can swim out of his reach or, when he gets too close, simply drop below the surface and speed away. A savvy "it," however, will lurk above or follow an underwater swimmer, waiting for her to come up for air. After all, she won't be able to stay down there forever.

Players who are tagged drop out of the game. The last untagged player is the winner and the new "it." The game may also be played with the stipulation that any player who is tagged immediately becomes "it."

Water Rope Tag

In this tag game, played with a piece of rope at least 4 feet (1.2m) long, one player is pursued and the rest are the chasers. The player who is to be chased ties the rope (clothesline is good) loosely around his waist, leaving a 2 to 3 feet (60 to 90cm) of rope trailing behind. At the signal "Ready, set, go!" the player begins swimming and the others give chase. The chasers try to catch the end of the rope—they may not touch the swimmer's body. The first player to grab the rope becomes the new rope wearer.

Tunnel Race

This race puts swimmers' underwater speed to the test.

Players: 6 to 10 (even number), plus an adult to supervise

Ages: 6 to 12 (at least novice swimmers)

Place: Swimming pool

Equipment: None

The Tunnel Race is a fun way for new swimmers to practice their underwater swimming skills. Because the game is played in relatively shallow water, participants need not be particularly strong swimmers. Kids invariably want to play this game over and over again—they seem to find endless fascination in the challenge of swimming through another person's legs!

Players divide into two teams of

three to five players. Each team then lines up, single file and spaced a few feet (about 1m) apart, in chest-deep water; players spread their legs apart, creating an underwater tunnel of legs. The two lines of players should be at least 5 feet (1.5m) away from each other. There should also be plenty of room–at least 15 feet (4.5m)–between the last player in each line and the wall of the pool behind.

At a signal from the adult supervisor, the player at the head of the line on each team turns to face her teammates, dives underwater, and swims through the "tunnel" formed by the players' legs. When the swimmer reaches the end of the tunnel, she stands at the end of the line. The player now newly at the head of the line then makes the same trip through the tunnel.

The race continues until every player on both teams has swum through the tunnel. The first team to complete the race wins.

Water Relay Race

This multi-participant race is a contest of swimming speed and teamwork.

Players: 6 or more (divisible into equal teams), plus an adult to supervise

Ages: 6 to 14 (strong swimmers only)

Place: Swimming pool

Equipment: None

If a relay race is a blast on land, it's doubly fun and challenging in the water. Although the classic water relay is purely a swimming race, there are numerous novelty variations that add to the fun. These races do require participants to be strong swimmers. As always, relay races encourage cooperation and teamwork.

For a classic water relay, participants divide into equal teams of at least three players each, and a captain is chosen for each team. The team members line up single file behind each captain at the deep end of the pool. The adult who's supervising can play the starter, yelling, "Ready, set, go!" as soon as everyone's in position. At the signal, the first player on each team jumps into the water, swims to the far end of the pool, tags the wall, and returns to the starting wall. The next player in line may jump in as soon as the first player touches the starting wall. The first team to have all its players complete the course is the winner.

In a classic water relay, one particular stroke that every swimmer must swim—like crawl, sidestroke, or backstroke—is selected before the race. But a free-for-all, in which each swimmer uses the stroke of her choice, is fine, too. In a Medley Relay, each team member swims a different stroke, with the first player on each team, for example, swimming breaststroke, the second swimming the butterfly, and so on.

Umbrella Relay

This race requires an umbrella, which should not have sharp points, for each team. The umbrellas are placed (closed) along the edge at the far end of the pool, opposite each team. To begin, the teams start out lined up in the shallow end of the pool. At the signal "Ready, set, go!" the first swimmer on each team swims the length of the pool—using whatever stroke he chooses—and reaches up to grab the umbrella. The swimmer then opens the umbrella and swims back to the start, holding the umbrella over his head. The umbrella is then handed to the next player, who swims down the pool with the umbrella over her head, then closes it, places it back on the edge, and swims back. When she touches the wall on her return, the next player heads for the umbrella.

Hoop Race

This relay variation requires a hula hoop, a piece of string (as long as the middle of the pool is deep), and a heavy stone or brick for each team. The string is tied to the hula hoop at one end and secured to the stone at the other end. The hula hoops are then placed in the middle of the pool, where they float anchored to the stones. The teams line up in the shallow end. At the signal "Ready, set, go!" the first player on each team swims to the team's hoop, wiggles through it, and then swims back to tag the next player, who does the same.

Water Balloon Race

This variation calls for one balloon for each team. With the teams lined up in the shallow end, the balloons are blown up and set afloat just in front of the first swimmer on each team. In the race, swimmers must literally use their heads to push their team's balloon all the way to the wall at the opposite end then back to the starting wall. Players may not use their hands to control the inevitably erratic movement of the balloon.

Pebble Carry

The Pebble Carry requires three pebbles for each player. Swimmers line up in the shallow end. At the signal "Ready, set, go!" the first swimmer on each team must swim to the opposite end of the pool balancing the pebbles on the back of his hand. This works best by swimming the dog paddle or side-stroke using one hand and holding the hand with the pebbles above the water. If any of the pebbles fall off, the player must dive down and retrieve them from the bottom of the pool, come straight up, and keep swimming to the end of the pool.

Waterball Carry

For Waterball Carry, each team needs a beach ball. Beginning in the shallow end, swimmers must navigate the length of the pool and back with a

beach ball clenched between their knees. This, of course, prevents any kicking and makes for a very buoyant bottom half. If the ball escapes, the swimmer must track it down and resume the race; at no time may she move forward unless the ball is in place. A player may use her hands only to put the ball in position and to hand it off to a teammate.

Sweatshirt Race

A sweatshirt is required for each team in this relay. With the teams lined up outside the pool at the deep end, the first swimmers put on their sweat-shirts. At the signal "Ready, set, go!"

they dive in and head across the pool. When they return, each must spring out of the water, strip off the soaking sweatshirt, and pass it on to the next teammate—who must put on the sweatshirt before diving in.

Potato Race

Each team gets a potato and a table-spoon for this race, which starts in the shallow end. The challenge is to swim the length of the pool and back hold-ing in one hand the spoon with the potato balancing on it. If the potato falls off the spoon, the swimmer must dive down, retrieve it, and then keep swimming to the end of the pool.

Diving for Distance

This cleaner the dive, the farther the glide in this contest.

Players: 2 or more, plus an adult to supervise

Ages: 8 to 14 (strong swimmers and divers only)

Place: Swimming pool at least 8 feet (2.4m) deep at one end

Equipment: None

Diving for Distance is a contest that measures the players' diving and breath-holding skills. Only strong swimmers and good divers should play this game. And the pool should be cleared of all other swim-mers before the competition begins.

Players line up at the deep end of the pool and take turns diving in. (Never dive into water less than 8 feet [2.4m] deep!) After her dive, the swim-mer glides underwater, arms in front of her, for as long as she can, trying not to come up for air until absolutely

necessary. Arms and legs must be kept straight throughout the glide. The goal is to do a long, relatively shallow dive, which allows the swim-mer to glide to the surface. If, howev-er, a swimmer needs a kick or an arm-stroke to surface, he must come straight up.

When the player finally emerges, her distance is marked from the tips of her fingers. The player who manages

to travel the longest distance is named the winner.

Cannonball Contest

Instead of competing for the longest underwater glide, Cannonball Contest participants vie to make the biggest splash. Players take turns doing "cannonballs" into the deep end—jumping into the pool, either off a diving board or simply from poolside, with knees clutched to the chest. The player whose cannonball sends the most water spraying up into the air—as judged by the adult supervisor—is the winner.

Treasure Diving

In this race, players dive deep
to retrieve a sunken treasure.

Players: 6 or more, plus an adult to supervise

Ages: 8 to 14 (strong swimmers only)

Place: Swimming pool

Equipment: Small, brightly colored object that doesn't float (coin, large marble, plastic bottle cap, painted stone, etc.); stopwatch or timer with second hand; pencil and paper for recording times (optional)

Treasure Diving is a challenging race that calls on underwater-diving skills, powers of observation, and the ability to hold one's breath. Players compete to snatch up an object from the bottom of the pool as quickly as possible. Because it must be played in deep water, this is an activity for strong swimmers only.

Players may compete individually or divide into two equal teams. The adult supervisor begins by throwing into the water a "treasure"—any small but sinkable object that is bright enough to be seen under water. Coins, play jewelry, marbles, plastic bottle caps, and small painted stones all work well. At a signal given by the supervisor, the first player jumps or dives off the side of the pool and swims down to retrieve the treasure. The supervisor times the diver with a stopwatch or a timer with a second hand; when the treasure breaks the surface of the water, the clock is stopped.

Each player takes a turn fetching the same treasure from the same depth and keeps track of her time. The player can come up for air and dive down again, but if she hasn't recovered the treasure within 2 minutes, that becomes her official time.

If played individually, the player with the fastest time is the winner. If played in teams, the times of all the team's players are totaled and the team with the lower total is the winner.

Water Keep Away

Interception is the key in this fast
and furious passing game.

Players: 3 or more, plus an adult to supervise

Ages: 7 to 14

Place: Swimming pool

Equipment: Beach ball or other soft inflatable toy

Water Keep Away is an action-packed game that can be played in the pool or at the beach. An ocean or lake is actually a great playing field since the game requires no boundaries or starting or finish lines. Although strong swimming skills aren't necessary when playing Water Keep Away in shallow water, players must avoid wild and reckless behavior as they leap about after the ball.

With one player holding a beach ball (or other soft inflatable toy), participants spread out across a shallow-water playing area. One player (who is not holding the ball) is chosen to be "it." The other players then begin playing catch and try to keep the ball from being intercepted by "it." Players must also avoid being tagged by "it" while holding the ball (lending the flavor of Hot Potato to the game). Other than tagging, no physical contact is permitted—the ball may not be pulled from another player's hands but can only be intercepted when it is in the air or floating on the water.

Any player who is tagged while holding the ball, or whose pass is intercepted by "it" or picked up by "it" after a bad throw, takes the place of "it" in the next round.

Poison Balls

This game is a sort of fast-paced Hot Potato for the pool.

Players: 6 or more (even number), plus an adult to supervise

Ages: 7 to 13

Place: Swimming pool

Equipment: 12 or more light floatable balls (tennis balls, whiffle balls, table tennis balls, beach balls); pool-length piece of rope; pool-wide piece of rope (for nonswimmers)

Poison Balls, sometimes called Dingball, is a fast and furious race in which each team tries to unload balls into its opponent's territory. The balls are "poison." Strong swimmers relish the challenge of playing Poison Balls in deep water. Less skilled swimmers can enjoy the game in waist-deep water. The more players participating, the faster and more challenging the action.

First, a rope is stretched across the length of the pool to divide it in half. The rope serves as a "net," dividing one team's territory from the other's. For nonswimmers, another rope should divide the pool in a way that restricts the playing area to the shallow side. Players then form two equal teams, and the teams arrange themselves on opposite sides of the net. At least a dozen floatable balls are thrown into the water, divided evenly between the sides. They are off limits until play begins.

At a signal from the supervisor, the players on both teams start throwing balls from their side over the rope to the other side. Whenever a ball from one team lands on the other team's side, that team picks it up and immediately throws it back over again. Each team's aim is to rid its side of as many balls as possible. The players splash, swim, and swoop through the water, trying to pelt each ball over to the other side as soon as it lands, trying to keep their side of the pool free of balls. Any ball thrown out of the pool must be retrieved by the player who threw it. (No running in the pool area, though!) After retrieving the ball, the player may throw it again only after getting back into the water on his own side.

Any team that gets rid of all its balls automatically wins the game. Otherwise, after 5 to 10 minutes, or another agreed-on amount of time, the supervisor stops play, and the team with the fewest balls wins. After a short rest, teams switch sides for another round.

Water Ball

The speediest ball snatchers have the advantage in this rowdy throwing and catching game.

Players: 6 or more, plus an adult to supervise

Ages: 7 to 13

Place: Swimming pool

Equipment: Tennis ball

Water Ball is a great game for pool parties because it is best with a big group of players. In this game it is every swimmer for herself. The water will be an ocean of children trying to catch or intercept a ball as it sails back and forth over the pool. Water Ball should be played in shallow water to allow for the greatest throwing and jumping action, and if there are nonswimmers or beginners, play should definitely be restricted to the shallow end.

The players divide into two groups, which need not be exactly equal because the groups are not teams. The two groups line up facing each other from opposite sides of the pool. Players should leave several feet (about 1m) of space between themselves and their neighbors.

The game begins when a player from one group throws the ball across the pool and, while the ball is in the air, calls out the name of someone on the other side. If the person for whom the ball is intended does in fact catch it, both she and the thrower score a point. But this is not so easy, because the other players on her side try to intercept the ball—and a player who makes an interception gets a point.

After each throw, the players return to their original positions against the sides of the pool. Whoever caught the ball gets to throw now. If no one caught the ball, it is returned to the original thrower, who throws again. Play continues in this way—as fast as possible—with each thrower calling out the name of someone on the opposite side as he tosses the ball toward that person. As the points accumulate, smart throwers will aim toward players with lower scores, in hopes that they will catch the ball and return the favor.

The first player to score 25 points is the winner.

Water Baseball

Water Baseball is a wet and wild version of the popular land game.

Players: 8 or more (even number), plus an adult to supervise

Ages: 8 to 14 (strong swimmers only)

Place: Swimming pool

Equipment: Beach ball or volleyball (or smaller ball for advanced players); towels or similar markers for bases

Water Baseball is an organized aquatic baseball game that requires the pool to be cleared of any nonplayers. The game is based on the land version, but only some of the rules apply. No bat is used and players are not required to travel from base to base in a straight line: they may plunge underwater to avoid capture. Because the whole pool, including the deep end, is used, players should be strong and confident swimmers. Water baseball is best played with a beach ball or volleyball, although advanced players may prefer a tennis ball or a small rubber ball.

Before playing, a Water Baseball diamond must be laid out in the pool. Home plate is in the middle of the shallow edge of the pool. First base is halfway along the edge to the shallow end's right; second base is in the middle of the deep-end edge; and third base is halfway along the remaining edge. Towels or something similar should be laid poolside to mark the bases. Of course, players can also use ladders and diving boards and other structural elements as bases.

The players divide into two equal teams. One team starts "in the field," with one of its players serving as pitcher. If the teams have only a few players each, the other team can provide the pitcher. He stands in shallow water a few feet (about 1m) in front of home plate. Another player should hold on to the edge near first base. The rest of the team spreads out throughout the pool.

The other team is "at bat." They now count off to determine the batting order, or a captain sets the order. With the other players sitting along the shallow edge of the pool, the first batter stands in the water, in front of home plate, and the pitcher throws the ball toward home plate. The batter

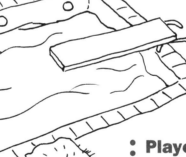

may wait for a pitch she likes, but she only gets one shot at it. She must hit the ball with her fist or open palm. If she misses altogether or hits it to the side or out of the pool, she's out and rejoins the rest of her team at poolside.

If, however, she hits it out in front of her and inside the pool, it's a "fair ball." She races, running through the water or swimming, to first base. If the ball is caught before it hits the water, she's out. Otherwise, the players in the field must dash to the ball and try to get the runner out before she reaches first base in one of two ways: throwing the ball to the first baseman (who must have one hand on first base) or tagging the runner with the ball. (Throwing the ball at the runner is not permitted.)

A runner can be tagged only when she's above the surface, but a savvy fielder may block her progress to the base to make her come up for air. The stronger a runner's lungs, the better chance she has of swimming around or under the fielder and making it to the base.

Depending on how far she's whacked the ball (or how smoothly the other team has fielded it), the runner may continue swimming from base to base, stopping when she thinks she can't go any farther without getting caught. She stays on the base she's reached and runs when the next player at bat hits the ball. A run is scored when a player makes it safely around all the bases.

Players continue coming up to bat until there are three outs. The teams then switch positions and the batting team takes the field. When each team has had a turn to bat and a turn to field, one inning is completed. The game usually continues for five innings. The team with the most runs at the end of the game is the winner.

Player at Bat

There are only two bases in this variation of Water Baseball, home plate and a base on the opposite side of the pool. This game can be played with as few as four players, and participants play to score individually rather than as teams. One player is up at bat and the other players are in the field, with one serving as pitcher. After the batter hits the ball, he tries to swim to the base opposite home plate without being tagged out. If the batter makes it, a run is scored; he returns to home base and gets to bat again. If not, the batter changes places with a player in the field. The player who has scored the most runs after everyone has had a chance to bat a predetermined number of times is the winner.

Water Basketball

Water Basketball is like One-Goal
Basketball played in the pool.

Players: 2 to 10 (even number), plus
an adult to supervise

Ages: 9 to 14 (strong swimmers only
for deep-end game)

Place: Swimming pool

Equipment: Aquatic basketball goal;
volleyball

Water Basketball requires an
aquatic basketball goal,
which can be bought at any
pool supply or toy store. The goal is
fastened to the edge of the pool, and
the hoop stands 4 or 5 feet (1.2 to
1.5m) above the surface of the water.

Because it is difficult (impossible,
really) to mark boundary lines in the
water, Water Basketball is a much
more free-form game than its counterpart on land.

It's certainly feasible to buy two
goals and set them at both ends of a
pool for a full-court Water Basketball
game. But more common is the half-
court version, played either in the
shallow or the deep end. Obviously,
the deep-end version is considerably
harder, and children participating
should be quite strong swimmers. The
rules below are for a team game, but
they can easily be modified for a one-
on-one contest.

For a half-court game, players divide
into two equal teams. The game begins
with one team taking possession of
the ball at a point about 15 feet (4.5m)
or so down the pool, away from the
basket (the "backcourt"). The object
of the game is to score points by
shooting the ball through the basket
while trying to prevent the other team
from doing the same. Players may
shoot the ball from anywhere in the
pool, and when a basket is sunk, 2
points are scored.

As players look for an opportunity
to take a shot, the ball may be passed
from player to player on the same
team. But a player may not move
while holding the ball. If she does, it's
called "carrying" and if a player is
caught carrying the ball, the other
team takes possession in the backcourt. So it's up to a player's teammates to splash about in an effort to
get open for a pass. (In a one-on-one
game, this rule doesn't apply.)

Meanwhile, as one team tries to get
near the basket, opposing players may
try to intercept a ball that is being
passed. If a ball is thrown or knocked
out of the pool, the team that did not
touch it last gains possession—at
the point where the ball went out
of bounds.

Whenever a basket is scored, the
other team gets possession of the ball,
again in the backcourt. Whenever a
shot is missed, however, both teams
may scramble for the ball as it
rebounds off the rim or backboard. If
the team that didn't shoot manages to
control the rebound, the ball must be
taken to the backcourt before a player
may shoot. If the shooting team
snatches the rebound, however, they
are permitted to shoot again without
returning to the backcourt.

Players may not bump or push the
player with the ball in an attempt to
steal the ball or prevent a shot. This is
a foul. There are many different ways
to deal with fouls in Water Basketball,
but here's a simple and fair approach:
When a player with the ball is fouled,
play stops and he is allowed to take a
"free throw," that is, an uncontested
shot from about 10 feet (3m) in front
of the basket. If he makes it, the basket is worth 1 point. But whether he
makes it or not, his team retains possession of the ball, starting in the
backcourt. In other instances of
excessive jostling, the fouled player
simply takes possession at backcourt.

The first team to score 21 points is
named the winner.

Water Volleyball

Water Volleyball players are sure to get wet while trying to hit the ball over the net.

Players: 4 or more (even number), plus an adult to supervise

Ages: 10 to 14

Place: Swimming pool

Equipment: Volleyball or beach ball; net or rope, plus additional rope for marking playing field

Volleyball takes good coordination, aim, and strength on land. Playing in water makes running harder and jumping easier. Since the game is best played in relatively shallow water, great swimming ability is not crucial. Kids 10 or older, who generally have greater hand-eye coordination and arm strength than younger children, especially enjoy Water Volleyball.

Before beginning, a playing area is established in the shallow end by stretching a rope across the width of the pool; then a net or another rope is stretched lengthwise across the playing area to divide the court in half. Players are split into two equal teams, which stand facing one another on opposite sides of the net. If there are enough players, the teams should arrange themselves into two or three rows. Otherwise, they should simply spread out on their side of the court.

The game begins when one player—standing in the back right corner of her team's side—serves the ball over the net by smacking it with the side of her fist or the heel of her palm. (A server is allowed two tries to get the ball over, or the other team gets a shot.) Once the ball is served, the other team tries to hit it back over the net before it touches the water. A player may hit it back with any part of his hand or arm—including fingers, fists, closed palms, wrists, or forearms—except he cannot use an open palm.

(This exception can be eased for beginning players.) If one hit isn't enough to get the ball over, another player on the same team may hit it again. In all, a team is allowed three hits to get the ball over the net. One player may not, however, hit the ball twice in a row.

The teams continue hitting the ball back and forth over the net, swooping and splashing in graceful leaps. Players can be a lot bolder with their jumps in the water than on land because falling on one's face is usually a pleasure, not a problem. The volley ends when one team fails to get the ball over the net or hits it out of bounds (or when one person hits it twice in a row). If the team that served commits the error, the opposing team gets to serve. If the nonserving team commits the error, however, the serving team scores a point and serves again.

When both teams have served and it is time for the first team to serve again, a new player gets a chance to serve. The first team to score 21 points (or another predetermined number) wins, as long as they are ahead by at least 2 points. If not, the game goes on until one team does win by 2 points.

Chicken Fights

Players try to knock opponents off other players' shoulders in this wacky water war.

Players: 4 or more (even number), plus an adult to supervise

Ages: 8 to 14

Place: Swimming pool

Equipment: None

Chicken Fights, also known as Horse and Rider, is a favorite pool activity. Kids find it great sport to ride around on friends' shoulders trying to dunk their opponents. Special attention must be paid, however, to ensuring that the game is played safely. Young children should not play this game because their shoulder muscles are not strong enough to support another body. Opponents should be equally matched in size and strength, and players should not try to carry children larger than themselves on their shoulders. Chicken Fights are best held in waist-deep water, far away from the sides of the pool or anything a falling player could hit her head on. Finally, kids should be cautioned not to fight too aggressively—combat should be limited to gentle pulls and pushes.

An even number of players is required for Chicken Fights, since the battle is fought in pairs. Each player selects a partner and the smaller of each pair climbs onto the larger child's shoulders. The bottom player should grasp the top player's legs to keep him steady. The pairs spread themselves out across the pool's shallow end. Then, at a signal from the supervisor, it's every chicken for herself. The double-decker couples go after one another with the aim of bumping, wrestling, or pushing the player on top off his partner's shoulders and into the water. No hitting, biting, hair pulling, or other "fowl" play allowed. Before long, someone is bound to make a splash. Once a chicken has fallen, that pair must move to the side of the pool.

Players continue to do battle until all of the chickens but one have fallen into the water. The team left standing is the winner. If players are of equal sizes, they change positions for the next round.

Tube Polo

Splashes and spills are all part of the fun as two teams compete to score a goal.

Players: 4 or more (even number), plus an adult to supervise

Ages: 7 to 14 (at least elementary swimming skills)

Place: Swimming pool

Equipment: Beach ball; inner tube or similar ring for each player; towels or similar markers for establishing goal boundaries (optional); pool-wide piece of rope (optional)

Tube Polo is a great team sport for swimmers from the elementary level on up. The players all sit in rubber or plastic tubes, so strong swimming ability doesn't matter. What counts is teamwork, as players try to pass a beach ball back and forth to their teammates while steadily kicking and paddling across the pool toward the opposition's goal area. Players should, however, have beginning swimming skills because in this game dumping a player out of his tube is one line of defense. With less experienced players, it's best to keep the game in the shallow end of the pool.

Before play begins, two goals should be set up on opposite sides of the pool, with two towels or similar markers placed about 3 feet (90cm) apart to define the goal area. If play is to be restricted to the shallow end, a piece of rope should be stretched across the pool to establish the playing area.

The players divide into two equal teams, get seated in their tubes, and arrange themselves along opposite sides of the pool, on either side of their goal. If there are more than four players, each team may want to designate a goalie to stay near the goal area and block the ball from going in. With the shout "Ready, set, go!" the

supervising adult throws the ball into the center of the pool and the game begins. In a mad scramble each team races to take possession of the ball. Players may propel themselves in any fashion that works, as long as they keep their bottoms inside their tubes. Once a player grabs the ball, she may pass it to a teammate or carry it in her lap or under her arm while paddling toward the opposition's goal. The opposing team may try to stop her in several ways: by intercepting or disrupting a pass, by blocking her path toward the goal, or by tipping over

her tube. Only one player at a time may try to turn over another player's tube, however, and no direct pushing or shoving is allowed—only the tube may be touched. Should the ball-carrying player get dumped, she must release the ball, which is now up for grabs. The overturned player must climb back into her tube before joining in play again.

To score a goal, a player must throw the ball so that it hits the wall within the defined goal area. If he misses and the ball stays in the pool, whoever retrieves the ball gains possession.

However, if at any time the ball goes outside the pool or playing area boundaries, the team that did not touch it last gains possession—at the point where the ball went out of bounds. Also, if a player disobeys any rule, the opposition automatically gets the ball, at the spot where the error was committed.

When a goal is scored, the opposing team gains possession of the ball, from a point to the side of their goal area. The game can go on for as long as the players want. The team with the most goals wins.

Pool Polo

This competitive game tests players' swimming endurance as well as their ball-throwing skills.

Players: 4 or more (even number), plus an adult to supervise

Ages: 9 to 14 (strong swimmers only)

Place: Swimming pool

Equipment: Beach ball; towels or similar markers for establishing goal boundaries; pool-wide piece of rope (optional)

In this simplified version of water polo, team members "dribble" and pass a beach ball as they swim toward and try to shoot at their opponent's goal. Best played in the deep end of the pool, this fast-paced game requires strong swimming skills. A player in possession of the ball is not allowed to let her feet touch the bottom of the pool, nor may she rest at or even touch the sides of the pool. (These rules can, of course, be relaxed a bit for less skilled swimmers.)

Before play begins, a rope should be stretched across the pool to set

off the playing area in the deep end. Two goals should then be established on opposite sides of the pool by placing towels or similar markers about 3 feet (90cm) apart in the middle of each side.

The players divide into two equal teams and arrange themselves along

opposite sides of the pool, to the left and right of their goal. If there are more than four players, each team should designate a goalie to guard the goal area and keep the ball away. To begin the game, the supervising adult yells, "Ready, set, go!" and throws the ball into the center of the pool. Players from each team race to grab the ball. Once a player gets the ball, he tries to "move" it, either passing it to another player or dribbling it by pushing it ahead with one hand at a time while he swims. His aim is to get the ball near enough to his opponents' goal for someone on his team to take a shot. His opponents, in turn, try to intercept or disrupt any passes or dribbling. Players may not, however, tackle or otherwise touch each other.

To score a goal, a player must throw the ball so that it hits the edge of the pool within the defined goal area. If she misses and the ball stays in the pool, whoever retrieves the ball gains possession. However, if at any time the ball goes outside the pool or playing area boundaries, the team that did not touch it last gains possession—at the point where the ball went out of bounds. Also, if a player disobeys any rule, the opposition automatically gets the ball, at the spot where the infraction occurred.

When a goal is scored, the opposing team gains possession of the ball, starting from a point immediately to the left or right of their goal area. The game can go on for as long as the players want, but it's a good idea to have a brief rest period after every goal or at least every 5 minutes. The team with the most goals wins.

Road Games

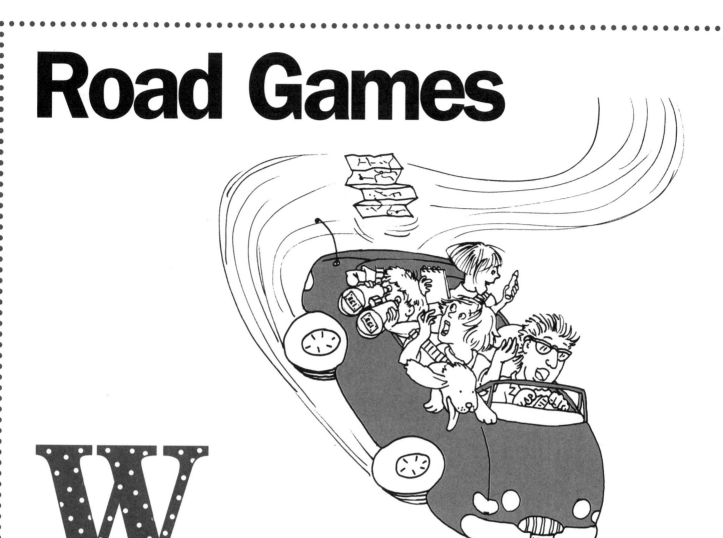

When are we going to get there? Anyone who has ever traveled with kids knows the answer: "Not soon enough!" Interesting and absorbing games for road trips are lifesavers for restless children as well as beleaguered adults. Although many games *can* be played in a car, plane, or train (check out the chapters on Mind Games, Word Games, and Pencil-and-Paper Games), the games in this chapter, for the most part, *must* be played in a car or on a bus. (A few exceptions, like Name That Tune, can be played just about anywhere.) Most of these games demand that players concentrate on things they can see outside the car, such as license plates or billboards. Few require parents to drag along extra equipment, although maps or pencil and paper are needed in some cases, as noted.

Alphabet Objects

Players name the objects that they see
in alphabetical order from A to Z.

Players: 2 or more

Ages: 4 to 14

Place: Car, bus, or train

Equipment: None

Alphabet Objects is a perfect
game for long car, bus, or train
trips, during which kids have
plenty of time to gaze out the window
at scenery. The game may be quick or
slow, depending on the ages of the
players and the composition of the
landscape. But the good news is that
it can be played over and over again.
Alphabet Objects is also a good learning tool for kids who are just becoming familiar with their letters.

In Alphabet Objects, players try to
spot, in the passing scenery, objects
with names starting with each letter
of the alphabet, in order. First, participants look out the window—things in
the vehicle don't count—for something that starts with the letter A. For
families on the road, automobile is
often an easy A.

Usually the game is played competitively, with each player trying to find
objects for every letter. In this
version, the moment a
player identifies an
object, she calls it
out and immediate-
ly moves on to
the next letter.
(Once an item
has been called
out by one play-
er, no other play-
er may use it.)
Letter by letter,
players make their
way through the alphabet. A barn
might be found for B, a cow for C, and
so on. An actual letter on a license
plate or a sign may also be used. The
D in a McDonald's sign, for example,
is fine. Difficult-to-find letters like Q,
X, and Z may be eliminated, although
keep in mind that on some highways
"Exit" and "No Passing Zone" signs
are fairly common.

In the competitive version, the first
player to finish the entire alphabet
wins the game. The game can also be
played noncompetitively, with each
player being responsible, in turn, for
finding something that begins with the
next letter of the alphabet.

Billboard Alphabet

Road signs provide the letters for this
alphabet hunt game.

Players: 2 or more

Ages: 6 to 14

Place: Car, bus, or train

Equipment: None

The more signs along the side of
the road, the more interesting the
game of Billboard Alphabet. In
this game, players must track down
all the letters in the alphabet, in
sequence, on passing billboards, as
well as road and building
signs. If there's no Dairy
Queen around, players
might ride for a hundred
miles searching for a Q.
But they should keep their
eyes open for such other
possibilities as "quiet,"
"square," and "equipment."

To play, participants
scan signs (but not license
plates or anything else
attached to vehicles) in
search of the letters of the
alphabet from A to Z. When a player
spots a letter, she points and says it
out loud: "A in Holiday Inn," for
example. Once a player has found
the letter she

needs, she moves on to the next one in the alphabet.

A player may use only one letter from each sign, and each sign may be used by only one player. A player must call out his discoveries quickly to claim a sign that has letters both he and his opponents want. The first person to complete the alphabet is the winner. Players may also choose to collaborate on this journey through the alphabet.

Travel Scavenger Hunt

Players survey the landscape to find items on their Scavenger Hunt lists.

Players: 2 or more, plus an adult or older child to prepare lists

Ages: 6 to 14

Place: Car, bus, or train

Equipment: Pencil and paper for each player

Travel Scavenger Hunt is a great way to keep children of many ages occupied (for hours!) while traveling in a car or on a bus or train. Although it's most interesting if the trip takes the players through several different landscapes (city and country, for example), almost any journey offers ample opportunity for a good Scavenger Hunt.

Before the trip, an adult or older child prepares a Scavenger Hunt list and makes enough copies to give one to each player. Depending on the ages of the participants, the lists may be simple and relatively short or much longer and more

detailed (listing a "black horse," for example, rather than just a "horse"). The lists should be tailored to the type of terrain that will be traveled through—it's pointless, for example, to include the "ocean" on a drive through the Midwest or a "cow" on a trip through the city.

To play, each child is given a copy of the list of items to find. The first player to spot an object calls it out and gets to cross it off her list. Only the first child to see a brick house, for instance, gets credit for it, but others may get credit for brick houses that they spot down the road. At the end of the trip, the player who has found the most items on the list is the winner. Of course, if someone lucks out and finds all the items on the list, he is immediately declared the winner.

Automobile 21

Players scan license plates to find the numbers 1 through 21.

Players: 2 or more

Ages: 4 to 12

Place: Car or bus

Equipment: None

As its name suggests, Automobile 21 is a game to play in the car or on a bus. The object is to be the first to find the numbers 1 through 21, in order, on the license plates of passing cars—a task that becomes ever more challenging in this age of customized plates. This game is a mild challenge for older kids,

and it's great for teaching little ones their numbers.

As players work their way up to 21, the numbers they see may be used in a variety of ways. Any single-digit or any double-digit number on a license plate is fair game. Also, any numbers in a sequence on a license plate can be added together. If, for example, a license plate has the number 415 on it, the individual digits (4, 1, and 5) are all available to any player who needs one of those numbers. But so is the number 10, because the three digits add up to 10; and so is 19, because 4 plus 15 equals 19. Part of the fun of this contest is figuring out combinations that give a player the number he's after.

Players call out the numbers as soon as they spot them, pointing at the passing cars and doing any necessary math out loud. Any individual license plate may be claimed by only one person and may be used for only one number.

The first player to find all the numbers is the winner. The game may also be played noncompetitively. In this version, each player must try to find only the number that comes up on her turn.

If the players wish, they may continue the game after reaching 21 by going back down to 1 again. Advanced players may also opt to play to a higher target number.

Motor Bingo

Players scan license plates to locate the numbers on their Bingo cards.

Players: 3 or more

Ages: 4 to 14

Place: Car or bus

Equipment: Pencil and paper for each player

Motor Bingo, which some players prefer to call Bingo on Wheels, is a simplified Bingo-type game that is perfect for keeping kids busy on long car trips.

Before the game, each player prepares a Bingo "card" by drawing a large square on a piece of paper and then dividing it into nine boxes of equal size (see diagram). A different two-digit number is written in each box. The numbers should increase in value from left to right and decrease in value from top to bottom. (In this way a number will always be lower than the one directly above it.) Cards may be prepared before the trip for younger players—or for those who have trouble writing while the car is moving.

One player is designated as the caller. If there are more than two players, the caller should not participate in the game. The caller starts the game by selecting a passing license plate and calling out the number given by the first two digits on the plate

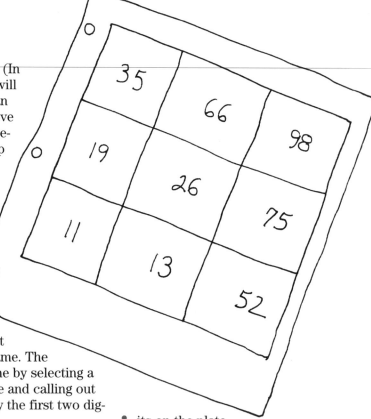

and then writing this down for future reference. If that number appears on a player's card, he gets to cross it out.

The first player to cross out a line of numbers—either horizontally, vertically, or diagonally—calls "Bingo!" This player is declared the winner—but only after her card is checked against the caller's list, to make sure there aren't any mistakes. For a longer game, a player must cross out all the numbers on the card to win.

Ten Pairs

In this number search game, players try to spot license plates bearing pairs.

Players: 2 or more

Ages: 6 to 14

Place: Car or bus

Equipment: None

License plates seem to supply an almost unlimited number of game opportunities, and Ten Pairs is a good example. In this game, players try to spot license plates that have double (or, if they're very lucky, triple) digits of a number of their choice. Ten Pairs provides excellent practice in addition as well as a work-

out for youngsters' memory skills.

Each player picks a different number between 1 and 9. This is the number the player will keep an eye out for throughout the game. The object is to spot all the license plates that bear at least two occurrences of the number he has selected.

Participants check passing license plates for their numbers. Each time someone spots a plate that has two of her digits (484-DAW, for example, for a player who chose 4), she points it out and scores 1 point. If the numbers appear consecutively (B58-447), she scores 2 points. If she spies a triple repeat (EK-444), she earns 3 points. If a plate contains pairs or triples for more than one player, it earns points for them all.

Players keep a running mental tally of their own scores. The first player to get 20 points is the winner.

License Plate Spelling

In this creative game, players use the letters on license plates to spell words.

Players: 2 or more

Ages: 6 to 14

Place: Car or bus

Equipment: Pencil and paper for each player

License Plate Spelling is a versatile game that can be played at two different levels of difficulty. Young kids can search plates to find letters for words that they've written down by themselves or with the help of an adult, while older children can incorporate the letters found on the plates into new words. Either way, License Plate Spelling is an entertaining pastime and a good spelling lesson for kids of all ages.

In the first version, geared for 6- to 8-year-olds, players begin by writing down the same three- or four-letter word—a word that either they have chosen themselves or has been chosen for them. The players then scan passing license plates for the letters in this word, crossing them off when spotted. The letters must be

identified in sequence. (If, for example, the chosen word is "girl," the player must find a G first, then an I,

an R, and an L.) Each letter must come from a different license plate, and no two players may claim a letter from the same plate. The first player to complete the word is the License Plate Spelling champion.

In the game's more sophisticated version, one license plate is chosen, and all the participants must try to form words using its letters. From the license plate 179-SNR, for instance, players may spell "sunrise," "sooner," or "snore." The first player to think of a word scores a point. If players call out a word at the same time, the longest word wins.

The game continues for as many rounds as desired with the highest-scoring player taking the License Plate Spelling title. Or players can compete to be the first to reach a predetermined score, such as 10.

License Plate Phrases

In this more difficult variation of License Plate Spelling, players compete to come up with a phrase using the license plate's letters, in order, as the first letters of the words in the phrase. For example, the letters on the plate T6B-48C4 (T-B-C) could be used as the initial letters in the phrases "The Big Cat," "Teach Babies Carefully," "Toys Bother Children," and "Ten Black Cars." The plate 99KB-R9N (K-B-R-N) could be used for "Kill Bugs Right Now," "Kids Bring Red Napkins," or "Koala Bears Read Nothing." The phrases can be familiar expressions, if they work, or they can be completely made-up combinations, so long as the invented phrases make at least some sense.

Imaginations are encouraged to run wild. The more letters there are, the tougher the task. And, of course, some letter combinations are bound to be harder than others (try Q-X-Q-L!).

Players take turns choosing license plates to work with; it's a good idea to start with three- or even two-letter phrases and work up. The first player to come up with a phrase scores a point. As with License Plate Spelling, the game can continue for as long as desired, with the player with the most points winning, or victory can go to the first to reach an agreed-upon number of points.

One Hundred Points

Quick thinking on wheels is necessary for this game of motor math.

Players: 2 or more

Ages: 7 to 12

Place: Car or bus

Equipment: None

One Hundred Points is a math lesson in disguise, which requires sharp eyes, a quick mind, and good adding skills. A good memory also helps, since players need to remember their changing point totals from round to round. The object of the game, as indicated by its name, is to be the first player to add up 100 points from numbers found on passing cars' license plates.

To play, participants take turns examining the license plate of a passing car and adding up all the digits on the plate. If, for example, the first player's plate reads 825-DWG, he would quickly tally up the digits for a total of 15 (8 + 2 + 5). The second player takes the next plate and adds up her sum, and so on through the

rest of the round.

When everyone has had a turn, the first player goes again, adding the sum from his next license plate to his old total. If the plate reads 7Q7-9Z this time, he adds 23 (7 + 7 + 9) to 15 for a new total of 38 points. When someone reaches 100 points (or more), play continues until the end of that round (so everyone has the same number of turns), and then the player with the highest score is pronounced the winner.

Since there will probably not be a math teacher around, it's up to the players themselves to check each other's arithmetic.

Find All 50

Players vie to "collect" license plates
from all the states.

Players: 2 or more, plus an adult or
older child to prepare lists

Ages: 6 to 14

Place: Car or bus

Equipment: Pencil and paper for each
player

Find All 50 is a visual hunt for the license plates of every state on the map. This game is sure to occupy many on-the-road hours and give informal lessons in geography and observation. Kids must be able to read well to play this game.

Before the game, an adult or older child prepares a checklist of all 50 states for each player. As he puts together the lists, the preparer may even challenge the kids to see who can name the most states. The best way to set up the checklist is to write the names of the states alphabetically along the left side of the page and then make two columns labeled "plates" and "slogans/symbols." Players earn bonus points for spotting license plates that include state slogans and/or symbols.

Not all license plates have slogans or symbols. New York, for example, has neither. Connecticut's standard plate bears the slogan "Constitution State" but no symbol. License plates in Pennsylvania, however, include both a slogan ("Keystone State") and a symbol (a keystone).

Once each player has a checklist, the players start scanning the roads for license plates. The license plates may be found in any order, but only the player who spots the plate on any vehicle may claim that plate for her checklist. Contestants score 1 point for finding a plate from a particular state and 3 points for a plate with a slogan and/or symbol. A bonus point is earned for a "nonstate" plate, such as the District of Columbia, Guam, or any foreign country, such as Canada or Mexico.

At the end of the trip, the numbers are added up and the player with the highest score is the winner. (Although finding plates from all 50 states is the goal, spotting a Hawaiian plate in the continental U.S. is next to impossible, especially on the East Coast—but players should figure this out for themselves!)

Bordering Plates

An imaginary trip across the country is mapped out and traveled via license plates.

Players: 2 or more

Ages: 9 to 14

Place: Car or bus

Equipment: Map of the United States or atlas; pencil and paper (optional)

ordering Plates is an interesting and educational game for older children. Not only does the game keep travelers occupied, it teaches geography, map reading, and route planning. Each child plans an imaginary cross-country trip, which is then carried out by identifying license plates from each successive bordering state. Depending on the traffic, an imaginary trip from Washington, D.C., to Seattle in the state of Washington might take longer than the real thing. The game is best played on large interstate highways, where it's most likely that cars from many parts of the country will be seen.

To prepare for the game, each child chooses a starting point on one side of the country (say, Portland, Oregon) and a destination on the opposite side (say, Boston, Massachusetts). Another option is for all players to choose to take the same journey. To begin the trip, each player must find a license plate from the state of his departure. Only one player can claim each plate, so the first to call it out gets it.

After the player finds a plate from his starting state, he searches for one from a bordering state in order to move toward the destination state. A map of the United States is indispensable to solve disputes along the journey. The route to Massachusetts may be direct (Oregon to Idaho to Wyoming, for example) or more indirect (Oregon to California to Arizona). Players continue trying to advance by finding one bordering state's plate after the other. They may move in any direction they wish, so long as they move to a bordering state. It's up to the players themselves to consult the map in order to make sure no one tries to get credit for a nonbordering state.

The first player to reach her destination is declared the winner. If nobody makes it all the way, the person who comes the closest wins. If it seems impossible to complete a full coast-to-coast journey, a shorter trip, north to south, for instance, can be substituted.

License Plate Poker

License plate numbers supply the hands in this cardless poker game.

Players: 2 or more

Ages: 9 to 14

Place: Car or bus

Equipment: Pencil and paper for each player

t's hard to play cards on the road, but License Plate Poker is a great substitute. This challenging game requires players to assemble poker hands from letters and numbers found on license plates. No betting is involved, and it's not possible to hide your hand or bluff. Kids should have a good working knowledge of the various poker hands and their relative values (see next page). The game helps sharpen memory and develop the capacity for abstract thinking.

To play, participants study passing cars, searching for license plates with five letters and/or numbers that make up a poker hand. Each digit represents a numbered card from a regular deck (0 stands for Ten). Some letters represent face cards: J stands for Jack, Q for Queen, K for King, and A for Ace. No other letters count. There are no suits (clubs, diamonds, hearts, or spades).

As in regular poker, players are looking for a plate ("hand") on which the chosen five letters or numbers will provide them with two-, three-, or four-of-a-kinds (the higher the better). When a player spies a plate with good "cards," he claims it and calls out the hand, then writes all the characters from the plate on a piece of paper. Players should have a time limit in which to choose a hand; otherwise, cunning players might wait until a four-of-a-kind plate passes by.

On a busy road, a minute is usually enough time to choose a hand. (On a quiet road, it might actually make more sense for players to be assigned hands in order, as the cars come along.) No two players may pick the same license plate. When every player has picked a plate, they all compare their hands. Here is a list of possible License Plate Poker hands, in order of least to most valuable.

One Pair: Two of any number or face card (KS-858, for example)

Two Pair: Two pairs of matching numbers or letters (669-KMK, for example)

Three of a Kind: Three matching numbers or letters (725-677, for example)

Full House: Three of a kind and two of a kind (JJ3-633, for example)

Four of a Kind: Four matching numbers or letters (G44-244, for example)

Straight: Five numbers (or numbers and letters together) that can be arranged in a perfect sequence (SQJ-098, for example, which contains Queen, Jack, Ten, Nine, and Eight)

The player with the best hand wins.

In the absence of any combinations, the player with the highest "card" wins (438-KWG beats 921-QED because a King beats a Queen). Aces are high. If two players have combinations of equal value, the highest second card in each hand determines the winner. This game can go on with players alternating who goes first.

Name That Tune

Players try to identify songs after hearing as few notes as possible in this musical guessing game.

Players: 2 or more

Ages: 8 to 14

Place: Anywhere

Equipment: None

Like the old game show that inspired it, Name That Tune challenges players to identify songs after hearing only the first few notes of the main melody. Although Name That Tune can be played just about anywhere, it's a terrific travel game. A good ear for music is a great help in playing, as is a wide knowledge of songs.

One player is chosen to be the first clue giver. She begins the game by thinking of a song and humming or whistling the first note—or better yet, singing the notes with a neutral syllable, such as "da." Players should stick to tunes that everyone in the group is familiar with. The other players now try to guess the identity of the song, which, of course, is nearly impossible to do after hearing only one note.

The hummer or singer performs the beginning of the melody again and again, adding one note each time, until someone calls out the correct name of the song. The person who identifies the song is the winner and becomes the new clue giver.

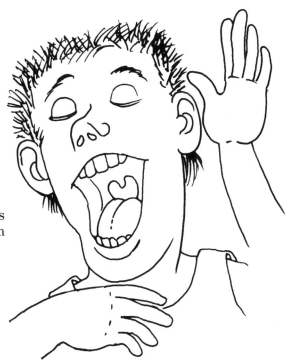

Car Snap

Players compete to spot the most examples of the car of their choice.

Players: 2 or more

Ages: 4 to 12

Place: Car or bus

Equipment: Pencil and paper for keeping score (optional)

In Car Snap each player has a chance to scan the highway for the car of her favorite make and color. Players must be old enough to recognize the makes of cars, but the game can be simplified for younger kids by asking them to choose only a color.

The game begins with each player selecting a color and make of car. A few possibilities include a blue Volkswagen, a gold Cadillac, a red Jeep, and a black Rolls-Royce. No two players may select the same combination in any round. Immediately all the players look out the window, eyes trained on the road in search of their chosen cars.

When a player's car comes into view, he at once points it out and exclaims, "Snap!" The snapper scores a point. The players then all choose new cars, and a new round begins. The player with the highest score after five rounds is the winner.

Color Collection

This variation may be played with two or three players (ages 7 to 12), who each choose a primary color (red, yellow, or blue). Players earn points by spotting a car of their chosen color. But there's a twist: players score points not only for finding cars sporting the chosen color (including multi-colored cars), but also for finding cars of a hue that contains their primary color. A purple car, for example, earns a point for a red player or a blue player. All players can score on brown, gray, and black cars (all the colors mixed together). An appropriately colored car can count for more than one player. The first player to score 10 points—or the player with the most points after a predetermined period of time—is the winner.

Name the Car

Players compete to be the first to correctly identify the makes of oncoming cars.

Players: 2 or more

Ages: 9 to 14

Place: Car or bus

Equipment: None

Name the Car appeals to players who are good at and interested in identifying a car by its make and model. Children who are really good at this (and many are) have such sharp and quick eyes that they leave adult competitors in the dust.

The goal of Name the Car is to identify as many cars as possible—whether they be Dodge Caravans, AMC Pacers, Porsche 911's, Jeep Grand Cherokees, or Toyota Corollas. As an oncoming car comes into view, the players compete to be the first to call out its correct make and model. Each player gets just one guess, and players can determine the right answer as the car passes. A player scores a point for every correct guess.

The game continues for as long as the players wish. At the end, after a predetermined amount of time, the player with the highest total score is the winner. Or the first player to reach a certain predetermined score—say, 10—is declared the winner.

Time and Distance

In this challenging road game, players try to predict the distance to faraway landmarks.

Players: 2 or more, plus adult driver to check odometer (if used)

Ages: 9 to 14

Place: Car

Equipment: Car odometer or watch

Time and Distance, sometimes called Miles to Go, is an interesting challenge for older children who understand the concepts of—that's right—time and distance. The object is to guess how far away a landmark is in either miles or minutes. After some practice, players are likely to become surprisingly accurate in their predictions.

First, someone chooses a landmark somewhere on the horizon—this could be anything from a bridge to a

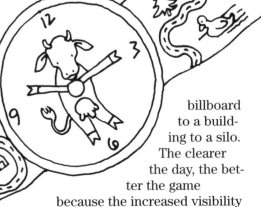

billboard to a building to a silo. The clearer the day, the better the game because the increased visibility allows players to see landmarks that are farther away. Once the landmark is chosen, each player guesses the distance that must be traveled before reaching the destination, to the nearest tenth of a mile or kilometer. (The same distance may not be selected by more than one player.) The driver watches the odometer to determine the actual distance traveled to the landmark.

The game may also be played with the participants guessing the time it will take to get to the destination rather than the miles or kilometers traveled. In this case, one person times the journey on a watch after everyone has made a prediction to the nearest minute.

The player with the closest guess— in time or distance or both—is declared the winner.

How Far Have We Gone?

In this variation, players try to estimate the distance they have traveled from a certain spot. The driver gives them a signal to start, and then, after a good amount of time has elapsed, asks them (making sure they can't peek at the odometer), "How far have we gone?" Each player takes a guess, and the one who comes the closest to the actual distance wins the game.

Index of Games by Name

Index of Games by Number of Players

1 PLAYER

2 PLAYERS

3 PLAYERS

4 PLAYERS

5 TO 9 PLAYERS

10 OR MORE PLAYERS

Index of Games by Age

AGES 3 TO 5

AGES 6 to 9